Wicked Valuations

Traditional valuation approaches are increasingly recognised as being insufficient to address the wicked valuation problems of the diverse peoples and groups that inhabit the globe from north, south, east to west. This book demonstrates the limitations of science and, in particular economics, as the foundation on which valuations are traditionally based. It demonstrates the importance of and provides justification for the personal, cultural values and norms which underpin our assessment of "value", and the fact that these vary across the world. In *Wicked Valuations* Michael McDermott develops a means of engaging with highly complex valuation problems. His autoethnography provides a lens to draw on knowledge and experience from his 40 years in land valuation in Africa and the Asia-Pacific, while documentary analysis is used to draw in the views of other valuation practitioners and scholars who are becoming increasingly aware of the need to develop ways to adapt land valuation processes to the complexity of our contemporary landscapes. These two threads are woven together as McDermott discusses his professional career in valuing real property rights, and the effects such rights have had on the peoples in countries across six continents. Drawing on lessons that emerge from this reflective journey, the book develops and pilots a tool which is specifically designed to address wicked valuation problems through engagement with small groups, particularly, but not exclusively, value juries.

This transdisciplinary work seeks to provide a fundamental challenge to how value is understood, measured, and practised and should be read by all those with an interest in valuation and real property rights, social problems, globalisation, and development studies.

Michael McDermott, PhD, is a Land Policy and Valuation International Consultant based in Australia.

Routledge Complex Real Property Rights Series
Series editor: Professor Spike Boydell, University of Technology, Sydney, Australia

Real property rights are central to the global economy and provide a legal framework for how society (be it developed or customary) relates to land and buildings. We need to better understand property rights to ensure sustainable societies, careful use of limited resources and sound ecological stewardship of our land and water. Contemporary property rights theory is dynamic and needs to engage thinkers who are prepared to think outside their disciplinary limitations.

The Routledge Complex Real Property Rights Series strives to take a trans-disciplinary approach to understanding property rights and specifically encourages heterodox thinking. Through rich international case studies our goal is to build models to connect theory to observed reality, allowing us to inform potential policy outcomes. This series is both an ideal forum and reference for students and scholars of property rights and land issues.

Land, Indigenous Peoples and Conflict
Edited by Alan Tidwell and Barry Zellen

Beyond Communal and Individual Ownership
Indigenous Land Reform in Australia
Leon Terrill

Strata Title Property Rights
Private Governance of Multi-owned Properties
Cathy Sherry

Property Rights and Climate Change
Land-Use under Changing Environmental Conditions
Fennie van Straalen, Thomas Hartmann and John Sheehan

Property, Place and Piracy
Edited by James Arvanitakis and Martin Fredriksson

Wicked Valuations
People and Landed Property
Michael McDermott

Wicked Valuations
People and Landed Property

Michael McDermott

Routledge
Taylor & Francis Group

LONDON AND NEW YORK

First published 2019 by Routledge

2 Park Square, Milton Park, Abingdon, Oxon OX14 4RN
605 Third Avenue, New York, NY 10017

Routledge is an imprint of the Taylor & Francis Group, an informa business

First issued in paperback 2021

Publisher's Note

The publisher has gone to great lengths to ensure the quality of this reprint
but points out that some imperfections in the original copies may be apparent.

British Library Cataloguing-in-Publication Data
A catalogue record for this book is available from the British Library

Library of Congress Cataloging-in-Publication Data
Names: McDermott, Michael, 1946- author.
Title: Wicked valuations : people and landed property / Michael
McDermott.
Description: Abingdon, Oxon; New York, NY : Routledge, 2018. |
Series: Routledge complex real property rights series | Includes
bibliographical references.
Identifiers: LCCN 2018005464 | ISBN 9781138584785 (hardback :
alk. paper) | ISBN 9780429505751 (ebook)
Subjects: LCSH: Real property—Valuation.
Classification: LCC HD1387 .M395 2018 | DDC 333.33/22—dc23
LC record available at https://lccn.loc.gov/2018005464

ISBN: 978-1-138-58478-5 (hbk)
ISBN: 978-1-03-217865-3 (pbk)
DOI: 10.1201/9780429505751

Typeset in Goudy
by Keystroke, Neville Lodge, Tettenhall, Wolverhampton

Contents

Foreword

Real property rights are central to the economy and provide a legal framework for how society (be it developed or customary) relates to land and buildings. Property rights are both institutional arrangements and social relations. We need to better understand property rights to ensure sustainable societies, careful use of limited resources and sound ecological stewardship of our land and water.

Land conflict is all around us – from corporate and political corruption over land dealings in the developed world, to land grabbing in developing countries, to compromised indigenous property rights, to resource exploitation. At a time when global food security, water security and shelter are paramount, an understanding of property rights is key to sustainability.

Contemporary property rights theory is dynamic and this series strives to engage thinkers who are prepared to step beyond their disciplinary limitations. "Property Rights" is a broad term that is fundamentally about social relations. Real property rights, obligations and restrictions can be found in and change across the full range of human societies, both in time and space. Property rights research has emerged from a broad range of disciplines including (but not limited to) archaeology, anthropology, ethics, sociology, psychology, law, geography, history, philosophy, economics, planning, and business studies. What makes this series special is that it facilitates a transdisciplinary approach to understanding property rights and specifically promotes heterodox thinking.

In *Wicked Valuations: People and Landed Property* Michael McDermott expands our understanding and shatters our preconceptions of property rights at the nexus of people, place and property. Mike achieves this by taking us on a journey into valuation, property rights and land policy that is both deeply personal and personally deep. Let me elaborate.

I first met Mike in 2002 when I was convening the FAO/USP/RICS Foundation South Pacific Land Tenure Conflict Symposium, which attracted over 150 delegates from the Pacific Islands, Australia and New Zealand to investigate the land-related conflict associated with the clash between traditional communal values and capitalist aspirations. At that time, Mike was a Commonwealth advisor consulting on land policy and valuation legislation in Vanuatu, and he made a major contribution to the behavioural versus empirical debate amongst the Symposium delegates. In 2007, Mike contacted me again after reading an article of mine (mentioned herein) that lamented my disillusion and dilemma at the absence of robust theoretical foundation for valuation and property within the academy. That was a catalyst to discussions with me and Jason Prior, which led Mike to progress the research that has evolved into this book.

Mike is one of the most travelled and best-read scholars that I have had the privilege to know. This means that he draws on an enormous transdisciplinary lexicon, which enables him to interrogate the insufficiency of traditional valuation thinking and the flaws in prescribed land policy interventions in a way that superficially can seem very challenging but ultimately leaves you way better informed. Indeed, this volume promises to change the way you look at property rights, valuation and land policy. You will want to keep his essential glossary close to hand, but please persist and allow his thought process to transform your understanding of people and landed property.

Given Mike's extensive experience in valuation and land policy (and as a transglobal tour guide), I take full responsibility for encouraging him to draw on that lived experience and expertise to adopt an autoethnographic approach to this book. This means that in taking us on a journey into complexity, property rights and wicked valuation problems autoethnography provides a lens to draw on his knowledge and experience from over the past 40 years in land valuation in Africa and the Asia-Pacific. He combines this with documentary analysis to draw in the views of other scholars and practitioners who likewise are increasingly aware of the (often urgent) need to develop ways to adapt land valuation processes to the complexity of our contemporary landscapes. These two threads are interwoven through Mike's narrative as he analyses his career valuing real property rights, and the effects such rights have had on the peoples in countries in which he has worked and travelled during his fascinating career.

In *Wicked Valuations: People and Landed Property* Mike McDermott permits us to observe the incremental evolution of his own particular response to the demonstrated limitations and failings of taking a positivist, reductionist and juridical prescription to land policy. The outcome is the testing and refinement of the "McDermott protocol" (what he refers to as his HVN↔HBA pilot tool) which takes an holistic approach to the wicked problems encountered in land policy and the valuation of real property rights. It does so by harnessing both the emotional and the logical dimensions of the brain to address the wicked problems encountered. Mike argues that the complexities at the nexus of law, economics and culture can be optimally addressed through protocols that integrate not only the ability of the left hemisphere of the brain to engage with our environment(s) and the capacity of the right hemisphere to make sense of them, but also our whole-headed and whole-hearted engagement with ourselves, our collaborators and all communities impacted by the wicked problem – the identity constructions of communities. He emphasises that respecting the complexities within wicked problems endemic in the development and implementation of land policy interventions, as well as the valuation of complex real property rights, is preconditional to transcending any of our left hemispheres' hard-wired tendency to premature assumptions of competence. Enjoy the journey, and don't look back!

Spike Boydell, General Editor
Sydney, April 2018

Acknowledgements

I wish to thank my supervisors for my doctoral degree, Professor Spike Boydell and Associate Professor Jason Prior, who showed me patient guidance well beyond my own capacities. I would also like to thank my wife Anne and the rest of my family for their support through these years of my monomania. In particular I thank my son Blake, who has achieved the impossible, and made my writing intelligible to him without my catastrophising even once.

My thanks are also due to the designers and supervisors of my Master's Degree, which with its emphasis upon adapting insights from complexity and chaos research for application in social sciences profoundly influenced the development of this work. In particular I express my gratitude to Dr Vladimir Dimitrov and Dr Lesley Kuhn.

I also thank Professor Kenneth Stanley and the University of Central Florida for permission to use the image titled the *Picbreeder Butterfly*. The original image is found in K. O. Stanley and J. Lehman's *Why Greatness Cannot Be Planned: The Myth of the Objective* (Springer, 2015).

Abbreviations

ABC	Australian Broadcasting Corporation
AHAL	All Hextants, All Levels framing: my adaptation of AQAL
AQAL	All Quadrants, All Levels framing to interrogate reality (Wilber 1995)
CAS	complex adaptive systems
ECLET	emergent-cyclical levels of existence theory
EIC	(The British) East India Company
FAO	Food and Agriculture Organization
GDP	gross domestic product
GIGO	garbage in, garbage out
HBA	HIDEGRE BIES ADALAS

HIDEGRE (for framing and principles)

H	Hextants: The division of a holon's functional circle highlighting six domains that must be engaged to address wicked problems
I	Identity: the identity of the holon
D	The interhextal developments of the holon to respond to the wicked problem, and its developments
E	Emergence: the identity's responses to the wicked problems through levels of emergence, every new emergent providing novel qualities and new simplicities.
G	Goldilocks: development may only occur within a limited zone of challenge intensity required to pace the responses.
RE	Related evolution: All evolution is co-evolution, and requires engagements with all hextants and in conformity to the above principles to occur.

BIES (for navigation)

B	Butterfly effects and black swans. A reminder of the essential unpredictability and non-linearity of both holons and wicked problems.

I, E, and S   These signify three forms of valuation to be considered in the holon's resolution of its wicked problem: the intrinsic value, the extrinsic value, and the systemic value of matters of concern. Market value may emerge from these and other variables as defined by the IVSC.

ADALAS (for exploring the landscapes)

AD   All domains, dimensions and degrees of the holon and its wicked problem (For example, drilling from heuristic to ansatz to science).

AL   All levels of complexity and lines of development of the holon and its wicked problem.

AS   All scales and systems of the holon and its wicked problem.

HVN   The primary ontological heuristic of the trans-ontological process: "Being" as a web of changes, of holarchic vortex networks in heterarchic fields

I2S   integration and implementation sciences

IVSC   International Valuation Standards Council

LEI   Land Equity International

LIS   land information system

MHC   Model of Hierarchical Complexity (Commons 2008)

NDS   national development strategy

NECSI   New England Complexity Science Institute

NSEW   north, south, east and west (pronounced, "en sew").

PECAPDISHD   The PEdagogical Counter-Apartheid-rule Psychological DIstortions on the Significance of Human Dignity.

PTSD   post-traumatic stress disorder

SEAP   Swaziland Environmental Action Plan

SNL   Swazi Nation Land

TDL   title deed land

TRA   tenure, rights and access

UNDP   United Nations Development Programme

UNEP   United Nations Environment Programme

Glossary

"Definitions/explanations of key terms" in Chapter 1 points out why I have to use unusual words in this book, and also why I have to employ words with particular meanings from within their broader range of meanings. One example of why I need these words is my use of the word "heterarchy" (q.v.), which is both an unusual word, and here employed in a particular way. An example of my using words with both their general and particular meanings is the word "field", which I use both in its general meaning, and the specific meaning used within HVN↔HBA, as defined below.

Ansatz   An educated guess, an expert first approximation to begin engagement with a problem.

Anthropological machine   The dissociating from other holons, in particular other humans, on the basis of their being less worthy of concern by dint of their otherness – race, tribe, religion, nationality etc. (Agamben 2004, pp. 33–38) or their species. It produces "not only subhuman homo sapiens who supposedly therefore deserve their subjugation and enslavement, but also other subhuman species that also deserve their subjugation and enslavement" (Oliver 2007, p. 11).

Antifragility   Becoming stronger as a result of addressing a challenge (Taleb 2012).

Arrow   The double-headed arrow (↔) as an indicator of a complex adaptive system with feedback loops. For example, I use it in HVN↔HBA to indicate that HBA is an emergent of HVN, and must constantly refer back to HVN, as HVN changes ceaselessly.

Artefact   An inanimate manufactured product, which can be simple or complicated, but not complex. It can be in any hextant, but not all (cf. holons below). Artefacts include artificial persons, being "a collection or succession of natural persons forming a corporation" (Osborn 1964, p. 240).

Autotelic and autotelaxic   "Autotelic" is an existing word meaning "self-purpose", some existent with a purpose. "Autotelaxic" is a neologism I have devised for the purpose of this work, to describe some existent both purposeful and meaningful in itself. It is cognate with another neologism here, "telaxiology" (see below). It also imputes "telax", a noun meaning "valuable purpose", adj. telaxic.

"Big V" valuations My term (McDermott, 1992) to distinguish value judgements from merely monetary ones. I mean them as defined in 2015: "Any social practice where the value or values of something are established, assessed, negotiated, provoked, maintained and/or contested" (Doganova et al. 2015, p. 87). That is, "Big V" values transcend and include market values.

Clumsy theory From cultural theory, clumsy theory looks to discoveries emerging "from a messy, noisy argumentative process; a constructive engagement between the three 'active' ways of organising: hierarchy, individualism and egalitarianism" (Thompson 2013, p. 430).

Complex and complex Respectively, complex knowledge and complex values.

Compliplex and compliplax Respectively, complicated knowledge and complicated values.

Confirmation bias The tendency to acquire or process new information in a way that confirms one's preconceptions and avoids contradictions with one's prior beliefs (Allahverdyan and Galstyan 2014).

Development The process of maturation and learning over time (Paul Bloom in Brockman 2013, p. 161). It always involves movement from a state of relative globality and lack of differentiation towards one of increasing differentiation, articulation and hierarchical integration (Werner 1957). Here, "differentiation" refers to the degree to which a system is composed of parts that differ in structure or function from one another, "integration" refers to the extent to which the different parts communicate and enhance one another's goals (Csikszentmihalyi 1993, pp. 156–157), and "articulation" the way the differentiated and integrated parts join or interrelate. In this work, the main focus is on the animate, not the inanimate, so the focus is on holarchical integration, not hierarchic (see below).

Evolution The constructive process of natural selection through time (Paul Bloom in Brockman 2013, p. 161).

Existents A term from ontology meaning phenomena "having being". I use this unfamiliar term where "thing" is usual as it is more appropriate to the HVN trans-ontological process approach of this book. The term is preferred by ontologists because "things" imply stasis and existents include processes and their relationships and values (Lawson 2014a, p. 2). I consider this a very important differentiation for the purposes of this work, as the word "thing" can be both a mis-description and a collapse of contexts, segueing over intrinsic and systemic value to privilege extrinsic value. Consequently, within this work, unless within a quotation, I am using "existent" instead of "thing", including avoiding words like "something" and "nothing", except in quotations.

Extrinsic value Use or utility value: what an existent is good for.

Field Components' interactions in time and space, dependent upon kinetics and neighbours (Goodwin 1994, p. 49).

Fitness landscape The capacity of an organism in its environment, an emergent from its situative adaption. In this work, its meaning is expanded to refer to the capacity of all existents, in particular land policies, valuations, and the artefacts of real property rights, in their environments.

Fractal Similar at different scales.

Framing "A frame is a way of looking at the world that is value laden" (Hoggan and Litwin 2016, p. 67). "Frames are mental structures that shape the way we see the world. As a result they shape the goals we seek, the plans we make, the way we act, and what counts as a good or bad outcome of our actions" (Lakoff 2004, p. xv).

Gestalt A structure, configuration, or pattern of physical, biological, or psychological phenomena so integrated as to constitute a functional unit with properties not derivable by summation of its parts.

Goldilocks zone A term derived from a children's story called Goldilocks and the Three Bears. Astronomers use it to describe the zone where water may be in its liquid state and therefore life may exist. Here I use it to describe the limited zone of challenge intensity wherein development may occur.

Ground value The value of an existent simply by dint of existing.

Heterarchy This key term derives from "Hetero", meaning "other", and "archy", meaning "rule". Here, "heterarchy" means "an organisational form somewhere between hierarchy and network that draws upon diverse horizontal and vertical links that permit different elements . . . to cooperate (and/or compete) while individually optimising different success criteria . . . [It is] a system of organisation replete with overlap, multiplicity, mixed ascendancy, and/or divergent-but-coexistent patterns of relation [in which] different kinds of power relations may exist between the same elements at the same time" (Normand 2016, p. 76). This differs sharply from Wilber's use of the term, which in his meaning refers to "differentiation without integration . . . heaps not wholes" (Wilber 1995, p. 21). He thereby sees heterarchy as destroying quality and reducing everything to mere quantities. In contrast, I mean it to describe inter-relationships between various levels inside and between holons and inside and between their hextants, because such a discernment is vital for my intrinsic valuation purposes. Stark (2000) refers to heterarchies as "a new mode of organization", enfolding "lateral accountability and organizational heterogeneity", responses to the increasing complexities of strategy horizons or fitness landscapes (ibid., p. 6). They are "complex adaptive systems . . . of competing and comparing value systems" (ibid., p. 8). Here, I mean the term to enfold relationships between all existents and their hextants, including those within and between hierarchies and holarchies.

Hextal helix Just as DNA requires a double helix, this work articulates that development requires a hextal (6-strand) intertwining and inter-relating helix).

Hextant One-sixth of a circle, dividing from the centre. Used here to highlight six domains of holons that must be engaged to address wicked problems.

Hierarchy A system in which members of an organisation or society are ranked according to relative status or authority. It is often loosely used to include "holarchy" or "heterarchy", but their differentiation is important in this work.

Holarchy An organisation of holons of various emergent levels of increasing complexity, the latter enfolding the former. A "ranking of orders or events according to their holistic capacity" (Wilber 1995, p. 17). Wilber uses "hierarchy" and "holarchy" interchangeably because he also differentiates between pathological and normal hierarchies, while observing that many have a visceral reaction to all hierarchies because of the pathological (dominator) hierarchies. However, I repeat that in this work differentiation between hierarchies, holarchies and heterarchies is of critical importance (Stark 2000; Lamont 2012).

Holon A whole that is also part of some other existent. Here, I limit the word to mean the animate and complex: a pan-hextal gestalt of gestalts, in order to differentiate life from the inanimate. It means human and biological "clumped patterns" within the Panarchy (Gunderson and Holling 2002, p. 405). Above, I define artefacts, while recognising that they, too, can be a whole and a part of other existents, as inanimate.

Homeorhesis A dynamic system's return to a developmental trajectory.

Homeostasis A system's return to equilibrium.

Identity The tendency in human beings, individually and in groups, to establish and maintain a sense of self-meaning, predictability and purpose (Northrup 1989, p. 63).

Intrinsic value A valuation based upon the development and complexity of an existent: how many levels of emergence it enfolds, and how differentiated, articulated and hierarchically integrated the existent is.

Land "Land is a delineable area of the Earth's terrestrial surface, encompassing all attributes of the biosphere immediately above or below this surface including those of the near-surface climate, the soil and terrain forms, the surface hydrology (including shallow lakes, rivers, marshes, and swamps), the near-surface sedimentary layers and associated groundwater reserve, the plant and animal populations, the human settlement pattern and physical results of past and present human activity (terracing, water storage or drainage structures, roads, buildings, etc.)" (FAO/UNEP 1997).

That is an objectivist, single vision, definition. As such, it is true as far as it goes; it just does not go far enough in a work about people's relationships with land:

"For people around the world, land is a source of food, shelter, and livelihoods; it's an economic asset, a crucial safety net, a link with culture and social identity, even a living relative or ancestor" (Cordes 2017).

Together with at least some environmental psychologists (Proshansky, Fabian and Kaminoff 1983), from my lived experience I further claim that land is not just a link with culture and social identity, but often fundamental to individual identity.

Land policy A set of coherent decisions about land with common long-term purpose(s) (adapted from International Livestock Research Institute 1995).

Land tenure The way real property rights are held.

Landscape   The word is used to mean both the land under consideration and a particular area of activity, such as a fitness landscape (q.v.). The title refers to both meanings. Hence "places" (q.v.) are included in the term "landscape", but not in the term "land" (q.v.).

Machine   "A combination of resistant parts, each specialized in function, operating under human control, to utilize energy and to perform work" (Mumford 1967, p. 191). Such parts may include holons, including people, whereby "the body is constituted as a part of a multisegmentary machine" (Foucault 1979, p. 164).

Machinism   Machinism conflates machines and people, artefacts and holons. Per se, it does not differentiate between a machine, that functions, and an animal, that lives and restructures its own world and body (Merleau-Ponty and Séglard 2003, p. 162).

Market value   "Market value is the estimated amount for which an asset or liability would exchange on the valuation date between a willing buyer and a willing seller in an arm's-length transaction after proper marketing wherein the parties had each acted knowledgeably, prudently and without compulsion" (IVSC n.d.).

Master and emissary   Respectively, the terms for the functions of right and left hemispheres of the brain used by McGilchrist (2009). In this work's terms, the Master better addresses the Landscapes, and the Emissary, The Machine.

Meme   Imitated existents in the psyche hextant, similar to genes in the soma hextant.

Memeplex   A coadapted complex of memes (Speel 1995).

Multiplex and multiplex   Respectively, wide-ranging knowledge and wide-ranging values

Natural capital   Natural capital consists of those components of the natural environment that provide a long-term stream of benefits to individual people and to society as a whole (Costanza et al. 2006, p. ii).

Necessary fallibility   "A term related to the chaos theory that explains the unpredictability of events results in nonlinear, noncoupled, nondeterministic systems" (McGraw-Hill 2002).

North, south, east and west (NSEW)   Here, the four directions, when capitalised and quoted together, have their cultural and economic meanings rather than directional:

North: The developed world
South: The underdeveloped world
East: Asia
West: Europe, North America and Australasia.

Octo   My name for an imaginary holon (q.v.), derived from the eight points of a cube, which I introduce in Chapter 5 to make a distinction between the external world, as perceived by the holon concerned, and the external world as inclusionary as we can make it.

Omniplex and omniplax   Respectively, all knowledge and all values

Ontology   "The branch of metaphysics concerned with the nature or essence of being or existence", and at another level "a rigorous and exhaustive organization of some knowledge domain" (Cruickshank 2004; Carrithers et al. 2010; Pedersen 2012).

Orthogenic Principle   The principle that all development proceeds from a state of relative globality and lack of differentiation to one of increasing differentiation, articulation and hierarchical integration (Werner 1957). In HBA, I refer to this as the "Development Principle", but substitute the word "holonic" for "hierarchic" when it comes to holons, and retain "hierarchic" for machines.

Place   "A place is a space where one can imagine living, a home to which values, in ethical and aesthetic terms, are attached" (Lovino 2014, p. 102).

Psyche   The mind (including imagination, intellect, desires, will, emotions, etc.).

Real estate   "The physical land and those human-made items, which attach to the land. It is the physical, tangible 'thing' which can be seen and touched, together with all additions on, above, or below the ground" (IVSC n.d.).

Real property   Immovable property which could be recovered by a real action. "Including all the rights, interests and benefits relating to the ownership of real estate. An interest or interests in real property is normally demonstrated by some evidence of ownership (e.g., a title deed) separate from the physical real estate. Real property is a non-physical concept" (IVSC n.d.).

Rights   Recognised and protected interests. Note that in this work the term enfolds formal (legally protected) and informal (otherwise socially recognised) rights, the term "formal property rights" being adopted when they alone are being referred to.

Simplex and simplex   Respectively, simple knowledge and simple valuations.

Simplex, complex, multiplex, omniplex etc.   Simplex, multiplex and omniplex are words adopted by Stewart and Cohen (1995), "simplex" meaning simple knowledge, "multiplex" wide-ranging knowledge, and "omniplex", all knowledge. To these, I have added "compliplex", to maintain the vital distinction for this work between complicated and complex, and "simplax", "complax", "multiplax" and "omniplax" as the axiological equivalents of Stewart and Cohen's terms.

Social imaginary   "A general belief about the world that has 'no ontological status' but comes to exist through the distinctions and intersections that constitute ordinary life and the various means we invent to appreciate and measure the differences that exist between individuals and cultures" (Dick 2013, p. 4). I use it neither to condemn nor to embrace, but rather to identify social imaginaries as a means towards valuing them.

Social messes   Heaps of wicked problems (q.v.).

Soma   The physical body.

Spatial imaginary   A subset of social imaginary, it is the space that "is visible or thinkable for each society and culture, that which grants meaning to the social, to the individuals and their experiences" (adapted from Cornelius

Castoriadis's definition of "social imaginary" in Castro Nogueira (1997, p. 16). As such, it is a core part of a person's umwelt (see below).

Spirituality "Spirituality is a state of interconnectedness with the Other – the divine, the self, the human, the natural, or any combination thereof – that nourishes the soul (the integration of mind, will and emotions), resulting in a state of security with a sense of worthful purpose in life" (Rosado 2003). Note the definition neither privileges nor refers to any religion: They are hextally distinct phenomena. Nor does it ascribe spirituality to natural or any other causes: It simply recognises it as fundamental to the behaviour of many humans, and absent from machines.

Systemic value The value of a holon or artefact in the context of its role as part of a system working towards how existents should be.

Telaxiology The study of meaningful purpose (a neologism for this work, following Vallicella (2009), by which I mean differentiating evil, trivial and futile purposes from good, significant and useful ones in their various contexts and scales. Also see "autotelaxic" above.

Theory Generally, a theory provides an explanation for some existent based on some research. More particularly, it provides a general explanation for observations made over time, explains and predicts behaviour, can never be established beyond all doubt, and may be modified but seldom has to be discarded if thoroughly tested. However, sometimes a theory may be widely accepted for a long time and later disproved (Dorin, Demmin and Gabel 1990).

Thintelligence A word coined by Michael Crichton for seeing the immediate situation, thinking narrowly and calling it "being focussed", and missing both the surround and the consequences.

Thomas theorem If one defines situations as real, they are real in their consequences (Thomas and Thomas 1928; Merton 1995).

Tool "A practical method to achieve a defined objective in a particular context" (Selabalo 2016).

Transdisciplinary Weak transdisciplinarity is conflational with interdisciplinarity, but not with multidisciplinarity. Here, I mean it in its strong sense, involving three pillars: levels of reality, the axiom of the included middle, and complexity (Max-Neef 2005). So multidisciplinarity refers to many disciplinary "silos", not necessarily relating to each other themselves. The silos relate in interdisciplinarity, and with the complex interactions of its three pillars, a transdisciplinarity process may emerge. As such, multi-, inter- and trans-disciplinarity are "better treated as complementary rather than being mutually exclusive" (Brown, Harris and Russell 2010, p. 21).

Trans-ontological process The term was first coined by Enrique Dussel as part of his trans-modernist decentralisation of The Machine (and its valuation of machinism as epistemically totalitarian) (Irvine 2011). Following Whitehead's process philosophy (1978), Heraclitus, the Taoist and Buddhist insight of impermanence Unger's (2007, pp. 85–86) rejection of ontology, and McGilchrist's (2009) analysis of the West's imbalanced emphasis of left hemisphere's machinism, HVN↔HBA as a trans-ontological process is a rejection of the "thinging" (Bateson 1979, p. 112) aspects of ontology *as prime*. However, the term as used here further recognises that our minds require imaginals to address realities, and transcends and includes them within HVN↔HBA to examine landscapes, The Machine and their interrelationships. That is, a trans-ontological process is permanently impermanent and provisional, a process not a thing.

Ubuntu As with many foreign words and phrases Ubuntu is not directly translatable into English, but involves the recognition of the high intrinsic value of one another's common humanity. Moreover, in contrast to the Cartesian "I think, therefore I am", Ubuntu means "whatever happens to the individual happens to the whole group, and whatever happens to the whole group happens to the individual. The individual can only say: 'I am, because we are; and since we are therefore I am'" (Mbiti 1990, p. 106).

Umfeld The world that objectively influences an organism.

Umwelt The world as perceived by an organism; all the semiotic processes of an organism as perceived in its innenwelt (inner world). The circumscribed portion of the environment which is meaningful and effective for a given species (English and English 1958).

Usury In this book, I use this term for the lending of money at an exploitative rate of interest (either immediate or accruing) not its broader meaning of lending money at any rate of interest whatsoever.

Welt German for "world".

Wicked problems Difficult or impossible complexly interrelated problems. "A wicked problem is a complex issue that defies complete definition, for which there can be no final solution, since any resolution generates further issues, and where solutions are not true or false or good or bad, but the best than can be done at the time. Such problems are not morally wicked, but diabolical in that they resist all the usual attempts to resolve them" (Brown, Deane, Harris and Russell in Brown, Harris and Russell 2010, p. 4).

Wisdom Integrated thought (Labouvie-Vief 1990). "The ability to make sense of complexity, context specificity, and to integrate moral perspectives, balancing part and bigger systems" (Mulgan 2014 at 29:57).

1 Framing the thesis of this book

Introduction

The primary purpose of this book is to be a knowledge-building document which includes the knowledge that knowledge itself can never be enough to address its subject.

That subject is policy development at all scales from personal to global, and in particular our land-related policies, laws, institutions and valuations.

Furthermore, I here argue that what I term "The Machine" is not only insufficient to address the performance of the International Valuation Standard's definition market value. That definition is fundamental to this book, particularly in its emphasis on *willing* buyers and *willing* sellers, because machines do not have wills:

> Market value is the estimated amount for which an asset or liability would exchange on the valuation date between a willing buyer and a willing seller in an arm's-length transaction after proper marketing wherein the parties had each acted knowledgeably, prudently and without compulsion.
>
> (IVSC 2016)

As explained later, we require *organisms* to find "willing" existents – holons, not artefacts, complex, not merely simple or complicated. They have to be so in order to value in the first place, and to address wicked problems. But they also create wicked valuation problems, particularly in the contexts of the North meeting the South, and the East meeting the West, because they employ heuristics called ideologies, and "ideologies exist spatially" (Emerson 2005), as tracked by Arredondo (2013) via his focus on the history of the USA.

As an example of ideologies existing spatially from the area of particular focus in this book, that of land policy, I note that "Land surveys in the 19th century began to help divide the country for settlement and political division by drawing patterns on the land. The notion of 'land ownership' invades the West with devastating effects on Native Americans" (Rumsey 2005, 10:19–10:26): "This is sort of the American experience: everything is rationalized, surveyed, contained" (ibid., 10:55–10:57). The process Rumsey described in the North

American context was repeated globally, and goes for out mental maps as well as our paper and digital ones. Yet there is a difference between them. As Lewis Mumford stated in *The Myth of the Machine*:

> Unlike an organism, which is an open system, subject to chance mutations and to many external forces and circumstances over which it has no control, mechanisms are closed systems, strictly contrived by the inventor to achieve clearly foreseen and limited ends. . . . By contrast, even the lowest species of organism . . . has remarkable potentialities that no machine can boast: it can alter its species' character and re-program itself, so to say, in order to seize new opportunities or resist unwanted external pressures. That margin of freedom no machine possesses in its own right.
>
> (Mumford 1970, p. 97)

I am asserting that ignoring or undervaluing how crucially important this difference is, and thinking exclusively inside the framing of "the mechanics of this" and the "mechanics of that", is a requisite gullibility for one to be confined within the myth of the machine. With Arredondo (2013), I contend that it was preconditional to man-induced climate change and the potential extinction of our species by that and other means (including nuclear war), and similarly the past and ongoing extinctions of thousands of other species on our planet.

That is because markets involve not only fact perceptions, but also value judgements, with value judgements actually directing the search for facts through framing what one seeks and finds in the first place (McGilchrist 2009, pp. 9 and 29, Lakoff 2004): "Values come first, facts and policies follow in the service of values. They matter, but they always support values" (Lakoff 2016). Once the basic needs in Maslow's hierarchy have been met (see Box 5.2, p. 202) there may be great differences in such value judgements between cultures, and therefore great differences in what constitutes a market value agreement within and between them (Henrich, Heine and Norenzayan 2010).

For that reason, in the context of framing our searches for facts and values and their inter-relationships it is necessary to include references to philosophers and scientists, including physicists. Philosophers are of central concern, but we are not to limit ourselves to philosophy: the central quest here is that of addressing wicked valuation problems. However, many philosophers provide useful guidance in that quest. One such, Charles Taylor, made a core perception in the context, that of a *social imaginary* (Taylor 2001, 2002, 2004). Using reductionism in what I consider to be its legitimate function as a highlighting device, rather than its illegitimate function as a cutting-off device, the "truth about stories is that's all we are" (King 2003), meaning that the "we" thus defined is a social imaginary.

Physicists are important not only because they have been the most influential in framing machine thinking, but also because many of them are at the forefront of revealing its limitations. Poets, politicians and activists are also important to reveal framings and value judgements. However, it is not only philosophers, physicists, poets, politicians and activists who are important to reveal framings and value judgements. In fact, everyone is, starting with oneself, particularly in relationships. Hence my emphasis on identity here, and the provision of my own identity construction as my best-known example of that process.

While McGilchrist and other recent researchers (for example, Nielsen et al. 2013) dismiss several popular hemispheric/personality lateralisations dating from the 1970's, they equally confirm that genuine lateralisations remain. McGilchrist's work still results in framing the right hemisphere's domain being that of all value judgements but the extrinsic/utilitarian ones (McGilchrist 2009, pp. 72 and 93). In turn, value judgements frame and power the philosophical, propositional and analytical choices of all peoples everywhere, whether they realise it or not. In this work, I am not mainly concerned with which hemispheres or neurons do what, but with McGilchrist's and Lakoff's insights into the relationships between fact perceptions and value judgements as they may apply in arriving at market agreements, particularly inter-cultural ones.

Many such culture-shaping value judgements are expressed through myths. As Diamond points out:

> A myth is one way we give meaning to our existence – no myth, no meaning. What we have come today scientifically to call models or paradigms are actually myths: cognitive constructs we create in an effort to better comprehend our universe and ourselves.
>
> (Diamond 2006, p. 186)

As Horkheimer and Adorno put it, "Myth is already enlightenment, and enlightenment reverts to mythology" (2002, p. xviii).What I term The Machine is born through the myth of mechanism, and comes into reality via the Thomas Theorem – "if one defines situations as real, they are real in their consequences" (Thomas and Thomas 1928; Merton 1995).

Those two terms, "myth" and "machine" were brought together decades ago by Lewis Mumford, on his above-quoted two-volume work, "The Myth of the Machine" (1967, 1970). The implementation of this myth – via the Thomas Theorem – has been and is still prompted by "a series of intentional choices made in the pursuit of power, power over nature and power over other humans". These engender "an increasing tendency towards mechanization that often [comes at] at the expense of humaneness" and leads to the machine becoming "an end in itself" and being "treated as if it were the creative principle instead of just one possible creation" (Carlo 2013). The myth enacts "the social consequences of increasing physical power" without necessarily having any "commensurate increase in intellectual insight, moral discipline, social awareness, and responsible political direction" (Mumford 1970, p. 232).

This myth, a philosophical expression of which is machinism (Merleau-Ponty and Séglard 2003, p. 162) developed what Mumford termed the megamachine, driven by what he termed "The Pentagon of Power", that pentagon being power, profit, productivity, property, and prestige (Mumford 1970). Via that pentagon, machinism provides an enboxing of complexity which provides a comforting closure and power-rush for its employers. That emotion of dominance is gained irrespective of its truth value. As such, is a facilitator of left-hemisphere dominance for some of the processually less aware. While this book concentrates on property, the other four ends of the pentagon remain inseparable throughout.

I also argue that the Myth of the Enlightenment (a sub-myth of the myth of the machine for knowledge, too, is power) – in particular, its deliberate disregard of intrinsic valuation – highlights weaknesses of The Machine in both its sources and its drivers.

While of vast extrinsic value in a myriad of contexts, the megamachine, which I shall hereinafter term "The Machine", is of no more intrinsic value than any other machine, such as a stapler, because as explained below machines are never complex, only simple to highly complicated. McGilchrist claims that "Not only does the right hemisphere have an affinity with whatever is living, but the left hemisphere has an equal affinity for what is mechanical" (McGilchrist 2009, p. 55). While not referring to brain geography but to the mental phenomena McGilchrist addressed over 60 years later, Lewis Mumford noted of mechanist mindsets that "their failure is due to the fact that they are seeking to discover, by abstraction and definition, something that is a complex product of varied, never-ending natural and human processes" (Mumford 1946, p. 161). Living holons are wickedly complex; inanimate machines are simple to complicated: "Biological and social systems are open, therefore understanding them in mechanical terms will not work" (Sardar and Abrams 2004, p. 69). As stated by Cobb:

> The entire issue serves to illustrate what I believe to be the central intellectual challenge of our age: We live in complex systems, but we do not understand them. Just admitting this might help us find our way forward on so many problems that now plague us.
>
> (Cobb 2011)

As distinct from just an intellectual problem, Arredondo (2013) considers what Mumford described as Myth of the Machine's "totalitarian triumph of scientific megatechnics" (Mumford 1970, p. 312) to be "the greatest problem that we face", with its "regression toward primitive forms of total domination and the nihilism that underlies it".

I contend that these problems are intimately enmeshed, and that attention to this interplay of value judgements and fact perceptions is core to addressing wicked valuation problems. I have developed HVN↔HBA to facilitate wise action in addressing that interplay. That is, I am introducing HVN↔HBA as a candidate for being a due diligence protocol in addressing wicked valuation problems.

This book, then, is by a practitioner of real property valuation who believes that the current valuation processes (strongly influenced as they are by mere rationalist economic theory which is, insofar as it is merely rationalist, unreasonable) are inadequate in addressing the complex landscape of property valuation. While my professional field is about reducing all relevant complexities to a market value of real property rights, this work is about addressing wicked valuation problems by respecting their complexities and irreducibilities. As Vandana Shiva puts it, "for anyone who says it's too big or too deep, unless we go there even smaller problems won't be solved" (ABC RN 2015a, 53:16).

Therefore I look outwards and upwards from my real property valuation base towards emerging disciplines such as Valuation Studies (Helgesson and Muniesa 2013), environmental psychology (Proshansky, Fabian and Kaminoff 1983), Complexics (Bastardas-Boada 2015), Integration and Implementation Sciences (I2S) (Bammer 2013), Clumsy Theory (Taylor 2015; Thompson 2013), Critical Systems Thinking (Pollack 2013), Post-Normal Science (Funtowicz and Ravetz 1990, 1991; Tognetti 2013) and others such as social identity and self-categorisation theories (Sindic and Condor 2014).

As obliquity is a recommended approach towards addressing complexities (Kay 2011), in so doing I shall introduce the subject with a story about the sea, a machine on it called the *Endeavour*, and the encounter of the machinism-focussed minds the *Endeavour* housed with a very different mind. I do so as an illustrative dichotomy towards the idea that there are many approaches to addressing the topic of this book in addition to those of the currently dominant machinist economic paradigm, and that to acknowledge their existence is not to recommend any dominance by any of them, but rather to employ them when optimal in the context.

In 1769, in the Society Islands, Joseph Banks encountered a man called Tupaia. Banks brought him aboard *Endeavour*, a ship captained by James Cook that was there to observe the transit of Venus as part of an expedition to discover *Terra Australis*. Later, the *Endeavour* discovered Australia's east coast for the British Crown, which led to the kinds of problems addressed in this work.

A major reason for observing the transit of Venus was that it would help British navigators accurately calculate their longitude: a vital cog for their ships to find their way around the globe. Their reasons for their voyages were centred around trade. Empire was about what Moore terms "the Law of Value" (Moore 2015), which he regards as fundamental to capitalism: to commonalise or otherwise externalise the costs, and privatise the profits – a process of exploitation via capitalisation, and appropriation of that value to themselves. The context of Cook's endeavour was to find in order to exploit more of a major requirement of that process, Cheap Nature.

By "Cheap Nature" Moore means "the ongoing, radically expansive, and relentlessly innovative quest to turn the work/energy of the biosphere into capital (value-in-motion)" (ibid., Kindle location 368). It asserts that "the web of life can be fragmented, that its moments can be valued through calculations of price and value" (ibid., Kindle location 1269), the "genius of capitalism's cheap nature strategy [being] to represent time as linear, space as flat, as nature as external" (Moore 2014, p. 286). Moore sees that approach as the West's inflection of what Haraway termed "the God Trick" – "seeing everything from nowhere" (Haraway 1988, p. 581), but which Blake would have seen as the Urizen Trick, passed from Urizen to Newton.

Tupaia was of particular interest to Banks because he could navigate without nailing down longitude. For him, as for other Polynesians, the planet was "a living force" (Strongman 2008, p. 72), a view more compatible with that of some modern scientists than that of eighteenth century mechanists: "The universe . . . is organic . . . a process, not a thing" (Cole 2001, p. 185). In contrast, the educated gentlemen on the *Endeavour*, facilitating what their contemporary William Blake described as Single Vision and Newton's sleep, navigated by a combination of a (then merely clockwork) astronomy and "Mr. Kendall's watch" (Sobel 1998, p.150).

One interpretation of Blake's "single vision" is seeing merely materially. Twofold vision means seeing not only materially but also the "perception of the human values in all things", threefold "the creative state", and fourfold "mystical ecstasy" (Damon 2013, pp. 469–470). Another interpretation is that they are a "loose hierarchy of psychical conditions, consisting in ascending order, of reason, energy, love and genius, each state containing the preceding ones" (Beer 1969, p. 27).

Single vision sees "things", and their being "either/or", with itself as their ultimate arbiter. In contrast, the higher levels transcend but include the lower. In the introductory chapter of their work *Tackling Wicked Problems through the Transdisciplinary Imagination* (Brown, Harris and Russell 2010), the chapter's authors note that this period of history was "the last time Western knowledge as a whole gave serious consideration to imagination as the premier way of knowing" (ibid., p. 9), that its rejection was a "false premise", and that "imagination plays an essential role in decision-making on complex issues" (ibid., p. 5). Instead, they looked at science from Midgley's perspective (ibid., p. 9) of science as "the huge, ever-changing imaginative structures of ideas by which scientific inquiry contrives to connect, understand and interpret its observations" (Midgley 2004, p. 3), not "just as an immense store-cupboard of objective facts" (ibid.).

One matter in this context is that Blake's imaginative mythmaking was "centred upon then different degrees of perception or insight" (Antal 2013, pp. 176–177). His "dark Satanic mills" were thought by those of literalist single visions to refer to the mills of the industrial revolution. While with the wisdom of hindsight they may be thought Satanic by some (those literal dark mills blackened England's skies and began anthropocentric climate change (Klein 2014, p. 157), Blake meant those mills as just artefacts of what he considered the truly Satanic; *the arresting and "shackling" of the mind* (Stevenson in Blake 1988, p. 11): he saw Satan as the state of mind of the fallen ego, obsessed with power.

Today, we would not use the same language. In a reversal of Susan Blackmore's Meme Machine (1999), we might call that arresting and shackling of the mind, "the machine meme" whereby we count beans, tick boxes, and goosestep. While Katya Walter recommended analogue truth as a sophrosyne, ratio/proportionality way of conceptualising reality that "offers the West something we need to expand the limits of our linear, logical reality" (Walter 1996, p. 181), valuing "relational quality over finite quantity . . . [and preferring] proportional shifts in nuance over summary statements" (ibid., p. 194), she recognised that:

The strange face of analog truth can be especially frightening to a rigid, impermeable, brittle western ego. A logic-bound ego expects only demons beyond its limits. It marks the map of its psyche with warnings: "Beyond these gates there be monsters."

(Walter 1996, p. 23)

Furthermore:

(a) ego, or self, is an organisation of knowledge,
(b) ego is characterised by cognitive biases strikingly analogous to totalitar-ian information-control strategies, and
(c) These totalitarian-ego biases junction to preserve organisation in cognitive structures.

Ego's cognitive biases are egocentricity (self as the focus of knowledge), "beneffectance" (perception of responsibility for desired, but not undesired, outcomes), and cognitive conservatism (resistance to cognitive change) . . . There is much evidence for the operation of these biases in . . . the human self or ego . . . as well as in two extrapersonal knowledge domains-paradigmatic scientific theory and totalitarian propaganda. The biases' predilection for fabrication and revision of history entails costs.

(Greenwald 1980, pp. 603, 615)

Mumford, too, noticed "the peculiar fascination automated systems would have for autocratic minds" (Mumford 1970, p. 189). But markets are not so confined; machines don't make markets: people do: *willing* buyers and *willing* sellers. Insofar as they are shackled, I see those minds as fuel for the Empire of The Machine. Insofar as they are not, I see them as possessing potential for addressing the complex aspects of wicked valuation problems.

In accord with the scientific studies quoted herein, this work is neither limited nor beholden to the linear, box-ticking strategies of the machinist meme in its approaches or even its formatting. Rather, it looks towards climbing Blake's interpretation of Jacob's ladder to ascend from single to four-fold vision and real freedom (Antal 2013, pp. 176–177), autoethnographically employing clumsy theory (Thompson 2013) in its relatively analinear, heterarchical formatting as a necessary but insufficient precondition to address the topic of this work.

Antal adds to Damon's explanation above that single vision included abstract-ing, and that twofold emerges from an apprehension that there are existents beyond the finite and reasoning abstracted from it, and they include contraries. Blake's threefold vision recognises the contraries can both be true, and fourfold vision refers to mystical ecstasy (Antal 2013, p. 176). With Francis Bacon and John Locke (referred to in Chapter 3 below), Newton's "mechanistic universe" and Locke's "mechanistic psychology" fitted together with Bacon's experimental-ism to form, in Blake's vision, an "infernal trinity", the trouble being that "it left out God, man, and all the values that made life worth living" (Damon 2013, p. 329).

It is vital to point out that Newton may not have considered his single vision/ monological gaze deficient. After all, it proved enormously powerful. Newton would further object to Blake that God was at the very core of his concerns. Newton was a natural philosopher, man of astonishing insight, one I always thought a genius, but, according to Beer, Blake put at the opposite end of his vision spectrum.

When I read selections from his works (Newton 1974), albeit seeing them as manifestly monological, they gave me no hint of the infernal. However, in his introduction to a book of such selections (ibid.), John Herman Randall Jr. admits the validity of the question, "did Newtonian mechanics add much to wisdom beyond that already given to the West by the Greeks thousands of years before?" He adds that Newton would be delighted his mode of thought was considered a necessary stage in the development of science. He would be even more cheered to hear it called "a gleaming pinnacle in the moral and religious life of Western culture" (ibid., p. x), with its "ideals of benevolence, tolerance, intellectual freedom, cosmopolitanism, and peace" (ibid., p. xi). Moreover, both Newton and his later critics would all be appalled at:

> The more recent contention that natural science has nothing to do with "values", that it can and should remain "value free" [and that] those seeking a direction for human life have nothing to learn from our best knowledge of the nature of things.
>
> (Newton 1974, p. x)

In Blake's fertile imagination, his "infernal trinity" were vessels of a state of mind he anthropomorphised as Urizen, the Ancient of Days, the Satanic slaver (ibid., p. 422), the "stern and sterile god of reason" (Ghiţă 2008, p. 25), the fallen ego as the eternal enemy of imagination and man's true identity (ibid., pp. 26, 54). Blake portrayed Newton as engaging a similar approach to Urizen, both of them measuring to abstract as portrayed below. In Urizen's case, he formed:

> The whole into another world better suited to obey
> His will where none should dare oppose his will himself being King
> Of All & all futurity be bound in his vast chain
> And the Sciences were fixd and the Vortexes began to operate
> On all the sons of men and every human soul terrified.
>> ("The Four Zoas", Night the Sixth, lines 118–123;
>> Blake 1988, p. 126)

Habermas and Foessel warn that:

> our western standards of egalitarian and individualistic universalism . . .often served, and still do serve, to cover up the practice of double standards – both

in the hypocritical justification of repressive regimes, and in the imperialist destruction and exploitation of foreign cultures", and that one must be wary of "the increasingly high-pitched appeal by politicians to 'our values' [which] sounds ever emptier".

(Habermas and Foessel 2015)

Midgley (1995, p. 250), sees Blake as seeing Reason as a colonial "imported governor" over the passions in the tradition of Plato, the Stoics, Descartes, Spinoza and Kant. However, Urizen's flaw was his arrogant single vision, the kind of Greek intellectualist arrogance that Midgley observes in Plato and Aristotle (ibid.), which was to be remedied by developing fourfold vision. From fourfold vision, Blake may well have agreed with Midgley in considering reason as "growing out of and completing a natural balance of parts" (ibid.). My approach to wicked valuation problems involves valuation within different contexts, and dissociation from a context prevents that.

The above myopia, if not hypocrisy, concerning collateral effects is *per se* single vision, and I contend below that Blake's objection to it remains robust to this day. By shutting out so-called "externalities" rather than valuing their possible influences, single vision is directly responsible for many of the wicked problems we have to address today, including climate change, mass extinctions, and the like. Tupaia's approach was in dramatic contrast to that of Urizen's follower Newton, and to Newton's followers on the *Endeavour*, whose:

approach was simply this: reduce what you are trying to think about to the minimum required by its definition; visualize it on paper, or at least in your mind . . . Then you can measure, that is, count the quanta. Early modernity's epoch-making abstractions were registered through the era's new cartographies, new temporalities, new forms of surveying and property-making.

(Moore 2015, Kindle locations 4756–4760)

As that approach as Master rather than Emissary is a major cause of the wicked valuation problems this book addresses, the work cannot be confined within that approach; that is because such a framing "presumes separation of humanity and nature" (Moore 2015, Kindle location 7186). Rather, this work "presumes a dialectical unity that proceeds from the distinctiveness of humans (among many other species) within the web of life" (ibid.).

From this framing I adopt Ghiţă's (2008, p. 13) phrase of an "unsystematic system" to describe Tupaia's approach. Catamarans were faster and sometimes larger than the *Endeavour* (Taonui 2012). On them, he would read the complex interplays between marker islands, the sidereal compass, wave orientations and refraction patterns, kinds of sea phosphorescence and clouds (including the green underbelly of clouds), bird kinds and behaviours, sea marks and stars (ibid., pp. 70, 80–81), and derive meanings from their combinations. He could chase stars across the night sky that he knew would emerge from related points of the horizon, with seven to 12 stars seeing him through a night (ibid.). Thereby, he was able to navigate on the *Endeavour* to islands that the British could not, because they had not then nailed down their latitude and longitude.

However, once those in the *Endeavour* had the islands' positions nailed, they did not need Tupaia's navigation anymore. *Nor would anyone else* ready, willing and able to use Captain Cook's charts and instruments. This is an instance of the wicked valuation problems arising that this work sets out to address: "technical environments defeat ancestral cognition . . . But the consequences of rewriting ancestral cognition cannot be anticipated in advance", thereby creating a wicked valuation problem (Bakker 2015). A few scratches on charts made Tupaia's previously high extrinsic value obsolete; an example of technological unemployment.

William Blake was a teenager when Captain Cook met Tupaia. If, when he had matured, Blake had seen portrayals of Polynesians including the spirals on and between the faces of Tupaia and his ancestors, he would have been impressed. For Blake, spirals represented an awareness of infinity, the vortex serving as a gateway to a new level of perception (Antal 2013, p. 176).

While impossible to dis-invent either mechanistic (single vision) thinking or ignore the often-colossal extrinsic value machines provide, that does not prevent us from asking, "Who, or what, navigates our ship, of state or of any other kind, and to what purpose? What baby was thrown out with that bathwater then, and since then?"

I do not mean just on the sea, but by what anti-Imperialists such as Tagore, Gandhi, Liang Shu-Ming and others (Mishra 2012) referred to as "The Machine" on land; a machine of power, enfolding nation-states and corporations, with "its mental slaves hypnotized into believing that they are free" (Tagore 1918, pp. 26–27).

Strongman saw the lives of priestly Polynesians such as Tupaia as cognitively more complex than those of their visitors from afar, and "capable of understanding and interpreting a more complex array of signifiers from the phenomenological world than the Europeans" (Strongman 2008, p. 73). He also submitted that for them "navigation was a state of being" (ibid., p. 98), with "self and environment co-existent and co-creative" (ibid., p. 99), resulting in their "whole self in navigation" (ibid., p. 100). This is an example of the adaptability to situational challenges that was also evident in Melanesian navigation, and which Strongman considers was endemic throughout all mainly non-Machine societies (Suchman 1987), and which I submit has much (but not all) to teach us about addressing wicked problems.

The Empire Cook worked for was one of what Mead refers to as the "maritime powers" (the USA being another). Mead suggests they remain the key to world power by their "Protocols of the Elders of Greenwich". Those protocols are:

- Develop and maintain an open, dynamic society at home
- Turn the economic energy of that society out into world trade
- Protect commerce throughout the world and defend the balance of power in the world's chief geographical theatres

- Open the global system to others, even to potential competitors in times of peace
- Turn the system against one's opponents in war
- Promote liberal values and institutions whenever one can (Mead 2007, p. 360).

Liang Shu-Ming and others saw The Machine that empowered these protocols as "the devil of the modern world" (Mishra 2012, p. 255). Gandhi said, "The state is a soulless machine ... [which] ... can never be weaned from violence" (Tendulkar 1960, vol. 4, p. 11); "What I object to is the craze for machinery, not machinery as such [but that] ... much machinery merely helps a few to ride on the backs of millions" (ibid., vol. 2, p. 161); "If India becomes the slave of the machine, then, I say, heaven save the world" (Gandhi in Gandhi, Prabhu and Rao 1968, p. 404).

While the Congress party did not follow Gandhi's views, Deendayal Upadhyaya did, whose views were foundational to the Bharatiya Jana Sangh (BJP). He was very wary of what he termed the "machinism" of the Imperialists, and vowed to fight it by Dharmarajya (Moral Rule), democracy, social equality and economic decentralisation (Upadhyaya 1988–1989). Nor were such cries confined to nationalists such as Upadhyaya. The American philosopher and scholar of Eastern art Ernest Fanollosa contrasted Western machinism and Eastern aesthetics, considering the latter to contain "critical information for our methods of education" (Williams 2014, p. 99). At Fenollosa's time, the late nineteenth, early twentieth century, he diagnosed a pathological imbalance within education, favouring analysis over synthesis. He warned of "the 'mental stiffness' with which 'the mechanical or the savage mind clings to its narrow traditions'" (ibid.).

They were no fools. What were they thinking? I consider that they were thinking from different value frames, and that we need to be aware of these value frames as well as our own in order to address wicked valuation problems. In particular, I mean those problems that are the focus of this book: those when the North meets the South, and the East meets the West (the when, but in this context the "when" also encompassing the where, why, who and how of when NSEW meet). In so doing however, it is important to realise that everyone throughout NSEW has brain hemispheres that function to varying degrees, so it's a species issue, and that the recent dominance of Western versions of The Machine is a historical aberration likely about to end: The Machine is not dependent on the North, South, East or West, but the most fit for purpose in the context.

Turning to contemporary thinkers, Jerry Ravetz and Silvio Funtowicz, the founders of the field of postnormal science, observed that "In pre-chaos days, it was assumed that values were irrelevant to scientific inference, and that all uncertainties could be tamed" (Ravetz in Sardar and Abrams 2004, p. 156), "But in a world dominated by chaos ... We confront issues where facts are uncertain, values in dispute, stakes high and decisions urgent ... In post-normal science,

Quality replaces Truth as the organising principle" (Funtowicz and Ravetz 1991, pp. 156, 159).

The last is an odd comment: quality and truth are hardly mutually exclusive. I quote it because qualities require valuation, and truth evaluation, and both can be engaged in a co-evolutionary dynamic.

As this Machine is also the system created through the "single vision" insights of Blake's infernal trinity, perhaps there is more to discover in general, and in the context of clashes in values in particular? Does the dazzling Enlightenment via a single vision necessarily endarken two-fold, three-fold and four-fold vision? More particularly in this work, does it endarken two-fold vision, which enfolds humane values, and what light, if any, might this throw upon the East's and South's concerns with the West and North?

So by "valuation" in the title of this book, I mean to enfold what I later herein call the "Big V" values – an especially topical example of the kind being the protection of the environment. The emerging discipline of Valuation Studies addresses such "Big V" values (Doganova et al. 2015, p. 87), as does the World Values Survey. At both levels of the term "valuation", valuations can affect and effect societies, environments and economies. While all three are relevant to it, my base discipline of the market valuation of real property rights is more focussed on economics than either the societal or the environmental valuation domains. I call such economic values "small v" values.

In the HVN↔HBA model I articulate below, the HVN's physical expressor is the Universe. Within an identity it is as apprehended by the right hemisphere of the brain (the hemisphere which emphasises "betweenness", with an "open, receptive, widely diffused alertness to whatever exists" (McGilchrist 2009, p. 25), and whereby the organism "is not separated from either the spirit or the real world itself" (Hughes 1992, p. 159). However, separation/dissection for analysis is the *modus operandi* of the left hemisphere, and to do so grasps aspects of reality as they fly past (McGilchrist 2009, p. 55) and which may even come to believe that its consequent constructions actually comprise the world (!) (ibid., p. 219). HIDEGRE and ADALAS are the analytical tools I am recommending the left hemisphere employs to approach wicked valuation problems in its proper role as the right hemisphere's Emissary.

These hemispheres represent "two individually coherent, but incompatible, aspects of the world" (ibid., p. 94). While both sides are required, McGilchrist claims that for optimal brain functioning the right hemisphere, repository of all values but utility (extrinsic) value, is to be the Master, and the left whose only valuation is extrinsic value – "what is this thing good for" – is to be the Emissary. He further claims that the West now has that relationship backwards, which I see as a major contributor to the wicked valuation problems this work addresses.

In terms of The Machine and the landscapes it confronts, according to McGilchrist the right hemisphere's task is to apprehend landscapes, and the left hemisphere's task is to facilitate machine thinking in order to operate upon the landscape and for the holon to flourish thereby. To address wicked valuation problems at the meetings of the North, the South, the East and the West I am here submitting that whole mind functioning is a necessary precondition, with McGilchrist's left hemisphere explanation better equipped to address complicated issues, the right to address complex ones, and both required to address wicked valuation problems by means of their co-evolution of emergent understandings. Interpretation of the landscapes means we must think big, and "mythic thinking is macrothought. Think big and you think myth" (Thompson 1989, p. 47). That is not an injunction, it is an observation. One cannot think big without engaging myth, which is a right hemisphere function. Myths provide "an image used to make sense of the world, used to integrate . . . and select other experiences. According to your myth, so is what you notice as being important" (Watts 2014, 7:00). That is, they draw "Big V" values to one's attention.

BIES is meant to provide a bridge between the two sets of analytical tools and the HVN, with the warning signs to be aware of black swans and butterfly effects designated by "B", and the "IES" being representative of what I term "Big V" values, which in an optimally functioning mind I consider both frame and drive the interplay between the two hemispheres.

As part of my valuation course I studied Economics 101, which according to the Nobel Laureate Robert Solow is most or all of what you need to give practical policy advice (Easterly 2013, p. 245). However, in the decades since I have come to doubt if even some of economics 101 was particularly useful in that context – at least, the more machinist, single vision aspects I was taught. Our major text was Paul Samuelson et al.'s *Economics: an Introductory Analysis* (1970), characterised by Sedlacek and Havel as "We present to you the mechanical machine *Economics*" (Sedlacek and Havel 2011, p. 257). Its oft-repeated single vision abstraction qualification was *ceteris paribus* (all other things being equal). In contrast, this Holarchic Vortex Network within Heterarchic Fields, a complex adaptive system with which I submit we should engage with a far more ecologically rational approach (Gigerenzer and Brighton 2009) when addressing wicked valuation problems in the context of this work. I call this approach HIDEGRE BIES ADALAS, and its feedback relationship with the Holarchic Vortex Network within Heterarchic Fields (HVN↔HBA). This feedback approach enfolds the truth that *ceteris paribus diu numquam*; all else is never equal for long.

Part of this long learning curve was in my encountering development eco-nomics, most intensively since my arrival in eSwatini (herein referred to by its name when I was there: Swaziland) in 1993 (see Chapter 2). In April 2015, I learnt that my concerns had been articulated by Easterly (2006, 2013); in particular, what Easterly terms autocracy/authoritarian development (Easterly 2013, p. 6). Authoritarian development regards the economy as a complicated machine.

Easterly (ibid., p. 32) looks more to the emergence of solutions from complex adaptive systems (CAS), rather more like Tupaia's approach than Captain Cook's. Viewed from this perspective, "an economy is always in the process of becoming. From this it follows that the notion of equilibrium as depicted in mainstream economics is incoherent" (Bromley 2008b, p. 219). Similarly:

> By its very definition, equilibrium filters out exploration, creation, transitory phenomena: anything in the economy that takes adjustment – adaptation,

innovation, structural change, history itself. These must be bypassed or dropped from the theory.

(Arthur 2014)

Neoclassical economics employs axioms that are "positively *contradictory* to observations in societies and experimental research of human behaviour in the laboratories" (Csaba 2009, p. 31).

In what he terms the "ludic fallacy" of attempting to mathematically model economic behaviour, Taleb agrees with Brian Arthur that the world is far too complex for economics (Taleb 2007, p. 155). Yet "the people who make decisions about macroeconomic policies are usually either professional economists or advised by professional economists" (Poteete 2003, p. 528). Tony Lawson also sees the formalistic mathematical models used as often very silly, and notes that some economists seem to be rather in awe of mathematics but often not very good at it, making irrelevant assumptions and being quite unaware that there are limitations to the uses of any specific form of mathematics. Michael Hudson, too, bemoaned "the replacing of the history thought" in economic courses "with mathematics which were essentially trivialised using junk statistics to create a junk economics to create a bubble economy" (Emmanuel and Fitzgerald 2011).

Lawson also sees the world more like Tupaia than Captain Cook – as open, processual – but notes that in order to get mathematics going, you have to treat the world as if it is isolated, abstracted, quite different from the way it really is (Lawson 2014b; also see Das 2011, p. 146). "The world of logic is a dead world" (Mini 1974, p. 213), part of the dead world of single vision. Lawson adds that the great proportion of economics is taught via such mathematical modelling, which he considers to be useless. He claims it gets in the way of genuine insights because the world is interrelated, not atomistic, and their models are not. In consequence, he sees the claims of economists as unrealistic (Lawson 2014b, 30:20–32:00), and concludes that by studying ontology one can come to see under what conditions mathematics might become useful (ibid., 34:00).

Similarly, Paul Ormerod has been criticising conventional economic theory for decades. For instance, in his *The Death of Economics* he devoted a chapter to such mechanistic modelling (Ormerod 1994, pp. 92–112). Twenty years later, he deconstructed the fundamental assumptions upon which the entire edifice of macroeconomics has been built, that:

- people choose in isolation (stating that without making that false assumption, their maths fails);
- people only make decisions on the basis of price;
- preferences are fixed, not affected by others; and
- people choose on objective attributes (which he claims is not wrong, but incomplete) (Ormerod 2014).

These fundamental assumptions that Ormerod criticises are also at odds with my decades of lived experience of investigating the circumstances of sale in landed property transactions. More importantly, they are uninformed by the insights of complexity theory (Arthur 1994, 2013, 2014) and, except among those trained to behave in that manner, counter to the empirical discoveries of behavioural economics (Kahneman, Knetsch and Thaler 1986; Kahneman 2003, 2011).

In summary, this thesis is consistent with the observation made in a review of a book published in June 2015 (Allen and Hoekstra 2015[1]) that "One day soon ecology and ecological perspectives will have to embrace and contain economics and become the dominant lens through which we look at the human condition" (Hurst 2015).

As such, this work submits that the emerging and process-based complexity paradigms in general and HVN↔HBA in particular are more realistic means of developing a framework to address the subject of this book than the currently more predominantly static-based foci. Especially, this approach is more realistic than neoclassical equilibrium-based economic theories which have "little to do with any real world economic situation" (Nelson 2002, p. 58). While still endemic in the development field, equilibrium-based economic theories are seen from this perspective as internally contradictory from the ground up (Fellman et al. 2004).

Furthermore, the concept of optimal efficiency in economics is illegitimate in a complex system because such a system does not allow an optimal decision; there are too many variables (Molloy 2004). In contrast, cooperative coevolution is a fundamental assumption in evolutionary optimisation (Yang, Tang and Yao 2008; Stewart 2014).

Note that I do not read these attacks on the sufficiency or even relevance of much mainstream economic theory as attacks on the many brilliant economists who have internalised them. Rather, by dint of their brilliance, they may transcend them. As Sedlacek and Havel put it, "one will never be a good economist, who is only an economist" (Sedlacek and Havel 2011, p. 6).

There are other criticisms of neoclassical economics from non-complexity-based ontologies (for example, see Stark 2000; Fullbrook 2004, 2007; Nussbaum 1997; Splash 2012; "Modern economics resembles a Ptolemaic system" – Das 2011, p. 148; "The tenets of mainstream economics are made-up, no more real than Medieval astronomers' crystalline spheres" – Orrell 2018):

> Virtually every aspect of conventional economic theory is intellectually unsound; virtually every economic policy recommendation is just as likely to do general harm as it is to lead to the general good. Far from holding the intellectual high ground, economics rests on foundations of quicksand.
>
> (Keen 2001, p. 4)

While obviously defended by some, neoclassical economics does not even recognise natural resources and the ecology as fundamentals, instead enfolding them within capital as one of four variables, the others being output, labour, and knowledge. Energy, drawn from natural resources, is similarly deprioritised. The economic sociologist David Stark notes that neoclassical economics misses any assessment of judgement (Stark 2000, p. 3), reducing everything to calculation (ibid.), whereas "values are a kind of anti-matter to calculation" (ibid., p. 4), and in reality "all economies have a moral component" (ibid., p. 5).

One such defender is Katzner (2015). However, Katzner also conceded (from within his microeconomic context) that many of the criticisms were legitimate, and had been recognised as such by economists for a very long time. The question for them was what to do about that, so they mainly resorted to the mechanistic metaphors that had so much success in physics. For reasons described below, this work proposes that mechanistic method, at least as a monological gaze, to be even more inappropriate to addressing wicked valuation problems than it is to examine one influence among many of such wicked problems, economics.

In the field land tenure, Elahi and Stilwell identified two counterfactual fundamental assumptions of neoclassical economics: firstly, that of people being selfish by nature, and secondly, that dominance by private property is axiomatic to economic performance (Elahi and Stilwell 2013). They then claim that customary land tenure demonstrates conceptual bias in this context by such economists. As such, we may view customary land tenure as more in tune with the cooperative coevolution of evolutionary optimisation than neoclassical economics.

From the perspective of this work, some economic historians have a particularly interesting take on neoclassical economics. Mason Gaffney considers neo-classical economics to have been a stratagem against Henry George (Gaffney 1993), and that it remains a corruption of economics (Gaffney and Harrison 1994).

In the nineteenth century, Henry George had proposed that a land value tax, based on land value increases being primarily societally rather than individually bestowed, was a just tax that could cover all government expenditure (George 1920), a contention much later supported by the Henry George Theorem (Arnott and Stiglitz 1979), and recently repeated by Foldvary (2006), Harrison (1983 and 2009), Anderson (in Ingram and Hong 2012, pp. 123–139) and Adams (2015). In general principle, it had been supported centuries before by Adam Smith (Smith 1776, book V, chapter 2, article I). John Dewey called George "one of the world's great social philosophers, certainly the greatest which this country has produced" (Dewey 2008, p.302), but Clarence Darrow presciently remarked of his land value taxation ideas:

> The "single tax" is so simple, so fundamental, and so easy to carry into effect that I have no doubt that it will be about the last land reform the world will ever get. People in this world are not often logical.
>
> (Darrow 1913)

Despite its theoretical and empirical sense, "its premise, however, was socializing land rents through taxation. Its very strengths were its undoing, then, by evoking a powerful, intransigent, wealthy counterforce" (Gaffney and Harrison 1994), which allegedly devised neo-classical economics as a counter (Gaffney 1993). However, Georgism is as yet still not quite undone, as Georgism-influenced organisations remain, and HVN↔HBA could assist in determining its potential in different contexts.

The biases of neoclassical economics have been revealed in other fields. For example, while Elahi and Stilwell assert the "self-interest" part of the "rational self-interest" trope of neoclassical economics is a far too reductive account of human behaviour, the emerging disciplines of behavioural economics and behavioural finance have revealed that the fundamental neoclassical assumptions that the "rational" part of that trope is at best a special case (Kahneman 2003). "Economists increasingly recognise the limits of the canonical assumption of self-interest" (Meyer and Braga 2009a, p. 1). Others go further and call it "incoherent" (Wilson 2017). "People do not necessarily vote their self-interest. They vote their identity. They vote their values." (Lakoff 2004, p. 19). Wang and Christensen characterise neoclassical economics as "a confusion between price and value . . . [and] based on value monism whereby all values can be transformed into money . . . [and] the economics way of thinking knows the price of everything and the value of nothing" (Wang and Christensen 2015, pp. 6–7).

I trust I have sufficiently pressed the futility and wastage of single vision economics. If the reader wishes to pursue the matter further, Lars P. Syll provides a succinct entry point (Syll 2014). All in all, I claim that conventional economics is quite inadequate for examining the subject of this work. Taleb's view – that such economics is a fable of some use in inspiring practice but should not direct or determine practice or advise policy (Taleb 2012, pp. 211–212) – appears robust in this context, and we must "attempt to convince the economic rationalists that their world view is too narrow. And if we can't convince them of this or replace them from being the primary advisers to government, we're in deep trouble" (ABC RN 2015a, 5:50).

Therefore, instead of conventional economics, this work is a response to a call made in a survey of papers related to evolutionary optimisation in uncertain environments, for future research topics to address:

1   Various uncertainties in multiobjective optimisation problems.
2   More than one aspect in one problem.
3   The inherent relationships between the different topics and, thus, to benefit from each other.
4   The relationships between uncertainties and multiobjectivity (Jin and Branke 2005).

It does so because this book does not explore policy making from an evolutionary computation approach but instead has its own complexity-based trans-ontological process. It therefore differs from mainstream economics, which is criticised as being developed upon contested bodies of work, not following its supposed epistemology, and lacking an explicit ontology (Splash 2012, p. 45). I recognise that much of current land policy making shares the following characteristics with other policy making. It:

•   is reflected in vast, sprawling policy debates requiring understanding both of the big picture and the details

- depends on data that are changing frequently (often daily in complex, scientific and political areas)
- has many stakeholders, organisational and personal, each with conflicting goals, values, and pressures
- involves individuals and organisations with overlapping roles
- requires decision-making based on guesses or forecasts that in turn are based on structural constraints of organisations, frameworks of policy in place, differing logics and world views, and distinct organisational or societal cultures
- is swamped by a high degree of unknowns and unknowables
- is wrapped in constant political power struggles
- involves communication with a wide variety of publics through the filter of the media
- involves a society or organisation becoming involved in an ongoing process of social learning and continuous change
- requires the ability to bring participants up-to-speed when they have missed meetings (Horn 2001, pp. 4–5).

As such, it is a *wicked problem* – that is, one that is very hard and potentially impossible to solve because of its multilayered complexities and the lack of information about them. When you solve one part of a wicked problem, you raise others. Furthermore, it is but one wicked problem in what in the developing world is generally a "Social Mess", which Horn defines as:

> A set of interrelated problems and other messes. Complexity – systems of systems – is among the factors that makes Social Messes so resistant to analysis and, more importantly, to resolution.
>
> (Horn 2001)

Unlike simple problems, wicked problems and social messes may not have simple solutions (Ashby's Law of Requisite Variety, Ashby 1956). They may, though; there are constants that may apply in quite unexpected contexts. For example, Feigenbaum's constant in chaos theory (showing ordered patterns emerging out of non-linear situations: Sardar and Abrams 2004, pp. 66–68), and those tracking the emergence of butterfly effects through cascading processes in behavioural dynamics (Yu et al. 2015).

I have therefore designed HVN↔HBA, informed by such approaches, to interrogate the subject of this work, and then employed it to address wicked valuation problems – not just market valuations, but general valuations, focussing upon intrinsic, extrinsic and systemic valuations.

My reason for addressing this subject from that perspective is that land tenure is a fundamental component of land policy, which currently faces massive challenges, including those stated in the problem statement below. Reactive and simplistic ("band aid") solutions might only make a wicked problem worse. Some may provide short-term gain at the cost of long-term pain, others short term pain for long-term gain, and others still variations of those spectra in different domains.

Over recent years, there has been a rise in the influence of psychology and similar behavioural sciences in the development of public policy (Jones, Pykett and Whitehead 2013). This work embraces and channels that trend, but towards the benefit of the relevant citizens as distinct from that of authoritarian governance. As such, it seeks an awareness of default bias manipulations and other instances of heuristics internalisations in such contexts (for example, see Wodak et al. 2009). I seek this awareness as a means of discerning the motivations of the manipulations, and the authentic from the inauthentic. That is, I do not intend to dismiss default bias manipulations (which is impossible), but for individuals to be equipped to properly value them within their own identity constructions.

To this end, this work examines whether the approach recommended can provide a richer methodology towards addressing wicked problems than those prevailing, with a view to establishing more robust due diligence protocols for that purpose. I start from the premise that to solve such problems we do not need to choose between Tupaia and Captain Cook's approaches to navigation. We need them both and more approaches besides. Therefore, this work is a journey navigated more in the style of Tupaia than of Cook, with my whole self in the navigation. Therefore, as Tupaia looked for complex interplays between many natural phenomena to navigate, so (in keeping with what all valuers do as market readers) I look for complex interplays between many facts, fact perceptions and value judgements. And as Tupaia used the stars to guide him through the dark, so I use the scholars cited to guide me through the unfamiliar kingdoms I need to navigate to arrive at my journey's end.

Problem statement

I began this book in response to challenges presented by the late Kenyan scholar Okoth-Ogendo (2000). He identified four major land policy challenges in the African context in the twenty-first century:

- To design truly innovative tenure regimes to suit the variety of complex land use systems that characterise the African landscape.
- To provide a framework within which customary land tenure and law can evolve in an orderly way.
- To find ways to democratise land administration systems and structures.
- To design a framework to codify customary tenure rules and integrate them into statutory law.

However, my research gradually made it apparent to me that not only is this challenge not confined to Africa, but also that it cannot be adequately addressed by law alone. I came to see it as a call for a legal framework to facilitate the meeting of NSEW globally, and that any such attempt must take much more into account than legislative changes.

One example of its universality is Davidson and Dyal-Chand's observation from their USA-focussed examination of the role of property in the global financial crisis. They note that property theorists trace ownership across a spectrum from public through community to ever more exclusive control, with the opposite end of the spectrum being some existent "like Blackstone's sole and absolute dominion" (Davidson and Dyal-Chand 2010, p. 1614).

To address Okoth-Ogendo's challenges by application of the complexity paradigm in the context of land, law and its implementation is clearly of major importance. However, this work is primarily valuation, not legislation, focussed. So legal framing remains a major objective, but in this book I expand his challenge beyond the necessary but insufficient legal domain, and into values. This expansion includes reference to the contexts in which tenure regimes occur.

The magnitude of the problem when extending into values is indicated by Kevin Cahill's worldwide land tenure review in 2007, which claims that 37.5 per cent of the planet was owned by 147 states, 21 per cent is owned by 21 people (26 monarchs claiming 20%), 41.5 per cent is owned by one per cent or less of the planet's population, and 85 per cent of the planet's population owns no land at all (Cahill 2007, p. 34).

At least at the high level orienting generalisations with which these figures are generally prepared, Cahill's estimates are consistent with those provided for wealth in general (not simply as held in land). In its 2014 Global Wealth Report (Stierli et al. 2014), Credit Suisse noted that one only needs $3,650 (in USD, and including the value of one's house) to be in the top half of the world's population in terms of wealth. Over $77,000 will get you into the top 10 per cent, which accounts for 87 per cent of the world's wealth, and $798,000 will mean you are in the top one per cent, which accounts for 48.2 per cent.

An Oxfam Report (Fuentes-Nieva and Galasso 2014) adds that the richest 85 people on Earth own as much as the poorest half of the world's population. Seventy per cent of the world's population live in countries where inequality has increased over the last 30 years, and that such countries include citizens of the USA. There, 95 per cent of the wealth increases since the GFC were captured by the wealthiest one per cent, and the bottom 90 per cent became poorer over the same period. Moreover, seven ruling families in one of the planet's most volatile regions own oil deposits worth $9,252 billion if valued at $20 per barrel (Hiro 2003, p. 447).

Without her actually identifying it as such, this process has been tracked by Chua (2004), who points out how the introduction of free markets and democracy has so often empowered an ethnic minority without empowering the majority, which she considers to be a major cause of anti-Americanism worldwide. The subtitle of her book *The World on Fire* is *How Exporting Free Market Democracy Breeds Ethnic Hatred and Global Instability*, and she addresses strategies to ameliorate or even remedy the situation. She highlights four of the main strategies available:

- Redistribution through tax and transfer programs
- De Soto's strategy: grant the poor formal property rights

- Find ways of giving the world's poor majorities part ownerships in the relevant corporations
- Government interventions to apply affirmative action to the poor majority (ibid., pp. 268–269).

I believe that these strategies could be best implemented with a HVN↔HBA approach.

These contexts are where so many of the wicked valuation problems that are the subject of this work are shaped. I approach them by emphasising the greater necessity of a transdisciplinary approach for human, as distinct from artefact, development. That is, I see the transdisciplinary imagination requiring the adoption of wisdom from philosophers of all stamps, and being informed by philosophical schools such as social constructivism or postmodernism rather than frame this HVN↔HBA process approach within any one of them. In this book I am focussing on the process of facts engaging our value judgements and vice versa, and valuations engaging both the facts we seek and the philosophies we adopt in terms of their facility in addressing wicked valuation problems.

Meyer and Braga have stated that:

> Most recent developments in the study of social dilemmas give an increasing amount of attention to cognition, belief systems, valuations, and language. However, developments in this field operate almost entirely under epistemological assumptions that only recognise the instrumental form of rationality and deny that "value judgements" or "moral questions" have cognitive content. This standpoint ignores the moral aspect of the choice situation and obstructs acknowledgement of the links connecting cognition, inner growth and moral reasoning, and the significance of such links in reaching cooperative solutions to many social problems.
>
> (Meyer and Braga 2015, p. 1)

Similarly, Kauffman has called for:

> [A] new conceptual framework that allows us to speak of life in interwoven language and metaphor, recognising the richness that, in fact, we know, feel, sense, intuit and act.
>
> (Kauffman 2016, p. 255)

When it comes to valuations, it has been established that often "market value is just one factor among many that motivate owners and is often not at the forefront of their decision-making" (Penalver and Alexander 2012, p. 840). In attempting to establish the normative standards in reading market behaviour to apply the IVSC definition in the relevant market, it is important to understand whatever those other factors are. For example, Small and Sheehan (2005) point out that "customary title is incomparable to Western conceptions of property value". Yet sometimes properties under customary title have to be acquired for public works.

What is to be done? This book describes a protocol to give due consideration of such matters, which I have found to be of far broader applicability.

My problem statement is how to address the above insights of Meyer and Braga, and of Kauffman and McGilchrist, in a land valuation and policy context: that of landscapes and The Machine. Recognising that even the best land policy responses to these challenges will be true but partial at best, the problem I am addressing here is how to engage in valuation in a way that is more inclusive of all the spectrums of cognitions, belief systems, valuations, languages and, in particular, all the spectrums of identity constructions around the globe. That requires not falling into the traps caused by monological gazing that Blake warned us of above, or those of Sedlacek and Havel's monocultural "mechanical machine *Economics*" (Sedlacek and Havel 2011, p. 257). Instead, I look to what tools or methods could be developed to facilitate this engagement, and how such tools or methods could constantly improve from application in a context when NSEW meet.

A benchmark for the scale of the problem at the global level happened in 2007, when for the first time in history the urban population of the planet exceeded the rural population (United Nations 2014). While there are many causes and consequences of this, both positive and negative, the positive consequences include "the biggest economic transformation the world has ever seen as the populations of cities in emerging markets expand and enjoy rising incomes" (Dobbs et al. 2012, p. iii). The challenges to be met there include that within about a dozen years builders will have to produce about 85 per cent more than all the residential commercial and building stock currently in existence (ibid.).

Real property rights are a fundamental component for both land policy and land valuation, and equally fundamental in considering how such challenges are to be met. The difference between the cost and the added value of those real property rights can be preconditional to such development happening in the first place, and their sustainability is a crucial factor in their value. This difference is at "the heart of all economic activity" (Ring and Boykin 1986, p. 1). Understanding land valuation is indispensable as a factor in determining land policy (Davy 2012, p. 90), and valuation's "polyrational" approaches could be beneficial as a grounding for land policy development (ibid., p. 95).

Background to the research

This work incorporates an autoethnographic approach interwoven into the traditional objective narrative of books such as this. It therefore presents a distillation of my quest to address the challenges encountered in life in general. These include those of not only over forty years' practice of land valuation-related activities at a professional level, but also almost a decade of leading many groups of travellers. This required my having to make sense of those countries, and communicate that understanding to my fellow travellers. I performed that role in around 60 countries, visiting many of them several times.

That decade was my own personal equivalent to Darwin's voyage of the *Beagle*, and again speaking only at the personal level possibly as enriching to my later life as that voyage was to his, providing the stimulation, ground and framing for much of the research herein. As this research covers considerable span and depth, in accordance with the Goldilocks Principle described in Chapter 5 below I have chosen autoethnography as a means of better addressing the complexities involved than I could manage adopting a wholly traditional approach.

That requires a looser and more discursive narrative style than is traditional in a book of this nature, which style I see as being better able to engage the right hemisphere, with its predilection for broad and deep vision and values. This narrative style I also found to be more amenable to Klein's injunction "think big, go deep" (Klein 2014, p. 26). This may frustrate the readers' left hemisphere's because:

> As things are re-presented in the left hemisphere, it is their use-value that is salient. In the world it brings into being, everything is either reduced to utility or rejected with considerable vehemence, a vehemence that appears to be born of frustration, and the affront to its 'will to power'. The higher values of Scheler's hierarchy, all of which require affective or moral engagement with the world, depend on the right hemisphere.
>
> (McGilchrist 2009, p. 161)

It is values such as Scheler's that I want to see engaged in the subject of this work. We need to develop a capacity to value values. To do so, Scheler's hierarchy of values – those for use and pleasure at the lowest end, with values of vitality above them, values of the intellect above them, and holy values at the summit (McGilchrist 2009, p. 160) require "affective or moral engagement with the world [and] depend on the right hemisphere" (ibid.). As McGilchrist further emphasises, these values are not those of the left hemisphere, and not subject to the left hemisphere's utilitarian requirements of Universality, Replicability, Control, Measurement, Validity, Reliability, Credibility and Falsifiability. Those requirements are to be the Emissaries', not the Masters', because they are "impossible to reconcile with understanding based on the implicit, context-bound nature of things as delivered by the right hemisphere" (ibid., p. 182).

However, in that role of higher values engaging with the world, they can be invaluable as Emissaries when addressing wicked valuation problems. As such, they are often essential in weighing fact perceptions and value judgements during the HBA process. They are tools to be engaged where appropriate in the HVN↔HBA process, but any claim to universality on their part is spurious in this context. Ben Goldacre explains in *Bad Science* (2008, p. 129) that those claiming the certainty sought by these requirements are "basically wrong" in even complex areas, let alone when building Procrustean beds in the wicked valuation contexts being addressed by this work. They are particularly dangerous when ignorantly applying them as if holons were machines which, as explained below, is also basically wrong.

Similarly, while writing this book I also found it to be basically wrong that autoethnography is sufficient in itself to address the subject, or to explain the design of a robust and rigorous framework to address wicked valuation problems, of the type I consider HVN↔HBA to be. However, in being more right hemisphere friendly, I still consider autoethnography to be a necessary but insufficient precondition to that end. So I continue the autoethnographic approach up to the literature review, and thereafter that takes the "back seat", as it were, to anyone's addressing of wicked valuation problems via HVN↔HBA, any autoethnographic references then being meant to provide examples of its potential applications, and their strengths and weaknesses.

I have also chosen it to highlight the realisation that whatever contributions this work may make to knowledge are necessarily emergent from, or consequences of, my own identity construction.

That is why my autoethnographic narrative spans Chapter 2, followed by a literature review in Chapter 3. My autoethnographic voice will reappear at moments throughout this book, but I will then couple this voice with a more structured voice common to a traditional work addressing such issues.

Ethnography is "a loose method for exploring the world through an open-ended, experimental, and initially nonjudgmental mind to understand how it actually functions" (Braverman in Blomley, Braverman, Delaney and Kedar 2014, p. 124), and autoethnography involves applying that process to oneself. As such, it employs autobiography in a "critical narrative as pedagogy" manner (Goodson and Gill 2014). Here, I am observing my own identity construction and its homologies with those of others via Collaborative Developmental Action Inquiry (Torbert 2013), including how narrative so often trumps data in that process, such that, as succinctly put by the comedian Tim Minchin, "Science adjusts its views based on what's observed. Faith is the denial of observation, so that belief can be preserved" (Minchin 2011).

In this case, the faith in question is that of the identity constructed, even in cases when the construction enfolds adjusting one's views based on what is observed while the observer itself is not observed. That is, retaining an identity solidity as a ground for observing reality, rather than the identity permeability recommended below (Metzinger and Windt 2015) via action inquiry.

Consequently, this book narrates how these two apparently very different paths of tour leading and real property valuation/land policy facilitation have provided a developmental dynamic in my identity imaginary (Taylor 2002). I present this as being a potential contribution to knowledge applicable to property valuation and land policy development at all scales, from local to global.

Its background, then, is the lived experience of one person out of the billions on this planet affected in some way by real property rights or their lack, and the values appertaining to them. That person was tasked at the end of the twentieth century with facilitating land policy reform in one very small southern African country, but did not succeed in seeing the draft policy adopted. This experience involved investigating into how best to facilitate land policy in general, and land tenure policy in particular, for land tenure was a core concern in Swaziland then and remains so now. I focus the insights from the co-evolution of experience and theory upon addressing the land policy/land tenure policy context within this

work's more general theme, and submit what general lessons might be extrapo-
lated from my experiences into wider geographic, legal, political, social, cultural,
economic and environmental situations – all of which are affected by land policy.

Research problem, propositions/research issues and contributions

While fractally applicable, I mainly mean HVN↔HBA as a protocol towards
harnessing trans-ontological teams, deliberative institutions or ad hoc as appropriate, towards addressing wicked valuation problems. In addition, they are to be
able to access additional professional and technical advice as required. I consider
such teams, not individual experts, in general to be the optimal means to effect
that purpose.

Transdisciplinarity has three pillars:

- firstly, the recognition that there are different levels of reality;
- secondly, the axiom of the included middle, which is a fundamental insight of fuzzy logic (Kosko 1994); and
- thirdly, the recognition of complexity as different in kind from complicated (see below) (Max-Neef 2005; Nicolescu 2006).

The first insight is developed in Chapter 5. The second differentiates that axiom
of Aristotle's in logic to the reality of landscapes. Like non-Euclidian geometry
changed Euclid's laws, so this changes Aristotle's Law of the Excluded Middle,
with similarly dramatic new worlds being shown as a result. However, it confirms
another observation of Aristotle, made in his *Nicomachean Ethics*: "it is the mark
of an educated man to look for precision in each class of things just so far as the
nature of the subject admits" (Aristotle, *Nicomachean Ethics*, bk 1, paragraph 3).
This is an essential point, because attempting machine-like precision may be
worse than useless when attempting to address wicked valuation problems.
Rather, one should go just so far as the nature of the subject admits, and in such
contexts fuzzy may be more relevant and resilient than crisp. The third point,
about difference in kind, means that transdisciplinarity is not a matter of heaping
up isolated single visions, be they from economics, law, environmental studies
or any other fields of inquiry. They must be not only differentiated and articulated, but also hierarchically integrated and, in HVN↔HBA, dynamically and
heterarchically related.

Hence the preponderance of quotations in this book. They are mainly from
specialists contributing to the transdisciplinary approach required to examine
this subject meaningfully. As a transdisciplinarian, I cannot claim competence
in all the relevant domains, but as a valuer I have spent my professional career
weighing the influences of many disciplines upon market values. I therefore consider it both appropriate and respectful to allow the specialists in their own
domains to speak within this book as directly as possible via direct quotes, and to
speak as directly as possible from my own.

Okoth-Ogendo's challenge inspired me to embark upon this work. However, I found that to address his challenge I had to broaden my topic, even beyond a complexity-based transdisciplinary approach to provide a developmental template to facilitate the integration of real property rights into different fitness landscapes (Di Robilant 2013). To increase real property rights' capacity to nurture intrinsic value, I had to transcend but include different ontologies.

As such, the mindscape of this work is dauntingly vast in scope, similar in that respect to the story about Alexander the Great and the Gordian knot. I will use neither a sword nor another extrinsically valuable but intrinsically cheap sharp object, Ockham's Razor, but look for a means whereby, with the appropriate balance of approaches, "the knot which you thought a Gordian one will untie itself before you" (Jefferson 2008).

Although made more accessible by the use of computers, this new approach has a pedigree going back millennia before Jefferson. For example, it is an attempt to apply the ancient Greek concept of *sophrosyne* (balanced proportionality, judiciousness in action) to the complexities of this topic. While Alexander's approach may be more emotionally satisfying and have more immediate extrinsic value, Jefferson's more sophrosyne recommendation is more sustainable and has the potential to express greater intrinsic (qualitative) value.

Michio Kaku makes a useful distinction in this regard. He notes that there are two principles that are diametrical opposites, yet both are also consistent with everything we know of science (Kaku 2014, p. 323). Firstly, the Copernican Principle – that which enabled Captain Cook's navigation – states that there is no privileged position for humanity in the Universe. Secondly, and on the other hand, the Anthropic Principle notes that life as we know it only exists because of many fine tunings that were all required for the emergence of life, and these fine tunings extend "to every atom of the body" and that "life is precious and a miracle" (ibid., pp. 324, 325). Later, he observed that the perfectly deterministic philosophies that attached themselves to the Copernican Principle are *just plain wrong*: "A combination of uncertainty and chaos makes a perfectly deterministic world impossible" (ibid., p. 340).

I intend HVN↔HBA to facilitate the finding of such tunings in the situations under scrutiny. It includes epistemological, telaxiological and other concerns. It promises an entirely different approach from the predominant Western epistemology as applied to land policy: "Descriptive disciplines are always wedded to an epistemology . . . Such an epistemology at once determines how we come to know the world and constitutes the range of what is knowable" (Euben 1999, p. 4).

By adaptation of HVN↔HBA, I seek to provide a far more spacious and inclusive framework within which theories, laws, and generalisations can be formulated than can the classical scientific and pre-scientific paradigms. These paradigms clash in wicked valuation problems of land policy development in general, and land-related value judgements and its real property rights aspects in particular. As this work proceeds, it engages a focus on becoming rather than being, of approaching real property rights as engaged in processes rather than part of a stasis. I reference pioneering works towards this emerging paradigm, including Peter Corning's *Holistic Darwinism* (2005), *Toward a Unified Ecology* (Allen and Hoekstra 2015), Gunderson and Holling's *Panarchy* (2002), Ken Wilber (1980, 1995, 1996, 1999, 1999a, 1999b, 2000, 2003, 2012), the strongly Wilber-influenced Sean Esjborn-Hartgens and Zimmerman (Esjborn-Hartgens and Zimmerman 2009), and many others.

Central to HVN↔HBA is the study of complexity, described by Stuart Kauffman as being essentially the science of emergence (Waldrop 1992, p. 88). Some of these emergents were described by Anderson (1972, p. 393), who noted that you could think of the whole universe as a hierarchy, the position of an entity determinable by the number of levels of emergence contained within it. Thus, atoms have emergent properties not possessed by quarks. They transcend and include quarks. Humans have emergent properties not possessed by human cells. They transcend and include human cells. Moreover, Anderson observes that these emergents' new qualities require *"entirely new laws, concepts and generalisations"* (ibid.) to address.

Similarly, in Beer's interpretation each of Blake's four visions enfolds the previous ones. Genius enfolds love, love enfolds energy, energy enfolds reason (Beer 1969, p. 27), and each has different qualities and needs entirely new laws, concepts and generalisations from the previous vision. That is, as defined in my Glossary and as differing from Wilber (1995), Blake's vision is holarchic, not hierarchic, and so is HVN↔HBA.

The study of complexity further involves the study of change in dynamical systems, and as such is centrally concerned with the dynamics of evolution and development rather than with stasis. With that emphasis, it is required to address the environment within which such evolution can occur, and that relationship is called the *fitness landscape*.

It thereby adopts an entirely different approach to addressing problems, recognising that a change in one participant's fitness landscape will result in changes in another participant's fitness landscape (Ruhl 1996). As such, complexity has already provided rich new insights into evolution in several apparently widely differing contexts.

I mean HVN↔HBA to facilitate the application of the lessons from complexity and chaos research to wicked valuation problems related to land policies, land-related valuations and real property rights. The HVN↔HBA approach is my response to the challenges of global conditions, characterised by Sardar (2010) as *complexity, chaos and contradiction*. I do so critically, but in the spirit of Bruno Latour, towards "A stubbornly realist attitude . . . but a realism dealing with matters of concern . . . whose import will no longer be to debunk, but to protect and to care" (Latour 2004, pp. 231, 232).

The submission of this book

I am not speaking from within a mindset of seeing the world as a mass of machinery. That is but one of very many ways to view the world. Yi-Fu Tuan's *Topophilia*

(1990) provides a broad overview of land-related perceptions, attitudes and values. Tuan's main foci (ibid., p. 3) include to:

1   Look at environmental values and perception at different levels (Chapter 5 of this work).
2   Articulate differences between the environment and our topophilia (love of it) to show how each contributes to our valuations of environments (also addressed in chapter 5).
3   Introduce the concept of change via European history (or that history most relevant to the domain concerned).

Topophilia's subtitle is *A Study of Environmental Perception, Attitudes and Values.* I see Tuan, and others cited here such as Corning (2005) and Fraser (1999), as being exemplars of three- or four-fold vision. Consequently, I have combined several of Tuan's insights with my own lived experience and my researches to address wicked valuation problems.

As a trans-ontological process, I mean HVN↔HBA to be a means of framing those complexities, that chaos, and those contradictions, in a manner that can facilitate the imaginative, valuational and cognitive complexities required to creatively address these challenges. By transcending the hegemony of the "thinging" (Bateson 1979, p. 112) of machinism, I hope to facilitate understanding of the relationships between the various components of HBA, and hence towards those in the HVN. Others, such as some designers of things, are now commiting themselves to "the Political Values of Post-Thing Centered Designing", towards "defending values by design" (Tonkinwise 2015, pp. 1, 10) and thereby addressing wicked problems through Transition Design (Irwin, Kosoff, Tonkinwise and Scupelli 2015).

I designed the HBA section to introduce its practitioners to the HVN type of trans-ontological awareness, which in turn feeds back into HBA's application. Hence the "↔" in what I intend as a tool towards facilitating creativity in the user, not as a substitute for it.

The philosophical underpinnings of this approach are cited throughout the report, but as an orienting generalisation they have strong affinities with A. N. Whitehead's process philosophy as articulated in *Process and Reality* (1978). On page xiii, Whitehead identified and repudiates nine myths and fallacious proceedings that, at least in my lived experience, remain endemic barriers to facilitatory insights in land reform:

- *The distrust of speculative philosophy* – to counter this defect, I have, for example, engaged Pirsig (1974, 1991) in my autoethnographic narrative. Whitehead's following points have been similarly engaged.
- *The trust in language as an adequate expression of propositions.* While this is directly cognate with Taoism's "the name that can be defined is not the unchanging name" (Lao Tzu 1972), there are still degrees of accuracy in vocabulary. However, we have both other perceptual apparatuses and other prehensions available to ourselves, not just language.

- *The mode of philosophical thought which implies, and is implied by, the faculty-psychology* (by which he means enboxing/isolating human faculties such as reason and emotion; we respond to experiences at different levels, scales and dimensions; this fallacy is addressed by HVN↔HBA in this work).
- *The subject-predicate form of expression* (mistaking abstractions for reality, breaking existents up into isolated things).
- *The sensationalist doctrine of perception* (that sensory processing is primary; instead, Whitehead admits a prehension of reality, sensation being secondary).
- *The doctrine of vacuous actuality.* (That objects have no subjective experience). This fallacy is addressed by the holonic/hextal approach in this work, and their *necessary* inter-relationships in terms of HVN↔HBA.
- *The Kantian doctrine of the objective world as a theoretical construct from purely subjective experience.* Once again, the hextal approach is intended to highlight the difference between reality and such theoretical, subjective and/or intersubjective constructs and their interplays.
- *Arbitrary deductions in ex absurdo arguments.* This relates to throwing the baby out with the bathwater. One flaw does not necessarily result in everything discovered being discarded.
- *Belief that logical inconsistencies can indicate anything else than some antecedent errors.* Logical inconsistencies can arise from anywhere. Gödel's (1995) incompleteness theorem demonstrated that all logical systems are essentially incomplete if they are not infinite.

There are varying interpretations of Whitehead. Of these, my trans-ontological process is closest to the ecstatic interpretation, which saves Whitehead's universe of value (Henning 2005) and which, rather than being subject-object centred, recognises *superjects* (the emergent actual occasions from which value is abstracted). Whitehead employs the term "ecstatic" in the sense of being out, away from, static, with the present emerging unpredictable from the past, an advance into novelty (ibid., p. 457). In particular, the interpretation stresses the core importance of intrinsic valuations in recognising, appreciating and affirming the intrinsic value of others. "Every entity has some value not only for itself but for the whole universe [from which insight] morality becomes possible" (ibid., p. 465).

Applying an evolutionary complexity trans-ontological process to an established subject requires not only new insights and terms to describe them, but also different emphases upon old ones. Insofar as it has developed – and it is a moveable feast, dogmatism is per se of little intrinsic value – this complexity-based approach can provide insights that may be relevant in terms of the application of HVN↔HBA in different geographic, economic, social, and environmental contexts.

The approach is not one of subversion of existing approaches, neither the scientific method nor other cherished (that is, identity-cored) tribal, religious and other mindsets that have demonstrated value in fitness landscapes, but to transcend and include them all into a larger whole. I am looking for neither a silver bullet nor a golden hammer, but to providing functionally fitting and sustainable recommendations to address Okoth-Ogendo's and the other wicked valuation problems when NSEW meet.

For example, one might pose the question, "are property rights that are appropriate in highly developed social systems necessarily appropriate to facilitate the developmental health of less highly developed societies?" One would think not, on Anderson's abovementioned dictum that "entirely new laws, concepts and generalisations" are required for each emergent level. Without sufficient insight into the relevant fitness landscapes, except for chance how can the appropriateness of such a policy intervention be determined?

Morin (2007) claims that most answers to such questions are attempted from the classical scientific paradigm, which rejected complexity based on three basic explanatory principles:

- universal determinism;
- reductionism; and
- disjunction – isolating and separating cognitive difficulties from one another (which led to disciplines becoming hermetically sealed from one another).

In contrast to the first explanatory principle, complexity science looks to a principle or principles concerning the relations between order and chaos and how the former emerges from the latter. In contrast to the latter two principles, complexity science looks to a principle of distinction and a principle of conjunction – maintaining distinctions but establishing relations (ibid., pp. 10–11).

Moreover, Ruhl (1996) points out that reductionism is mainly premised on five specious premises:

1   Small, gradual changes in causes give rise to small, gradual changes in effects.
2   Deterministic rules of behaviour give rise to completely predictable events.
3   All real-world truths are the logical outcome of following a set of rules.
4   Complicated systems can always be understood by breaking them down into simpler parts.
5   Surprising behaviour results only from complicated, hard-to understand interactions among a system's component parts.

Ruhl concludes that these principles, which mainly underpin current legal institutions, "are a fantasy" (ibid.).

While Ruhl's perception enfolds – and therefore also applies to – the current legal institutions of formal real property rights, his critique of reductionism applies far more broadly than that, and in particular to the subject of this book. There are pragmatic reasons for such fantasies, related to the necessity for heuristics (Gigerenzer and Todd 1999) in the context of the cognitive expenses of information costs (Long 2004). However, due diligence in such sensitive domains as this work addresses requires more rigorous treatment than is available when embedded within reductionist fantasies. For example, in resource management circles it is becoming increasingly apparent that traditional scientific [reductionist] approaches not only do not work; they actually make problems worse (Gunderson and Holling 2002, p. 118; Allison and Hobbs 2012).

That has been interpreted as being because, almost without exception, large scale interventions destabilise. In turn, that is because they disrupt existing socio-economic interdependencies and by adoption of reductionist fantasies the interventions can become blindly entangled by and in those interdependencies. As Mary Midgley (1995, p. 181) states, "there is nothing rational about using simple premises for complex subject matter", a mistake made by the economists that Amartya Sen called "rational fools" (Sen 1977). Similarly, "there is nothing natural about turning things into monetary equivalents" (Fourcade 2011, p. 1727). Abraham Maslow (1966, p. 15) once commented, "If all you have is a hammer, everything looks like a nail". If all we have is a limited capacity to reason about a small number of variables, we want to hit every existent with that "golden" hammer. But it simply is not so.

We have many capacities other than reason, and computers have the potential to not only enhance our capacity to reason about millions of variables, but help in valuing and weighing them as well. Once processes are put into the mix, what the complexity sciences offer to this work is that "insights into pattern formation and evolutionary dynamics" may help to develop more skilful means in such contexts (Bar-Yam 2005, p. 1).

For this to happen, insofar as they are hermetically sealed, we also discard the last of the three fundamental explanatory principles: disjunction. Instead, interdisciplinarity and its emergent, transdisciplinarity, are required (Max-Neef 2005; Nicolescu 2006).

Bromley and Yao (2006) develop this insight towards the production of this book by observing that mechanisms are not needed. Instead, they look toward development of a theory of institutions and institutional change built upon "prospective volition – the human will in action, looking to the future, contemplating the ways in which the future might and should unfold" (Bromley 2006, p. 15). In this context, that means looking to how these wicked valuation problems should be addressed in the future. As recommended herein, they thereby include the domain of values (axiology) and their co-evolving belief systems and how they "inform and shape the norms, rules, and entitlements (property relations) in an economy" (Bromley and Yao 2006).

This work adds to that quote how such belief systems inform and shape the economy, how values are "a real emergent property of situations in the world" (Midgley 2014, p. 86). Therefore, they must be considered in this context, as must *telaxiology* at ADALAS (see Glossary). It follows that inappropriate property rights can facilitate the damage or even destruction of environments. These may include the very senses of identity of the persons involved, and thereby their value to themselves and others.

Schools of developmental psychologists claim that this process of identity construction has emergent levels of complexity. Through the Model of Hierarchical

Complexity (Commons 2007) concerning identity and its components, and information-theory-based measures (Fernandez, Maldonado and Gershenson 2013) concerning all else, it further introduces a means by which one may determine which levels of emergence are higher or lower than others in terms of complexity and hence intrinsic valuation. Barnett (2000, p. 48) notes that these social arrangements include:

- nomadism;
- cultivating occupied land as a community;
- feudal ownership (lords and serfs);
- private occupation and production to market the produce;
- trading in land; and
- ownership by social artefacts such as nations or municipalities (ibid.).

He further notes that the ways that land is held (tenures) impact on a great variety of matters. These include those that have only developed at high levels of emergence in our species, such as religions, law, morality, social-scale violence, economics, history, politics and our reactions to these and their interactions, and that to reduce these to animal territorial behaviour is ludicrous (Barnett 2000, p. 49). That is not to say, however, that animal territorial behaviours played no part in their emergence.

Similarly, what if the hard facts that are the claimed domain of reductionism are not the major drivers of property rights, but rather values and beliefs are? In that case, we need Blake's second vision. Then, a major question to be addressed is: "Remember that property rights are mental artefacts of potential extrinsic value to facilitate intrinsic values, but they are not of intrinsic value themselves. In that case, which property rights facilitate which values and beliefs? And which of these have which consequences in terms of human development, and why?"

After all, many of the problems are similar across the globe (Toulmin and Pepper 2000). What are these similarities, and is it possible to place them in a developmental holarchy? If at each level of complexity, entirely new properties appear [and] entirely new laws, concepts and generalisations are necessary, what are they in terms of appropriate land policies, land-related valuations and real property rights?

Furthermore, it is pointless to switch from cheap reductionism (Lane 2014) to cheap inflationism such as "we are all one", or "everything is connected", which provide little or no explanatory depth. While having a role as ansatzes,[2] both reductionist and inflationist single vision approaches require development towards addressing phenomena by skilful means, at the appropriate level of complexity to address the problem. That may not be the highest level of complexity that the problem has achieved, but nonetheless (as articulated below) that highest level must be recognised by intrinsic valuations when deciding what to do.

Justification for the research

The United Nations has reported that:

> The emerging disciplines of complexity science and network science provide an increasing body of knowledge which, however, has typically not been considered by policy makers to date, in large part because it is not readily accessible knowledge. Yet, this knowledge has become increasingly important, in view of the global scale that man-made networking has reached.
>
> (UNDP 2015, paragraph 2.1.8, p. 43)

Similarly, progressive economists have made similarly relevant statements to this work, for example that:

> For understanding of complex outcomes that result from a variety of interactive processes and are shaped by various, often contradicting rationalities, *developing a complex analytical framework and a nuanced interpretation has become a must.* . . . A more attentive stance to other disciplines is now in the self interest of economics if it wants to escape the very real danger of being relegated to a socially and academically irrelevant, *self-referential* intellectual activity. Being attentive and receptive to the findings of others is part and parcel of the professional minimum.
>
> (Csaba 2009, p. 28; italics in original)

These confirm that unlike Tupaia in this story, who had only one sea and one sky to navigate, we have seas of information in all sorts of dimensions, domains, lines, levels and scales to address the wicked valuation problems when the NSEW meet. We now have to make policies in a world now known to be far more uncertain than we had previously understood (Swanson and Bhadwal 2009). Because of globalisation and technology, we have moved into postnormal times (Sardar 2010) – times characterised by complexity, chaos and contradictions, not so much one of integration and global identity construction as one of fanatical tribalisms, resurrected resentments and antipathies, with new ones piling atop the old ones (Mishra 2012, pp. 295–296). The contradictions include that (despite the availability of land information systems) land administration is generally one of the most stagnant and corrupted areas of activity in the developing world (Van der Molen and Tuladhar 2007; Wren-Lewis 2013). Moreover, the property-rights-catalysed global financial crisis has prompted scholars to call for a fundamental review of property rights, seeking a period of "proactive, systemic efforts to conceptualize the structure of property" (Davidson and Dyal-Chand 2010, p. 1658). The crisis has triggered a "property moment" – "critical junctures of significant institutional change" (ibid., p. 1617), "times of crisis that call foundational concepts into question" (ibid., p. 1612).

While the global financial crisis triggered this property moment, land policy is not confined to only financial matters. In the spheres of law (Ruhl 1996) and economics, all fundamental assumptions have been called into question (Nussbaum 1997, pp. 1997–1998). The whole antifoundationalist Western discourse, centred upon "how to construct a just society without the transcendent foundations thought to have previously sustained it" (Euben 1999, p. 2), has found itself to be quite inadequate to address valuations other than market ones, such that market based fundamentalist approaches are being attacked by other fundamentalists, particularly but not exclusively Islamic fundamentalists:

> The tried and true tools with which we in the West study political life may distort our understanding of practices cross-culturally. But it also suggests that many of our descriptive and theoretical tools are inadequate to the task of understanding foundationalist political practice.
>
> (Euben 1999)

In particular, the tools appear unable to appreciate the *strengths* of beliefs in traditional values.[3] For instance, Sayyad Qutb's main stated reason for opposition to the West was its alleged bankruptcy in the values that foster *true* human progress and development (Qutb in Euben 1999, pp. 55 and 210). While many in the West are demonstrably not bankrupt in values (traditional or otherwise), many who could never agree with Qutb's remedy of Islamist violence have made similar assertions, and all are relevant in land policy development worldwide. For those, Qutb's problem remains. There is still no "convincingly universalist approach" to this Western amoral problematic, and many of the West's interventions have been "dangerously unsuitable in large parts of the world" (Mishra 2012, p. 306). As described below, that includes interventions in land policy:

> Recent models of individual behaviour lack any internal structure that could be used to link the plurality of subjective representation defined by a model with the associated behaviours in a given situation.
>
> (Meyer and Braga 2007, p. 2)

This "lack of a theory of human valuation" (Meyer 2010; Meyer and Braga 2009, 2011, 2015) not only "hinders both prediction of agents' variable responses to similar incentive structures and the development of a more general theory of collective-action" (Meyer and Braga 2009, p.1), it makes them "virtually impossible" (Meyer 2010; p. 1, Meyer and Braga 2011, p. 1).

Moreover, even the old image of science itself, "where empirical data led to true conclusions and scientific reasoning led to correct policies", is "no longer plausible" (Sardar and Abrams 2004). Some even go so far as to say that science was never generally legitimate in the first place, only in special cases, wherein they do not include complex issues. The reasons include that:

- There is no universal uniform formal model of the world or its phenomena.
- Modern science is of fractured heterogeneity (starting with the breach between the natural sciences and humanities).

- Mankind's limited information and conceptual space holds us back.
- Science is inaccurate in principle.
- Initial concepts such as the concept of property are indistinct (Sosnitsky 2011, pp. 83–84).

The second-last reason includes that science is always chasing behind reality, which is subject to butterfly effects and black swans. Essentially, reality is unpredictable above certain levels of complexity, a criticism Eucken also applied to economics (Eucken 1992, p. 306).The last reason means that "All the existing definitions are essentially illegal and, hence, all the system of Science is nonlegitimate by definition [a fact that is] hushed up by its apologists (ibid.).

On the one hand, data is increasing exponentially; Wang and Ranjan (2015) estimate that by 2020 there will be about 5.2 gigabytes of data for every person on Earth. On the other hand, the most entrenched scientific procedures such as the "slow and costly scientific publication process, criticism of the peer review system and the challenge of reproducing research results due to lack of re-useable and replicable data" (Sosnitsky 2011) continue. Similarly, despite all this data social development experiments have high failure rates and uneven progress, and a main part of this is probably due to misguided "value configurations and incommensurability of values" (Wang and Christensen 2015, p. 4).

To address these multifarious challenges, the HVN↔HBA may facilitate not merely new approaches, but the emergence of new mindsets – paradigms – to select our approaches from. They should include what we mean by "I", "we" and "our" in these approaches. With Cohen, I consider that any such paradigm must take into account the way our minds work, and the intrinsic and extrinsic value of their responses to circumstances, and that while such an awareness is "of increasing relevance to economists and sociologists, [it] may matter most of all to policymakers" (Cohen 2005, p. 2).

When looking out through such paradigms, I intend to look at land valuations and policies under both formal and informal institutional arrangements. Social capital aside, real property rights contain a very high proportion – perhaps even the majority – of the wealth of humankind, often between a half and three-quarters of national wealth (World Bank 2013). This premise alone is sufficient justification for this research.

However, when so doing it has been further noted that most sustainability policies cannot alone promote sustainable management of natural resources (Gerber et al. 2009, p. 799), that heterogeneous demands on land are both the most common and the most problematic to analyse (ibid., p. 800), and that most policy failures are attributable to the property rights regimes (ibid., p. 801). Furthermore, in the institutional economics frame that Bromley addresses, economic production is largely defined by the rules that specify the relationships, rights and duties between people with respect to the use and control of land (Bromley 2006, p. 41). That is, property rights in general, and real property rights in particular, not only define wealth storage, but are also fundamental to environmentally sustainable economic performance.

As such, interrogations arising from the paradigm-enfolding HVN↔HBA articulated below may have the potential to generate significant economic consequences, as it is intended to generate better functional fits between the practically infinite actual complexities of our environments (and the fitness landscapes therein) and the limited capacities of our minds to address them. Furthermore, as real property rights – including those for the exploitation of natural resources – are also fundamental in social and environmental fields, the consequences of misapplication of reductionist approaches can be even worse in those fields than are the more readily measurable economic ones.

The real world is one of bounded rationality in unbounded complexity, a contest of limited minds that cannot "store, compute or adapt" to the demands of their environments (Mahzarin Banaji in Brockman 2013, pp. 94–95). If these observations about the traditional scientific economic and legal approaches from the old paradigm are correct, then such reductionist practices would have directly contributed not only to the wastage of hundreds of millions of dollars in foreign aid, but also to massive social disruption (Caufield 1998; Easterly 2006; Hickel 2017).

A major feature of this examination of fitness landscapes is the examination of the mindscapes that shape not only them but also, in turn, the landscape itself. This can have dramatic results. For instance, World Vision's chief food security adviser, Anthony Rinaudo, recounted how a community leader in northern Ethiopia told him, "If your objective is to transform landscapes, you will fail. But if your objective is to change mindsets and hearts of people, then you'll succeed" (Rinaudo 2014).

As far as I am aware, no one has yet attempted to apply the insights of a complexity-based approach to this subject. However, I am aware of complementary land-related initiatives, such as those land-management-related research initiatives at the new James Hutton Institute in Aberdeen. Consequently, my particular focus within this general topic is to establish a robust and rigorous framework to examine the environments and fitness landscapes for various forms of real property rights valuations, including both market value and "Big V" valuations. I have arrived at understanding that the general topic is essential to frame my particular one. I intend that focus to facilitate more sensitive and practical development and implementation of land policies, land-related valuations and real property rights.

This will require a framework for institutional and broader analysis and facilitation of imaginative syntheses that is applicable to all relevant scales from macro to micro, and from the simplest appropriate levels of complexity to the most complex. Therefore, this work may be a contribution to Bastardas-Boada's proposed new transdiscipline called *complexics* (see Box 1.1).

What makes the lived experience of one person tasked with facilitating land policy reform in one very small southern African country worthy of research in such a broad context? Is it the relationships between informal tenure and formal tenure? Is it that Swaziland happens to be a crucible of a core arena of concerns not only throughout Africa, but also in many other countries, including Australia?

**Box 1.1   Bastardas-Boada's proposed transdiscipline
of complexics**

The abstract by Bastardas-Boada introducing his proposed discipline is so
relevant to this work that I quote it in full, as follows:

> The proposed transdisciplinary field of "complexics" would bring
> together all contemporary efforts in any specific disciplines or by any
> researchers specifically devoted to constructing tools, procedures,
> models and concepts intended for transversal application that are
> aimed at understanding and explaining the most interwoven and
> dynamic phenomena of reality. Our aim needs to be, as Morin says, not
> "to reduce complexity to simplicity, [but] to translate complexity into
> theory". New tools for the conception, apprehension and treatment of
> the data of experience will need to be devised to complement existing
> ones and to enable us to make headway toward practices that better
> fit complexic theories. New mathematical and computational contri-
> butions have already continued to grow in number, thanks primarily
> to scholars in statistical physics and computer science, who are now
> taking an interest in social and economic phenomena. Certainly,
> these methodological innovations put into question and again make
> us take note of the excessive separation between the training received
> by researchers in the "sciences" and in the "arts". Closer collaboration
> between these two subsets would, in all likelihood, be much more
> energising and creative than their current mutual distance. Human
> complexics must be seen as multi-methodological, insofar as necessary
> combining quantitative-computation methodologies and more qualita-
> tive methodologies aimed at understanding the mental and emotional
> world of people. In the final analysis, however, models always have a
> narrative running behind them that reflects the attempts of a human
> being to understand the world, and models are always interpreted on
> that basis.
>
> (Bastardas-Boada 2015)

It is more than that. These relationships are an important area of concern
because land tenure underpins any society's social, environmental and economic
performance (Ring and Boykin 1986). Land tenure is foundational in social,
environmental and economic arenas every bit as much as land itself is foundational
for a building, and with similar potentially catastrophic consequences to all that is
built upon real property rights should any existent go wrong.

Existents have gone very wrong, and they continue to do so. The central thrust
of this work is that one major reason for it is an undervaluation of the fact that
when we are addressing land policies we are addressing humans and other
organisms. Yet when it comes to legal definitions of persons, "objects of rights and

duties . . . capable of having rights and of being liable to duties" they are of only two kinds. A kind of holon called a human being, and several kinds of artefacts (artificial persons). Under the maxim of legal interpretation *expressio unius personae vel rei, est exclusion alterius*, one may imply that means that no other holons but humans may have any rights. However, lawyers regard the maxim as "a valuable servant but a dangerous master" (ibid., p. 131), and the assumption that the natural world has no rights against what Tagore and others described as "The Machine" is a manifestation of just such a danger – a danger by no means confined to that particular maxim.

In my experience, so much is viewed through the pervasive Western philosophy of machinism, as if we were addressing machines with skin. Such views are endemic, machinism to most Westerners being as unnoticed as water is to fish. This is of particular importance in this context, as mechanistic thinking is pervasive in economics (Ormerod 2014) and law (Ruhl 1996). Humans are spiritual existents, not things (Rosado 2003), and machines are not. While mechanisms can be extremely useful and often necessary, machinism is a fantasy. I am submitting that a mechanistic approach cannot ever be sufficient under any land-related policy circumstances, because humans are holons, and complex; corporations are artefacts, and simple to complicated.[4]

Rather, just as Tony Lawson insists that one must go to ontology to decide where mathematics may and may not be useful (Lawson 2014b, 34:00), I propose the HVN↔HBA processual trans-ontology in general, and Complexics and Valuation Studies in particular, as being potentially far more useful to address the wicked valuation problems that are the concern of this work. My "Big V" and "small v" values differentiation (McDermott 1992) is now the subject of a new journal (see Box 1.2).

Box 1.2   About valuation studies

From the first article in the first edition of the journal *Valuation Studies*:

> The aim of the journal is therefore to be plainly a hub for work from the variety of disciplines and approaches that are related to the study of valuation as a social practice. . . . We therefore envisage a duality of a focussed scope on valuation as a topic, while focussing a broad scope as to what kinds of valuations are empirically examined or indeed how valuations are approached empirically and methodologically. A slight majority of the thus far submitted contributions are in the realm where economic aspects are central to the valuation practices examined. This is all fine and very welcome. We will, however, encourage and make efforts to make Valuation Studies a site with a scope as broad as possible when it comes to the valuation practices under scrutiny.
>
> (Helgesson and Muniesa 2013, p. 4)

I am further submitting that often we policy facilitators have been using the wrong tools for the tasks at hand. Or rather, we have been applying tools that are useful in one context to another where they are not. For example, the Copernican Principle worked very well for Captain Cook's navigation, but its single vision completely ignored Anderson's point that entirely new laws, concepts and generalisations are required for each emergent level of reality. We must have means of discovering what are the most suitable approaches and tools for the tasks at hand, and be competent to apply them appropriately.

The fruit of this research is this new HVN↔HBA approach to addressing wicked problems when the NSEW meet. I am proposing HVN↔HBA in a valuation studies/land policy context, focussing back from that broad perspective onto my core discipline, the market valuation of real property rights.

As it turned out, HVN↔HBA could have broader applications in terms of addressing other wicked problems and even social messes. Such potentials for broader applications are as suggested in Chapter 7, which addresses the global current affairs situation from land policies, land-related valuations and real property rights perspectives. That said, the fitness to purpose of HVN↔HBA to other wicked problem areas is a matter for those with the most relevant competencies in the context to determine, and if useful they should if necessary change it to make it more so.

Methodology

Methodology is "probably the most significant component [to address the topic of this work, as it] provides the substrate for establishing our knowledge of the world" (Braverman in Blomley, Braverman, Delaney and Kedar 2014, p. 120), and "tried-and-tested linear policy solutions are increasingly inadequate or failing" (West, Haider, Sinare and Karpouzoglou 2014). As Aldwin put it:

> Science is in the midst of a Kuhnian paradigm shift, from causal, deterministic models to more probabilistic ones that emphasize systems approaches. In the developmental sciences, this shift has been manifesting in relational developmental systems theories (RSDTs) which ... highlight multilevel analyses, interindividual differences in intraindividual change, and coaction with the context.
>
> (Aldwin 2015, p. 189)

Therefore, in conducting this research, it became apparent that I would have to approach it from a new trans-ontological process facilitating an integral approach that combines research across a broad array of disciplines.

The methodology emerging from the trans-ontological process is composed of elements derived from the application of complexity theory to social behaviour. This approach is of value not only in applying complexity science's lessons to pursue social issues more effectively, but also to "encourage a reassessment of the nature and prospects for social policy itself' (Gilbert and Bullock 2014, p. 2). USAID is also developing a complexity-based approach to monitor and evaluate their projects (Britt 2013). Through a qualitative framework addressing levels of complexity, HVN↔HBA will differentiate and articulate the interplay between scales and levels of behaviour within the area of investigation, and their likely resultant dynamic behaviour patterns.

Homologies exist between the methodology independently derived in this work and the research taken by others engaged with addressing complex problems. Seven researchers who have done so emphasise the need for adaptive approaches transcending "traditional units of analysis such as ecosystems" and instead could be characterised by "interconnectedness and emergence", and furthermore that such methodologies are *necessary* as "approaches to complex problems" (McGowan et al. 2014, p. 36).

A useful articulation of part of that methodology has been devised by one of the four scholars who designed and conducted a Master of Arts degree on using insights from complexity and chaos sciences to address complex social problems, which I completed in 2005: Hodge (2007) articulated four kinds of complexity and considers that complexity *enfolds values* (positive and negative), science and non-science, academic and non-academic meanings: "With folds/differences and relationships so dynamically related that no aspect is totally independent. This complex field is the minimum context in which to explore claims about a 'complexity revolution'" (ibid.).

Hodge's four complexities are:

- *Complexity 1:* "composed of many interrelated parts", or problems "so complicated or intricate as to be hard to deal with" (ibid.).
- *Complexity 2:* the presenting complexity of problems, which science will strip down to underlying simplicity.
- *Complexity 3:* a revolutionarily more positive attitude to complexity in science that does not seek to be reductive.
- *Complexity 4:* the complexity of the humanities: acknowledges and celebrates the inherent complexity of texts and meanings.

Note that Hodge's Complexity 1 is superficially only complicated, not complex, as defined by Glouberman and Zimmerman (2002) and quoted below. However, Hodge's Complexity 1 does not necessarily *exclude* complex parts – that is, those with emergent properties. As elaborated below, complex enfolds complicated, and complicated enfolds simple, but not the other way around. However, identity construction often requires the fallacy that they do enfold the other way around as an extrinsically valuable means of addressing challenges, but that is no reason to lose sight of that reality.

While accessing all four of these complexities, this work places particular emphasis on Complexity 4, because as Hodge (2007) states it has remained a refuge for the irreducibly complex. As such, "it takes for granted that real-life problems will always be too complex (with too many factors, interrelated in too many ways) to be reduced to the sort of problem that isolated disciplines could handle" (ibid.). However, "it is painters and poets who really look at the world" (Roszak 1972, p. 288), and "there is no truth greater than the truth of literature, the realm of beautiful lies" (Craven 2010). As Whitehead put it:

> In the present lecture, I propose in the first place to consider how the concrete educated thought of men has viewed this opposition of mechanism and organism. It is in literature that the concrete outlook of humanity receives its expression. Accordingly it is to literature that we must look, particularly in its more concrete forms, namely in poetry and in drama, if we hope to discover the inward thoughts of a generation.
>
> (Whitehead 2011, pp. 93–94)

Poetic metaphors allow "a sudden flinging open of the door into the world of the right side, the world where the animal is not separated from either the spirit or the real world or itself" (Hughes 1992, p. 159). Also:

> Only the right hemisphere has the capacity to understand metaphor. . . . Metaphoric thinking is fundamental to our understanding of the world, because it is the only way in which understanding can reach outside the system of signs to life itself. It is what links language to life (ibid., p. 115) . . . all thinking, most obviously philosophical and scientific thinking, is at bottom metaphorical in nature.
>
> (McGilchrist 2012, Kindle locations 176–177)

And: "Poetry is the only way language can escape from its self-created prison" within the machine mind of the left hemisphere (ibid., p. 249). Moreover, films such as the Qatsi Trilogy demonstrate how words can be unnecessary to stimulate meaning-making in the viewer.

As both a painter and a poet, William Blake really looked at the world. Hobsbawm noted that Blake was among the first to foresee the "social earthquake" caused by The Machine, and that such poets often see "not only more deeply but also sometimes more clearly" (Hobsbawm 1996, p. 263). As such, Complexity 4 enfolds at least Blake's single and twofold visions, and arguably three and fourfold, but as this work attempts to address real life problems, it strongly focusses on Complexity 4 insofar as it enfolds twofold vision, and therefore includes both art and poetry where they provide more succinct explanatory depth than prose can alone.

With the appropriately developed trans-ontological process in place from such a base, HVN↔HBA will be better able to assess the current or prospective fitness of the various policies in a given environment.

As mentioned above, this work takes a narrative autoethnographic approach (Pace 2012). As such, I trust that the reader will be better able to understand how the lessons from my experiences have informed the creation of the HVN↔HBA process. I intend it to provide a more comprehensive framing for policy formulation than I have otherwise encountered. Moreover, as autoethnography is especially suitable for qualitative research, I intend the autoethnographic presentation of the development of this framing to inform the readers' weighing or valuation of the various matters in HVN↔HBA.

I intend HVN↔HBA to be a means of addressing – a trans-ontological framing – of the environment that property rights are embedded – or to be embedded – within. I do not see the environment as clockwork, or a machine. Rather (as described in Chapter 4), I see it as holarchic vortex networks within heterarchic fields, enfolding both machines and the memeplexes that create them within a far greater whole. Therefore, I have both that general trans-ontological process for the environment as the HVN, and the particular HBA approach for a means to address it.

The "V" in HVN stands for "vortex". Vortices appear at all scales, from the sub-atomic to the known universe, and diverse vectors drive these vortices. HVN↔HBA does not confine such vortices to the simple ones we see, such as a tornado, or water going down a drain. It sees all life as environmental vortices – not isolated things but existents in fields, created by those fields. Consequently, in HVN↔HBA existents are no more reducible to vortices than you are reducible to your atoms. I mean HVN↔HBA as a model to be employed as a tool – "a practical method to achieve a defined objective in a particular context" (Selabalo 2016). In this case, the defined objective is to address wicked valuation problems, designed to build in the realisation that models, including ontologies, are at best only approximations to irreducibly complex realities, and their purpose is to facilitate the evolution of cognitive complexity (Commons 2007) in their users, including valuations. This is a process that should not stop, either by collapsing into a reductionist fantasy, or by being blown up into an inflationist fantasy, or even by stopping at ontologies themselves. They are to increase intrinsic value for the intended policy beneficiaries by means of the skilful application of methods of extrinsic value to that task.

Even as an ontology HVN↔HBA would be a start, but once properly set out it can become a dynamic trans-ontological process by engagement of the six principles articulated in Chapter 5. In particular, the Goldilocks Principle – that development can only occur in a tolerable space-time frame – can be employed to provide insights into practicable solutions of wicked problems over a period – not only what policies are practicable, but also what resources to put into what areas at what time.

As my professional background was that of a valuer before I went to Swaziland, that skill of weighing the various components' influences in a valuation decision was already familiar to me in the narrower context of determining the market value of a property. I then adapted that skill to the much broader new fitness landscapes I encountered there. These fitness landscapes involved not only market values, but also many other kinds of valuations not reducible to a monetary consideration.

In addition to the above advantages, the autoethnographic approach allows me to emphasise one aspect that I consider undervalued in such processes.

The identity I can narrate is unique, but so is every other identity that land policies affect and, as shown later in this book, that affect can be dramatic, for good or for ill. In particular, the inter-relationship between identity and land is often underestimated. I think we made that mistake in Swaziland, because I now consider that the importance of tribal identity over personal identity was insufficiently addressed in Swaziland's land policy formulation. It is vital to recognise that the autoethnographic approach would entail a different narrative from every participant in that process, and that is what happens whether written down or not. I have created HVN↔HBA to address that reality.

Outline of the book

This book therefore takes the following form. After an account of my learning of an opportunity in Swaziland and a preliminary account of what I learnt there, I begin a narration of those parts of my own identity construction that I consider were the most important in shaping the evolution of HVN↔HBA. These include events showing a typically highly contingent sequence of events that led to my existing at all, and once that existence began the highly selective and contingent manner in which I set about constructing my identity narrative.

The purpose of this section is to engage the reader into considering not only the universality of this process, but that all its results are unique, in that each identity construction starts from a different time and place with a myriad of consequential differences. These include history, environment, values, genes, memes, languages, societal structures and so on that each one of us has to address.

When one enters the field of policy formulation, one looks for common decisions among all these different identities. Moreover, those policies are likely to have significant affects upon unknown thousands or millions, some of whom are unborn, just as my parents' and grandparents' activities caused my existence in the first place, and theirs were similarly caused, and so on back to the beginning of space–time.

To this end, Chapter 2 gives the back-story to introduce what capacities I had to engage in Swaziland's policy facilitation. While I had no previous experience there, I did have both my travelling experience and my valuation skills. When I began as a valuer, the then Commonwealth Institute of Valuers motto was "broad vision and balanced judgement", which I took very much to heart.

My narrative relates how, while by then I could have made a comparatively strong claim to broad vision from my previous experiences and that I attempted balanced judgement, I did not succeed in successfully facilitating Swaziland's National Land Policy. I now believe that one can have broad *and deep* vision and balanced judgement and still not succeed. We need more, and this book recommends a way.

In finding this way, I have had to move across multiple fields. That meant that I have had to include greater breadth than usual within the length confines of a book, and at times this has had to come at the cost of greater depth. A person with specialised knowledge in one or more of these fields might find this challenging, as they would naturally seek greater depth over breath in such domains. To them I offer HVN↔HBA as a consolation, as I consider that the methodology can be used to investigate to any depths they may require.

The chapter then describes my time in Swaziland, with the successes, defeats and lessons that triggered my eventual creation of HVN↔HBA. Finally, the chapter enfolds my autoethnographic narrative of my time after Swaziland, during which time I developed HVN↔HBA itself. It took a long time and a great many challenges to distil all that happened into a framework having the potential to enfold the lessons from all of the above experiences.

Chapter 3 then provides a literature review informed by that autoethnographic narrative, taking the form of a desktop revisitation of the places I had visited as road crew. Thus informed, the fourth chapter then introduces the high level HVN trans-ontological process, and the fifth introduces the HBA.

So then, in Chapter 6, I report upon my testing how robust the HVN↔HBA trans-ontological process is in providing a practical framing for policy formulation and implementation. I narrate its further development in conferences in Malaysia and Washington, how I presented it publicly for the first time at a symposium in the Solomon Islands, and developed it via a consultancy for UN-Habitat/ GLTN. I then proceed to interpret globalisation's effects upon the wicked problems of valuations and policies via HVN↔HBA, then employ HBA to inter-rogate the current International Valuation Standards Council (IVSC) definition of market value.

From there, I look to the global property scene, including an examination of legal geography via HVN↔HBA. I then proceed to specifically address Okoth-Ogendo's challenge at the African scale, and then use that same HVN↔HBA trans-ontological process to see whether or not there could have been a better outcome to Swaziland's National Land Policy initiative and, if so, how.

The seventh and final chapter of this book wraps together the conclusions, and suggests a methodology for both researching and addressing wicked valuation problems.

Definitions/explanations of key terms

I have been advised to keep this book's vocabulary as simple as precision permits. Yet "words make worlds" (Cornwall 2010, p. 1) and I have found the field of property to be as Kingsley Davis described: "forever a paradoxical thing, a blending of opposites, producing a perennial confusion of words and emotions" (Pels 1986, p. 15). If one is trapped inside a simple vocabulary, one is trapped inside a simple world which is inadequate to address the realm of property. It therefore required the attention of the right hemisphere, attention to the myths made that trap and, in particular, the *"Myth of the Machine"* (Mumford 1967, 1970). As Panikkar noted before McGilchrist articulated it as *the right hemisphere framing where the left directs its attention in the first place* (McGilchrist 2009, p. 187): "myth defies a further foundation. It is beyond any possible definition, because myth is a horizon which make the definition possible" (Panikkar 1989a, p. 12). Furthermore:

Panikkar stresses the distinction between creative word and scientistic term, where the creative, analogical and mythological function of the word is juxtaposed to the scientistic term of the Logos, which is devoid of symbolic echoes and of positive creative complexities. The scientistic term restrains and separates, pinning and limiting things to a specific and often univocal meaning that circumscribes and confines life into stereotypical patterns rather than opening up it to worlds of interconnected and dialogic significances.

(Riem Natale 2016, p. 8)

The similarities between these distinctions and the hemispheric distinctions made by McGilchrist and Lakoff are clear. Lakoff adds that words do not have meaning independent of metaphor, and "give meaning to the words we hear rather than the other way around" (Hoggan and Litwin 2016, p. 49). Moreover, the word "confusion" means "fuse together", and confusion is inevitable with an impoverished reductionist vocabulary. We need to be able to value the potential contributions of a wide variety of persons – poets, physicists, politicians, philosophers, activists etc. – and to do that we need to unfuse and articulate each of our left hemispheres' Logos from our right hemispheres' Mythos and recognise each of their essential contributions towards addressing the complexities of wicked valuation problems. As Bateson observed:

If this was the sort of message that could be communicated in words, there would be no point in dancing it. But it is not that sort of message. It is, in fact, precisely the sort of message that would be falsified if communicated in words, because the use of words (other than poetry) would imply that this is a fully conscious and voluntary message, and this would be simply untrue.

(Bateson 1987, p. 147)

This observation is not inconsistent with Wittgenstein's comment that "the limits of our language are the limits of our world" (Wittgenstein 1974, p. 56), because there are several other languages – means of communication – besides words. However, in this work I must largely confine myself to words, while at the same time realising their strengths and limitations in the context I am addressing.

Such recognition is sometimes undervalued in its consequences: for example, McGilchrist observed how "the words we use to describe human processes are highly influential ... for the values to which we hold" (McGilchrist 2009, p. 459), the reductive language of the "worn-out mode of scientific materialism" can blind people "to the very possibility that they might be dealing with anything other than a machine" (ibid.). "All the Nazi or Fascist schoolbooks made use of an impoverished vocabulary, and an elementary syntax, in order to limit the instruments for complex and critical reasoning" (Eco 1995, p. 8), and yet we now have "newly emergent standards of evaluation that privilege transparency, clarity, and simplicity ... as opposed to more classical academic virtues such as erudition, depth of understanding, and sophistication" (Lamont 2012, p.14).

To address wicked valuation problems, I submit that the classical academic virtues are far more relevant.

When it comes to words and property, the point made above by Davis that "property is forever a paradoxical thing, a blending of opposites, producing a perennial confusion of words and emotions" (as quoted in Pels 1986, p. 15) is particularly germane when addressing wicked valuation problems, as valuers value property rights over existents, not the existents themselves. Among the most fundamental definitions used in this book are those relating to Western conceptions of property. In common law, "real property" means "immovable property which could be recovered by a real action" (Osborn 1964, p. 234), and a right is "an interest recognised and protected by law" (ibid., p. 247). In this book, when I say "real property rights" I am referring to all such rights, not only those under common, statutory or civil law but also those under all socially accepted forms in any particular culture. I do so because with regard to land-related vocabulary in the context of Austronesia, Reuter notes:

> The terminology we use to designate different territories and social relations to land in Western societies – words such as "estate", "village", "domain", "territory", "proprietor", "tenant" and their reflexes in other European languages – are not suitable to serve as universal categories for the purposes of cross-cultural comparison.
>
> (Reuter 2006)

The reason Reuter gives is that the meanings of words (such as "real property rights") are socially embedded, in not only Europe and Austronesia, but everywhere. As Lakoff put it, "All words are defined relative to conceptual frames. When you hear a word, its frame (or collection of frames) is activated in your brain" (Lakoff 2004, p. xv), and this work has to address widely varying societies, their languages and their frames. In particular, the meanings of key words in a society arise "from their conceptual relation to the local cosmology and idiom" (Reuter 2006). To which I add that it is not only their conceptual relations, but also relations between values. I further add Whitehead's abovementioned repudiations of nine myths to Reuter's insight, in particular the myth of mere language as an adequate expression of propositions. As defined below the real world is a mix of simple, complicated and complex, and in addressing any existent beyond the simple, "the greatest problem of all is dumbing down" (Goldacre 2008, p. 338).

In the introduction to *The Mystery of Values: Studies in Axiology*, the author notes that once the term "axiology" emerged, "a new realm of reality, previously ignored or at best restricted to other domains, was discovered" (Grunberg 2000, p. 12). Similarly, to find such domains veiled by inappropriate verbal imprecisions, it is sometimes necessary to disentangle concepts from their "close etymological siblings" (Mason 2015, p. 12).

To disentangle this Gordian knot, I am introducing a new word, *telaxiology*, in the hope that it may open up still more worlds than one of its parent words, axiology, did. The other parent word is "teleology": The study of purpose. I coined the neologism following a blog post (Vallicella 2009) wherein Vallicella pointed out that while life is meaningless without purpose, one can gain a feeling of purpose in one's life by evil, trivial or futile activities. That can apply to Csikszentmihalyi's *Flow* (1990), which is often the payoff in playing computer games. So while Csikszentmihalyi points out that "The best moments in life are those spent attempting something difficult and worthwhile" (1990, p. 3), that is as it seems to the person. Vallicella rejects a solely subjective assessment of meaning. Therefore, while the meaningfulness of a person's existence can only be discovered by an integration of teleology and axiology, the person may feel meaning by experiencing autotelaxic flow regardless; a key factor in their manipulation in markets.

While one is entitled to be carelessly telaxiological in monitoring and evaluating one's own existence, one must be more careful about judging others. As an autoethnographic instance, most nights I go for walks along Casuarina beach, in Darwin. On the way to the beach, the path goes through where Aboriginal homeless people, called "long-grassers", usually gather. I used to reflect on how little our umwelts touch – much less than anywhere else I had ever been. It is as though we lived in utterly different ghostly parallel worlds, with only the occasional greeting or other communication through the screen (so far, never hostile either way). Later, I discovered the concept of different white and black "spatial imaginaries" in the book *How Racism Takes Place* (Lipsitz 2011), which fits perfectly with that perception, and concretises and contextualises it by giving me the vocabulary to both file it in my identity construction and communicate it to others. In my case, I probably ignore places along my walk that could be central, even sacred, to long-grassers. As Niklas Luhmann put it:

> Pieces of information don't exist "out there", waiting to be picked up by the system. As selections they are produced by the system itself in comparison with something else ... The communicative synthesis of information, utterance and understanding is possible only as an elementary unit of an ongoing social system.
>
> (Luhmann 1986)

Similarly, there are simple words and phrases that close inquiries (for example, "'this' is 'nothing but' 'that'") and simple words that open vistas (such as the Jewish proverb, *we don't see things as they are; we see things as we are*). All observation is, always and necessarily, theory-laden (Cronin in Brockman 2013, p. 157). Hence the desirability of peer review, and of HVN↔HBA being a collaborative team, transdisciplinary approach, not simply that of one individual.

The importance of this insight in development studies – and thereby to the topic of this book – can be implied by the above-quoted "words make worlds" being the first words on the first chapter of the book *Deconstructing Development Discourse: Buzzwords and Fuzzwords* (Cornwall in Cornwall and Eade 2010). By rubrics such as attempting to make complex issues intelligible to a disinterested child, language becomes cut off from reality. So paradoxically, in order to attempt precision, a large vocabulary is required of both the writer and the reader. Without the right word, the right meaning has little hope of being conveyed; "when you lack words, you shut down new insights and lines of reasoning" (Passuello 2007); hence a large vocabulary being the single best indicator of professional success (Shand 1994). Moreover, the same words and terms can have differences in meanings in different contexts, or the same contexts in different domains, which can lead to misunderstandings, including in property valuation (Fischer 2000, p. 293). This lack of extent and precision in vocabularies precipitated the fate facilitated by "newspeak" in George Orwell's *1984 in fiction*, and by changes in educational policy in the 1960s *in fact* (Singal 1991).

As is consistent within the Goldilocks Principle described in Chapter 5, people learn words best that are slightly beyond their vocabulary frontier (Shand 1994, p. 2). I am unaware of the readers' vocabulary frontier so – while being acutely aware of my own deficiencies in vocabulary – I have tried to err on the side of caution in presenting these definitions and explanations of key terms.

One such, the term "fitness landscape" arose in evolutionary biology (Wright 1932), and refers to the capacity of an organism in its environment. I am using it in a sense expanded in the discipline of evolutionary optimisation (Sarker, Mohammadian and Xin Yao 2002), expanding it to matters such as economics (Fellman et al. 2004) and to the telaxiology of land policies, real property rights in this work.

I use the term "fitness landscape" because unlike "environment", "umwelt" (the world as perceived by an organism) and "umfeld" (the world that objectively influences an organism) it emphasises that when one component of a participant in an environment changes, other components may respond to that change, and those changes then impact upon other components and the landscape itself (Kauffman 1993). Furthermore, the umwelt impacts upon the innenwelt, and vice versa. That is, I am approaching the subject from the fundamental proposition that we are addressing an arena for the "co-evolution on mutually interdependent or reciprocally deformed fitness landscapes" (Holbrook 2003, p. 22), in which "we are all each other's fitness landscapes" (Brand 2013, p. 124). Therefore, the interactions between land and ourselves provide the fitness landscapes affected by, and affecting, wicked problems when NSEW meet.

Confusingly, another key word has several definitions: Ontology (Cruickshank 2004; Carrithers et al. 2010; Pedersen 2012). It derives from the Greek "onto", meaning "being", and "logos", usually interpreted in English as "science" (Lawson 2014a, p. 1). At one level, it is defined as "the branch of metaphysics concerned with the nature or essence of being or existence", and at another level "a rigorous and exhaustive organization of some knowledge domain". As such, it differs from a "paradigm", which means a scientific consensus – common tools, methods, technologies, jargon etc. unifying theory with practice (Fischer 2000, p. 293). I use "ontology" in both meanings in this book, and by the nature of HVN↔HBA, it cannot be a fixed and static "thing", but is necessarily a trans-ontological process (Sohst 2009) to be able to compare ontologies.

The "Holarchic Vortex Networks within Heterarchic Fields" (HVN for short) fulfils the above high level meaning of "ontology", but by being a trans-ontological process opens up new worlds of understanding and value. In fact, if complexity science is to be believed, that trans-ontological process is far more reality-centred that my quotidian level of consciousness can comprehend. So that level needs HBA as articulated in Chapter 5 as my framing towards tackling the topic – the second level of the definition of "process ontology".[5] I say "towards" because the ideal of the topic being able to be both rigorously and exhaustively treated is unattainable, because the subject is a wicked, not a simple, problem. Hence, also the need for a trans-ontological process.

Another major definition is that of complexity, which Waldrop defined as "the science of emergent properties" (Waldrop 1992, p. 8). In common parlance it can be confused with complicated, such as complicated matters being adopted by Hodge (see "Definitions/explanations of key terms" above) as Complexity 1. That is fine in general, but in this work it is vital to know the distinctions. Table 1.1 explains the meaning of these terms in this book. These different systems require markedly different approaches to address (see Table 1.2).

This provides a reframing of the criticism by Easterly that I elucidate in Chapter 2, is consistent with McGilchrist's neurological evidence of the differences between the functioning of the left (addressing complicated) and right (addressing complex) hemispheres (McGilchrist 2009), and shapes the approach of this work and the application of HVN↔HBA. Blake's single vision is great for

Table 1.1 Examples of simple, complicated and complex

Simple	*Complicated*	*Complex*
Example: Following a recipe	*Example: Sending a rocket to the moon*	*Example: Raising a child*
The recipe is essential	Formulae are critical and necessary	Formulae have a limited application
Recipes are tested to assure easy replication	Sending one rocket increases assurance that the next will be OK	Raising one child provides experience but no assurance of success with the next
No particular expertise is required. But cooking expertise increases success rate	High levels of expertise in a variety of fields are necessary for success	Expertise can contribute but is neither necessary nor sufficient to assure success
Recipes produce standardised products	Rockets are similar in critical ways	Every child is unique and must be understood as an individual
The best recipes give good results every time	There is a high degree of certainty of outcome	Uncertainty of outcome remains
Optimistic approach to problem possible	Optimistic approach to problem possible	Optimistic approach to problem possible

Source: Glouberman and Zimmerman (2002, p. 2)

Table 1.2 Different leadership tasks for different systems

Simple and complicated systems	Complex adaptive systems
Role defining – setting job and task descriptions	Relationship building – working with patterns of interaction
Decision-making – find the 'best' choice	Sense making – collective interpretation
Tight structuring – use chain of command and prioritise or limit simple actions	Loose coupling – support communities of practice and add more degrees of freedom
Knowing – decide and tell others what to do	Learning – act/learn/plan at the same time
Staying the course – align and maintain focus	Notice emergent directions – building on what works

Source: Allen (2013), from Anderson and McDaniel (2000) and Snowden and Boone (2007)

simple and complicated, but inappropriate for complex. HVN↔HBA requires the wisdom and compassion to apply "horses for courses" in addressing wicked problems when the four directions meet. That requires many more differentiations than those of Tupaia's and Captain Cook's approaches.

As John Kay noted, the approaches of many so-called rationalists such as machinists are not rational at all if they attempt to apply their methods where entirely new ones are required, because they are employing a "false and oversimplified picture of the world" (Kay 2011, p. 8):

> Directness is appropriate when the environment is stable, and objectives are one-dimensional and transparent, and it is then possible to determine when and whether goals have been achieved. And only then. . . . [Not] whenever complex systems evolve in an uncertain environment and whenever the effect of our actions depend on the ways in which others depend upon them.
> (Kay 2011, p. 179)

Grint (2013) further developed these differentiations and integrations by defining distinctions between managers, commanders, and leaders. Noting that these are definitions, not means of straightjacketing people with all sorts of varying competencies into one role, he sees the commanders' role is to address critical problems (for example, "we are being invaded; follow me! We must defend our territory!"), the managers' role as addressing tame problems – ones with known causes, which can be competently addressed by following recipes and formulae, and the leaders' role as addressing wicked problems, as articulated above, noting that dramatically different skill sets are required for each role.

While the above distinctions are best made in Grint's 2013 work, previous works by Grint (2008, 2009) have further articulated aspects of the above, and also adopts aspects I have adopted elsewhere in this book. For example, Grint defines heterarchies (Grint 2009, p. 4) as embracing emergence (ibid.).

That is not to say that there are no roles for command and management approaches in addressing wicked problems, or that wicked problems are necessarily free of simple and complicated components. Clearly, if a fingernail grows too long, that is a simple problem which is resolved by trimming it. Holons are far more likely to include all to varying degrees. For example, as long ago as 1975 medical practitioners recognised that they make mistakes not only through ignorance and ineptitude, but also by some existent they termed "necessary fallibility" (Gorovitz and MacIntyre 1975). Therefore, to minimise fallibilities, the importance of checklists to address complicated matters was recently re-emphasised by Gawande (2010), but the distinctions between complicated, complex and wicked were not drawn. However, Gawande makes a useful distinction for my purposes between throwing an ice cube into a big fire (it's highly predictable that the ice cube would quickly melt in fires of a certain scale, and extinguish fires in other scales) and the necessary ignorance that exists when trying to track the path of a hurricane. Ignorance and ineptitude can apply across this entire spectrum of simple, complicated, complex, wicked problems and social messes. Therefore, instead of atomistic crispness, some words have a *necessary fuzzibility*, because they apply to complexity and wicked situations (Rowson 2014, p. 17).

While even interlocking complicated systems result in an intervention having quite unexpected consequences in a different place (Goldacre 2008, p. 101), with complicated systems they can be tracked. Necessary fallibility and necessary fuzzibility, only apply to the complex, wicked problems and social messes. Simply put, in such complex domains "anyone who ever expresses anything with certainty is basically wrong" (ibid., p 129). While simplex, snake oil reassurances can be reassuring and thereby lucrative and empowering, and even engender the placebo effect, the truth of the matter is that "complex problems often have depressingly complex causes, and the solutions can be taxing and unsatisfactory" (ibid., p. 153).

These distinctions also influence conventional academic protocols. For example, Shipman (2014) considers that, to be considered good research, research should be reliable, valid, generalisable and credible. That rubric is applicable to the simple and complicated, but *per se* inapplicable to the complex and wicked, which are precisely the natures of many of the problems to be addressed in land policy and even real property valuations. Therefore, while such research can be invaluable in discerning what aspects of a problem are simple and complicated within complex and wicked situations, they are impotent beyond that. In such contexts they may become "cheap reductionism . . . not very worthwhile . . . reductionism is quite useful in the right domain . . . Reduce too much and we lose. Don't reduce and we inflate too much" (Lane 2014). Similarly, we can conflate too much in our mental sets, racism being among the most pernicious examples.

For the purposes of framing this work, it is necessary to define further terms to go with the above. The first is *simplexity*. It refers to the tendency of a simpler order to emerge from complexity (Stewart and Cohen 1995). It has a companion word, *complicity*, similar to Blake's contraries, without which there is no progression, and which is part of what I refer to as Related Evolution in my HBA trans-ontology below. Another two, *wicked problems* and *social messes*, were defined in the introduction. A description has been collated (Cox, Pinfield and Smith 2014) from the original 10 defining features of such problems (Rittell and Webber 1973; Horn and Weber 2007) as shown in Box 1.3.

They say wicked problems should be addressed holistically – that is, by emphasising the importance of the whole and the interdependence of its parts. Therefore, it requires a fundamental understand of the difference between the whole and the total – another example of the importance of vocabulary. Emergent

---

Box 1.3   Sixteen defining features of wicked problems

The first ten defining features of wicked problems below are those Rittel and Webber (1973):

1   There is no definitive formulation of a wicked problem. Different approaches to the problem see it differently. Different proposed solutions reflect the fact that it is defined differently.

2   There is a "no stopping rule". Unlike in an experiment where you can stop natural processes and control variables, you cannot step outside a wicked problem or stop it to contemplate an approach to answering it. Things keep changing as policy makers are trying to formulate their answers.

3   Solutions are not true or false, rather they are good or bad. There is no right answer and no one is in the position to say what is a right answer. The many stakeholders focus on whether proposed solutions are ones they like from their point of view.

4   There is no test of whether a solution will work or has worked. After a solution is tried the complex and unpredictable ramifications of the intervention will change the context in such a way that the problem is now different.

5   Every solution is a "one-shot operation". There can be no gradual learning by trial and error, because each intervention changes the problem in an irreversible way.

6   There is no comprehensive list of possible solutions.

7   Each wicked problem is unique, so that it is hard to learn from previous problems because they were different in significant ways.

8   A wicked problem is itself a symptom of other problems. Incremental solutions run the risk of not really addressing the underlying problem.

9   There is a choice about how to see the problem, but how we see the problem determines which type of solution we will try and apply.

10   Wicked societal problems have effects on real people, so one cannot conduct experiments to see what works without having tangible effects on people's lives.

The Horn and Weber (2007) additions follow:

11 As well as there being no single definition of the problem, there are multiple value conflicts wrapped up in it.
12 There are also multiple ideological, political or economic constraints on possible solutions.
13 There is great resistance to change.
14 With social messes, in addition to the complexity of the problem itself, data to describe the problem is often uncertain or missing. It may be difficult actually to collect information. There is no one expert with the answer.
15 Because the problems are complex, there are multiple possible intervention points.
16 "The consequences of any particular intervention are difficult to imagine" (Cox, Pinfield and Smith 2014).

wholes come with new levels of simplexity, so I am referring to a hierarchy of wholes, both nested and separate – a holarchy that relates heterarchically – when addressing wicked problems.

While Glouberman and Zimmerman (2002) classify problems into simple, complicated and complex, Stewart and Cohen (1997) offer a high-level orienting framework towards finding those best able to address such tasks. They divide cognition levels into simplex, complex, and multiplex, each of which has different capacities in addressing wicked problems (to which I add compliplex to maintain the distinction between complicated and complex).

When it comes to these wicked valuation problems, "a simplex mind cannot cope" (Stewart and Cohen 1997, p. 296), and simplex vocabularies are not up to the task either. Stewart and Cohen assert that today, "simplex management of scientific research is futile and counterproductive . . . our scientific extelligence will fall apart if research is allowed to be managed by simplex minds" (ibid., p. 296).

Under the Goldilocks Principle described below, simplex minds are good to address simple problems that would be far too boring to occupy the attention of a complex or multiplex mind for the requisite period.

Stewart and Cohen began by asking the question, "What is the most important thing in the universe?" They then state that any mind that gives an answer to that is a *simplex* mind, which is precisely the "nothing but" approach that I criticise in this book as being insufficient to address the complexities involved. Many religious leaders and politicians focus at this level (Stewart and Cohen 1997, p. 291).

They describe two other levels of mind:

A complex mind can perceive the many intertwining strands of cause and effect that combine, within some consistent worldview, to constrain and control the unfolding of a particular selection of events. Complexity is a state that is inaccessible to the vast proportion of the human race, but as the global village shrinks, more of us take the complex view. Rarer still is the multiplex mind, which can work simultaneously with several conflicting paradigms. It sees not just one interpretation of reality, but many, yet it sees them as a seam-less whole. Such a mind is untroubled by mere inconsistency: it is comfortable with a mutable, adaptive, loosely coherent flux . . .

(Stewart and Cohen 1997, pp. 289–290)

I see this multiplex sort of mind as required in land policy formulation and imple-mentation, but still insufficient as there is no reference to values: "A wise person . . . is . . . a critical ingredient for fundamental transformation" (Gunderson and Holling 2002, p. 91). At the other extreme, using the example of the growth of a town, Stewart and Cohen show how simplex thinkers think that there is only one important rationale for its growth, and that they know what it is. Complex think-ers would not, but look at existents multiperspectively (Stewart and Cohen 1997, p. 292). However, a multiplex mind would examine the town's phase space, and see the many different routes that could have been taken as well as what happened. It would also see the town as a system, a process, involving what fitness landscapes for what peoples, what valuations by what people, and "not make the mistake of attributing features that are important on an individual level (such as purpose) to the system as a whole" (ibid., p. 292).

While humanity exists, with its holons enfolding so much of the story of evolution within them and active still, there "will always be tribal groups, nations, wars, just as there are still bacterial ecologies and anthills" (ibid., p. 299). This is a given for a complex mind, and necessary to consider in addressing wicked valuation problems.

There has been proposed a "fourth type of mind, omniplex, embracing the Cosmic All" (ibid., pp. 289–90), but that is a simplex thought, however big it may be: plenty of span, but no depth. In contrast, the Taoists recognise that "The Tao that can be known is not the eternal Tao" (Lao Tzu 1972). That is, while logical structures can be internally consistent, their bridge to reality is symbols – words, mathematical and otherwise – and their applications are thereby both inevitably imprecise and, moreover, inevitably in the past tense (Libet et al. 1983). Consequently, while one may construct conceptual framings, they cannot enfold life in general, or optimally address wicked problems in particular, via their abstractions, any more than one can catch the wind. As Émile Durkheim put it, "to live is not to think, but to act, and the consequence of our ideas is . . . a reflection of the stream of events which perpetually unravel in us" (Durkheim 1887). The more a mind is able to fully internalise that understanding, that is, the more optimal its functioning McGilchrist's terms, the more it is able to transcend and include the multiplex. There are significant differences in competencies in this regard (Steufert 1978; Streufert and Streufert 1978).

However, Stewart and Cohen's ladder is all about epistemological lines (see Chapter 5), not telaxiological. It is complicated, not really complex at all in terms of the above nomenclature, not even at the level of Blake's twofold vision. As such, it begets confidence beyond competence when addressing wicked valuation problems. That is why:

> Whatever the deficiencies in the Australian aborigine's habits of observation or in his symbolic formulation of his experience ... the Australian's "primitive" view is in fact far less primitive, biologically and culturally speaking, than that of the mechanical world picture, for it includes those many dimensions of life that Kepler, Galileo, and their successors intentionally excluded, as spoiling the accuracy of their observations and the elegance of their descriptions.
>
> (Mumford 1970, p. 70)

To get to twofold vision involves a rebalancing act. The development of wisdom requires one such. In India, the process is referred to as *karunā-prajñā*. For example, in Buddhism, "prajñā gives rise to karunā, and karunā gives rise to prajña" (O'Brien 2015). Also similarly, Armstrong observed, "if feelings are not to degenerate into indulgent, aggressive or unhealthy emotionalism, they need to be informed by critical intelligence" (Armstrong 1993, p. 394).

The omniplex may still be like Urizen's, dissociated from intrinsic values. Those ensnared within reductionist/machinist paradigms often sneer at compassion as being sentimentalist and impractical. "Bleeding hearts" is their usual term of abuse, as if hard and bloodless hearts are somehow superior to compassionate ones. However, when they are asked to provide examples they are often of unwise behaviour, rather than being the fault of compassion itself. More practical people than they are see compassion as "a practical and evolved ethic" (Ramp and Bekoff 2015; Gilbert 2007; Gilbert and Choden 2015). In the context of recognising the intrinsic value and sentience of nonhuman animals (Ramp and Bekoff 2015, p. 2), Ramp and Bekoff note that such deficiencies of empathy in decision-making "can, in part, be attributed to" [avoiding] "the perceived difficulty in comparing complex and competing sets of values" (ibid., p. 1). While some consider that compassion can be both sufficiently defined and nurtured, and call for "basic research on these essential aspects [empathy and compassion] of human development" (Greenberg and Turksma 2015; Mascaro, Darcher, Negi and Raison 2015; Gilbert and Choden 2015), others see compassion as "hard to define, impossible to mandate", but nonetheless crucially important (Chadwick 2015).

However achieved, the co-evolution of wisdom and compassion develops sophrosyne (skilful means), which is an essential in matters as sensitive and important as land policy, and sophrosyne is a component of what is meant by wisdom in several traditions, described by Kidd (2007) as including the qualities summarised in Table 1.3.

Misplaced concreteness, misplaced abstraction, and dissociation and disdain can topple the potential for such balanced discernment and embrace. I submit such discernment as the best our species can achieve towards identifying and addressing the subject of this work.

Table 1.3 Qualities indicative of wisdom

Source	Qualities indicative of Wisdom
Modern Western Bertrand Russell (1956, p. 160); Labouvie-Vief (1990); Mulgan (2014, 29m 57secs)	(1) a sense of proportion; a comprehensive vision; (3) an awareness of the end of life; (4) *intellect combined with feeling*; (Diaz) impartiality in attitude; (6) love, not hatred; (7) a pacific temper of mind, not war-like; (8) a cosmopolitan outlook as the citizen of the world. Integrated thought. The ability to make sense of complexity, context specificity, and to integrate moral perspectives, balancing part and bigger systems.
Chinese	(1) creativeness; humaneness; (3) reasonableness, in the sense of intellect and feeling perfectly blended; (4) timeliness and flexibility or situationalness; (Diaz) harmony and equilibrium; (6) authenticity as the way to enlightenment implying each other; (7) care and concern; (8) practice or experientialism.
Ancient Greek Matthew Arnold (1916)	The happy and gracious flexibility, or the happy and right mean, characterised further by (1) lucidity of thought; clearness and propriety of language; (3) freedom from prejudices and freedom from stiffness; (4) openness of mind; (Diaz) amiability of manners.
Indian	An emergent from the combined operation of *prajñā* and *karunā* (wisdom and compassion). They urge us to be free from greed, anger, and attachment (e.g., infatuation, obsession etc.). Supreme eloquence is not as good as supreme silence.

Source: Kidd (2007), with Mulgan reference added; the numbers are from Kidd, and may be ignored in this context

Study limitations and research suggestions

Demolishing is easy. Building is hard. One inevitable limitation of any trans-disciplinary approach, and even more so this HVN↔HBA approach to addressing wicked valuation problems, is that no one person can be an expert in all the fields that are to be enfolded in any transdisciplinary purview. Instead of absorbing information and developing it into understanding and wisdom, they would drown in it. In general, any one of us will be well outside our own Goldilocks Zones (as described in Chapter 5) when we attempt to grapple with the complexities that should be respected to sustainably address wicked problems and social messes.

What that means in the HBA context is that its conclusions in any one discipline must always be open to critiques from those best capable of forming an opinion in that discipline, and that the participants should meet Midgley's standard of rigour, which requires understanding the discipline "so fully that one can relate them to those needed for other enquiries. We do not just have to verify our hypotheses carefully, but also to form them intelligently" (Midgley 1995, p. 22), such that we can connect them to matters outside our fields and with the collaboration of others of widely different knowledges and values. Such contri-butions to the HVN↔HBA process have to be valued on intrinsic, extrinsic and systemic bases (as described in Chapter 5), and experts in those disciplines are to be made aware of all relevant valuations' criteria.

So this work's major limitations and research suggestions are both around the same issue: To devise means of ensuring machinism engages in the service of the co-evolution of wisdom and compassion in addressing wicked valuation problems. In the HVN↔HBA trans-ontological process, I see this as preconditional to addressing wicked problems as best we can. That is, by addressing them with all the equipment that evolution has given us, not just the mechanist methodology so extrinsically valuable but intrinsically and systemically so blind, deaf and dumb.

For this to occur, the submissions of this book require more grounding in practice, with accompanying empirical research which can only be uncovered by attempting the process. In so doing, I recommend following Bruno Latour's recommended process in *An Inquiry into Modes of Existence: An Anthropology of the Moderns* (2013), in which he traces a process of moving from debunking to protecting and to care (Latour 2004, pp. 231 and 232).

He recommended that any approach to his subject must answer four questions to be acceptable (ibid., p. 475):

1 Can the experience detected be shared?
2 Does the detection of one mode allow us to respect the other modes?
3 Can accounts other than the author's be proposed?
4 Can the inquiry mutate into a diplomatic arrangement so that institutions adjusted to the modes can be designed while a new space is opened up for comparative anthropology by a series of negotiations over values?

While his book is published, it has not been confined to a static "thing" but remains a process – an "augmented" digital book – via a community of inquiry.

It is possible that the HVN↔HBA could be adapted to wider challenges, such as Latour's or (in a more epistemological, less axiological context) Gabriele Bammer's Global Network for Research Integration and Implementation via an online community of inquiry methodology such as their respective ones, but that still requires further research in accord with the Development Principle (Chapter 5).

I consider that a major potential arena for discovering limitations and areas for further research on developing HVN↔HBA while at the same time grounding Latour's process in applying the insights of Whittal and Barry (2005) in the geomatics domain towards addressing the concerns of this work. Whittal's thesis is to apply the change management principles of John Kotter (1996), Liam Fahey (1994), Helena Dolny (2001) and others to Geomatics.

Kotter articulated eight stages in change management:

• *Stage 1*: establishing a sense of urgency;
• *Stage 2*: creating the guiding coalition;
• *Stage 3*: developing a vision and a strategy;

- *Stage 4*: communicating the vision;
- *Stage 5*: empowering broad-based action;
- *Stage 6*: generating short-term wins;
- *Stage 7*: consolidating gains and producing more change; and
- *Stage 8*: anchoring new approaches in the culture (Kotter 1996; Whittall and Barry 2005).

Her paper with Barry adopts the above, and addresses identifying the forces driving the system change through Fahey (1994). It also adds four issues from Dolny: organisational and extra-organisational politics and public relations, engagement with adversaries the interrelationships of law and change, and the importance of race and gender relations. The paper was centred upon a case study of fiscal cadastral reform in Cape Town. This was about change management in the technical mass valuation process, as distinct from the micro professional valuation processes required in the context of compulsory acquisition and compensation. At that more heuristic level, the reform was to address both poverty and inequality through systemic reform of property valuation and taxation.

From that study, Whittal and Barry noted that Dolny's four added issues are overriding ones that apply throughout Kotter's eight-stage process. I therefore see a similar role for HVN↔HBA to Dolny's for those attempting change management. In Chapter 7, I comment further on this potential way forward within my valuation context from the perspectives gained through this work.

Chapter summary and the way forward

This chapter has set up the framing of all that follows. It looks at the world through the lens supplied to me by my profession, which looks to both the fact perceptions and value judgements made in examining evidence to see whether or not a sale is admissible as evidence of market value. That process revealed that "Big V" values are major components in real property markets, and consequently such markets are not reducible to what I have termed "The Machine". In accordance with the IVSC definition of market value, machines do not hold or make values, or markets: people do.

That Machine framing was provided to me before I set off on my travels, and when I looked at the world from within it, it became particularly clear that most transactions are very distant from compliance with that definition, which compliance would be of considerable benefit if more general in world affairs. Many of today's problems are exceptionally complex, and yet most of the means of addressing them are simplistic in the extreme – simple to complicated, when the problems themselves are simple to complicated and complex to wicked. The reduction of complex and wicked problems to simple to complicated ones often exacerbates them, with such matters being dismissed by The Machine as "externalities", thereby being able to commonalise or otherwise externalise the costs, and privatise the profits. That appears to be a major deficiency in wisdom, one which seems inevitable when framing every existent as nothing but an object for exploitation by The Machine. Machinism is simply not up to the task of addressing complex to wicked problems. Its psychiatric causes have been identified by McGilchrist (2009), and they have caused (and will continue to cause) much harm.

In contrast, the masters I completed in 2005 (about applying the insights from complexity and chaos sciences to social questions) starts from recognising that there is a necessary fallibility to us all in addressing complex to wicked problems. That recognition implies the need not only for interdisciplinary approaches, but that transdisciplinary teams would be needed to engage the rigour, skills and diligence due for optimal engagements with problems of that nature, and that such teams would need both adequate vocabularies to mutually address the challenge, and full recourse to their available capacities in the manner described by McGilchrist. I defined and explain key terms from that perspective, and provided study limitations and research suggestions towards doing the best we can in these circumstances. I have also outlined the chapters to follow, which trace, firstly by use of an autoethnographic approach and later add more traditional approaches, the development of HVN↔HBA as a way of addressing wicked problems to that end.

Notes

1 The book itself adopts several of the principles within this work: "the authors present a new synthesis of their core ideas on evaluating communities, organisms, populations, biomes, models, and management. The book places greater emphasis on post-normal critiques, cognisant of ever-present observer values in the system. The problem is how to work holistically on complex things that cannot be defined, and the book continues to define an approach to the problem of scaling in ecosystems. Provoked by complexity theory, the authors add a whole new chapter on the central role of narrative in science and how models improve them" (Hurst 2015). This chapter (ibid., ch. 8, Kindle location 6415) contains an appendix (ibid., pp. 355–356, Kindle locations 7391–7498) which includes many questions potentially relevant to the addressing of wicked valuation problems by the communities of inquiry and practice for which I have designed HVN↔HBA.
2 I prefer the term "ansatz" to "abductive development theory" because Holdheim (1985) says that "no single English term could possibly convey the multifariously refracted shades of meaning that the German word suggests" – which openness is precisely what I want – and goes on to further articulate ansatz's meaning, including the terms "expanding", "growing", "not mechanistic but temporal", a way to "open up the whole", including "an excursion into personal intuition" regarding knowledge being "neither illusory nor absolute, it is approximate, exposed to the risk of uncertainty" (ibid., pp. 627–628). In contrast, I interpret abductive theory development as more linear, mechanistic and formal, more exclusively left hemisphere.
3 Lally (2000) has pointed out that value juries are particularly useful to assess strengths of beliefs. As such, they would be useful in determining *épreuves* – "contests in which different constructions of the value of an entity conflict and are measured against one another by social actors" (Lamont 2012, p. 213).
4 Note however that, be they holons or artefacts as restrictively defined in the Glossary – animate (holons) or inanimate (artefacts, including material machines machine-plexes, and mental memes and memeplexes) – "it is probably impossible to describe any one thing in the world exhaustively without mentioning everything else as well"

(Rucker 1997, p 142). Following Speel (1995) with "memeplexes", here I mean the word "machineplex" to mean a coadapted complex of machines.

5 The word "ontology" is now also used in computing and information science to catego-rise "a formal language purposefully designed for a specific set of practical applications and contexts or environments" (Lawson 2014a, p. 1). HBA is towards that meaning as well, but in a transdisciplinary context – not within any one science.

2 The narrative begins
Gestating HVN↔HBA

Introduction

This narrative has two basic intentions. First, to provide an example of what one person's identity construction may bring to the table in the context of this work, while essentially recognising that all those at the table bring their own identity constructions as well, all of which have potentially both greater and lesser value in different contexts. Second, it is intended to provide a means of introducing the complexities involved in addressing these wicked valuation problems in a manner reasonably compatible with the Goldilocks Principle (see Chapter 5).

The turning point

"Hey, Anne! There's an ad here; they're looking for a valuer to work in Swaziland as part of the team for an urban development project."

I looked across the kitchen table at my wife. This was in 1992. We had first met in 1979 in Kathmandu, when I was the courier for a coach trip going from there to London via countries not quite so easy to visit any more – countries including Pakistan, Afghanistan, Iran, Iraq and Syria. Even way back then there were dangers, as I was to encounter on that trip and others. Anne is a feisty lass, and ready for any existent. She did not hesitate: "Go for it!"

So I did, and I got the job. Two kids in tow this time, and years ahead of us in a country we had never been. Despite both having visited 60-plus countries by then, we had scarcely even heard of Swaziland. We knew that it was small, and somewhere in Southern Africa, but that was about it.

We were about to find out a whole lot more.

My back story

My journey to that position was circuitous, but for reasons that will become clear later, vital in terms of understanding what I am bringing to the table in the development of HVN↔HBA.

It was not my original intention to address wicked valuation problems by this autoethnographic approach, but learnt that it would be the most facilitatory path to come to grips with such a complex subject. Such a subject requires process description, and it is to process philosophy I turn to describe the subject. That is because the method recommended in this work attempts to respect the true complexity of addressing land policies. As such, it necessarily acknowledges the interior spaces of all stakeholders involved in the policy development process, whom in turn are to acknowledge the interior spaces of all affected parties and, in particular, their identities.

While my interior is of necessity not the most important one in that process, it is the one I can address with the most authority. I trust that readers of this book will recognise that all stakeholders bring different perspectives into policy formulation by dint of their different narratives. All of us are flawed, all of us valuable, in our own different ways and degrees, simply by being stakeholders. The result of our interrelationships can be unique as well. My strong claim is that only with that insight can one begin to understand the depth and complexity of issues around land policy, and that the lack of such understanding has been, and still can be, catastrophic.

Childhood

When my grandmother was a toddler (she was born in 1872), she got lost. Local Aborigines found her and returned her to her family. That is all I heard of the incident. I do not know whether or not she was in mortal danger, but obviously if she had died, I would not exist today. This radically contingent nature of events, explored in the mathematical discipline of combinatorics (Rucker 1987), is a fundamental observation of a complexity and chaos based paradigm. In dramatic contrast to the clockwork paradigm of the universe, chaos theory has brought to our attention that, like a collapsing wave function, we emerge from trillions of contingent situations, a lottery of far greater odds than any formal one. Just as all of life on Earth owes its existence to exploded stars, if my grandmother owed her life to those Aborigines, then I do too. This radicality requires an equally radical response, one opposite to the clockwork paradigm. I here propose a recognition of our common humanity to be a necessary but insufficient precondition to addressing wicked problems. That recognition includes that all of us have life narratives that may frame and shape our perceptions of the problems concerned, and which will all be different in degree and kind from each other – even between twins. I include my own life narrative here not because I expect it to be of any value to the reader, but to emphasise that other narratives apply to all other living creatures, including those of the reader, so they can more accurately monitor and evaluate their roles in Collective Developmental Action Inquiry (Torbert 2013) in themselves, their collaborators, and parties affected by wicked problem. So it is not presented as an exemplar, but an example of such radical contingency and our ordering of it.

My father had been born in India in 1900, so in my child-mind I had associated that country with him. His parents had been part and parcel of the British administration of the subcontinent, but after the loss of more than half of their children to disease, they migrated to Australia in 1908.

He died when I had just turned one year old. When I was eight years old, and my sister Alice eleven, our mother bought us a set of Arthur Mee's children's encyclopaedias. They opened up the world to me, albeit from the perspective of the more enlightened levels within the British Imperial world view. They also set in train a passion for learning that has continued to this day. In particular, they provided me with images of India, which again I associated with my missing father and his parents because of my grandfather's service for the Empire in India. I lived in those volumes, which provided far more in terms of meaningful education than I managed to extract from my school education. The latter was an excellent exemplar of that described in Foucault's *Discipline and Punish* (1979), a school in which the "fundamental reference was not to the state of nature, but to the meticulously subordinated cogs of a machine, not to the primal social contract, but to permanent coercions, not to fundamental rights, but to indefinitely progressive forms of training, not to the general will but to automatic docility" (ibid., p. 169), and wherein I behaved as a typical "gifted underachiever" – self-reproaching, prone to guilt, lonely and brooding (Khan 2005). But while the recurring theme in my report cards was "could try harder", in fact, I could not: I was fully engaged with other identity construction concerns.

While I later blamed this inattention on my formal education providers, with the wisdom of further hindsight it was more the fourth major influence that caused my major disconnect within my then fitness landscape. That was the lingering death of my mother from bowel cancer when I was 14. Despite all the evidence, I had remained in denial until a teacher told me of her death, which happened a few days after my last visit to her. Had such a diagnosis been available at the time, I would have assuredly been diagnosed as suffering from post-traumatic stress disorder (PTSD) throughout all my subsequent teenage years and into my early twenties.

I read many books in attempts to come to terms with life's challenges. For example, I recall reading Carl Jung's *Man and his Symbols* while on holidays (Jung 1964) which, as the Guardian review quoted on the back cover noted, insisted that "imaginative life must be taken seriously in its own right, as the most distinctive characteristics of human beings", thereby echoing Blake. Another book, from my school library, was written by a priest whose name and book title I have forgotten, but who had been to China. He may have studied Taoism, for he delivered the insights later developed by John Kay in his book *Obliquity: Why Our Goals Are Best Achieved Indirectly* (Kay 2011), in which he devoted the last third of the book to addressing complex problems by obliquity.

Of particular relevance, the poetry enfolded in Hodge's Complexity 4 was one of my consolations during my school years, and seeded many of the observations made in this book. I was particularly fond of British nature poets, one of whom, John Clare (1793–1864), made reference to "enclosures" in his poem *The Mores*. At that time, I had no idea what he was talking about. Nor did I come to terms with William Blake, who was way beyond my conceptual space at the time, and an interest in him was not encouraged at my school in any case. Now, at least insofar as this work describes, I better understand both poets.

Wordsworth was my favourite, although the full importance of his phrase "we murder to dissect" (Wordsworth 1798) did not hit me at the time. The works of Gerard Manley Hopkins also attracted and intrigued me. Following up on Hopkins' verse and others of his, I read W. H. Gardner's edition of Hopkins's *Poems and Prose* (Hopkins 1953). On p. xx of his Introduction, Gardner refers to Hopkins' coining of the terms *inscape*, which he used to refer to some existent's individual-distinctive form made up of sense data, and *instress* – that which "determines an inscape and keeps it in being". But not only that; instress is often the sensation of inscape: "a sudden perception of that deeper pattern, order, and unity which gives meaning to external forms" (ibid., p. xxi).

I here contend this is a major impulse that draws our identity from the astonishingly complex and chaotic events referred to above. To address this complexity, our minds evolved as *pattern makers and reality inhibitors* (Grove 1992, pp. 182–183). We derive our social (including our spatial) imaginaries that way through processes including sensory gating and brain filtering which, while essential for survival, block out the more expansive understanding (Woollacott 2016) which I consider to be preconditional to optimally addressing wicked valuation problems. We "spend our lives spotting patterns, and picking out the exceptional and interesting things" (Goldacre 2008, p. 251), manufacturing our own order out of chaos via that impulse. However, when we attempt to translate this impulse into our identity constructions often we see "patterns where there is only random noise" [and] "causal relationships where there are none" (ibid., p. 247).

Later, Gardner refers to Hopkins as valuing "the human spirit as the direct link between man and his Creator, a relationship which is part of that vast hierarchy of being which is made up of all creatures, animate and inanimate, with Christ as their summit" (Hopkins 1953, p. xxv). In the passage that Gardner refers to, Hopkins said, "we may learn that all things are created by consideration of the world without or of ourselves the world within" (ibid., p. 145); but then again, we may not.

Decades later, when discussing land policy and similar issues in Swaziland, these insights reminded me that everyone across the table carries a different narrative with them into whatever is being negotiated. We all have different inscapes, our own identities, and if they are attacked head on by dint of attacking views that we identify with, then the attack will be opposed with tooth and claw. However contrary they may be to our own, the role of identity constructions in land policy must be respected.

Young adulthood

In the absence of any PTSD formal therapy at the time, I eventually healed myself as best I could through the abovementioned bibliotherapy, track and field athletics, and listening to classical music. Track and field helped in two ways: firstly in my gaining the respect and companionship of my peers, and secondly exercise is now a demonstrated means of helping with PTSD (Rosenbaum et al. 2011). Classical music provided a different companionship – with composers from even centuries ago and far away, revealing a depth and breadth of emotions which provided a powerful catharsis for my own. Now, such music is also a demonstrated means of helping with PTSD (Gao 2013). My mother had exposed me to this form of music all my boyhood long. She had taught music at school and listened to classical music constantly on the Australian Broadcasting Corporation (ABC).

Eventually, I recovered enough to embark upon a course in property valuation. I had been motivated to that course by a chance meeting of a valuer at a party, and the fact that I had by then gained my inheritance and was a "man of property" inherited directly or indirectly from my grandmother.

My career was delayed a year after being asked by my future mentor Jim MacDonald why I wanted to become a valuer. I had replied that I wanted to explore not especially market values, but mainly human values – what makes us decide what some existent is worth in terms of some other existent.[1] That reply did not satisfy my interviewers, but when I re-applied again the next year they realised that I was serious, and appointed me. Among the first training I received from them was a list of questions to ask when analysing sales. When the first of them was "why did the vendor decide to sell, and the purchaser to buy?", I knew that I had come to the right place.

As a result of the excellent training then available at the now defunct Australian Valuation Office and my consequently good examination results, a private firm recruited me to the position of valuation manager before I was fully qualified. My new boss, Mr Noel Taplin, generously provided all the necessary transitional supervision, and a friendship that has lasted to this day (Taplin 2015, pp. 134, 179). In 1974, I qualified as an Associate of the Commonwealth Institute of Valuers (now the Australian Property Institute, of which I am now a Fellow).

My way of trying to make some sense of it all is largely attributable to those influences. The religion of Catholicism that my mother had strictly raised me within provided some structure and solace, but as I matured its premises seemed more and more questionable, and in consequence so did the legitimacy of both its structure and its solace.

After leaving school, the rebellious but sometimes spiritual zeitgeist of my generation was in flower, so when in 1970 I saw an ABC TV interview with someone I had not heard of before called Jiddu Krishnamurti, I was receptive to his revolutionary message of "drop it".

To Krishnamurti (1950) "it" meant an identity attachment to any existent, including one's identity itself, admitting that we do not know, but would like to find out. He pointed out that believing *in* is quite a different process from believing *that*. But unlike most versions that only looked out from one's identity, not inside as part and parcel of the same process, Krishnamurti's was an approach directed internally at the self as well as externally at the other. As an incentive to practice that, as Strongman said of Tupaia, Krishnamurti stated that there was a vitality and ecstasy available by living completely in the moment that was not accessible via screenings through the constructed identity. He viewed mindfulness meditation as being a state of such ecstatic awareness – in particular, a state not mediated by thought, that key of identity construction. At the time, "drop it" especially meant for me dropping my child-mind's yearning for my father, and my mourning for my mother, and with that at last snapping out of my passive – if not self-pitying – identity as a victim. Over four decades later, I encountered a YouTube account by a neuroscientist who was also a left hemisphere stroke victim (Bolte Taylor 2008). Her description of deep insights she gained thereby has several similarities with those Krishnamurti claimed would flow from dropping "it". I now see as dropping "thinging" as part of that process (Bateson 1979, p. 112), which has been identified by McGilchrist and others as a left hemisphere function of the brain (McGilchrist 2009).

Another book of the hundreds I had already read by then in my quest to make sense of the world prepared me for that warning about believing "in" as distinct from "that". In the first paragraph of the introduction, the writer of that book started with the observation that the trust that was once confined to doctors and patients and religious leaders seeking converts, was now one of nationalists, "who wish not only to confirm certain political beliefs within their boundaries, but to proselytise the outside world" (Sargant 1963, p. 13). That is, to link others to their social imaginary (Taylor 2002, p. 13).

After recounting a singularly depressing litany of abuse of both animals and people in efforts to change their minds, Sargant made a highly telling point to me at the time. He observed that for hundreds of years medicine operated from ontological frameworks to explain sicknesses, but when medicine dropped metaphysics and instead "simply set about examining the functional mechanism of the lungs, the heart, the liver, and finally the brain itself, its stupendous practical progress began" (Sargant 1963, p. 212).

Later I was to learn that despite their mechanistic mindsets "before 1935 doctors were basically useless . . . [and] that 'golden age' – mythical and simplistic though that model may be – ended in the 1970s" (Goldacre 2008, pp. 233, 235). In that decade, however, it was clear to me that Sargant's observations applied not only to medicine, but to science in general and even, as Krishnamurti had implied, reality in general.

It would be over thirty years after reading both Sargent's above quotations before I could contextualise them to my current satisfaction. As I shall outline, there is a direct line from them to the urgent need to address the topic of this book.

In the meantime, I found that realising Krishnamurti's insight was easier said than done: Being very aware in that Zen-like sense is very hard. However, when he spoke of being most alive in the sort of effortless, choiceless awareness you may have when you look at a sunset, I knew that had been true for me. He asked us to observe how thought only comes into our minds when we are less conscious than when we are in that enchantment in the moment, and that truth is a pathless land that we – in the form of our separate identities – may come to terms with to our current satisfaction, and encounter but can never capture.

Krishnamurti's "drop it" injunction, however, raised as many questions as it answered. In particular, to me it did not seem to address a particular form of soul hunger, a love hunger, or at least a hunger for the acknowledgement of one's fellows, for a recognised and relating identity; I eventually thought of it as a regard-recognition hunger. Over 30 years later Roberto Unger described what I had sensed as follows: "We ask of one another more than any person can give another; not just respect, admiration or love, but some reliable sign that there is a place for us in the world" (Unger 2007, p. 10).

Prior to my own, Lewis Mumford had made a similar insight: "The most important thing for a human being to know, from infancy onward, is whether he is welcome or unwelcome, whether he is being loved and cherished and protected or hated and feared" (Mumford 1951, p. 44). Several others, such as Jean Vanier, observed that "the deepest desire for us all is to be appreciated, to be loved, to be seen as somebody of value" (Jean Vanier, in Tippett 2016, Kindle location 1306). A related hunger, possibly subsidiary – and of particular interest to me as a valuer and "a man of property" – was the hunger for place, for territory, which then, for me, meant property:

> A territory is an area of space, whether of water or earth or air, which an animal or group of animals defends as an exclusive preserve. The word is also used to describe the inward compulsion in animate beings to possess and defend such a space. A territorial species of animals, therefore, is one in which all males, and sometimes females too, bear an inherent drive to gain and defend an exclusive property.
>
> (Ardrey 1972, p. 13)

Subsequent research has indicated that such a drive would be very useful in evolution, and resulted in a growth of mammals to exploit the fitness landscapes vacated by the dinosaurs. That is, all evolution is co-evolution (see Chapter 5), and environment specific (although often adaptable to different environments) (Morowitz 2002, p. 137).

Moreover, recent theories in consciousness studies include theories that consciousness itself emerged from that interactive dynamic between an organism and its environment (Rockwell 2005), thereby engendering its fitness landscape. There was no doubt in my mind that I held such a territorial imperative toward the house I had grown up in and had by now inherited. Territoriality was clearly a major component in the identity my own regard-recognition hunger had developed.

Furthermore, as a young man, I had keenly felt another observation of Ardrey's:

> Only in the wild does [an animal] face those pressures and opportunities which give expression to his total nature . . . Captivity has subtracted fear from his life, and substituted boredom. And it is for this reason that we should feel sorry for him.
>
> (Ardrey 1972, p. 34)

"Oh dear", I mused, "not 'poor me' again! Poor captured creature of the wild Earth: Enough!" Then I asked myself:

> Aren't such multiple impulses – for companionship, for territory, for the wild – as real as the one for food and drink, and isn't it so that they require

recharging through time, just as eating food does? In the nagging presence of many desires, how could one constantly live in choiceless awareness as Krishnamurti appeared to recommend?

These questions of mine were immersed in the spirit of the age. That spirit was expressed in the books I read by the Zen philosopher Alan Watts, who pointed out that injunctions such as Krishnamurti's "drop it", and those of Jesus such as "turn the other cheek", are useful precisely because they prompt the question, "why can't I do that?" They thereby set one out upon a course towards the Delphic injunction to "know thyself".

One of Watts' books was entitled *The Book: On the Taboo against Knowing Who You Are* (Watts 1973). In the very first paragraph of the Preface, written in January 1966, he proclaimed that we have a hallucination that we are nothing but separate egos enclosed in bags of skin, and that "this hallucination underlies the misuse of technology for the violent subjugation of man's natural environment and, consequently, its eventual destruction". He then went on to describe his own Vedanta/Western science "cross-fertilisation" concerning a better understanding of our identities, which is consciousness looking out from our eyes and those of all else conscious (see Chapter 5).

Later I encountered, at first via a front cover review in *Time* magazine and later bought, a book called *Zen and the Art of Motorcycle Maintenance* (Pirsig 1974). I had been interested in areté since my school days. Pirsig's book was about areté, which Pirsig translated as "Quality". Moreover, Pirsig was finding Zen not in using a broad and comprehensive system, but by a Krishnamurti-like, Sargant-identified, focus on the task to hand.

Pursuing such questions, I teamed up with a couple of others in Adelaide also intrigued by Krishnamurti, Jim Bald and Susunaga Weeraperuma. I told them I was thinking of travelling to India, and they told me of meetings that Krishnamurti held there, but also in Switzerland, in Saanen, an alpine village. Despite Krishnamurti constantly emphasising that no one should take existents on authority alone, and especially not his, I resolved to ask Krishnamurti about this environmentally shaped identity appetite of mine face to face.

At the time, my sister lived around the corner from me, and she had become friends with the couple opposite, Christine and Andrew Stephens. Once, Christine and I went to a session on Theravada Buddhism at Union Hall at Adelaide University, wherein the lecturer, a Buddhist nun, referred to disciplining the mind. I asked her, "What is the difference between a mind intent upon imposing discipline on itself, and a mind in conflict with itself?" This she was unable to answer, which led to an embarrassing halt: I rescued her by asking another question.

This intensity of this question was reinforced at a gathering at my place with Jim, Susu, my sister, Alice and Andrew. Andrew said to me:

> Mike, take a good look at yourself, and Jim and Susu! You are all single, and therefore know so little about real life that you can assume you know more

about it than others. You presume to philosophise about life, but unless you engage with it, what can you possibly learn of value? Get a wife and get a life. Have some kids! You can learn more from them about life than you will ever learn at the feet of some guru or even an anti-guru like Krishnamurti! As a spouse and a parent, you can gain wisdom that is simply unattainable from your precious books. Mike, you're heading down a dead end street. Even if the dead end is at the top of a mountain, you will be stuck there, cold and alone. Get engaged in life! Get real!

That advice resonated strongly with me, having been primed for it by the *Time* magazine review of *Zen and the Art of Motorcycle Maintenance*, with its reference to "the underlying quality of familial love", and the *Time* review's final sentence:

> What matters most is that he communicates how very much he cares about living as a whole man and how hard he has worked at it. Indeed, the special gift of the universal principle that Pirsig calls Quality is caring, even if one reaches for the heavens with grease on his hands.
>
> (Sheppard 1974)

Pirsig was pointing out that you could be both a whole person in one's environmental and religious setting and still set about examining the functional mechanism. Unlike what one might impute from Sargant's comment, there are dancing mechanics. It could be a both/and process; it did not have to be either/or:

> Areté implies a respect for the wholeness or oneness of life, and a consequent dislike of specialization. It implies a contempt for efficiency . . . or rather a much higher idea of efficiency, an efficiency which exists not in one department of life but in life itself . . . [Man] had built empires of scientific capability to manipulate the phenomena of nature into enormous manifestations of his own dreams of power and wealth . . . but for this he had exchanged an empire of understanding of equal magnitude: an understanding of what it is to be a part of the world, and not an enemy of it.
>
> (Pirsig 1974, pp. 386, 387)

However, as Pirsig said in *Lila*:

> Naturally there is no mechanism towards which life is heading. Mechanisms are the enemy of life. The more static and unyielding the mechanisms are, the more life works to evade them or overcome them.
>
> (Pirsig 1991, p. 142)

I see that latter understanding as being that which Strongman claims Tupaia had, and Blake claimed the infernal trinity separated themselves and others from. From this big "Zen" picture, Pirsig saw Quality not being "just a part of reality [but] the whole thing" (ibid., p. 252).

So what was in the space in between Sargant's dichotomy? How is one to find and address this empire of understanding both within and between the metaphysician and the mechanist, humanism and machinism, holons and artefacts, and beyond these dichotomies?

I did not realise it then, but in that space was an essential part of addressing wicked valuation problems arising when cultures from the NSEW meet.

I came to learn that understanding what property rights are for could be highlighted by looking in that space. For in admitting territoriality as a component of my own identity construction, I could recognise it in the identity of others, and the settling of resulting competing claims for territory to be the genesis of property rights.

I also did not know then what has been made clear by complexity and chaos sciences since; that while the scientific method can help greatly in the role Pirsig set for it, it can never entirely close that space.

Breaking free

So it was that in 1976 I booked an Asian Overland with a company called Capricorn, then booked accommodation in Saanen to ask my question to Krishnamurti, booked a much shorter European Tour than the South American one, and a flight back to Australia.

Kathmandu blew me away, blasted me beyond my single vision. No, it wasn't the drugs you could get there: I was too straight laced to get involved in that scene then, and have remained so. It was the place itself, and the faces shining through the poverty and grime. It was also the near total absence of so much that I had internalised in my upbringing as "the way things are". To paraphrase Sargant, the Nepalis were using a broad and comprehensive system of metaphysics to explain every existent, with synergies of Hinduism and Tibetan Buddhism that, in all their dazzling complexity from my perspective, seemed to provide some form of integrated sense and meaning from theirs.

Suddenly and at last, all I had taken for granted was thrown open for scrutiny in the way that Krishnamurti had recommended, an attitude of "I don't know, but I want to find out". What I had taken for granted had remained hidden as background assumptions until Kathmandu had revealed it by its countless contrasts with every existent I had taken for granted. The insides of people's heads could be vastly different from all I had falsely assumed from my own experience about the way all people are, and they could still thrive and be happy!

With my mind and senses blasted open, I drank in our trip through India like a man finding water after a long desert trek.

Nor did the trip pale beyond India. Even though the Taj Mahal and the beauty of Kashmir had no equals, places and peoples in and beyond India never failed to amaze.

Afterwards I did get to ask Krishnamurti my regard-recognition hunger question in Saanen, in a public meeting held there. His reply was insufficient, so after the meeting I asked him in private, but I still went away dissatisfied.

Krishnamurti had therefore, and it seems inadvertently, confirmed to me the wisdom of his injunction to abjure authorities, especially his. Yet there was still a long path for me from the general policy of acceptance of authority that was drummed into me by my Catholic upbringing to my acceptance of the epistemology of the scientific method as the best lodestone to truth. In my case, that acceptance developed from the opposite end of the spectrum from authoritarian religion, via Krishnamurti's advocacy of total doubt and discarding of all authority whatsoever to one of organised, quantified, qualified, and nuanced doubt, both epistemological and telaxiological: particularly, always have doubts about what won't let you doubt (Walter 1996, p. 19). In terms of Hegelian dialectic, my thesis had been Catholicism, and my antithesis Krishnamurti, and my synthesis what is contained here as HVN↔HBA, an emergent which, like oxygen and hydrogen with their emergent water, has qualities not possessed by either component. It evolved from what I later articulated as complexity epistemology, which in both its genesis and function has a necessary co-evolution with what I articulated in the same paper as complexity axiology (McDermott and Boydell 2010), and later found that both are means of addressing being, or process ontology. Hence their co-evolution facilitated the emergence of this HVN↔HBA trans-ontological process.

I returned to Australia after the European tour, and tried to settle back home again, but was feeling the truth of R.M. Williams observation, "there's a lot more freedom in a tent that there is in a castle". So when the driver of my overland trip came to Adelaide on a promotional trip and asked me if I wanted to become an overland courier, I asked myself the question, "Mike, imagine yourself on your deathbed; from there, what would you have wanted your answer to be?" I was away. Back to Kathmandu, where I met my trainers, the driver and the courier.

I had wanted wild. I found wild in the driver and courier. In front of this driver and courier was this bookish little smart-arse who came to Kathmandu having made friends with the passengers! What was Capricorn thinking? How on earth could anyone bring someone like that up to speed? The driver tested Ardrey, who had said: "An effective social organization in primate groups will be achieved through territory, or it will be achieved through tyranny. Contemporary research has revealed no third way" (Ardrey 1972, p. 240).

This driver ran his mobile territory, the Titanic, as a tyranny, to the extent that at one stage on the trip, the passengers start to prime me as Fletcher Christian, towards a Mutiny on the Titanic. But that tyranny of the crew became open to listening, and by the end of the trip we were all the best of friends. I had survived their deliberate baptism of fire, and many of the lessons they taught me were essential to the happiness and successes in the role I later enjoyed.

I worked as a courier years after that and had many adventures, including being caught up in the 1978 "Saur" revolution in Kabul, enduring robbery in the Khyber Pass in 1979, and taking trips through Iran before, during and after the revolution there. In those times, I discovered the truth in the saying that the thought of the noose concentrates the mind wonderfully. But in my case it was exploding bombs and looking down the barrels of guns from the wrong end that did the trick.

They concentrated my mind on why matters were as they were in those places, and because of my earlier insights re identity and territoriality and my then still unrecognised confirmation bias (Kahneman 2011; Goldacre 1999, pp. 247, 249–250), the answers I found included land reform, or its lack.

With my background as a valuer, I gravitated to an interest in such land reform matters in many countries I visited. I found that land reform had played an important role in the revolutionary history of several countries along the overland. In the case of Iran, it was possibly encouraged by the USA's land reform successes in Japan (facilitated by Emperor Hirohito). After the CIA facilitated revolution in Iran (Roosevelt 1979) President Kennedy recommended to the Shah that he undertake similar land reforms in Iran. So began the Shah's White Revolution. Although fair monetary compensation for land acquired was part of the land reform policy, the reforms triggered the enmity of many of Iran's large landowning families, one of which was Khomeini's.

It is not firmly established whether or not Ayatollah Khomeini spoke out directly against the Shah's land reforms (Keddie and Yann 1981, p. 360). After all, if he had done so, it would have been impolitic in terms of cultivating his support base. Instead, he focussed upon opposing the right of women to vote (Moin 1999, p. 75), which he branded as proof of the Shah trying to destroy Islam, and emerged with the same bitter enmity against the Shah that many of his peers shared because of those land reforms (Abrahamian 1989, p. 1).

On the other hand, while Afghanistan's President Daoud had engaged in moderate land reforms, the land reforms implemented by the regimes that followed that revolution were far more dramatic. Decrees issued immediately after the Saur revolution I had witnessed abolished usury and mortgages more than five years old, and forgave the debts of landless peasants. "This measure alienated many of the rural elites and disrupted the system of reciprocal rights and obligations around which rural life was organized" (Ishiyama 2005). "The rebellion that ensued from these and concurrent radical educational reforms, led to Soviet invasion and occupation" (Alden Wily 2003, p. 5).

In Afghanistan as in Iran, many of the Muslim clergy were rich landowners, and as in Khomeini's opposition to the Shah of Iran's White Revolution, many of those opposing Taraki did so because of Taraki's moves to emancipate women, outlaw child marriages, teach women to read, outlaw bride price, and so on (Ishiyama 2005). Some such fanatical opponents of both land reform and female emancipation came to be known as the Mujahedeen. Their funding mechanisms included the cultivation of opium in the tribal areas between Pakistan and Afghanistan.

While there are others, as a final modern history example from the Asian Overland, I will mention the country the other side of Iran from Afghanistan: Iraq. Between the period of British domination and the control of the Ba'ath party in Iraq, there was a period now seen by some as part of a Golden Age (Zaman 2012, p. 108) – the rule of Abd al-Kareem Qassem (1958–63). He instituted a four-point revolution towards a welfare state, the first of which was Agrarian Reform. The others were social and cultural plans, industrialisation, and renegotiation of oil revenue agreements (Gabbay 1978, p. 108). Although he killed to acquire power and was killed in losing it, he is still remembered for his attempts to help Iraq's peasantry with land reform and other measures.

By this stage I had realised that land reform is very important, and that "revolutionary land reform is always an extremely complex and precarious undertaking even under the best of conditions" (Blum 2004, p. 340). For example, three years before I was born a book was published in Melbourne called *Seven Pillars of Folly*. Although a polemic, not a scholarly work, from my authoethnographic context and also as they are germane to this work I am retabling some observations.

The seven pillars Crockett identified were:

1 our wrong concept of wealth;
2 the profit system;
3 the private issue and control of money – private money;
4 the debt system – interest;
5 the private ownership of land and natural resources;
6 the corruption of education and opinion; and
7 unrepresentative government (Crockett 1943).

Going further than Henry George (see Chapter 1), James Crockett wanted land reform to take the shape of no private ownership of land value[2] as it is community created, but to permit ownership and rental of improvements as they are owner created:

> Private land has one main purpose – to entitle Land "owners" to Rent. I put "owners" in inverted commas because to "own" land is, like to "issue" Bank credit, wholly a fiction, an effective fiction, because enforceable at law – the landlord-made law-of-property ... In essence, what is owned is the Land-value, that which produces Rent, not the land as land.
>
> (Crockett 1943, pp. 152, 145)

For existing land in private ownership, Crockett proposed resumption over 50 years, not to change the user or the use (ibid., p. 152). "That change should be seen as a process of evolution ... Haste means cataclysm, and cataclysm means reaction – and worse" (ibid., p. 256). Crockett thereby displayed awareness of identity issues, the Goldilocks Principle and scale, but arguably not to the extent a HBA reflection would consider necessary. He claimed that his seven follies were equal rights "fundamental only to a plutocracy", "rights per unit of humanity, but, in our set-up of scarcity, the power is per unit of riches" (ibid., p.3), and used the example of India to show its pernicious effects which, he predicted, will overtake Australia (ibid., pp. 153–156). A recent book has repeated Crockett's call for public ownership of land value (Adams 2015).

Therefore, the question began to form in my mind:

> *If land reform is often necessary for people to develop out of poverty, but it is extremely complex and precarious, what is required to both address that complexity and avoid the dangers involved?*

The approximately 12,000km drives between Kathmandu and London gave me ample time to both study and consider such concerns. We had lots of time on the long days' drives and in long nights' conversations to explore matters dear to us. We had a large box on the coach where people could put their books after they had read them, and there I found a passenger's book that I now raise in this context. It was Gregory Bateson's *Mind and Nature: A Necessary Unity* (Bateson 1979).

I must confess that I did not absorb anywhere near the lessons in the book at the time that I did when re-reading it for the purpose of this work. As earlier with William Blake, at that stage of my adult development I had not developed the conceptual space to accommodate his paradigm (Commons 2007). I recall Bateson's reference to "*the two great contraries of mental process, either of which by itself is lethal. Rigor alone is paralytic death, but imagination alone is insanity*" (Bateson 1979, p. 242). At the time, I was yet to encounter Mary Midgley's definition of rigour, which as also mentioned above requires attaining a level of understanding in one's discipline sufficient for fruitful interdisciplinary co-operation, and engagement in understanding the general structure of human thought (Midgley 1995, p. 22). In addition, in the introduction to his book, Bateson highlighted the following phrase as the key to the work: "Break the pattern that connects the items of learning and you necessarily destroy all quality" (Bateson 1979, p. 8). That is, Midgley's version of rigour is required (Midgley 1995, p. 22) towards making one's discipline part of the "pattern that connects".

"Quality; areté", I thought, linking the two as in Pirsig's book; "so broadly, Bateson is saying that to break the pattern which connects is to necessarily destroy areté. So single vision necessarily destroys quality. What follows is that if you work only in the way that Sargant (1963) recommended, that is, a reductionist focus on one existent, not on the pattern which connects, *you necessarily destroy quality*". So while Tupaia did not necessarily destroy quality, Captain Cook necessarily did.

So in the current context, if that pattern which connects is not informing land policy, where does that leave the quality of the land policy? Bateson warns that the profound, deep nonsense of personalising artefacts has the correlated nonsense of "thingifying people" (Bateson 1979, p. 112). Thingifying people has now been shown to appear at the foundational level of much twentieth century economic theory (Kahneman 2003) and much else besides, for as Bateson put it:

> The truth of the matter is that every circuit of causation in the whole of biology, in our physiology, in our thinking, our neural process, in our homeostasis, and in the ecological and cultural systems of which we are parts, every such circuit conceals or proposes those paradoxes and confusions that accompany errors and distortions in logical typing.
>
> (Bateson 1979, p. 121)

That much I had gleaned at the time. In the intervening thirty-plus years I have learned a great deal more, until now at last I can integrate Bateson's insights into HVN↔HBA.

During my years on the overland it turned out that what I learned in my training trip combined with my previous interests (following the directions given to me by Arthur Mee all those years before) was a winning combination in the courier context. When returning to London, I would go to the library of London University's School of Oriental and African Studies to both answer those concerns and find that special piece of information that could stimulate the interests of my passengers. In so doing, I discovered that the above instances of the importance of land-related issues in Afghanistan, Iraq and Iran in the modern era had uncounted precedents throughout history (Frankopan 2015).

For instance, following my 1976 overland I had developed a strong interest in the Silk Road between the Chinese and Roman Empires, which began over 2,100 years ago. It followed various trails, depending on the security, trade and environmental circumstances of the time. One such trail used the Via Maris, an even more ancient route network between Damascus and the Mediterranean. Herod the Great had constructed a trading port at Caesarea, arguably in an attempt to gain a foothold in the rich trade in silks and spices from the East, a competing terminus for which was Tyre, not far north. In AD 66, an event occurred at Caesarea that has had resonances down to the present that can be seen as a manifestation of the butterfly effect.

At that time, Caesarea was a mainly pagan city, but with a significant population of Jews. However, a Greek owned all the land around the synagogue. The Jews offered to buy his land at well above its market value, but their offer was knocked back and bad blood came between the parties, such that the Greek began to restrict access to the synagogue. The Jews then offered eight talents of silver to the procurator there, Gessius Florus, who made promises to sort it out in the Jews' favour, and then absconded with the money. When the Jews chased him to fulfil his promise, he had them thrown in jail and demanded even more money.

That was the last straw. The corrupt land administration was a catalyst for the revolt that led ultimately to the destruction of Jerusalem and the scattering of the Jews. That scattering then lasted almost two thousand years, until the Zionist movement of the nineteenth century led to the establishment of the state of Israel in 1948.

Earlier that century, the Jews were being crushed by the oppression of two "kingdoms": Herod's kingdom of Rome and the kingdom of the temple. The Romans, The Machine of the day, administered the area by appointing local rulers such as Herod who had to collect taxes on two bases: a land tax (*tributum soli*) and a poll tax (*tributum capitas*). Non-payment of either was tantamount to rebellion, and Herod instituted his massive construction projects such as the new temple in part from taxes he collected beyond the tribute levels, which he could keep for himself.

To pay the taxes, oftentimes the peasants would have to take out loans from the Temple elite and other moneylenders, using their land as collateral. These two 'kingdoms' exploited the peasantry to such an extent that many peasants lived at the edge of destitution. Loans were made that could not be repaid, the land was confiscated by this means, and the priestly elite "in Galilee and Judea therefore became the controlling force of most private land" (Van Eck 2011, p. 50). The "great absentee landlords were stealing the land and freedom of the Israelites, and thus their destiny" (Hudson 1993, p. 42). Their confiscated holdings were consolidated into commercial scale agricultural holdings, leaving the peasantry both resentful and desolate.

That may have been a motivating force for Jesus's attempt to introduce a third 'Kingdom', the Kingdom of God, where the peasants would be fairly treated, their stolen land returned, and so on. As such, it may have been similar to that which Taraki had violently attempted in Afghanistan immediately after my last trip there. He had cancelled peasant debts and abolished the form of usury "by which peasants, who were forced to borrow money against future crops, were left in perpetual debt to money-lenders" (Blum 2004, p. 340). Jesus's motivations can therefore be interpreted as including land reform and as such a direct precedent for the twentieth century Liberation Theology initiatives in Latin America repressed by Pope John Paul II (Lynch 1994).

It was at the London end of the Overland that I found a similar land reform to that objected to by Jesus. It went back centuries into British history. That was the process of enclosure of open fields that were once shared but then fell under exclusive ownership referred to in the Clare poem *The Mores* I mentioned above. The fields were then entitled or deeded to that ownership. The Europe-wide process began in England early in the second millennium, and was practically completed there by the end of the nineteenth century.

Apart from John Clare's poem *The Mores*, my first knowledge of this practice can be dated to 1966, because a movie of the time, *A Man for All Seasons*, prompted me to read Sir Thomas More's *Utopia*, which condemned the then "peculiar to England" practice of enclosure (More 1516, pp. 24–25). Described as "a plain enough case of class robbery" (Thompson 1963, p. 218.), "the lords and nobles . . . were literally robbing the poor of their share in the commons" (Polanyi 1957, p. 35), the practice of enclosure was repeated in Ireland and other lands throughout the British Empire.

In Ireland the law was the instrument of "class robbery", via enclosures. These changes from property rights in Celtic Irish Law (Peden 1977) came at great cost to the Irish:

> Amongst the many bitter injustices inflicted upon Ireland and the Irish by the English conquest none has had more cruel or more far-reaching effects than the abrogation of the Brehon law relating to land-tenure and division of property.
>
> (Hyde 1907)

For instance, while a series of potato crop failures in the 1840s were the proximate cause of the destitution, deaths, and migration of millions of Irish, the land tenure system, enriching rent-seeking absentee landlords and their middlemen exporting millions of tons of grain through the period of the famine, was an ultimate cause (Smith 1993). This was known then, and in 1866, Isaac Butt suggested a remedy:

I have traced, I believe, clearly and satisfactorily, this spirit of disloyalty [of the Irish] to that system of land tenure which makes the law of landlord and tenant a code of conquest and enmity to his home.

(Butt 1866, p. xiv)

Butt saw the specific base evil being the tenant farmers' insecurity of tenure. Instead, Butt called for tenant farmers to be given sixty year leases with the rent to be determined by valuation, not by the landlord (who could change the rent at whim), as remedy for this (ibid., p. 6). Westminster rejected his suggestion.

For centuries, beneficiaries and economists have tabled economies of scale and other advantages tendentiously. They have been used to say that the end – of greater productivity – justified the means – of enclosures (for example, Ernle 1912). Over recent decades, these alleged benefits have been called into question (Allen 1982, 1992), although this remains in dispute (Turner 1986; McCloskey 1972, 1991).

This was repeated to such an extent that an associate of mine in Swaziland and later a colleague of mine in a consultancy in Lesotho, the late Patrick McAuslan, made the strong claim that "colonialism was basically about land tenure" in one of his books (McAuslan 1985, p. 19). This was expanded by Mbembe to claim that colonial occupation was about taking control of geographical areas, and then "writing on the ground a new set of spatial relations", developed over time into "boundaries and hierarchies, zones and enclaves" (Mbembe 2003, pp. 25–26). This was also described as "the first stage of capitalist growth": "'discovering' new territories and grabbing land without paying for it, then extracting riches from the earth without compensating local populations" (Klein 2010, p. 57). That is, *privatising the profits and commonising the costs*.

That was all a logical follow-on from the enclosures of British lands. Thereby, the landowners gained the capital to finance industrial ventures, and by the dispossessed having to migrate to the cities, they then provided an essential ingredient – the cheap labour – needed to start the industrial revolution (Patriquin 2004). They also began the social aspects of human fitness landscapes which Marx and Engels analysed to produce the Communist Manifesto with its statement in ch. 2 that "in this sense, the theory of the Communists may be summed up in the single sentence: Abolition of private property" (Marx and Engels 1985 [1888]: 96).

However, it was often to gain private property that many such dispossessed migrated to America, Australia, Africa and elsewhere, themselves becoming the beneficiaries of the dispossession of the indigenous people in those places. While it would be precisely the sort of oversimplification that I will later attack in this book to say that it was the sole cause of half the world's population now being in urban areas, it was nonetheless a significant one.

From the background of Arthur Mee's children's encyclopaedia, I had internalised a romantic and benign concept of the British Raj. Those pressures and opportunities that gave expression to my total nature along the wilds of the overland included reading Kipling's *Kim*, which described a Lahore that, although the

British Empire's rule is over and the Hindus practically banished, still had strong echoes in the Lahore I visited so many times.

Once, I was told by an Indian friend of mine that I and my passengers were pilgrims. While I disagreed then, I agree now. As pointed out by Cavanaugh, a pilgrimage "required a disorientation from the trappings of one's quotidian identity in order to respond to a call from the source of one's deeper identity" (Cavanaugh 2011, p. 80), and that, I found, is why many travellers went overland.

Roszak (1972) claims poetry can communicate resonances to the reader not found in prose. As such, a great poem can be a pilgrimage too. Following McGilchrist, finding that deeper identity involves poetry because some poetry provides a verbal bridge from the left hemisphere to the right hemisphere. The left hemisphere has no capacity for metaphor, but the right hemisphere has a great affinity for it, and poetry's "indirect, connotative" language in contrast to the left hemisphere's explicit, direct language, is the portal to metaphor, and metaphor "*underlies all forms of understanding whatsoever*" (McGilchrist 2009, p. 71; italics in original). In particular, the right hemisphere is essential to understand what others mean (ibid., p. 70).

Poetry and metaphor are therefore essential to engage in the resolution of wicked valuation problems. Like Cavanaugh's pilgrimages and unlike prose, poetry too has resonances of a call from the source of one's deeper identity which, as McGilchrist recently confirmed, must remain unknown for those resonances to both be retained and of use in this endeavour.

However, I was to find that the history of British India had aspects to it well beneath the noble aspects of Arthur Mee's view of the British Empire in his Encyclopaedias and Kipling's sacrificial sentiments in the *White Man's Burden* (Kipling 1899), which squarely related to its colonial land-related revenue policy.

I mentioned the Taj Mahal above. To this day, for many Westerners, myself included, it epitomises the romance of the East. However, I discovered that with the exception of a brief and partial respite by the comparatively enlightened Mughal ruler Akbar the Great, the grandfather of Shah Jahan (the builder of the Taj Mahal), the thousand-year history of Muslim rule in India was horrendous. In the words of Will and Ariel Durant, it was "probably the bloodiest story in history" (Durant 1935, vol. 1, p. 459). It was not only a period of massive bloodshed, but also one of profound cultural destruction, including the burning of the Library of Nalanda, which effectively destroyed Buddhism throughout the region (McKay et al. 2008, p. 311).

Before the British came, these property relations of the Mughal Empire involved intermediaries between the rulers and the peasants, local landlords called zamindars. These went from rajahs, nawabs etc. down to just above peasant level, the peasants themselves being divided into peasants with occupancy rights, and vagrant peasants (Bandyopādhyāÿa 2004, p. 8). At that time, there was no private property in land there. Then as now, self-governing village communities called panchayats had to hand over a large share of the year's produce.

According to John Maynard Keynes in *Essays in Persuasion* (1931), the British came to India in the form of the East India Company (EIC) from the plunder of

Sir Francis Drake from Spain (which had plundered it from the Native Americans). Queen Elizabeth I had been a major investor in Drake's enterprises and from her share was able to pay off her foreign debts and, with the remaining fortune, founded the Levant Company, which profited and gained a Royal Charter for the EIC from the Queen (Keynes 1963, pp. 361–362).

Given its Royal Charter in 1600, the EIC's original aim was to trade with the East Indies (now mainly Indonesia). However, the Dutch East India Company gained and held that environmental niche in the imperial fitness landscape, so the EIC turned its attention to India, and was graciously received at the court of Jahangir, the father of Shah Jahan. It established several trading posts around the Indian coastline, notably Calcutta in Bengal in 1690, but as the Mughal Empire declined following the reign of Aurungzeb, the fundamentalist son of Shah Jahan, power niches opened that the EIC was quick to fill. The EIC's transition from trader to ruler can be dated to the Battles of Plassey (1757) and Buxar (1764), leading to eventual control by the EIC of "one fifth of the world's people . . . revenue greater than the whole of Britain and . . . a private army a quarter of a million strong" (Robins 2003, p. 79). It fell upon Bengal, and via tax farming and other means bled Bengal of its resources even more rapaciously than had the former overlords, multiplying the land taxes many-fold from its acquisition in 1765 in just five years.

In the fourth of those years, 1769, the monsoon failed and there was full-blown famine. Reserves that may have sustained the peasantry had been taxed away, and "an estimated 10 million people – or one-third of the population – died, transforming India's granary into a 'jungle inhabited only by wild beasts'" (Robins 2003, p. 84). Yet Hastings noted, "Notwithstanding the loss of at least one-third of the inhabitants of the province . . . the revenue . . . was violently kept up to its former standard" (Dutt 2000, p. 53). As such, the EIC, and later the British government, repeated the strategies that Jesus apparently objected to some 1,800 years before, with iniquitous land taxes (Dutt 2013) and other "laws affecting property and debt, not adapted to the condition of the people [having effects including] suffocating burdens of peasant indebtedness to moneylenders" (Gray 2006, p. 204).

With so much devastation following the 1769 famine, the violently extracted revenues were unsustainable, and the EIC found itself in trouble at both ends of its trading pipeline, with a devastated Bengal at one end and depression in Europe at the other. It was on the verge of bankruptcy, but managed to save itself by means of cash crops.

One was tea, which was grown in China and traded to Britain by the EIC (which had a monopoly on the trade) and from there went to Britain's colonies. Another cash crop was opium. This was not from China, but Bengal (Brook and Wakabayashi 2000). While tea was a lucrative crop, it had to be paid for, and the Chinese wanted no existent the British could sell them. So the EIC increased opium cash crops in Bengal (which had formerly been traded from there to China by the Dutch), and sold it there to other British trading companies who would smuggle the illegal crop into China. Over the years, the effects of the drug on China's population and the funding of the EIC's interventions in China from the opium trade via ports such as Shanghai and Hong Kong wreaked massive destruction on that country as well.

Land tenure reforms introduced by Lord Cornwallis in India further facilitated this growth of opium and other cash crops (especially indigo). Although apparently well intentioned, Cornwallis's reforms had unintended consequences. These included the creation of a land market among the zamidars, and the zamidars becoming absentee landlords. Cornwallis introduced a British style tenure system with the state as the ultimate owner, but with individual peasant land ownership under that umbrella. He then introduced a fixed tax, irrespective of crop yields. In other words, the British adapted the process of enclosures they had developed in England to these new lands under the name "Permanent Settlement".

Instead of just tax-farmers, the zamindars became proprietors, and Bengal's 20 million smallholders were deprived of all hereditary rights. The Permanent Settlement of Bengal in 1793 was "a particularly brutal and doctrinaire attempt to establish unitary proprietorship over land" (Greer 2012, p. 365). The results included that instead of about 40 per cent under the Mughals, almost two-thirds of a rural peasant's income would be taken from the household (Robins 2003, p. 85).

The Permanent Settlement land policy was implemented all over India. The Great Indian Arc of the Meridian, begun in 1800 and hailed as "one of the most stupendous works in the history of science", was the backbone for the Survey of India, the most important role of which was "assessing local and agricultural taxes which made India such an attractive country to rule. For [this] maps were essential" (Keay 2000). Other parts of the British Empire were similarly enclosed, including colonies in Africa.

Such practices, and similar famines, continued through the time of the Raj, the effects of which were often exacerbated by the fixed and high nature of the land taxes imposed (Dutt 2013, p. 1). The last of the famines under the Raj went from 1943 to 1944, which killed an unknown number of Bengalis, but with estimates running into the millions (Mukerjee 2010). Once again there was a combination of causes, but they included preventable ones that were not addressed because of other wartime priorities.

Uncounted millions had perished in the famines in between. According to Will Durant, the "British rule in India", which my grandparents had been party to, was "the most sordid and criminal exploitation of one nation by another in all recorded history" (Durant 1930, p. 2). Moreover, property taxes were at its heart.

These and other appalling events, many involving mass slaughter, not merely mass deaths for preventable reasons, led me to recall Ardrey's view of a tyranny-territory relationship. While clearly there were a myriad of causes, attributable to different degrees in different cases, my view was strengthening that clearly there was a thread worth following here. That thread was the relationship between the regard-recognition hunger I first had gone overland to ask Krishnamurti about, and my own professional field's base, that of placing market and market rental values on real property rights.

I continued looking for such examples over the next few years, which facilitated other insights into the places we visited which in turn made my talks on the countries we visited more interesting. Certainly, those trips were the best time of my own life to that point, and correspondence with passengers since then has confirmed that it was the "trip of a lifetime" for so many of us.

Over my last few stays in Kathmandu, I became friends with Hubert DeCleer, a former Penn World courier who had become even more blown away by Nepal than I was, and in particular the Vajrayana form of Buddhism that was practised there. We had many hours of wonderful discussions, often in the coffee lounge of the Blue Star Hotel, which the overland companies that I worked for used, and where we would stay between trips. He paid me the compliment of writing down what I said from time to time, and referred to me as "my Taoist friend". I do not specifically recall him doing so, but it is highly likely that he explained Vajrayana's emphasis on developing a powerful imagination, identifying with the deities imagined, and then dissolving them (Beyer 1978). This may be a very useful methodology for understanding not only the power of the imagination, but also realising Bateson's observation that "imagination alone is insanity" (Bateson 1979, p. 242). This practice is reified by the creation and dissipation of the Kalachakra Sand Mandala (Bryant 2003) such as I was later able to see in Ladakh.

Hubert's enthusiasm was infectious. I studied the subject over the decades since, including learning that the patterns of thought of Hua-Yen Buddhism, integral to the construction of Borobudur, are also integral to the Vajrayana Buddhism Hubert and I discussed all those years ago (Odin 1982, p. 146). Furthermore, they are also consonant with Whitehead's process philosophy (ibid.), and Hua-Yen Buddhism was itself strongly influenced by Taoism (Oh 2000, pp 278–297).

After the Asian Overland closed, I lead similar overlands across South America for a couple of years. Throughout that period, I continued my deliberations concerning the role of identity. For instance, a poem I wrote in 1982 concluded:

But if you seek, and thereby find
You are not
Perhaps at a stroke, you can unwind
That Gordian Knot.

Once again, I found that the attention or otherwise to land reform issues had played a major role in the history of the countries I had led trips through.

One example was in Brazil, where peasants from the *Latifundistas* (large ranches) went to the Amazonian rainforest in search of their own land, but found they had to slash and burn (Luna and Klein 2001). Large landowners were clearing much of the rest of the Amazonian rainforest. I learned that Joao Goulart, the son of a wealthy landowner and the President of Brazil from 1961–1964, had attempted (and failed) a land reform programme that would have expropriated and redistributed any landholdings larger than 600ha and allowed only one house per person in urban areas (Stedile 2010). His government was overthrown and a right-wing dictatorship came into power; it was of the harsh kind that dominated

South America during my trips there from 1980 to 1985 (for example, in Argentina and Chile). In 2006, it was claimed that Brazil had the highest concentration of land ownership in the world, with almost half the land being owned by one per cent of the population (ibid.).

After that I led some tours through North America, finding similar land dispossessions there as in Australia, India, Africa, Latin America and elsewhere, and later still began working for a company called Explore Worldwide. That had arisen from the ashes of the British overland operator that had employed Hubert: Penn World. The resurrection was thanks to the efforts of a team led by a man I had first met during the Saur revolution in Kabul, Travers Cox.

One of their tours I led went to Rajasthan, where as part of the tour there was a camel trip lasting a couple of days through the desert. It finished at the beautiful and romantic desert trading town of Jaisalmer. However, back in the days of the Raj it was one of the cities along an overland route of the trade in opium from Malwa. Many of Jaisalmer's exquisite palaces were built from the profits of the opium trade, as were much grander and larger buildings still in Mumbai: Opium was "the crucial factor in the emergence of Bombay as a metropolis" (Farooqui 2006).

In between such trips, I was waiting for the next one at the Ranjit Hotel in New Delhi, when I met the owner of a tiny shop there packed to the ceilings with a vast array of books of interest to travellers. She suggested that I read a book she had for sale called *The Atman Project*, by Ken Wilber (1980). Wilber was to become a major influence on me for many years.

Like my grandparents, I married in India. Anne and I were married in the gardens of the Australian High Commission in New Delhi. We then joined Travers in Sri Lanka to lead my last trip and have our honeymoon there before returning to Adelaide to settle down again in my late grandmother's beachfront home. By this time I had led tours in about 60 countries, with multiple visits to most of them, and had familiarised myself with the dominant paradigms – including the cultures, historical narratives, religions etc. – of many of them. These included places stretching from Bariloche to Vancouver in the Americas, and religions from Arianism to Zoroastrianism in Eurasia. They also included knowledge of many of the most ghastly crimes in history, ranging from those of the ancient world throughout the Middle East to those of the West, many of them land-related.

Having had to address the problems of my passengers on trips of up to 90 days together, I had also gained deeper insights into human nature than could have been available to me in almost any other context. Both were to serve me well in my later career as a land policy consultant.

However, I did not close the door on any of what I had learned; it was an enormous meal to digest, both intellectually and emotionally. So my explorations continued.

Settling down

With the help of my former colleagues at the Australian Valuation Office in Adelaide, I was able to resurrect my valuation career and was quickly promoted to Darwin, but once again was headhunted by the private sector. I became valuation manager for Hillier Parker back in Adelaide, and in 1989, having sold my grandmother's house we moved into the Adelaide Hills to be close to a school there that we felt would be best for our children. It had a philosophy as far away from that of my own school as I could find. It was like Ardrey's territorial societies, whereas my school had been a tyranny.

Later, I became the South Australian managing partner for Herron Todd White, and later still I was asked to present one of four papers at a property conference held by my professional institute in Adelaide in July 1992. I did so before 160 people on the subject "The Environment: Static or Dynamic?" My sister recently rediscovered the paper and newspaper reports about it at the time. It is of interest in this context because it encapsulates several points that I have developed over the years into the framework for this work.

It begins:

> "Value": A big word, "value"; the more you think about it, the bigger it gets. For this paper, it is important to distinguish between three levels of the term – Value, economic value, and market value.
>
> At its biggest, I submit that the value of an existent to a person – an idea, or an animate or inanimate object – can be defined as how central it is to one's sense of being. Defined in this way, it can be seen that maintenance of a set of values is often far more important than maintenance of one's physical existence. This has been proved countless times in history – from Socrates to Christian martyrs to kamikaze pilots. People don't die for their beliefs – they die for how central these beliefs are to their sense of being. We can be so blinded by our splendid vision that we never know or care what effect it may have on our neighbours, or we may die and kill for Values. These can be termed the "Big V" values. An especially topical one is the protection of the environment.
>
> (McDermott 1992)

My sister's rediscovery of the paper revealed that I had retained that interest in such values as I termed "'Big V' values" since my interviews with Jim MacDonald back in the sixties:

> Abstract as it may sound, attention to the "Big V" values is the central point to bear in mind when examining strategies for the 90s in the context of the property business and the environmental movements . . . People operate on the "Big V" values, not just a subset of them, "economic value".
>
> I think that there is already a good definition of economic value: that to be found in Murray's book, *Principles and Practice of Valuation*, as being "the benefit conferred by ownership, which includes not only the possibility of exchange for other commodities, but all the satisfaction which may arise from possession" (Murray 1969). That is, "Big V" values don't operate in a

vacuum. They are formed by our natural needs, attitudes and gifts interacting with circumstances, including economic ones.

It is within the framework of economic value that the professional valuer operates. His "holy grail" is the concept of "market value". It is a pretty elusive holy grail.

(McDermott 1992)

The paper then went on to interrogate the relationship between "Big V" (especially environmental) values and market values. In a later newspaper report on the subject – also kept by my sister – I was quoted as saying:

Ultimately the environment and the economy are interdependent. There must be more dynamic cooperation and less static confrontation to ensure their mutual survival through the uncharted waters of the 1990s.

(*Mount Barker Courier*, 22 July 1992)

Despite the success I enjoyed in my profession, I was still an animal that wanted to "face those pressures and opportunities which give expression to his total nature" (Ardrey 1972, p. 34). So when I saw that opportunity in Swaziland arise, I asked my wife, who felt the same.

During this period, I continued my search for answers to the questions that Sargant and Ardrey had posed. One book that I had read during that pre-overland period was Colin Wilson's *The Outsider* (Wilson 1956), a controversial book I had read while I was in my early twenties. In 1984, Wilson published another book, called *A Criminal History of Mankind*, which recapped much of what I had learned, and answered my call in noting that from:

The time of the Assyrians to the time of the Nazis, history has been full of ruthlessly efficient men who ended in failure. And it is of central importance to understand why this is so; for we are now dealing with the essence of crime.

(Wilson 1984, p. 153)

Wilson also referred to Turnbull's study of a dispossessed African tribe, *The Mountain People: the Classic Account of a Society Too Poor for Morality* (Turnbull 1984). He said:

Since the Second World War, the Ik have been driven out of their traditional hunting grounds by a government decision to turn the land into a game reserve . . . The result of this hardship is that they seemed to lose all normal human feelings.

(Wilson 1984, p. 52)

He also quoted from Cyrus the Great, as developed by Arnold Toynbee: "Soft countries breed soft men" (ibid., p. 276).

A complementary insight is Mary Midgley's lesson from the Ik, that "In the process of destruction ... more complex and advanced capacities will probably tend to go to pieces before its simplest and most primitive ones" (Midgley 1995, pp. 287–88). However, the main point that stuck in my mind from Wilson's book was the concept of "the Right Man" (introduced on p. 68), a dominator (Eisler 1995) whose self-esteem is dependent upon being considered by others absolutely right at all times.

Once such appears to have been Charles Trevelyan, who did not change his mind. After presiding over the great famine in Ireland, from his fixated idea from his laissez faire philosophy (Keynes 1926) of the alleged pauperising of gratuitous relief, he concluded that the starvation was facilitating a "wonderful social revolution" that was proceeding in Ireland, and that any relief would destroy the lesson they needed to learn (Gray 2006, p. 213).

Eisler (1995) takes this idea of the Right Man much further, embedding Right Men as a product of one of two basic ways of addressing the sexuality of our species: the dominator (for example, Saudi Arabia) and partnership (for example, Scandinavia) models (ibid., pp. 4, 344). She includes much Judeo-Christian-Islamic moral coding as a means of sowing tension and mistrust into our most intimate relations, and thereby having that inbuilt need to trust transferred to the dominators, and agreeing with Wilhelm Reich (1946) in seeing the authoritarian family as "the factory of [fascism's] structure and ideology" (ibid., p. 215). She asserts that a consequence of that dominator model that, globally, women only earn one–tenth of what men do, and own a hundredth of the world's property (ibid., p. 339).

Terrorists-type dominators often have an obsession with morality, especially sexual purity, presumably similarly motivated (Crenshaw 1981, p. 395). They thereby prop up the states they oppose, and "strengthen the old order" (Crenshaw 1983, pp. 148–49). Militant extremists' three major identifying characteristics are "Proviolence, Vile World, and Divine Power" (Stankov, Saucier and Knezevic 2010), a.k.a. "nastiness, grudge and excuse". Their nastiness is "akin to dogmatism and authoritarianism that are known to be hard to modify" (Stankov 2014), so being a dominator is a necessary but insufficient precondition for militant extremism. Historically, they have been the most destructive when they get their hands on the instruments of state. In contrast, "free institutions create free values, and vice versa, for a virtuous feedback loop" (Easterly 2013, p. 139).

Whatever costume they don, militant extremists appear to be unaware that new moralities emerge at new levels, quite as unable to answer my question, "What is the difference between a mind intent upon imposing discipline on itself, and a mind in conflict with itself?" as the Buddhist nun was. The importance of morality on the one hand and the immorality of imposing morality on another, when coupled with how much tolerance of intolerance a society should allow, are a wicked valuation problem when NSEW meet.

It seemed to me that, historically, the role of such Right Men has been arguably the major one in causing these wicked valuation problems, and I should watch out for it in land policy formulation and implementation as a potentially highly toxic ingredient in those domains.

All the negative examples of preventable famines, mass murder on an incredible scale and so on had hit me hard concerning our capacity for evil, all within our various identity constructions. However, by this time I had also learnt with Anne the truth of what Andrew Stephens had said, that one only finds oneself, becomes a whole person, a humane person, by loving others. I found that there are whole dimensions to life that are dormant until true love arrives, and more dimensions still when children do, all of which may kick in with astonishing force. As such, we also wanted our children to be able to grow up to be able to express their total natures, in the sense of achieving that telaxic integration of excellence of mind, body and spirit that I understood as being the modern view of areté.

In pursuit of that for my children, I went to a lecture by Miraca Gross in Adelaide which referred to an American psychologist called Mihaly Csikszentmihalyi, and followed up by buying a book of Csikszentmihalyi's called *Flow: The Psychology of Optimal Experience* (1990), which is the source of the Goldilocks Principle below.

It was from that background that I was selected and in early 1993 sent with my family to Swaziland by Australian Aid to assist in land-related matters, particularly in terms of upgrading fringe urban settlements as part of a World Bank funded Urban Development Project. Packing all our stuff away into a spare room, I noted that my collection of books had grown from Arthur Mee's 10 volumes and a few others to over a thousand. The several books that I took over there included Wilber's *The Atman Project* and several others by him, and Csikszentmihalyi's *Flow*.

Swaziland

Swaziland made me acutely aware of the conceptual and functional chasms between Title Deed Land (TDL) and Swazi Nation Land (SNL). Land alienation during colonial times had deeply penetrated the identity of the Swazi Nation (in fact it could be considered that in adopting Swazi identity you are adopting a trauma – a useful phenomenon for nationalists everywhere). A song still sung at traditional ceremonies is an example of how that is kept vivid to this day. Called *lelive ngelakho Mswati*, it is a song sung at the Umhlanga ceremony, and is about how the land was cut apart for concessionaries. It was addressed to King Mswati II, (not the current King Mswati III). A translation follows:

Lead singer:	The country is yours Mswati they are just bothering you!
Chorus:	Watch, watch, land concessionaires!
Lead singer:	It is for the King of the Swazis! For the King of the Swazis!
Chorus:	Watch, watch, land concessionaires!
Lead singer:	Mswati is the King at Hhohho at Hhohho!
Chorus:	Watch, watch, land concessionaires!
Lead singer:	The country is for the King, the King of the Swazis!
Chorus:	Watch, watch, land concessionaires!

Lead singer:	It is for the King of the Swazis! For the King of the Swazis!
Chorus:	Watch, watch, land concessionaires!
Lead singer:	They have spoiled it, spoilt it!
Chorus:	Watch, watch, land concessionaires!
Lead singer:	It will eventually come back, the Ngwane-land!
Chorus:	Watch, watch, land concessionaires!

(Wilcox 2013, p. 46; Masango 2009, p. 113)

The song highlighted the national identity trauma that resulted in the deep anti-pathy I was to find many (but not all) traditional Swazis held to non-traditional land tenure.

A World Bank overseer of the UDP, David De Groot (see Lowsby and DeGroot 2007) had shown me a Readers Digest article about Hernando De Soto, a Peruvian Economist who promoted the idea of giving property rights for the poor – exactly what the UDP was attempting by trying to allow 99-year leases over SNL. My diary noted that I finished reading De Soto's book *The Other Path* on the first of August 1993 (De Soto 1989). I had written on my copy at the time that "the problem is, it makes values a subset of economics rather than economics a subset of values. The same goes for economic rationalism in general. The central problem is how to get income distribution." I had made the last remark because mortgage finance requires both collateral to secure the loan, and enough income to service the loan. One without the other is insufficient. Therefore, while De Soto referred to formalised property rights as "the missing ingredient" (De Soto 2000), I then considered it to be "potentially *a* missing ingredient".

My interests in Csikszentmihalyi and Wilber also developed, the former through a book of his called *The Evolving Self* (Csikszentmihalyi 1993) and the latter a book that many still consider to be Wilber's Magnum Opus, *Sex, Ecology, Spirituality* (Wilber 1995) in which he introduced his "All Quadrants, All Levels" (AQAL) approach (I read it after I had sent in my NDS submission).

In view of its indebtedness to him, I sent Wilber a copy of my submission to the NDS. Wilber replied, we continued to correspond until about 2006. Although I visited him again in 2014, our lives, and drives, and values, and methodologies, have parted ways.

During all of the above, I observed how so much of what we did in the donor community emanated from Newton's single vision, resulting from what I have since understood as being attempts to solve wicked problems as if they were simple or complicated ones. I could see it generating the same suspicions and hostilities among so many Swazis as The Machine did to Tagore, and those abovementioned who considered it the devil of the modern world.

According to Easterly, such suspicions have been amply justified by the support of authoritarian development by those within the donor community he terms technocrats, who empower what he terms "authoritarian development" because of a false assumption that the main cause of poverty is a shortage of expertise. In contrast, he considers the main cause of poverty is a shortage of rights in the relevant domain, and in particular "the unchecked power of the state against poor people without rights" (Easterly 2013, p. 6).

He considers that "well-intentioned autocrats advised by technical experts" (ibid.) focussed on "technical fixes to technical problems" are not the solution, but the problem (ibid., p. 7).

On p. 74, he quotes the New Zealand economist J. B. Condliffe, whom he describes as one banished to the worst circle of hell reserved for those who are right ahead of their time (Easterly 2013, p. 76), in noting that:

> We face a new and more formidable superstition than the world has ever known, the myth of the nation-state, whose priests are as intolerant as those of the Inquisition. The struggle for the rights of the individual against the all-powerful and intolerant nation-state is the most difficult and crucial issue of our generation.
>
> (Condliffe 1938, p. 137)

This mythical creature "first arose in the eighteenth century and became prevalent only in the nineteenth century and following" (ibid., p. 11). As mentioned above, this is what Tagore claims holds "its mental slaves hypnotized into believing that they are free" (Tagore 1918, pp. 26–27): "The boundaries of a nation are fictive plots bandied about by real-estate agencies of the mind" (Shell 1993, p. 180). Similarly, empires were the instruments of Urizen according to that "Prophet Against Empire" William Blake (Erdman 1977), who saw Urizen as the eternal priest and Los as the eternal prophet (Bloom 1971, p. 75). However, the myth of the nation-state is but one manifestation of what is arguably the most pervasive myth of all in the North and West, "The Myth of the Machine" (Mumford 1967, 1970), traced by Mumford back to the earliest civilisations, and looking to the future, whereby in 1967 he foresaw that:

> The beleaguered – even "obsolete" – individual would be entirely de-skilled, reduced to a passive, inert, "trivial accessory to the machine". Technical surveillance and limitless data-collection – "an all-seeing eye" (Panopticon) – would monitor every "individual on the planet". Ultimately, the totalitarian technocracy, centralizing and augmenting its "power-complex", ignoring the real needs and values of human life, might produce a world "fit only for machines to live in".
>
> (Mumford 1967, p. 2)

There, Mumford voiced the concerns of many Swazis I spoke to over my years in that beautiful place, some of whom saw Westerners as more to be pitied than admired, and scorned for their discarding of, and disrespect for, their elders. In contrast, while taking what the West had to offer they also had a retreat from the West's towns, which was provided by lands allocated to them by their chiefs. In their view these lands provided not only sanctuary from the depredations The Machine would otherwise visit upon them, but also allowed a return to their traditions, some (not all) of which were more humane and respectful than our own. Here I again highlight what I mentioned in the introduction: that in the second volume of *The Myth of the Machine*, entitled *The Pentagon of Power* (1970), Mumford's five sides of that Pentagon were "power, profit, productivity, property, and prestige": hence the Swazis extreme sensitivity on the issue of property rights over land. In their culture, to a significant extent no Swaziland Nation Land equals no adult identity, and no place to hide from the ruthless and rapacious Machine, which would force them "to face the terrifying prospect of the destruction of their world and of their traditional forms of life" (Arredondo 2013).

As described in Chapter 5, when one gains identity by internalisation of social values, via the Thomas Theorem one becomes an instrument for making the myths of The Machine and the relevant nation-states, tribes etc. real. While nation-states are often founded by war, as described by Ian Morris they require peace within their domains (Morris 2014). To this end, they employ psychology and related disciplines in their governance (Jones, Pykett and Whitehead 2013). As with any artefact, such employments can be for good or ill, depending on who is in control and what checks and balances there are. We individuals can be quite dreadful to one another, and the restraining power of the state can be highly beneficial as well as pernicious. For instance, along with trade, increasing cosmopolitanism, women's rights and employment of reason, nation-states have played a pivotal role in the reduction of the percentages of violent deaths in their domains (Pinker 2011).

To frame his debate between freedom and autocracy, Easterly presented three dichotomies: a blank state versus learning from history, the well-being of nations versus that of individuals, and conscious design versus spontaneous solutions (Easterly 2013, p. 24). He devoted the sixth chapter of his book to "Values: The Long Struggle for Individual Rights" (ibid., pp. 129–154). Therein, he noted that "unconstrained power goes with collectivist values" (ibid., p. 138), and that "the difference between individualist and collectivist values is one of those great divides that help us understand how Europe pulled ahead and the rest of the world fell behind" (ibid., p. 144). He later remarked that one needs annoying dissidents insulting one's conformist views (ibid., p. 300) and concluded the book by observing that "unrestrained power will always turn out to be the enemy of development" (ibid., p. 351).

States are artefactual magnifiers of the power of certain individuals. They sorely test the capacity of many to remain wise, compassionate and honest against the pressures and seductions of such power. Hence the need for rigorous checks and balances on power.

Easterly also referred to the researches of Kahneman, Tversky and other behavioural economists and their finding of our wired-in need to personalise accomplishments to a hero, which he describes as a "fundamental attribution error". Elsewhere, the error is termed "correspondence bias", "the tendency to draw inferences about a person's unique and enduring dispositions from behaviours which can be entirely explained by the situations in which they occur" (Gilbert and Malone 1995, p. 21).

At that time, I sensed such insights via a discomforted feeling, but prior to this work was unable to articulate them.

That is where I sat back then, which is now over twenty years ago. Later, Ken Wilber formed the Integral Institute, and he twice paid for my return fares from Swaziland and my accommodation in Boulder, Colorado to attend meetings of the Integral Politics branch of the Integral Institute as a founding member. When I met him again in 2014, I asked myself:

> Since I first read Ken (Wilber 1980), how much have my own insights developed in terms of the definition of Werner's (1957) Orthogenic Principle as defined in the above Glossary? And could that development enfold Naisbitt's expanding concept of what it means to be human?

Despite our parting of the ways, I found that some of Wilber's framing still facilitated insights. For example, an article in the *Times* of Swaziland dated 7 November 1998 shows the potential for interpretative clarity that Wilber's framework can provide. One of the King's appointed parliamentarians "caused a stir during a parliamentary civic education workshop when he condemned the teaching of human rights to citizens, saying they were totally in conflict with Swazi law and custom . . . Swaziland . . . can do without the ideologies of countries that claim to be democratic". Wilber's framework interprets this as a mythic-level defence against the threat of a mental-level approach. However, I had come to realise there was rather more to it than that:

> The concept of God is a psychological strategy which only became necessary when certain human groups developed a strong ego structure. The development of theism was not the result (and the indication) of an evolutionary movement advance towards spirit – as Wilber believes – but the result of an accidental historical event which caused a movement away from it.
>
> (Taylor n.d.)

I mentioned at the beginning of this chapter that this time in Swaziland was a pivotal period in my becoming motivated to embark upon this work. That was for two reasons: my work in Swaziland, and the decline of Wilber's influence on my identity construction. The former sensitised me to the enormous problems involved in trying to change the status quo, as experienced by my first Principal Secretary and Honourable Minister, which continued, but less intensively, for the rest of my stay.

Along with my period on the Asian Overland, my Wilber period up to and including Swaziland was pivotal to my coming to understand the need to write this book. While all the above was going on, I had not yet moved on from Wilber, which I now have, albeit enriched and with (heavily qualified but still overall) gratitude and respect.

A large part of that differentiation emerged from my problem with Wilber's concept of some states, such as the USA, as "social holons" (Wilber 1995, 2003;

Kofman 2001), which, as applied by Bush and Cheney, resulted in what Anderson called Wilber's ontology: "An imperialist act of envelopment and disenfranchisement" (Anderson 2010, p. 32). Having been to Iraq many times and remained engaged with its events since, I see Bush and Cheney's invasion of Iraq as such. In contrast, Wilber saw it as an advanced social holon bringing a pathological one back into line. When I saw Ken Wilber again in 2014, I asked him about that: "What do you do after you have warned people over and over what would happen, then they go ahead and do it anyway, and it happens?" After looking at me for a long time, he answered: "I don't know".

Neither do I, Ken. It is a wicked valuation problem when NSEW meet.

Like Easterly cited earlier in this chapter, I have witnessed authoritarian development via these social *artefacts*, not holons, of states and corporations. As Caufield stated in her book about the World Bank, *Masters of Illusion*:

> Consultants who wish to make a life of it have to learn to close their eyes to certain aspects of the real world. Those who refuse to do so are not popular teammates. They slow things down with their disturbing questions and incessant worrying. Most international consultants – certainly, the most successful ones – have learned to narrow their vision, to focus only on their small piece of the puzzle, to ignore the larger questions and those that fall between the cracks, so that they can do their work quickly and efficiently, collect their substantial pay checks, and move on to the next mission without pausing to have a nervous breakdown.
>
> (Caufield 1998, p. 235)

In other words, they have degenerated into single vision.

I have also seen that the situation is a bit more complex than that. There are many consultants, and many working within the World Bank and other such institutions, who do not close their eyes in the way Caufield describes, who do not confine themselves to being cookie cutters for The Empire of The Machine's single vision. Rather, as far as I am able to discern, they have fourfold vision and implement it. They evince broad and deep vision, and balanced judgement. I have cited many of those in this work, and also consider many other consultants I have and have not met to be similarly equipped. One such I have not met is Craig Valters, whose Theories of Change in International Development Paper (Valters 2014) calls for many features addressed in this thesis, including more critical reflection, the need to "focus on process rather than product, uncertainty rather than results, iterative development of hypotheses rather than static theories, and learning rather than accountability", and calling for "a critical, honest and reflective approach, which takes the complexity of social change seriously" (Valters 2014a). I also know of many good people entrapped inside single vision who, with the best of intentions, know not what they wreak. For instance, I can see the relics of one such in the mirror.

This difference between Wilber's social holons and my social artefacts also applies, not to God, but to conceptions of God, which again I see as social artefacts. "It is the individual who is custodian and executor of the self-organizing drive of universe" (Dimitrov 2003, p. 16), not memes, not memeplexes, and not machinery, and therefore because and only insofar as, they are not machines. It is the individual as part of the pattern that connects, not that which disconnects and thereby destroys all quality (Bateson 1979, p. 8, Dimitrov 2003, p. 58). Similarly to Steve Taylor (n.d.) regarding the concept of god being a *moving away* from spirit, I suspect collateral damage in the historical separation of the social imaginaries produced into the artefacts of church and state in the West. While I personally consider that separation to have been highly beneficial in so many ways, perhaps a baby was thrown out with the bathwater. There may have been a moving away from recognising spirituality as a major attractor for the complex adaptive systems called humans.

My problem with Wilber's social holons, particularly as including the United States and other countries as such (Howard 2005, p. 52), is but one of a wider critique (Edwards 2002–2003; Smith 2001; Schwartz 2013). I agree with Schwartz:

> Grafting approaches proper to individual holons onto the analysis of social holons is a wayward form of methodological individualism" [and that] "the concept of a social holon remains undertheorised in integral theory.
>
> (Schwartz 2013, p. 163)

I have also taken on board many, but by no means all, other critiques of Wilber, including many by David and Andrea Lane (2006–2015) and several others. However, I remain in substantive agreement with many of Wilber's defenders against single vision attacks upon him, often based upon a visceral rejection of hierarchies (Morgan 2011, p. 811).

More nuanced critics have deeper points to make. Among those are the critiques of the late Tomislav Markus (2009), a materialist historian I see as fitting comfortably into Blake's Urizen narrative, but who also had a rather Edenic view of hunter-gatherer bands. He saw Wilber's Integral Theory as maintaining:

> Strong anti-naturalistic impulses because it often calls for a "rise above" our "animality" into the "higher level of spiritual life". This is essentialy (sic) a modern version of the ancient anti-naturalism of the axial religions, with which Integral Theory has many important connections.
>
> (Markus 2009)

Markus also saw the last 10,000 years of human history not as progressive but in fact regressive. He did not mean that in a moral sense, "but in the sense of a continual decline of the quality of human life and a continual increase of anthropogenic problems" (ibid.). In this paper's terminology, he saw ever more wicked problems now increasing exponentially, with a particular emphasis on civilisation's insatiable need for energy supplies (Markus 2010).

The original linking of the social imaginaries and their artefacts in the West via Steve Taylor's concept of god (Taylor n.d.) contributed to the Feudal system.

While that could well have strengthened both church and state in harnessing motivations and harvesting actions, their separation can be seen as both beneficial and damaging. Moreover, in adopting a spurious atomism to humanity, scientism threw the baby of spirituality out with the bathwater of religion, such that the mere raising of the role of spirituality in human behaviour can brand one as a sermoniser. That is a Western phenomenon, by no means global, and in this work we are addressing the NSEW, not privileging any one of them.

However we conceive a God or even if we do not, we are not closer to God by dint of being motorcycle maintainers, but for all practical intents and purposes of the concept of God, we are closer by being in the Zen state. We cannot assert that either Tupaia or Captain Cook were "closer to God". However, we can say the flow experience matches feeling that way, as the sixth of the eight characteristic dimensions of the flow experience is "a loss of self-consciousness, transcendence of ego boundaries, a sense of growth and being part of some greater whole" (Csikszentmihalyi 1993, p. 178). That may be a holonic feeling channelled into the concept of God, which concept is a mental artefact. Similarly, we cannot assert that everyone finds autotelaxic flow or spirituality to be an attractor, but we can assert that it is up to everyone to find out for oneself.

Even if such experiences are only interior, perhaps such experiences are as far as we can go towards God. And in any case it is as far as we need to go for current purposes. We need to go that far because of the role of the concept of God in identity construction at both the social and the personal identity scales (see Chapter 5). In particular, perhaps they are far enough to enfold the psyche hextant's competencies in HVN↔HBA, as described below, to address the wicked problems referred to in this work.

From that perhaps-far-enough position, we can see that, just like the Enlightenment paradigm and its subsequent development, some problems are rather more wicked than can be addressed by models of any kind, even ones as spacious as Wilber's.

After four years in Swaziland, I was appointed to a new position, this time funded by the British, as Swaziland's National Land Policy Facilitator – a position I held there until the initiative became stalled by several factors, including the drafting of a new Constitution; several of the land-related initiatives in the draft policy are now in Swaziland's Constitution.

Vanuatu and beyond

While I was still in Swaziland, the Commonwealth Secretariat suggested I apply for a position in Vanuatu. So I began in Vanuatu on 13 August 2001 on a two-year contract (later extended) to facilitate the introduction of two new Acts. The Ministry appointed me to the committee steering the formulation of the Administrative Policy for the Lands Tribunal Act of 2002, an Act facilitating the determining of land disputes by the traditional authorities. The Ministry also appointed me as a member of the Land Revenue Policy Committee. The government accepted the committee's recommendations, and they formed a major part of the government's 2004 plans to improve government revenues.

I returned to Swaziland after my stint in Vanuatu, in the hope that the NLP process would be able to proceed. However, it was still stalled (and remains so), so I took up a permanent position as a senior valuer in Darwin, but with permission to take leave for international consultancies as the opportunities arose.

In 2007, Land Equity International Pty Ltd (LEI) appointed me as their International Valuation, Fees and Finance Adviser to Palestine as part of Component 1 of Palestine's World-Bank-funded Land Policy Formulation and Development of Regulatory Framework of the Land Administration Project. We were based in Ramallah for 2.5 months from 11 February. While "[a]t the heart of the Israel/Palestine conflict lies the question of land and who rules it" (Global Policy Forum n.d.), this exercise was not intended to address that conflict. Rather, it was about how to manage the land under Palestinian administration. Even so, for me this was a pivotal consultancy in so many ways, including my path to this book. For example, in my report presentation, comprising only four slides, in the third slide I inserted the following comment:

> Development only occurs in a network of relationships of components in dynamic near-equilibrium with one another. We submit that the development of the valuation profession in Palestine requires the following five factors to be developed in that manner.

After enumerating them, I followed up with the diagram shown in Figure 2.1, which later developed into HVN↔HBA.

Subsequent consultancies took me to Indonesia, Vietnam, Timor Leste, Pakistan, Azerbaijan, Afghanistan and Peru. The Timor Leste assignment was in many ways the most challenging of them all, insofar as the country and its land records had been repeatedly devastated. With a few possible exceptions, it was ground zero on a world scale. The problems I had encountered in Palestine and Vietnam in particular were even worse here, so I had to address them with even greater intensity. This included further development of the use of heuristics (Gigerenzer 1999, 2007, 2013, 2014; Gigerenzer and Brighton 2009; Kruglanski and Gigerenzer 2011; Gigerenzer and Hertwig 2011; Haldane and Madouros 2012; Hertwig, Hoffrage and the ABC Research Group 2013; Todd, Gigerenzer and the ABC Research Group 2012). I wanted to develop heuristics into useful ansatzes towards valuations in markets where either no evidence exists, or where evidence does exist, but is kept in secret, especially from the state.

Chapter summary and the way forward

I told my own story in this chapter not so much because it is important to know how my identity has influenced this work and my thoughts, but because it is as a reminder that everyone has one's own life story, which similarly affects what they bring to the table in addressing wicked problems. While that appears blatantly

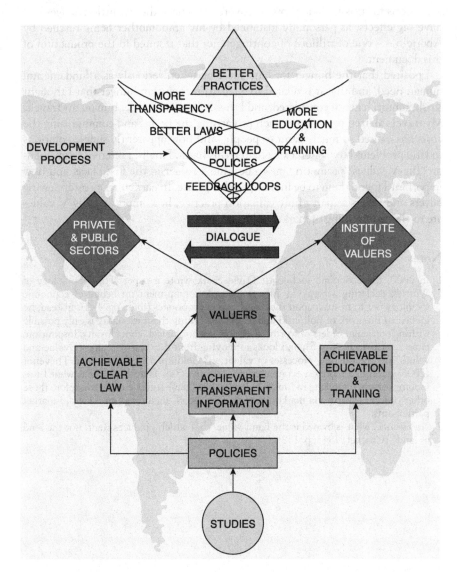

Figure 2.1 My diagram towards the evolution of valuation in Palestine

Source: graphics by my local counterpart, Osama Kasbari

obvious once stated, when operating in single vision I rarely gave it a single thought: I just looked for results by myself rather than with others. All stakeholders come with their own thoughts and agendas, and because they are to address wicked valuation problems that observation is of major consequence in this work. Furthermore, the autoethnographic narrative is meant to introduce concepts at what I hope will be a manageable rate for the reader.

Reasons for this include those uncovered by chaos theory: little changes can have big effects, as personally instanced by my grandmother being rescued by Aborigines – one of trillions of contingencies that resulted in the production of this document.

I posited that the hunger for land must be taken seriously as a fundamental human need, and that it is related to a regard-recognition hunger that I thought Krishnamurti had not considered, and I therefore went to meet him on my travels. My travels alerted me to how much privatising the profits and communising the costs has caused so much harm to people, and how apparently simple solutions to land problems have often exacerbated this harm. Finally, I referred to my focus on "Big-V values" prompting me to become a valuer in the first place, and how important I found them to be in how people operate. In particular, by interviewing buyers and sellers as part of my valuation practice, how important Big-V values are to the determining of market values.

Notes

1 In 2000, the economic sociologist David Stark wrote a paper "For a Sociology of Worth", declaring a break in Talcott Parson's commitment on behalf of economic sociology not to trespass upon the magisteria of economics (ibid., pp. 1–2). Instead, he looked to the work of Boltanski and Thévenot noting that rationality is only possible within "particular orders of worth" – market, technological, civic, loyalty, inspiration, fame . . . (ibid., p. 4, n. 5), and looks to moving from the "static fixtures of value and values" to "the ongoing processes of valuation" (ibid., p. 5). Boltanski and Thévenot (2006) published more on economies of worth in 2006. That discipline is what I was looking for when replying to Jim MacDonald, but I have still been able to explore those other orders of worth via market valuation protocols, including interviews of market participants.

2 "In essence, what is owned is the Land-value, that which produces Rent, not the land as land" (Crockett 1943, p. 152).

3 The law of the machine and global landscapes

Introduction

While there are many other wicked valuation problems when NSEW meet, following Patrick McAuslan's abovementioned observation about colonialism being basically about land tenure, this literature review focusses on The Machine's approach to property rights over land, and its consequences.

Professional valuers like me do not value land as such. They value the property rights over the land, and the value of those social artefacts depend upon what the highest and best legal use of the land is – what can be done with it, insofar as that effects the market supply and demand for that land, and how readily fungible any such rights are. That is, the legal framework, formal or informal, is a consideration at the root of all market valuations. Therefore, market value is a social imaginary atop the socially imagined artefacts of property rights over land.

One reason for choosing this focus is that this work emerges into transdisciplinarity from my career in the valuation of real property rights from within The Machine, and property rights are fundamental to its performance. Yet, while The Machine's property rights are complicated:

> Ownership is a woefully inadequate perception of what property is . . .
> Property is something we must collectively design and construct . . . Like
> music, property gets its sense of stability from the ongoing creation and
> dissolution of various forms of tension.
>
> (Singer 2000, p. 13)

Moreover, as other scholars have observed: "Property issues arise in interconnected physical, social, and legal environments. All indications point to legal connections that are complex, far-reaching in scope, multiscalar, dynamic and non-linear" (Arnold 2011, p. 167). Therefore, this chapter is similarly fundamental for later chapters as the framing from the previous chapters is to gain its import.

I begin by focussing on the time of the enclosures in England from before the time of Sir Thomas More, and through the era of John Locke (1632–1704), who was one of William Blake's infernal trinity and the philosopher who most influentially attended to those enclosures and to property in general. As the chapter continues, I string the literature along a line around the world, beginning in Australia then going across to Brazil and Peru and working up to North America, across to Eurasia, then down to Africa and back to Australasia and the Pacific.

The literature review includes a call from a modern Lockean scholar, James Tully (Tully 2008, vol. II, p. 72), for a twenty-first century political philosophy. I consider that call to be consistent with the evolutionary complexity trans-ontological process of this work.

The background

John Locke considered the state and property as being co-dependent (Locke 1764 [1690], ch. IX, §124). Beneath both the state and property is the commons, which Locke considered the natural state where every existent is owned by everybody. However, ownership becomes individualised by dint of a worker's input into the particular area of land. When the worker labours to put water in a bucket, the water becomes that worker's; when the worker works, plants or builds upon land, the worker can claim private ownership: Possession is nine points of the law. This same principle was applied by Locke (ibid., ch. V, §27) to land ownership.

The first chapter of one of the first popular science books about complexity theory has a crucial point to make about this assumption (Waldrop 1992, pp. 15–51). Entitled "The Irish Idea of a Hero", it relates the story of a founder of Complexity Economics, Brian Arthur (Arthur 2013) as he worked his way along what Hernando De Soto (De Soto 1989) described in a Christmas card to me as "the hard path of new ideas".

In Arthur's case, his idea was "increasing returns" (Waldrop 1992, p. 16), which was considered quite outrageously heretical by the economics establishment. Not against formalism, but against "formalism for its own sake" (ibid., p. 44), he had noted that tiny events could have massive consequences – a subject of another early popular science book, *Chaos* (Gleick 1987). *Chaos* popularised Lorentz's "Butterfly Effect", using the observation that the flap of a butterfly's wing in Brazil could set off a tornado in Texas (Lorenz 1972). Arthur did not see economics as flowing from some crystalline structure of laws and principles. He saw it as path-dependent, complicated, evolving, open and *organic* – that is, holonic-centric, not artefact-centric, starting from "small chance events" and becoming magnified by increasing returns. Just like bushfires, his economics processes can start from a single spark in the right fitness landscape, but do not start from every spark. Arthur sees this process as endemic in economic functions, and unaccounted for in classical economics (Waldrop 1992, p. 17).

Network studies are tracking Arthur's "positive feedbacks", much of the work being termed "The Matthew Effect", after the quote from the Gospel of Matthew saying "to everyone that hath shall be given" (Mt 25:29) (Merton 1995; Perc 2014; Waldrop 1992, p. 17). For the current narrative, I see increasing returns from locked-in historical events as being magnified by positive feedback flowing from that tiny initial assumption of Locke's. That firstly focussed on the individual – *not* the community of that individual – and then went straight through to commonwealths. Locke stated that "The great and chief end, therefore, of men's uniting into commonwealths, and putting themselves under government, is the preservation of their property" (Locke 1947 [1689], p. 184).

With reference to the former input-for-ownership idea of Locke's, he ignored scales of identity construction. He did not differentiate as to who the person acted for when taking the bucket of water. For example, he did not consider that the person that took that bucket of water from the river might have done so as a member of a family or a community.

Consistent with Blake's characterisation of Locke as one member of his infernal trinity, in Locke's single vision he only looked at it from one scale, that of the individual, assuming that individual to have an indivisible identity. Locke's focus on the individual was "unfriendly to claims of special rights for particular groups" (Russell 2006, p. 6). However, an individual can identify with families, sports teams, communities, commonwealths and governments, carry water on behalf of any of them, and have intra-individual divided loyalties and priorities.

Moreover, Locke's building block approach not only involved an unarticulated hierarchy of such a commonwealth concerning property; his age was unaware of the co-evolutionary dynamics of hierarchies and meshworks (DeLanda 1998), or holarchies and heterarchies. In seeing the event as an isolated individual doing it, and not enfolding such other levels of identity construction, Locke performed an act known as "anchoring" in behavioural economics (Kahneman 2011): becoming fixed on a possibly completely unrelated number as a reference point to address a situation. That anchored term then became the beneficiary of confirmation bias, and then set a snowball rolling that started an avalanche that spread throughout not only Britain, but also the British Empire (Lesjak n.d.).

Over a century before Locke's time, the Spanish and the Portuguese European used warfare technology and law to conquer Central and Southern America (Russell 2006, pp. 31–42). The British and the French set out with even more developed technology to conquer North America. The enclosures having provided the cheap labour to drive the industrial revolution, the extrinsically valuable but intrinsically trivial wave of mechanistic warfare and science had Locke's ideas ride upon it.

For both good and ill, that complex of waves, that multifaceted avalanche, swept over all sorts of other forms of holding real property that had evolved to address the fitness landscapes of the subjugated societies. Nevertheless, not all of them drowned, and they often formed an intrinsic part of the identities of the subjugated peoples. In these days, following the end of old empires, they are surfacing again.

Current property rights analogies

In the field of property rights law, one manifestation of this machinist, Lockean approach to real property was Henry Maine's "bundle of rights" approach to property law, wherein he traced the development of real property rights from status to contract, from communal to individuated tenure (Maine 2007, p. 59). He referred to individual tenure as a *universitas juris*, a university (or bundle) of rights and duties united by the single circumstance of their having belonged at one time to some one person. Thereby he saw it as the "legal clothing" of some given individual. He did not see it as formed by grouping together just any old rights and duties, but only constituted by taking all the rights and all the duties of a particular person (ibid., p. 60).

Here Maine, like Locke, was entirely focussed on a person. However, by thirty years after Maine's book, corporations were ensconced in law as persons too, artificial persons as distinct from natural persons, so at that stage corporations as persons could hold rights that communities could not unless the community incorporated itself.

We cannot blame that gap on Maine. Like us, he was a creature of his time. Maine's time was that of the second industrial revolution (Landes 1969), which was one of applied mechanics pervading the zeitgeist. That mechanistic zeitgeist broke wholes into parts, put them back together, and found them to work. That is a result rarely achieved with people, including the progenitors of concepts such as property rights as being, analogically, a bundle of sticks. However: "If a question is ill posed, ill stated, if the premises from which it issues cannot be accepted – then a direct answer to it will automatically be tantamount to falling into error" (Panikkar 1989, p. 11). In turn, once that snowballing error stream goes out into the fitness landscape, it is there subjected to the same processes that Brian Arthur describes. In that process, whether or not it is true may be less important than whether or not it suits agendas.

Hohfeld was another creature of his time: "As Albert Einstein published his theories of relativity, Wesley Hohfeld identified eight fundamental legal relationships, *each of which transformed itself in relation to the others*" (Andrews 2001). I have emphasised the comment to signal a possibly wicked problem resolution application, such as HVN↔HBA below. Hohfeld's eight fundamental legal relationships are shown in Table 3.1.

In the legal profession, these eight fundamental legal relationships remain to this day as a means of coming to grips with legal complexities. As with analogies (Czarniawska 2013, p. 17), even false dichotomies can be useful as interrogational entry points, providing those adopting them are capable of avoiding confirmation bias, which is much more difficult than generally recognised (Allahverdyan and

Table 3.1 Hohfeld's eight fundamental legal relationships

Jural	Opposites	Correlatives
Right	No-right	Duty
Privilege	Duty	No-right
Power	Disability	Liability
Immunity	Liability	Disability

Source: Andrews (2001)

Galstyan 2014). In fact, Mercier and Sperber hypothesised that the Enlightenment's god of Reason, what William Blake called Urizen, the mythical progenitor of "single vision and Newton's sleep", is effectively the servant of confirmation bias in its manifestation as what they term "myside bias" (Mercier and Sperber 2017). They see it as an argumentative faculty, often leading to "epistemic distortions and poor decisions" (Mercier and Sperber 2011, p. 57).

If Mercier and Sperber are correct, we can regard Maine and Hohfeld as reasoning within their mechanist confirmation biases. Maine's analogy and Hohfeld's relationships have both been widely adopted as orienting generalisations to understand property rights. Therefore, with Maine we can speak of that original bundle having the sticks of title, possession, selling and leasing being with the owner. The sticks of mineral rights, air rights etc. are with the government, those of occupancy rights are with a tenant; and so on.

However, that approach misses a great deal, both inside that zeitgeist and outside of it. For example, inside the zeitgeist a "bundle" says no useful existent about the differences between structure and organisation pointed out by Maturana and Varela in *Tree of Knowledge* (1987, p. 47). They articulate a more developed view, noting that organisation can remain while structural materials change, and vice versa. Moreover, modern scholars such as Di Robilant (2013) implicitly suggest moving beyond that zeitgeist insofar as they use the analogy of a *tree* of property rights – that is, a living organism of property rights instead of a bundle of static sticks.

In reviving this mid-twentieth century concept, Di Robilant noted that comparative property law is still a largely unexplored field, and claimed that a model was required that could better balance the social and individual elements of property (ibid., p. 907). It should also better account for the complex structure of property rights, and highlight "the wide range of values and interests implicated by ownership of different resources" (ibid., p. 909). Di Robilant further suggests that just as the branches share the trunk of a tree, property rights share a duty to perform social functions and duties concerning basic resources such as land (ibid., p. 931). Finally, she adds that a weakness of the analogy is that it does not give proper weight to the fact that property entails coercion (ibid., p. 931).

From the above-made distinctions, I would add that property rights are not holons like trees; they are abstract artefacts. However, as such they are still produced by holons, and thereby the analogy has at least as much legitimacy as does a bundle of sticks analogy and, I submit, a good deal more usefulness if applied from HVN↔HBA, because trees, like the law, are living, changing existents from a relatively consistent core.

All of the above, however, is intra-Western, and the range of this book is not. The crude insertion of Western-based modernist concepts on alien fitness landscapes has been criticised by Bromley as "the wrong prescription for the wrong malady" (Bromley 2008a). He condemns the advocacy of formal titles as imposing "ideational hegemony", notes that the rich often lack the conceptual space to imagine that the poor may *not* want to be just like them. He adds that a transplant of complex alien cultural practices and laws from one complex environment to another may not take and, just like an organ transplant, be rejected or "rarely work as imagined". He further notes that to think they will work as imagined is extremely naïve (ibid., p. 26).

I note that we may predict such attitudes from Mercier and Sperber's hypothesis of reasoning being the servant of argumentation from one's confirmation/myside bias (Mercier and Sperber 2011, p. 57).

However, that rejection of change is not necessarily so. After all, there have been successful transplants of many other cultural practices. For example, rap and hip-hop have penetrated cultures very different from those from which they sprang. One does not have to have the cultural background that developed a vehicle or a TV in order to use them, and one does not have to have the cultural background that developed vaccinations to benefit from them either.

That is not the only reason. Complexity science adds another scale of understanding to Bromley's insight that complex alien cultural practices and laws cannot work as imagined. It is also because, unlike artefacts, no complex existent can survive stasis for any non-trivial period. Bromley recognises that in his 2008 paper, referring to all legal arrangements being "evolved – and evolving – manifestations of a complex pattern of scarcities, priorities, power relations and local circumstances" (Bromley 2008b, p. 26).

Yet our minds need simplicities – heuristics or ansatzes – as an entry point for grappling with complex realities: "We cannot function without categories" (Eisler 1995, p. 305). The trouble is, while operating from inside Arthur's observation and confirmation bias we automatically draw them from the existing arsenals in our identity construction. Rather than looking with fresh eyes at a problem, as Krishnamurti had recommended, we resort to our previous experience of what works where we come from. So it is that Maine's "bundle of rights" manifestation of Lockean thinking still forms the initial framing of many current works, and thereby enboxing their perceptual space. For one example, see *Land Tenure Property Rights and Natural Resource Management* (USAID 2006).

Bromley is not the only voice raised against this modernist imperium (Arnold 2011; Fairlie and Boydell 2010; Boydell, Sheehan and Prior 2009; Boydell, Sheehan, Prior and Hendy 2009; von Benda-Beckmann, von Benda-Beckmann and Wiber 2006). Arnold diagnoses seven major flaws in The Machine's bundle of rights metaphor (ibid., pp. 175–176), the third being that "it disconnects property as an abstraction from its context" (ibid., p. 175). That is, it is an example of Blake's single vision, as painted by him in the portraits of Urizen and Newton in this book's introduction. Arnold concludes that the metaphor is therefore "ill-equipped to address the complex, multifaceted, and sometimes highly unpredictable impacts of nature and its processes and humans and society" (ibid., p. 176), and suggests a "web of interests" as a far more useful metaphor. I add that the inter-relationships between humans, society and nature at the scales addressed in this work make the bundle metaphor even less fit for purpose in this broader and deeper domain.

Property as a bundle of abstract legal rights with each right taken in isolation (Maine 2007, p. 59) acknowledges that a property right exists as a relationship between many entities with respect to a central property object (Arnold 2002; Zellmer and Harder 2007). The Web of Interests acknowledges the continuity of property elements such as land.

Another metaphor, the "Constellation of Rights", enfolds the relationships that exist between people, between people and objects and that these relationships may interact (Boydell, Sheehan and Prior 2009; Boydell, Sheehan, Prior and Hendy 2009; von Benda-Beckmann, von Benda-Beckmann and Wiber 2006).

These analogies do not exhaust the attempts to develop a better description. Once again, Anna Di Robilant (2013, p. 875) noted that "property is increasingly becoming a constellation of resource-specific regimes", but instead of taking the constellation model further, as mentioned above she revives a "Tree" model of property. That model had its foundations laid by French jurists in the beginning of the twentieth century, but had most of the craft work done in 1930s Italy.

Di Robilant (2013, p. 878) characterises the bundle of sticks model as regarding property as:

1   a set of analytically distinct entitlements,
2   relational in nature,
3   a bundle both assembled and backed by the state, and
4   a malleable bundle.

Di Robilant then characterises the ownership model as facilitating:

1   analytical clarity,
2   an efficient delineation strategy, and
3   insights into the morality of ownership.

Di Robilant (ibid., p. 891) also refers to yet another analogy created by the need for a better approach to property law. Merrill (2011) suggested replacing the Bundle of Rights analogy with a Property Prism, such as a glass tetrahedron, each side representing a class of persons, with the prism sending a colour message to them. For example, red for strangers – "keep out" – amber for potential transactors, green for persons inside the zone of privacy, and white for neighbours (white light containing a spectrum of potential colour messages) (ibid., pp. 250–252). Merrill's paper opens the rich vein of natural law tradition going back to medieval times, which emphasised the morality of ownership and exclusion because of the natural law obligation of self-perfection – the same morality that drives HVN↔HBA – and observes that the prism analogy "tells us that property is not a formless collection of random rights but has an inherent structural integrity whose shape can be explained by ideas like information costs" (ibid., p. 252). It concludes by dismissing the bundle of rights as "a primitive analogy, conjuring up a medieval peasant carrying a faggot of wood" (ibid., p. 252).

These analogies provide insights into the complexities addressed by this work. However, I see them all as exclusion strategies. Looking at some existent through one lens excludes looking at some existent through another one. As such, each can be "a convenient starting point, a rough first cut" (Di Robilant 2013, p. 891), but as with any ansatz the idea must be taken lightly so as not to fall prey to damaging confirmation bias.

One question to be addressed is "if they had been around at Locke's time, which of these if any would have allowed Locke to have addressed the community ownership level in his examples, not just the individual level?" Another issue is, as Arthur explains, that seemingly trivial events can have massive consequences. While we cannot identify all such trivia at their birth, we can some, and we can monitor and evaluate others as they emerge – providing the monitoring and evaluation methodologies are not confined to the monological gaze that led to the problematic blindness in the first place. What model, if any, can facilitate that awareness?

That question brings me back to Australia.

Australia

In addition to Ruhl's observation that the fundamental reductionist principles that underpin current legal institutions are a fantasy (Ruhl 1996), others have pointed out the monological nature of juridical thinking (Uhlmann 2001) and contrasted it with other approaches. For example, Armitage (2011) compares it to a questing humanist approach, seeing the former is monological, universalist and transcendent, and the latter as dialogical, contingent and critical. Sidebotham's point that "in relation specifically to land, the law excluded (and excludes) relationships with land that are different from its own conceptions of ownership", but Aboriginals' ways of relating to land emerged in Australia and "*cannot* be expressed in a form understandable by the law" (Sidebotham 2009, p. 54). I stress the word "cannot" because their real property rights approaches emerged from their own fitness landscapes, not England's.

Also in 2009, Sarah Maddison wrote a book on being within Aboriginals' complex political culture (Maddison 2009). I was a member of the audience at her book launch in Darwin and later wrote to her that I was writing this work as part of a complexity-based approach to related issues. I remarked that it requires a kind of thinking that is "a major departure from traditional science" (Finlay-Brian 2013), looking at how parts and systems relate to each other and interact to form a whole, rather than just looking at one part or system at a time. From this wide perspective, I particularly emphasised the limitations of prevailing Western approaches when attempting to introduce "our" forms of land tenure into the "developing world".

In developing the approach I described to Maddison, I found a book called *Do Komo* (Leenhardt 1979). On page 102, he states that a more culturally relevant approach than those prevailing:

> Has to result in a wholly different sociology from our own, based on rhythm and not on number, on the cadence of oscillation and not on quantitative measurement, and on the play of relationships between elements whose symmetry is revealed over time.

That is, an approach more like Tupaia's than Captain Cook's. Leenhardt wrote that in 1947, well before science established that the generally bicameral nature of the two hemispheres of the brain was along similar lines. Leenhardt does not leave that as a dichotomy, though. At the book's conclusion, anticipating McGilchrist (2009) by decades, he highlights myth and rationality as being "two complementary modes of knowledge", and asserts that "primitivity lies here, in this aspect of unilateral thought, which, by depriving man of the balance between two modes of knowledge, leads him into aberrations" (ibid., p. 194). That is, primitivity lies in single vision.

I take that undervaluation of myth *as a facilitator of the development of an identity's intrinsic value* as being a major reason why the Aboriginals' ways of relating to land cannot be expressed in a form understandable by the law. Within the Arunta culture for example, the whole landscape is one's "living, age-old family tree", with the stories of one's totemic ancestor being of what one's own identity did "at the beginning of time", saturated with ancestors who "for a brief space may take on human shape once more" (Strehlow 1968, p.30). As with other mythical level thinking in any culture (Sallustius in Murray 2003, p. 195), perhaps Aboriginal dreamtimes never happened literally but always are really, because the origin is ever present via the HVN: the instant we pin something down in writing, reality has already moved on. Westerners may immediately condemn that as ridiculously irrational, while failing to question the rationality of their own identity constructions.

From Maddison's book, I came to see both single visions as dangerous. The primitivity of myth without rationality as being the attractor dangerously dominant in her narrative of black politics, and the other attractor, rationality without myth, as being the even more dangerously dominant pole in Western politics. As Leenhardt put it:

> If the primitive had given himself up to the mode of knowledge provided by rationality alone, he would have . . . pursued his logical work to exhaustion, disgust and death. What is more logical than the organization of so-called total war?
>
> (Leenhardt 1979, p. 195)

Moreover, rationality without myth is integral to the reductionist fantasy. As Kay emphasises by placing the observation at the conclusion of the third of three parts of his book, with only his conclusions to follow: "By downplaying genuine practical knowledge and skill in pursuit of a mistaken notion of rationality we have in practice produced wide irrationality – and many bad decisions" (Kay 2011, p. 168).

From Leenhardt's (1979) framing, the "bad decisions" *as such* contributed to the disastrous two world wars, both of which began in Europe. Narrative, which is inevitably mythic in terms of its cherry picking of isolated incidents, also happens to be intrinsic to the scientific endeavour (Sheehan and Rode 1999): "The bottom line in science is narrative" (Lissack and Graber 2014, p. 192).

Leenhardt's co-evolutionary observations are consistent with my broader evolutionary framework. I see the interplay of the bodyself with socio-environmental challenges in a particular environment as how we construct our identities. That process involves interplay of all our minds' centres, with those centres reacting as if they were the ones most appropriate to address those challenges – often, alas, falsely.

Furthermore, there is no basis for claims of species exceptionalism in such behaviour. One cannot expect chickens to transcend pecking orders. Nor can we expect humans to do so without development beyond the primitivities of myth and rationality that Leenhardt described. Such development only happens by means of the process he described. That is, by dynamic engagements of myth and reason within a fitness landscape (and, I would add, by a broader range of knowledge than those two forms, because we possess several more than he knew of then).

For all our sakes, somehow we have to transcend the traumas that life has imposed on us. Not just Aboriginal identities, but those of all oppressed and oppressing peoples, which in the case of Aboriginals and of many indigenous peoples throughout the world had colonisation as a major factor. As Greer (2012, p. 385) as well as McAuslan (1985, p. 19) observed, the main business of colonising was to dispossess the indigenous and impose new property regimes (Greer 2012, p. 385). In consequence, addressing tenure is one aspect of facilitating development of those peoples' own higher levels of identity than that of their own tribe, religion, nation, or whatever unbalanced monological memeplexes may dominate their identities for now.

In the Middle East, traumas are now just as potent in this identity conflation as they were 1,000 years ago. In terms of absorption of a cultural identity, there is no reason whatsoever to consider that such traumas fade over time. Moreover, as Mandela pointed out, the victims are the oppressors, as well as the oppressed (Mandela 1994).

Although I did not realise it at the time, this was the background of the – sometimes quite spirited – discussion I had with Patrick McAuslan over dinner at the Calabash restaurant in Swaziland in 1997. I contrasted the fractal nature of Swazi social organisation and other African societies (Eglash 1999) with British common law, and suggested a parallel with the individual ownership of land in various systems, and ownership of land by nations. Speaking from within his Hohfeld-based juridical framework this was dismissed outright by Patrick, who quite rightly pointed out that nations have a different order of rights, most particularly that of eminent domain, so the comparison is illegitimate. Within his framing, that was true. Beyond his framing, his comment was partial to the point of being a non-sequitur.

If we were to continue that debate today, I would point out the above distinction made by Armitage. I would also state how necessary but how necessarily insufficient juridical frameworks are in policy formulation and implementation. Therefore, what is quite right within a juridical framework is not necessarily quite right beyond it, especially interculturally. Seen from other cultures the magisterial claims of law are every bit as much a fantasy as the reductionist and positivist premises that they are based upon, which was referred to by Russell (2006, p. 30) as "Western Imperialism and its Legal Magic". Moreover, however blind to them, legal magic is subject to the processes described by Arthur, the reductionist fantasies described by Ruhl, the inflationist ones described by Land as well as conflationist ones, the falling into error via answering inadequately framed questions as described by Panikkar, and the dynamics as described by DeLanda. It can also be highly pernicious in legitimising human suffering, as described by Veitch (2007). From within The Machine as distinct from Aboriginal culture, Crockett wrote in Melbourne over 70 years ago:

> The law-of-property which permits the private appropriation of community-created values is an unjust law. All rent is community-created value. Its appropriation by land "owners" is a public wrong, the original and greatest public wrong, the first and worst betrayal of common rights, the fundamental error in our law of property.
>
> (Crockett 1943, p. 144)

As Machiavelli put it, when it comes to governing the artefact of a Princedom:

> There are two ways of contesting, one by law and the other by force; the first method is proper to men, the second to beasts; but because the first is frequently not sufficient, it is necessary to have recourse to the second. Therefore it is necessary for a prince to understand how to avail himself of the beast and the man.
>
> (Machiavelli et al. 1997, p. 83)

Like anyone, jurists should know their role in a social artefact's fitness landscape, and know that while it is an essential administrative one they have higher responsibilities as well. These include being humane. There are good reasons for the separation of powers into legislative, executive and judiciary in Western states (including facilitating their co-evolution). There are similarly good reasons to differentiate and value the magisteria of the juridical, the humanist, and other responses to fitness landscapes in the contexts addressed by this work.

In the above discussion of models, Maine's bundle of rights still fits the positivist, reductionist, juridical tradition, whereas Arnold's and Boydell's looks beyond it, engaging in discussions of trans-juridical concepts including meaning (Boydell also in Nugapitiya, Boydell and Healy 2009; Beyer 2015), and looking towards integrating "GIS and spatial components alongside social, economic and legal information".

Does their constellation model really provide the conceptual space to achieve this? They make no such claim, instead tabling it as a first step along a path, a contribution to a work in progress. In looking for a more inclusive ansatz they are presumably also being careful not to miss some existent, which was crucial at the very beginning (as I claim Locke did). I further claim that our steps are along the same questing humanist path as that of political philosophers looking for a distinctive twenty-first century philosophy. Tully (2008) states that such a philosophy should combine the wisdom of the owl (in understanding where we are by understanding where we have been) with that of the raven, looking towards a transformative journey into our unknown future. As such, any existent staking a claim to being such a philosophy should test its robustness in the face of these wicked valuation problems.

When so doing, the philosophy must be able to understand and address the Aboriginal cry used as the title of Sidebotham's thesis (2009): "white man never wanna hear nothin about what's different from him". William Blake would have agreed, but added that the white man's ignorance is not necessarily racially based, but a result of their education down into "single vision and Newton's sleep". That Aboriginal cry not only echoes down in history: a great many of the colonised people in the world also could still repeat it when it comes to their own takes on these wicked valuation problems when NSEW meet, including the colonised minds in the West.

I now proceed to listening for echoes of that cry in many of the places I have referred to above.

South America

In South America, academics are proposing a similar basic approach to that which I stated when I embarked upon this book to address real property rights in the commons. Called the *integral approach*, Meyer (2008) applies the works of Chris Cowan – one of the co-authors of Spiral Dynamics (Beck and Cowan 1996) – and Ken Wilber (1996) to revisit the dilemma of the commons.

The similarities begin with the very first sentence – "How we frame the enquiry into any subject has decisive implications". Meyer then engages with the works of Elinor Ostrom towards describing an approach informed by Clare Graves (1981) and Ken Wilber. He then presents Graves' Emergent-Cyclical Levels of Existence Theory (ECLET) (Graves 2005) as a lodestone for implementing the prime directive for institutional change or intervention, that being if it is to happen at all it should be for awakening human potential – that is, human development – and that awakening has a path tracked from egocentrism to universal concern. Meyer further recognises that for that to happen it must be geared to what I describe below as the Goldilocks Zone part of HBA of everyone concerned (Meyer 2008, p. xviii).

In so doing, I see Meyer's approach to his task as complementary to my approach, especially when I embarked upon this work. However even though the original approach is similar, Meyer's thesis differs significantly in objective, scope and contribution to knowledge from that of this book. Moreover, this book has developed in unexpected ways since. Even so, for now Meyer's approach remains the closest I have found to this work in its core approach. While Meyer and his colleagues continue to develop their approach (Meyer and Braga 2009, 2009a, 2011, 2015; Meyer, Costa, Figuerdo and Braga 2013), thus far I have not found further discussion of Meyer's thesis, let alone further development, in the broader literature.

There is another approach originating in South America that has achieved far wider currency than Meyer's, that being the approach of the Peruvian economist Hernando de Soto (1989, 1993, 2000) and the Greek institutional economist Elena Panaritis (2007), whose first project on enabling property markets to work was located in Peru. De Soto saw the "missing ingredient" (De Soto 1993) as the recognition of de facto informal property rights de jure. These formal recognitions could then be traded, consequently have market value, and in further consequence then be used as collateral for loans, thereby considerably magnifying the potential for the human development of the beneficiaries. De Soto referred to these formal property rights as '*the* missing ingredient', not 'one missing ingredient', or 'the silver bullet', as some of his critics have averred (Bruce 2012; Van der Molen 2012).

As H. L. Mencken once observed: "Explanations exist; they have existed for all time; there is always a well-known solution to every human problem – neat, plausible, and wrong" (Mencken 1921, p. 158). On the other hand, a mechanist could retort: "If the missing ingredient in a car is the fuel, the car goes nowhere; if it is the brakes, the car might crash. Property rights are artefacts, like cars, and can therefore be analysed like machines can." While that is so, people are not artefacts; they are complex holons, where the application of machinism is only analogical. However, it can still be very useful but like fire makes a good slave but a terrible master and within single vision, it can become a master.

Comments upon De Soto's ideas have been both highly charged and varied. Strongly promoted by many of those applying a mechanist ontology to this field including Armitage's juridical monological, one-size-fits-all juridical framers, those who oppose it can be generally characterised as having Armitage's "questing humanist" approach, with its dialogical, contingent and critical framing, critical of any hegemony of representation balanced with an emphasis upon evidence as being more persuasive than ideology. Van der Molen (2012) has collated a literature review and summary of the critiques. These critiques allege that De Soto neglects that:

1 Experiences that show titling does not work.
2 Legal roles of customary tenure and management even exist.
3 Access to land is skewed in many countries.
4 Formalising land tenure is not as simple as just confirming informal tenure, as often the land was stolen.
5 Governments sometimes could not care less for their poor and are otherwise dysfunctional.
6 The poor are not homogeneous, but have vastly different circumstances and degrees of poverty that require individual solutions (Van der Molen 2012, pp. 6–7).

Despite the varied but all still significant degrees of legitimacy of the above critiques (and others that De Soto's assertions are not sufficiently evidence-based, and that the projects he cites in Peru did not achieve the results De Soto claimed) Van der Molen concludes that "much is left from the ideas of De Soto" (ibid., p. 9), and recommends a more gradual approach, an evolutionary one. I consider this recommendation to be consistent with Okoth-Ogendo's approach (which he referred to as 'ladder tenure' when conversing with me in New York after I presented at a tutorial of his at New York University), and that HVN↔HBA would facilitate determining when that was appropriate, and tracking its implementation.

Furthermore, at the top of Okoth-Ogendo's ladder is a pot of gold (or sometimes, as described in Hudson 2006, a golden poison chalice): The availability of finance. This is often viewed as one missing ingredient towards lifting people out of poverty; in this context, Grameen Bank's micro-finance is necessarily insufficient. Van der Molen (2012) notes that much titling is to facilitate credit from banks, which makes no sense where there is no banking sector in place. When the banking sector is allowed to co-evolve, it comes with its own rules, which are born of much practical experience.

From whatever mortgagor we are referring to – an individual, a household, tribe, community, trust, or corporation – there are three requirements for banks' due diligence. For them to engage in commerce with you, you need the three C's: cash flow, collateral, and character. The first is about servicing loan repayments, the second about security and thereby lower interest rates, and the third about trust, and requires reasons to trust that the loan will be repaid. There can be no commerce with anyone, not just banks, without a sufficient degree of trust (either between the parties, or in a system of recourse if one party proves untrustworthy). Moreover, any deficiencies in the desired degree of security on any one of these can mean that the bank will not grant the loan, or that a higher rate of interest will be required to compensate for the risk. The supposed beneficiary will then be handicapped in competition against those with lower interest rates available to them.

Banks have had their fingers rather badly burnt when departing from the three Cs, including in the developing world, and are not inclined to forget or forgive. Their duties lie elsewhere. When it comes to collateral, it is only of use to them if they can sell it or otherwise utilise to recover their losses, and that can mean the dispossession of the mortgagor. So, if the loan were to a community, that could mean the bank might have to evict the community, which politically no bank would readily countenance, meaning no loan. Security of tenure is only relevant to obtaining finance insofar as if a mortgagee takes possession it can get its money back, so security of *fungibility* is vital for finance. This is a matter that would require a complexity-based inquiry in general, and HVN↔HBA at both the philosophical and technical levels in particular.

North America

As far as technical implementation of HVN↔HBA goes, the most facilitatory approach I have yet discovered in this literature review is from further north, in the United States of America. However, it is from a South African now working there; one who had to address similar challenges at a similar time in South Africa to several I faced in Swaziland. Called *Talking Titler: Evolutionary and Self Adaptive Land Tenure Information System Development* (Barry et al. 2013), it would be a key instrument to facilitate HVN↔HBA developing from a trans-ontological process into an ontology appropriate to the local circumstances. Like HVN↔HBA is a tool for addressing wicked valuation problems, so talking tenure is a "tool for prototyping different designs and for developing land tenure information systems using evolutionary strategies" (ibid., p. 1) which emerged from practical experiences in peri-urban areas. While "flexibility in creating relationships between people and between people and their interests in land has been the primary design feature" (ibid.), it has uncovered a Goldilocks Principle problem (see Chapter 5). That problem is that the simpler the system, the more likely it is to be used, but also "the less likely it will provide an adequate model of complex tenure situations or address wicked problem situations, and, in a worst case scenario, it may exacerbate an already troubled situation" (ibid., p. 10). I therefore envisage a potential interface between HVN↔HBA's addressing wicked valuation problems, and talking tenure both alerting users of the HVN↔HBA to wicked problems, and being a means of better addressing them.

In so doing however, any user of such an instrument should recognise that although Sidebotham's (2009) observation that Aboriginals' ways of relating to land can't be expressed in a form understandable by the law, it could be immensely useful in the HBA context, but only providing:

1   it is realised that the final step on that journey can never be taken;
2   that every input is obsolete as soon as it is done;
3   it is framed in very different ways to actual human behaviour; and
4   it is deficient in being blind to Arthur's processes (at least in their early stages).

Each of these realisations are consistent with the evolutionary and self-adaptive nature of Barry's approach.

The USA provides several rich veins of literature for this review, the three main lodes I have mined being the World Bank, the Lincoln Institute of Land Policy, and the University of Wisconsin–Madison. As mentioned above, much of the literature there is still based upon developments from Maine's ansatz rather than either Arnold's or Fairlie's and Boydell's (USAID 2006). However, the veins are so rich there that for almost every example we could find a counterexample. Both the integral approach and much of the complexity and chaos sciences had their genesis in North America.

My familiarity with that fitness landscape began with a meeting I had with Professor James A. Graaskamp in the foyer of the Reserve Bank in Adelaide in the early 1970s. Unfortunately, while the James Graaskamp Landmark Research Collection has a record of his 1984 trip to Australia it does not have a record of that early 1970s one. Yet he made a statement to me at the time that has stuck with me ever since. He said that *valuation is a behavioural not an empirical science*.

I mention that as a personal example of Arthur's observation of tiny events having massive consequences. In this case, that applied within my own identity construction and my approach to valuation ever since. In particular, it has led to my emphasis on identity matters, and behavioural economics, in this book.

Graaskamp also lamented the absence of a theoretical foundation for valuation broad enough to include all that it requires (DeLisle and Worzala 2004), an absence that was addressed by Boydell (2007a) and which catalysed my embarkation upon this thesis. Without making reference to Graaskamp, as mentioned earlier its absence was also lamented by Cannone and MacDonald (2003), who suggested a new, five-disciplined science to be called "Timology" to address this absence. While I agree with that contention, I consider that the disciplines should be more complexity-based, not based upon reductionist, inflationist or conflationist fantasies. As such, they may yet emerge from a combination of the emerging disciplines of Valuation Studies (Helgesson and Muniesa 2013) and Complexics (Bastardas-Boada 2015).

As pointed out by Davy (2012 p. 90), "understanding and managing land values is indispensable for land policy if policymakers wish to promote a better use of the land". While Davy (2012, 2014) recommends a polyrational approach to that task – one considering many variables from many different domains and disciplines – following Cannone and MacDonald (2003) I consider that a "polytimological" or more precisely a "complexity telaxiology" approach is required as well. This is so complexity epistemology and complexity telaxiology might engage in a co-evolution within HVN↔HBA (McDermott and Boydell 2011).

That is, following Commons (2007, 2008), Graves (2005), Wilber (1995) and Meyer (2008), I add emergent levels to all the many rationalities the prefix "poly" is intended to enfold by Davy. Similarly, I add emergent levels to all the disciplines envisaged in Cannone's and Macdonald's proposed new science of Timology. I also add them to the constellation of property rights model suggested by Fairlie and Boydell.

Professor Graaskamp has had several illustrious successors at the University of Wisconsin Madison, two of whom, John Bruce and Dan Bromley, are of particular import to this work. I met John Bruce several times in the context of African land policy development. In 1987, Bruce published an overview of land tenure in all the countries of Africa. There have been updates since, but the 1987 is still largely correct.

Just as McAuslan (1985, p. 19) observed about Africa, the story of European conquest in North America was also basically about land tenure. As such, it contained several similarities to the colonisation of Australia and the Pacific, with consequent tenure concerns there (Yunupingu 1997; Lundsgaarde 1974; Crocombe and Meleisea 1994; Crocombe 1987; Greer 2012). One commentator noted that "among all the ways in which his values differed from the white man's it was between their respective attitudes towards land that there yawned the widest abyss" (Van Every 1961, p. 40). My understanding of that North American conquest is of it being opposed, in part, for similar reasons to its opposition to the imperium elsewhere. Namely, a visceral rejection of Locke's idea of ownership. Many considered the very idea of private land ownership "preposterous", and reacted with the abhorrence that added zest to the atrocities they perpetrated upon settlers (ibid., p. 41).

Among the fiercest defenders of their lands were the Apaches, and their attachment to land was succinctly stated by an Apache interviewed by Keith H. Basso as *Wisdom sits in Places* (Basso in Feld and Basso 1996, pp. 53, 67, 70; Basso 1996), a view which Basso predicts "may be found to exhibit transcultural qualities" (Feld and Basso 1996, p. 87). While Basso has been criticised by Ball (2002) for his Western philosophical interpretations of what the Apaches said to him, I find that ethnographically informative as well, and Ball does not question the veracity of his ethnography. Neither does Ball question the role of land emphasised in Basso (Feld and Basso 1996, p. 86) in Apache identity construction (Ball 2002, p. 462), nor that land is "the primary referent for all formulations of meaning and value within the culture" (ibid., p. 465).

Basso quoted an Apache rubric to their children: "Drink from places, then you can work on your mind" (Feld and Basso 1996, p. 76). That working is to be towards wisdom, and "it's difficult!" (ibid., p. 66):

> You will need to think about your own mind . . . You must make your mind smooth . . . steady . . . resilient . . . You must learn to forget about yourself . . .
> How will you walk along this trail of wisdom? Well, you will go to many places. You must look at them closely. You must remember all of them . . . then your mind will become smoother and smoother.
> (Feld and Basso 1996, p. 70)

Basso interprets a smooth mind as being uncluttered, unfettered, unobstructed, allowing them to "observe and reason with penetrating clarity" (ibid. p. 74): a quality which I recall as similar to that recommended by Krishnamurti.

I have seen evidence of the transcultural nature of attachment to land not only throughout my travels, but also within myself with respect to my former home on the Esplanade. Basso notes that senses of place are far from uniform within us, either in nature or intensity, "and that pervasive fact is part of what makes it interesting" (ibid., p. 84). It is complex, and it is complax: it is difficult, but worthwhile. It already existed in Strehlow's study of the Arunta (Strehlow 1968), and in the northernmost range of Tupaia's Polynesian culture, the USA's island state of Hawaii. There, Trinidad (2014) has proposed a Critical Indigenous Pedagogy of Place (CIPP), including indigenisation and reinhabit-ation, re-establishing sources of wisdom from place as a means of re-sowing the seeds of indigenous identity and flourishing and cure *cultural loss syndrome* – "deep grief and sorrow rooted in . . . collective sorrow and moral outrage" (ibid., pp. 2 and 5).

The visceral approach of indigenous North Americans was not on one side alone. While not verified in any scholarly journal, only by a tape recording, whether or not it is true the following report of a comment made by Ayn Rand in an address she made at West Point neatly encapsulates an alternative view:

> They didn't have any rights to the land, and there was no reason for anyone to grant them rights which they had not conceived and were not using . . . What was it that they were fighting for, when they opposed white men on this continent? For their wish to continue a primitive existence, their "right" to keep part of the earth untouched, unused and not even as property, but just keep everybody out so that you will live practically like an animal, or a few caves above it. Any white person who brings the element of civilization has the right to take over this continent.
>
> (Rand 1974)

Rand has a still powerful following in the USA, and her statement was consistent with Locke's approach to ownership. Compare that with a comment in that country's 9/11 report: "Terrorism against American interests 'over there' should be regarded just as we regard terrorism against America 'over here'. In this same sense, the American homeland is the planet" (National Commission on Terrorist Attacks Upon the United States 2004, p. 362).

In any sense, any social imaginary anthropic machine whose controllers consider it owns the planet in any sense at all qualifies under this work's area of concern. Compare this with a comment of Rabindranath Tagore, made well before Rand's: "[Western Nationalism] tries to pass off the cult of selfishness as a moral duty, simply because that selfishness is gigantic in stature" (Tagore 1994, p. 861). He adds that such an approach "not only commits depredations but attacks the very vitals of humanity" (ibid.). That smacks of William Blake's referring to the Satanic state of mind's strategy as being to teach "Trembling and fear, terror, constriction; abject selfishness" ("Milton", line 35 in Blake 1988, p. 188). Stannard (1992) provided an account of the costs of such visceral attitudes as Ayn Rand's "abject selfishness" prevailing in the USA.

I emphasise that, whether it is the USA's homeland or not, similar attitudes are present everywhere on the planet, because they are states of mind. They include but are not limited to those targeted in the 9/11 Commission Report, because every human alive enfolds the "rigid, obsessive, compulsive, ritualistic and paranoid" (Maclean 1990) characteristics of the reptilian brain, and is by nature inclined to engage them when insulted, be that insult directed at one's person, or through some "thing" one identifies with, such as a pet dog, a sports team, or a nation-state. In particular, that state of mind conflates the insulting person's state of mind with the whole person, a single vision blunder which in Blake's terminology is "the error of Ulro" (Blake 1904, p. 10).

Here, I stress that Rand's views were not those promulgated by the British Crown. In 1763, King George III issued a Royal Proclamation recognising the land rights of the Indian nations over those lands not expressly ceded to, or purchased by, the Crown (Russell 2006, p. 47), forbidding direct acquisitions by private individuals of tribal lands. The Crown's representatives convened a peace council, attended by about two thousand chiefs representing over 24 nations, at Niagara. This treaty was opposed by many settlers, one of whom was George Washington, who had wanted to sell Indian land to settlers, thereby providing another contributing motivation to the United States' war of independence some 12 years later (Calloway n.d.).

Like King George III, Phillip II of Spain also instructed his subjects to respect indigenous property rights, and as with elsewhere the colonists largely ignored those instructions (Greer 2012, p. 380). Many of those land claims, and others, are now being revived in the USA (Dunbar-Ortiz 2015). In this process of colonisation Greer also points out that Locke's description of it being one of enclosure of open commons was "anything but an innocent mistake" (ibid., p. 385). Rather, it was yet another instance of tendentious reductionist fantasising, this time of a fantasyland like Australia's *terra nullius*.

Locke's America "existed mainly in the imperial imagination" (ibid., p. 372). In dramatic contrast, Greer's overview of precolonial tenure in North America indicates, "America was a quilt of native commons" (ibid., p. 372). It further observed that it was the colonialists' commons that were the major facilitator of destruction of indigenous commons – "the prime instrument of dispossession" (ibid., p. 382) – with enclosures following in their wake, leaving practically no room for the indigenous inhabitants. Watch, watch, land concessionaires!

Moreover, that happened alongside the sort of population explosion of Europeans in North America (ibid., p. 378) similar to that of rabbits, foxes and other introduced feral animals in Australia. As with Australia, America's was a multi-species colonisation, with the European introducers and many of those species triumphing over time over the native populations.

Despite the riches available in North America, it is from my experiences in and reviews of literature from Asia that the addition to Fairlie's and Boydell's constellation model seemed to me to be more suitable to this HVN↔HBA. Because of the already dominant Western ontology, I specifically did not want the model to be of an exclusively Western origin.

Europe

European real property law varies widely, but for overview purposes has been divided into five families:

1   The Code Napoleon system (France, Belgium, Italy, Luxembourg, Portugal, Spain).
2   Common Law systems (England and Wales, Ireland, Scotland in many respects).
3   The Nordic countries.
4   The Eastern European states.
5   The German systems (Austria, Germany and Switzerland) (Schmidt, Hertl and Wicke 2005, p. 8).

Generally, real property law throughout Europe developed as various blends of tribal and feudal laws with Roman law. The word "feudal" is cognate with "feu", meaning a loan for use. In such systems, all land is owned by the relevant monarch, with the loan to be repaid by taxation (for example, a proportion of the crop) or by military or other service. The feudal system spread through Europe in the sixth to eighth centuries, eventually arriving in Britain with the Norman Conquest.

While it changed in Europe during the Enlightenment, the British system of freehold developed from conquest. The Crown remained the ultimate owner, but it granted the right for the land to be held free and forever. While Roman law had preceded the feudal system throughout much of Europe, it was revived to succeed the feudal systems via the great codifications of the 19th and 20th centuries (Schmidt, Hertl and Wicke 2005, pp. 11). When the Europeans became colonial powers, Roman law provided a different basis of ownership than either the indigenous or the common law systems did. For example, South African real property law is from a Roman-Dutch base, with Roman Law ownership as distinct from freehold.

The Western conception of ownership has been articulated into 11 rights (Honoré 1987), summarised in Table 3.2. Other systems beyond Europe may have different articulations, but may still be considered to be ownership in the system concerned.

Table 3.2 The Western concept of ownership

To possess	To control something to the exclusion of everyone else without your permission
To use	To personally enjoy and use the property
To manage	To maintain, lend, share, lease etc. the property
To gain income from the property	By working on the property, or gaining investment returns from it
To the capital	By selling, mortgaging, harvesting, destroying or otherwise using it to gain reward
To security	To retain ownership, or not have it taken away without just compensation
The incident of transmissibility	To be able to transfer it to another or others
The incident of absence of term	The right remains in perpetuity
The duty to prevent harm	The property right must not be used to harm others, even when another has the owner's agreed possession of it
The liability to execution	Owners are liable for their debts, and their property can be seized if needs be for the debts to be paid
The incident of residuarity	Repayments are prioritised according to the nature of the claimants (mortgagees etc.) to a property

Source: Honoré (1987, pp. 161–162)

The EU has not attempted to harmonise land law in Europe. Reasons include:

- It is generally recognised as reasonable for different states to have their own land laws.
- The land law of a state can only be understood in the general laws of the state.
- Land law is static. Mostly, the laws were sorted out in the nineteenth century.
- "In land law, as generally in property law, there is not only a channel, but an ocean between the continental systems on one side and the common law systems on the other side" (Schmidt, Hertel and Wicke 2005, p. 8).

Because these points in general, and the third in particular, are relevant not only in Europe but also in the countries to which the colonists exported their respective laws, I consider that they are of crucial note in creating a practical trans-ontological process for the purposes of this work.

Another aspect I am highlighting from within this review of Europe is the evolution of the abovementioned "tree" concept of property rights. The jurist Salvatore Pugliatti developed this aspect from within Fascist Italy. He did so for the specific purpose of resisting the absolutist Fascist concept of the state and providing an alternative to it (Di Robilant 2013, pp. 900–901). Pugliatti did so from his belief that property, more than any other existent, reflects the social and historical environment (ibid., p. 911), and wanted to make land available to all (ibid., p. 913). From my HBA perspective, "reflects" is too passive a word. Rather, it shapes much of the physical and social environment for good or ill, including wicked valuation problems such as those this book addresses.

With reference to the "identity" part of HVN↔HBA, a paper by Douzinas (2002) gave a significant boost to the development of my understanding of the importance of identity in addressing such wicked problems. The paper also first alerted me to the fact that Hegel had thought of my regard-recognition hunger model of identity construction long before I had, and that recognition of one's property rights is tantamount to an identity confirmation. As a corollary, the non-recognition of such rights is tantamount to an identity devaluation, dehumanisation, and oppression. A contemporary of Hegel's, Adam Smith, held a similar view (see Box 3.1).

At the identity/land nexus, many scholars in Europe besides Douzinos have made significant contributions to the subject of this work. As Hann (2007, p. 309) noted, there have been few disruptions in the history of humanity's land tenure as the ructions caused by the communists' abolition of private property and collectivisation, followed by decollectivisation and restitution following communism's collapse. From that experience, lessons have emerged that are similar to those upon which I base HVN↔HBA and which differ markedly from communism, fascism and the Western neoliberal paradigm.

Hann praises the development of Maine's "bundle of rights" into that which has been referred to as the constellation of rights, as manifested by von Benda Beckmann and Wiber and credited by Boydell and Fairlie above. Hann (2007)

Box 3.1   Adam Smith on regard-recognition hunger

In one part of his *Theory of Moral Sentiments* Adam Smith (1790) had limited regard-recognition hunger to that for *good* regard, the hunger to be loved and be lovely (ibid., III.I.8). Elsewhere in *Moral Sentiments*, Smith realises that a dark manifestation of that hunger in others, envy, can be harnessed to enrich those able to manipulate the others to their benefit:

> And it is well that nature imposes upon us in this manner. It is this deception which rouses and keeps in continual motion the industry of mankind. It is this which first prompted them to cultivate the ground, to build houses, to found cities and commonwealths, and to invent and improve all the sciences and arts, which ennoble and embellish human life; which have entirely changed the whole face of the globe, have turned the rude forests of nature into agreeable and fertile plains, and made the trackless and barren ocean a new fund of subsistence, and the great high road of communication to the different nations of the earth . . .
>
> (Smith 1790, IV.1.10)

I shall term this deception as employed by Smith, "Smith's smokescreen". Such tendentious sentiments condoning greed and envy in his work on *Moral Sentiments* grounded his later work *The Wealth of Nations*. However, in *The Wealth of Nations* he excoriated the British East India Company (Smith 1904) not by dint of the rapacious and corrupt behaviour of its employees, but by the dreadful destruction they, through it, wrought in India by its structural problem, by its very nature as a monopolistic joint stock company. He referred to such companies as "nuisances in every respect" (ibid., IV.7.194) and called for a waking up from their "golden dreams" of Empire (ibid., V.3.92). Instead, he recommended that they liberate colonies and trade with them, but also recognised the futility of his counsel (ibid., IV.7.152; Muthu 2008) against greed, envy, and vanity.

In India itself, the company would have been regarded by philosophers there as a vessel of samsara, just as it was, in his own way (by recognising the deceptive nature of the hunger), by Smith. To apply a comment by Wilber to our samsaric regard-recognition hunger, it: "is driven forward endlessly, searching in the world of time for that which is altogether timeless. And since it will never find it, it will never cease the search. Samsara circles endlessly, and that is always the brutal nightmare hidden in its heart" (Wilber 1995, p. 316).

Or, as Adam Smith's contemporary William Blake put it, "More! More! is the cry of a mistaken soul; less than All cannot satisfy Man" (Blake 1788). Such actions cause oppression. Therefore, like Smith's insights, analyses made back in Latin America by Paolo Friere in his *Pedagogy of the Oppressed* (1972) are still applicable. They include that a person's ontological vocation is to act upon and transform the fitness landscape towards a fuller and richer life for that person and that person's companions. Friere further noted that fitness landscapes are dynamic and we should engage with them to that end (Friere 1972).

Smith's smokescreen was to conceal that insight, and his success continues, with the secret of China's economic success being the introduction of a market economy and modern copy of his *Wealth of Nations* (Wang and Christensen 2015, p. 16). At the same time, it ignores or devalues public values such as the environment and social equality, and controlling political corruption (ibid., p. 13). If Wang and Christensen are right, the Chinese have fallen for the smokescreen that Smith built the *Wealth of Nations* upon.

describes it as being able to facilitate rigorous interrogation of how the private ownership "obsession" results in land policy failures, and how it can address the second of the six conclusions of Adams et al. below, concerning knock-on effects (ibid., p. 310). He calls for "more flexible property rules" (ibid., p. 289), questions whether the Western paradigm is sufficient to understand all humanity (ibid., p. 289), and argues for a "wider compass", noting the fractal nature of African tenure (ibid., p. 292). He also notes the need to consider emotional attachment to the land, morality and justice (ibid., pp. 294, 303), and other identity-related aspects considered in HVN↔HBA, including those such as Siberian hunters, whose cosmology strongly links their identities to the natural environment and expresses "a strong moral economy" (ibid., p. 297). Like Sidebotham, he asserts that titles "can never exhaust the social complexity of property relations" (ibid., p. 301). His review concludes that there is a need for "a new focus on the concept of value".

Moreover, like Leenhardt above, Hann recommends a Melanesian world view as being more suitable for thinking about property, and ownership in general, than the neoliberal one (ibid., p. 307), and that it is time to "abandon the seductive reductionism of the standard liberal model" (ibid., p. 308). In this, as mentioned in my introduction, he can find support from many modern heterodox economists, who at the high level share the following differences with neoliberalism's close relative, neoclassical economics. For example, Karagiannis, Madjd-Sadjadi and Sen (2013, p. 18) state that: "Neoclassical economics makes eight basic (but false) assumptions that lead them to an alternative formulation of democracy", whereas heterodox economists generally agree on a different set of tenets (Table 3.3).

From these and many other scholars, it is safe to conclude that in a land policy context it is time to devise more competent approaches to all those tasks, and I have designed HVN↔HBA as being a robust means of finding the best approaches for the particular circumstances.

Table 3.3 Differences between neo-classical and most heterodox economists

	Neoclassical	Heterodox
1.	Neoclassical economics is value free	Economics should be value laden
2.	Individuals act in their own rational self-interest	Individuals are *Homo sapiens*, not *Homo economicus*
3.	Markets self-equilibrate	Markets need assistance from governments to operate
4.	Markets move is an orderly fashion	Markets move chaotically
5.	Markets are naturally efficient	Markets are inefficient
6.	Markets are non-coercive	Markets are systems of power
7.	Property rights are sacrosanct	Property rights are granted by government
8.	Efficiency is the proper and virtually exclusive criterion for evaluating market versus state action	The choice between market and state must take into consideration questions of equity and access and not just efficiency

Source: Karagiannis, Madjd-Sadjadi and Sen (2013)

Asia and the Pacific

It was in Asia that HVN↔HBA began to emerge from the above base, firstly in Palestine in 2007, then in Indonesia, Vietnam, East Timor, Pakistan, Azerbaijan and Afghanistan. All of these consultancies involved recourse to academic literature. From the Philippines (Connolly 1992) through to the Mediterranean, there is an uninterrupted vista of less than optimally functioning property rights regimes. The literature reviews are therefore integrated into the overall narrative of this book. While the same applies for the Pacific, there is one book of particular relevance to this work in that it reviews territorial categories and institutions in the Austronesian World – a world populated by about 270 million people and covering a large proportion of the Earth's surface. Entitled *Sharing the Earth, Dividing the Land*, it is dedicated to:

> All the people of the Asia Pacific whose land has been alienated in the wake of colonialism, modernity and development, and whose traditional insights into human beings' relationship with their physical environment have rarely received the serious consideration they indisputably deserve.
>
> (Reuter 2006)

My contribution to that deserved consideration is, as described in Chapter 6, within my developing HVN↔HBA. For I consider those peoples for whom *Sharing the Earth, Dividing the Land* is dedicated have a more robust means of addressing wicked valuation problems in that:

> In many contemporary societies in the Austronesian world, one therefore finds a complex layered patchwork of territorial and other social institutions that can be traced to various stages in a historical movement towards

ever-increasing complexity. I will later return to the question of how relevant Austronesian territorial categories still are in the context of complex
modern nation states with rapidly globalising economies.

(Reuter 2006)

Africa

When returning to Africa, the best resources I have found to gain a high-level
understanding of the fitness landscapes of the different countries are the Common
Country Assessments of the UNDP. For land policies and real property rights
(and their valuations but not their market valuations), John Bruce's *Country
Profiles of Land Tenure in Africa 1996* (Bruce 1998) was a vital resource. Other
highly relevant overviews include those of Barume (2014), on indigenous land
rights in Africa, Payne (1997) concerning urban land, Liz Alden Wily (2000)
concerning forestry and tenure, and Palmer (2007), which retains the broader
geographical focus – albeit lower market value focus – on rural land. Lombard's
literature review (Lombard 2012) focusses on land tenure in the context of urban
conflict in general, not Africa in particular; but it still has much of value to say
towards the HBA approach in this book.

When conducting that review, I concluded what Davy (2012, p. 165) pointed
out: that many authors see the strength of human rights "mostly in moral strength
or public discourse", as distinct from intra-judicially. I consider that, while still
useful, Armitage's (2011) humanist/juridical distinction is an oversimplification
in the African context. In the parts of Africa I have direct experience in, neither
humanist nor juridical approaches are dominant in governance: Many other
agendas prevail. Moreover, there are few people I have met who have such high
humanist virtues as McAuslan, whose juridical approach was made manifest in his
facilitation of Tanzania's land policy by means of an 800-page law, but he also
recognised that social legitimacy is essential (McAuslan 2003).

In particular, he railed against the World Bank's approach to land as monologi-
cally gazing upon land as an extrinsically valuable ingredient in economic performance, thereby devaluing, even ignoring, its intrinsic values in facilitating social
relations (ibid.). It thereby also pays scant regard to what Payne observes: how it
"excites intense emotional and psychological attachment in a way that services,
materials and finance do not" (Payne 2001), which I attribute to its role in identity
construction.

With McAuslan's broader than merely juridical view, in his last book (McAuslan
2013), he observed that the juridical approach is not dominant in Africa at all.
In fact, he strongly asserts it to be an essential missing ingredient, but does not
thereby imply that it is the only one. Armitage had pointed out that this distinction was particularly unclear in empires. Armitage also noted "the difficulty even
Tully experiences in making claims on behalf of indigenous peoples without
falling into juridical language" (Armitage 2011).

This African component of the literature review establishes that so far there
are no effective responses to Okoth-Ogendo's challenge. In fact, as Dan Bromley

has observed, there has been major institutional decay in rural Africa such that information costs and the costs of arranging and enforcing contracts are too high to facilitate forward-looking economic behaviour (Bromley 2008, pp. 540–541). However, this review also reveals that there has been some limited progress to that end.

One of the monitors and evaluators of that progress is Martin Adams, who facilitated South Africa's land reforms under Mandela, recruited me for Swaziland, and worked with McAuslan and me in Lesotho. For many years, (even after I left Swaziland) he would ask me to contribute news from Swaziland to an annual review of land policy on the continent. Recently, with Rachael Knight he has contributed chapter 3 of a book specifically about "re-conceiving property rights in the new Millennium", and "looking towards a new sustainable land relations policy" (Chigara 2012).

Adams and Knight's chapter begins with reference to a paper that Okoth-Ogendo presented in Cape Town in 1998 (Okoth-Ogendo 1998). They use that paper as a starting point for their analysis of developments and setbacks since then, and point out that, while there has been both progress and setbacks since that 1998 paper, in the main stasis has prevailed.

The conclusion of the chapter is incisive. It mentions six main matters that require correction:

- Designing policies without adequate attention to how they can be implemented.
- Looking at problems on a problem by problem basis, without consideration of unintended consequences and knock-on effects.
- Inadequate or no consultation with affected parties at various or all stages of the process.
- Inadequate attention to the financial implications of implementation.
- The conservatism and lack of capacity to manage change of government land agencies.
- Underestimating the time frames required and losing momentum and political support when the time frames blow out.

I was already familiar with them all, and they have informed my design of HVN↔HBA.

While that was one chapter in the book, the book editor's major conclusion, and thereby an important and current consideration in addressing Okoth-Ogendo's challenge, is an initiative called PECAPDISHD (Chigara 2012, p. 221). PECAPDISHD stands for addressing the "pedagogical counter-apartheid-rule psychological distortions on the significance of human dignity". In other words, like HVN↔HBA its main focus is on remediating abused identity constructions. While consonant with (and referencing) Friere's *Pedagogy of the Oppressed* (1972), it seeks to transcend the oppressor/oppressed level in the way that Mandela expressed both in his book *The Long Walk to Freedom* (Mandela 1994) and in his governance.

The PECAPDISHD initiative is to comprise three steps: educational campaigns by the relevant governments and donors, drafting of supporting legislation, and the implementation of that legislation.

The Peace and Reconciliation Commission under Mandela's governance was consistent with William Blake's solution to man's disintegration, which was via reconciliation through forgiveness (Stevenson in Blake 1988, p.15). However, it did not arise from Blake, but on a major value already present in the region. Variously expressed and nuanced, it is generally known by its Bantu term, *Ubuntu*, meaning, "the humanity/humaneness in me recognises the humanity/humaneness in you", in stark contrast to the trope that one becomes more manly by behaving like a brute: rather, you then become a brute. Therefore, without Ubuntu a person is only "semi-authentic" (Chigara 2012, pp. 223–224), a so-called "tough guy", not a real man, and that a person can only become a real person through other persons. Generosity is considered an indicator that a person has become a real person. It is therefore not within the capacity of everyone to realise. Like I consider that Nora Bateson's "mutually alert care and attention to the wellbeing of all people and ecological systems . . . [which] requires the integrity of having gone through the dark night" (Bateson 2017) has homologies with Ubuntu, and that it is similar to the Buddhist loving kindness that is the philosophy behind Vairocana's Tower. Developing loving kindness was what Borobudur was intended to facilitate (Kwee 2010). I intend the HVN model to carry Ubuntu through to its applications via HBA in addressing the wicked valuation problems that are the concern of this work.

It is also what Walt Whitman in his *Song of Joys* called "the joy of that vast elemental sympathy which only the human soul is capable of generating and emitting in steady and limitless floods" (Whitman 1860), and what Western humanism and Leenhardt's balanced development were meant to facilitate. As it requires an evolutionary process from being only semi-authentic to becoming a vessel of Ubuntu, it is particularly cognate with evolutionary humanism (Huxley 1954, p. 20; Smocovitis 2014).

As such, it may require more than the three recommended steps in order to implement it in a population. According to some developmental psychologists (Commons 2007; Graves 1981), the co-evolutionary dynamic described by Leenhardt and other such co-evolutionary dynamics may take decades to achieve in a person, and may not manifest at all in some cases. On the other hand, manifesting loving kindness is hardly a rarity. How can the addressing of wicked valuation problems enfold elemental sympathy?

That question needs to be addressed from the various perspectives of the individual, the community, and social imaginaries such as the state, and their respective powers and stakes in the matter at hand. Following on, once those likely consequences are identified, how can one see how they can be best addressed? Ubuntu will not be enough; wisdom in its application will be required. Machines do not have Ubuntu. Insofar as they manifest as anthropological machines (Agamben 2004, pp. 33–38), in single vision and Newton's sleep, people do not manifest it either (Caufield 1998, pp. 60, 218, 229, 232, 296). Yet I agree with

Chigara about the need for Ubuntu in land reform, and in particular to address Okoth-Ogendo's challenges. I believe that great insight in its application will be needed to not only implement the three steps recommended in his paper, but also to determine what else is needed in which contexts, and how to skilfully implement the required measures.

As part of that insight, the HVN is to transcend the question of whether real property rights are intra or extra juridical, just as a city transcends the question. In so doing, it facilitates a framing for lessons learnt in one customary domain to be useful in another. For example, Bohannan's (1973) insights concerning African land tenure have been recently generalised to the Canadian Aboriginal context, in particular the Tsilhqot'in land claim (Jones and Barry 2016). They note that Bohannan defines land tenure not as merely judicial, but as being people's association between three concepts:

1   a representational map of how they relate to other people; and
2   a view of land as a thing that can be owned; or
3   a spatial manifestation of culture. (ibid., p. 8).

I consider the interface of groups regarding land as a commodity, a thing, and others regarding it as being "how social relationships are managed in the spatial context and lacks dependency on land ownership" (ibid., p. 9) to be very much a wicked problem context for the application of HVN↔HBA. Bohannan's original article concluded with the observation that:

> It is not enough to see "land-tenure" in terms of our own system. We must see it also in terms of the people who are approaching new economic and social horizons. And that very process makes it possible for us, as social scientists, to create what has in the past been completely lacking – a theory of land-tenure.
>
> (Bohannan 1973, p. 8)

To facilitate that, HVN facilitates the trans-juridical consequences of property rights. Further, in the telaxiological domain it implies that they are an emergent right by dint of the high intrinsic value of any human being, whether or not such humans possess high extrinsic or market value in a fitness landscape. As such, a more complex approach than the three steps may be more effective to achieve Chigara's splendid vision.

In 2012, Martin Adams led the team that wrote the FAO's *Strategic Evaluation Report on tenure, rights, and access to land and other resources* (FAO 2012). The report was to evaluate the FAO's recent work worldwide on tenure, rights and access (TRA) to land and other natural resources, and assess and develop recommendations on future directions and priorities for FAO's work in TRA (ibid., p. 12). Among its recommendations was a call for normative work informing the design of fieldwork, and for the fieldwork results to feed back into the development of normative products (paragraph 373). It looked to a more integrated approach (ibid., paragraph 374, for example by looking at the relationships between land-grabbing and deforestation). In sum how more attention should be paid to potential synergies in TRA work, and that we should "work together where it makes sense to do so; but don't force everything into one mould. There are plenty of differences and they need to be handled in different ways" (ibid., paragraph 389).

I consider that HVN↔HBA is well suited to address these and other recommendations of that report. For example, HBA would address paragraph 373 by reference to the co-evolution principle, and paragraphs 374 and 389 are at the very core of this book's approach to addressing these wicked valuation problems. Some lawyers seeking justice on behalf of those dispossessed observe that "local land grabbers are able to employ the apparatus of justice and law enforcement, sometimes violently" (Adonga, Ibreck and Bulla 2015), and claim that strengthening justice mechanisms is absolutely necessary. I add that even if such mechanisms functioned perfectly, they would still require valuations for compensation of the dispossessed, which would often involve wicked problems in such contexts. While the report makes sound recommendations, it does not say how to implement them. I believe HVN↔HBA would assist such a process.

If my abovementioned interpretation of Maddison's book is correct, then the emergence of Ubuntu still has some co-evolution to go in Australia. Clearly, persons on both sides possessed elemental sympathy, but it was neither ubiquitous nor robust enough to avoid terrible costs to the Aborigines. Nor is it yet so in much of the world, with similar costs to the oppressed on many fronts. There are also concomitant spiritual costs on the oppressor, in accord with the insights of Friere (1972) and Mandela (1994).

While thinking technically requires thintelligence, a narrow and specialised focus, those in The Machine still have their myths. As Bruno Latour put it, "lots of gods, always in machines" (Latour 2004, p. 247), and machines are extremely shallow in terms of intrinsic value. The scientific method locks out mythic thinking, but myths remain in our psyche whether or not we want them, or pretend them to be an "externality". Whether we are thinking big in the Bible or the Koran, Marx or Darwin, scientism or superstition, we think myth. In fact we live by myths (Samuel and Thompson 1990; Grant 1998; Midgley 2003; Byrnes 2012), adopt them in our identity constructions. Our own identity constructions and those of other stakeholders are therefore of core importance in addressing wicked problems when NSEW meet. For example, much of climate change and many other wicked problems are directly caused by artefact development, much of that development itself being driven via self-mythologising and thereby fragile identity constructions (Csikszentmihalyi 1981).

Back to Australia

Applying Thompson's insight, the two levels of meaning of the word "ontology" – the philosophical and the technical reality frames, the former for identity construction, the latter for computer programming – are homologous to this reason/myth dichotomy, and therefore could assist in addressing it. In returning to Australia, one returns to a property market being maintained by a well-functioning property market machine, with an accepting population, at least among the non-indigenous. Attempts to introduce that machine elsewhere include the works of Ian Williamson, whose machinism-based approach is typical in the North and West, and considered by powerful forces therefrom to be ideal for the East and the South as well.

An article to this end is by Jones (2013), which provides a link to a 2012 publication by Williamson, Enemark, Wallace and Rajabifard, *Land Administration for Sustainable Development* (2012).

As long as users of such approaches recognise that philosophical ontologies can transcend and include technical ones, then the recommendation that traditional land should be enfolded into land administration systems despite the difficulties (ibid., p. 143) has merit. However (as Sidebotham observed in the Aboriginal context), technical ontologies can never include all of philosophical ontologies (Sidebotham 2009, p. 54), any more than Blake's single vision can enfold two, three and fourfold vision. Therefore, it is more than a little problematic how this could be done and, I submit, HVN↔HBA or similar is needed to consider that "how", and the desirability of attempting that in the first place.

The book then proceeds to address land policy. Through the work of Payne (2001), it acknowledges that a monological gaze can never be sufficient in that domain, and proceeds to address the work of De Soto and recommend an evolutionary approach to the development of land markets.

The whole book "reflects the philosophy of Hernando de Soto" (Williamson et al. 2012, p. viii), and its philosophical ontology is developed from that, not from HVN↔HBA. However, it does contain elements of HVN↔HBA. For example, it notes, "the core ingredient of a complex property market is the cognitive capacity of its participants" (ibid., p. 158) – thereby recognising the need for a complexity epistemology and the development of "psyche" – the second of the six domains required for development to work in the HBA model. It also observes that such capacities require the articulation of "a broadly accepted philosophy and set of values to undergird the entire system" (ibid.), thereby calling for an axiology and an ontology.

However, its rightful focus in its context on the commodification of land ignores many of the pillars of HVN↔HBA. For example, HVN↔HBA looks to understanding and accommodating different sets of values, not just one. Despite making reference to the many complexities in the field, the book does not refer beyond the above for a different, complexity-based approach to address them. Nor does it recognise that from within such a complexity ontology there is a need for a complexity telaxiology to balance and co-evolve with a complexity epistemology, or recognise the need for a trans-ontological approach to allow the emergence of creative advances into novelty. Nor does it have any other references to emergence, or to other aspects of HVN↔HBA.

However, while not offering such an approach it does recognise values beyond merely market ones (ibid. pp. 132, 172, 186, 243, 391, 395), and observes that little research has been done on how to incorporate social and stewardship values into their approach (ibid., p. 156) – values which direct HVN↔HBA. It also recognises land's other roles beyond market-related ones, including in personal and social identity construction (ibid., p. 150), and that like other complex social and economic systems, land markets generate their own myths and shared understandings. In their context, that refers to thinking and talking about land as "mine" and "yours". The fact that "ours" is not mentioned is telling in terms of ignoring communal tenure. On the other hand, they recognise how we build land-related concepts and "embed these concepts in social behaviour, language, and the economy" (ibid., p. 160).

Similarly, it acknowledges the need to respect other ontologies: "how people conceptualize and value land needs to be documented. A full understanding can often take months, if not years" (ibid., p. 410). That came close to, but missed, Hann's (2007) and Sidebotham's point that technical ontologies can *never* include all of philosophical ontologies (Sidebotham 2009, p. 54). Finally, on its last page, about addressing the challenges ahead, it notes that the "idea of land as a mere physical object has been replaced by better appreciation of the cultural values and cognitive meanings of land" and looks towards a much broader understanding of the roles land plays in society and the economy (ibid., p. 465). That is, it looks forward to the emergence of twofold vision.

I therefore read the book as a looking out beyond from within its "toolbox approach" (ibid., p. 446) – that is, its mechanistic paradigm – and seeing the challenges ahead as being those which I have developed HVN↔HBA to address and addressing wicked problems, through that trans-ontological process. However, to me it seems to have only the first glimmers of recognition that the mechanistic paradigm is utterly incompetent to enfold others. I submit here that both levels of HVN↔HBA are necessary to meet that challenge, not either/or.

So I see Williamson et al. as true but partial: true in that little work has been done on incorporating social and stewardship values, but partial insofar as they may implicitly assume any magisterium of machinism. I have designed this trans-ontological HVN↔HBA process to address that gap. Furthermore, insofar as it is working from The Machine as being prime and other values being enfoldable within it, it has matters backwards in the manner described in McGilchrist (2009).

Conclusion

This literature review has revealed calls from the philosophical ontology level in the case of James Tully to legalistic ontology level in the cases of McAuslan and Russell to the technical ontology level in the case of Williamson et al. to look to a fresh, trans-ontological approach to address the complexities we face in the twenty-first century. Human valuations about land in the larger (trans-monetary) sense is a major feature, with many axiological systems internationally implacably opposed to the whole idea of private ownership of land, and hence land's commodification and market valuation.

In beginning to grapple with finding solutions, the literature looks to go beyond Maine's analogy of a bundle of rights, with a constellation of rights being tabled as a new step in that direction.

Chapter summary and the way forward

My valuation training is about valuing property rights over existents, and in my case that training has been overwhelmingly focussed on land. This chapter revisited some of the countries in which I have travelled, building on the general knowledge I gained from my earlier travels as described in the previous chapters to look more intensively at the real property rights in those places. I looked to those property rights as a valuer wondering how knowledgeably, prudently and freely those rights were acquired and employed, and whether the wisdom of hindsight can teach us anything about improving the fitness landscapes of the property rights there.

That revealed suites of wicked problems and social messes to me, a significant proportion of which (but by no means all) have emerged from the topic of this work, and in particular The Machine's facility in externalising costs while appropriating profits to its beneficiaries.

In looking forward, I contend that Arthur's new discipline of complexity economics and similar initiatives from other complexity-based sciences provide an entry point to engage with not only property rights but their fitness landscapes. I further claim that, with Hodge's enfoldment of values into complexity-based approaches, such engagements should therefore enfold Scheler's higher values via a return to the balanced mentality described by McGilchrist. That necessarily implies, because machines do not make markets but people do, and property is one of the five essentials in Mumford's myth of the machine, that revisiting property rights would be an essential part of addressing wicked valuation problems when NSEW meet.

However, in so doing, I stress that in transcending machinist thinking it would be equally essential to import Scheler's intrinsic valuations into the mix, thereby effectively valuing values in the context, including the loving kindness value of Borodbur, expressed in PECAPDISHD as Ubuntu, and in that vast elemental sympathy which, as Whitman noted, is accessible to all of us with the souls to know it and the wisdom to apply it. That requires Scheler's values to be no mere hierarchy of values, but complaxly integrated, working as an whole, holonically and heterarchically. That is not within McGilchrist's left hemisphere competencies; it is a means of the right hemisphere restoring the mastery of the left that McGilchrist advocates. The next chapters describe, based on all the above, how I think that challenge can be optimally addressed.

4 The new high-level trans-ontological process

Introduction

In this chapter, I am going to expand upon the sentence with which I began this book:

> The primary purpose of this work is to be a knowledge-building document which includes the knowledge that knowledge itself can never be enough to address the topic of this work.

In discussing the omniplex mind above, I quoted the first lines of the first chapter in the most prominent work of philosophical Taoism, the Tao Te Ching. While "the Tao that can be known is not the Eternal Tao" (Lao Tzu 1972) should now be apparent, for my purposes I must ask, "how much of the Tao of addressing wicked valuation problems when NSEW meet can be known?" And I must now further ask, "how much that cannot be known be engaged to address these wicked valuation problems?" From McGilchrist's framing (2009), another way of asking these questions is "how are we to optimally engage in tackling wicked valuation problems?" McGilchrist's framing concludes that to move towards not only broad but also deep vision and balanced judgement, we need more than the shallow, extrinsic values of the left hemisphere: we need to engage the deep, intrinsic values which are only accessible via the right hemisphere. As such, I see that emerging from the ecstatic interpretation of Whitehead's process philosophy, in the sense of being out, away from, static, and submit that process as being preconditional to Blake's fourfold vision.

Therefore, in this chapter I introduce HVN as a simulacrum for what McGilchrist ascribes to the functioning of the right hemisphere, which is to be McGilchrist's Master hemisphere, and not to be enfolded into the left hemisphere's magisterium. For that *not* to happen:

> attention needs to do something quite different. It needs both to rest on the object and pass through the plane of focus. Seeing the thing as it is depends on also seeing through it, to something beyond, the context, the "roundness" or depth, in which it exists. If the detached, highly focused attention of the left hemisphere is brought to bear on living things, and not later resolved

> into the whole picture by right-hemisphere attention, which yields depth and context, it is destructive ... Explicitness always forces this sheering away, this concentration on the surface, and the loss of transparency – or more correctly semi-transparency ... Metaphoric meaning depends on this semi-transparency, this being-seen-and-not-being-seen.
>
> (McGilchrist 2009, p. 182)

That is, HVN is a *purposefully non-explicit* metaphor to facilitate how may we bring all our capabilities to bear in that engagement via the right hemisphere. While the "model of the machine is the only one that the left hemisphere likes" (ibid., p. 98), "only the right hemisphere has the capacity to understand metaphor" (ibid., p. 115). HVN is meant to engage not only those capacities of the McGilchrist's Emissary (the left hemisphere), that can be known, but also bring in those of our own Masters, that cannot be known. But not only them. How do we engage the Masters and Emissaries in the minds of all those engaged with those wicked valuation problems, the Masters of which cannot be known by any of their Emissaries?

> The machine had for Fenollosa become an overarching metaphor for any system or formula designed to induce dissective, analytical thinking East or West ... the only means of defense against The Machine (whatever its form) were the synthetic, "artistic" ideals of Daoism and Buddhism, the very "core" of Eastern imaginative life.
>
> (Williams 2014, p. 100)

The natural sciences have been typified by some as machinist, exclusively composed of those imprisoned within the left hemisphere's single vision and Newton's sleep. Mythically, they are personified as Tantalus, who had a divine but hidden parent and a mortal one, and was condemned to always have the fruit he craved be just out of reach, and the water would recede when he tried to drink it. Once again, as Durkheim said, "to live is not to think, but to act" (Durkheim 1887), and the Tao that can be known, enboxed in some logically consistent abstractions, is not the eternal Tao. It completely misses life-energy, conflates complex with complicated, holons with artefacts, and is blind, deaf and dumb to the intrinsic value of living creatures. The myth of the machine simply doesn't get it. It never will get the Tao because it never can.

To rebut this machinist myth, this chapter draws from the natural science which the machinists claim is their citadel, physics. However much that may have been in the past – and even that is dubious – when it comes to genius in the sciences, Beer's interpretation of genius was manifest in many physicists of this and the previous century. For Beer, genius was at the other end of the spectrum from single vision: genius enfolding love, love enfolding energy, energy enfolding reason (Beer 1969, p. 27), and each having different qualities and needing entirely new laws, concepts and generalisations from the enfolded vision. For example, Einstein said:

I believe in intuition and inspiration. . . . At times I feel certain I am right while not knowing the reason . . . Imagination is more important than knowledge. For knowledge is limited, whereas imagination embraces the entire world, stimulating progress, giving birth to evolution.

(Einstein 1931, p. 49)

In that perception, Einstein was not just speaking like a Blakean; he was also speaking like someone whose two hemispheres were engaged in addressing the problems he was tackling.

While the answers for the unknowable cannot be known, but can be intuited and valued, the answer for the knowable part could come from the end of that first chapter of the Tao Te Ching: "Minuteness in minuteness is the gate whence comes the beginning of all parts of the universe" (Smarandache 2010, p. 433). That insight is as scientifically robust as anything single vision can provide. Modern science considers the beginning of the universe as coming from exactly that minuteness in minuteness, and Brian Arthur bases his complexity economics approach on that observation as well: "the alternative [to the Newtonian clockwork metaphor of classical, neoclassical and neoliberal economics] – the complex approach – is total Taoist" (Arthur, interviewed in Waldrop 1992, p. 330), and, as representative of the Tao that cannot be known, so is HVN.

Furthermore, we have now come to understand that:

We have reversed the usual classical notion that the independent "elementary parts" of the world are the fundamental reality, and that the various systems are merely particular contingent forms and arrangements of these parts. Rather, we say that inseparable quantum interconnectedness of the whole universe is the fundamental reality, and that relatively independent behaving parts are merely particular and contingent forms within this whole.

(Bohm and Hiley 1975, p. 102)

An example of complexity (Taoist) economics from property itself is the recent global financial crisis, where "seemingly minor changes can cascade in terms of property" (Davidson and Dyal-Chand 2010, p. 1639), and where the purported ascendancy of modern forms of property, "the humble single-family house . . . turns out to be central to the entire global economy" (ibid., p. 1640). American retirees saw the value of their pensions evaporate because of events in Maine and Bahrain (ibid., p. 1639). Consequently, a new way of looking at property is called for, away from a "reductive practical bundle" towards a vision that can include a perception of the holistic and interconnected nature of real property's environments. It should include real property's stability orientation, distributive protectiveness, its context and relativity, accommodation and community, "woven into an inextricable web" which facilitates community involvement in the management of that web (ibid., pp. 1611, 1638, 1645, 1652 and 1657).

Vairacona's Tower: a new analogy found in the East

Earlier, I referred to the influence Pirsig's *Zen and the Art of Motorcycle Maintenance* had upon me in my youth. In that work he had Phaedrus say: "Of course it's an analogy. Everything's an analogy. But the Dialecticians don't know that" (Pirsig 1974, p. 207). Analogies are used to show how seemingly quite different existents have similarities in the context under discussion. Metaphors such as the "clock-work universe" and "The Machine" are used as figurative subsets of analogies. Here, I introduce Vairacona's Tower as a metaphor to describe HVN.

In Chapter 1, I speculated that William Blake's confirmation bias would have caused him to misinterpret Tupaia's spirals as representing an awareness of infinity, the vortex serving as a gateway to a new level of perception (Antal 2013, p. 176). If so, for the autoethnographic narrative use I am making of William Blake in this book, he may not have been completely wrong. Gell noted that tattooing is about "the exteriorisation of the interior which is simultaneously the interiorisation of the exterior" (Gell 1993, p. 39), and the basic schema of Torbert's development action inquiry is similarly focussed on awareness of the interplay of one's interior with exteriors (Torbert and Associates 2004). Furthermore:

> The idea of culture-in-motion, arising from the interplay between time, place and human action, is thus the central idiom of Austronesians' "models of" their own societies, and of the cosmos as a whole.
>
> (Reuter 2006)

I consider this dynamic and complex interplay is a foundational part of what the Austronesians' traditional insights into human beings' relationship with their physical environment can contribute to addressing wicked valuation problems.

Of all the frames to approach those problems, the most useful one I have found at the global scale is *Vairocana's Tower*. Borobudur was built in Java as a manifestation of that Tower.

"Vairacona" means "Universal Light" (Miksic 1990, p. 23). Vairocana's Tower is a model developed in the Hua-Yen school of Mahayana Buddhism:

> Within the tower there are hundreds of thousands of towers, each one as exquisitely adorned ... and each one, while preserving its individual existence, at the same time offering no obstruction to all the rest.
>
> (Loy 1993)

It is "fractal-like – a tower with many recursive towers within towers" (Jackson 2004, p. 34).

Like Indra's Net (Loy 1993), like Arnold's web of interests, every component of the net contains and reflects every other part, all existents shining, just as when you address one aspect of a wicked problem it has consequences in other aspects. Towers have hierarchical levels, which makes this a preferable model for my current purposes because complexity has levels of emergence, and Indra's net is silent on those. Furthermore, the Hua-Yen school bears notable resemblances to Whitehead's philosophy of organism (Odin 1982, pp. 1–6). However, there are crucial differences, albeit not core to this application. What is crucial in this context is that they both, like this HVN imagery, are attempts at syncretic harmonisation patterning within fields. The Hua-Yen school sees sunyata transcending and including all ontologies, and for current purposes, it is best to regard all ontologies as heuristics.

As a Chinese-based Buddhism, the Hua-Yen school was influenced by Taoism (Oh 2000), which saw the world as being like fractals and Leibniz's monads: it assumes a holarchy where "every part reproduces the whole" (Fraser 1999, p. 83).

With the wisdom of hindsight, the genesis of HVN goes back within my own psyche to before those discussions with Hubert DeCleer at the Blue Star Hotel to watching the dynamics of those sunsets on the Esplanade at Somerton Park that were, in terms of the insights of complexity economics, a cause of my own genesis. I had mused that while the time of the sunset is precisely predictable, the precise nature and configuration of clouds that provide the show are unpredictably different every time.

Similarly, if you look deeply at a property right, you will see it is no stand-alone "thing", but part of a greater whole reproduced in it; that it emanates from connections having connections, and so on ad infinitum (Rucker 1997, p 142). Moreover, they are not static, as Borobudur had to be, but dynamic.

By that circuitous route – in itself a journey through Whitehead's process philosophy, a Taoist network of vortices, Dimitrov's re-conceptualisations of *vorticity* (Dimitrov 2003, pp. 43–54), a demonstration of a complexity economics approach and the other approaches referred to herein – I submit a pragmatic model that enfolds what I require as an ansatz for HVN↔HBA.

Knowing that:

- All the so-called hard facts of science "are informational transformations by the viscoelastic brain" (MacLean 1990, p. 5) but never "nothing but" that
- People "might think up fresh ontologies, but they are ultimately a mental climate" (Kenji, n.d.) but never "nothing but" that . . .

Developed from all the above, and compatible with and possessing the qualities of Vairocana's Tower *but being processual not static, a web of changes through time*, I am adopting a *Holarchic Vortex Networks within Heterarchic Fields* trans-ontological process (HVN):

> In the Taoist perspective, the world, that web of time and change, is a network of vortices like a moving and dangerous torrent of water; the ideal Taoist is a person who has learned to use all her senses and faculties to improvise the shapes of the currents in the world, so as to harmonise herself with them completely. Meanwhile, the person remains an individual, a unique individual, who owns her ever-increasing senses, faculties, and ways of representation.
>
> (Feuerverger 2005, p. 189)

These vortices and their heterarchical co-evolutionary mesh networks and their ADALAS (see Chapter 5) relationships represent the universe, with vortices ceaselessly emerging from ADALAS energy fields, relating and dissipating. Overton (2013) noted that the:

> Cartesian-Split-Mechanistic scientific paradigm . . . has been progressively failing as a scientific research program. An alternative scientific paradigm composed of nested metatheories with relationism at the broadest level and relational developmental systems as a midrange metatheory is offered as a more progressive conceptual framework for developmental science.
>
> (Overton 2013, p. 22)

Like Overton's model, I intend HVN↔HBA to assist in transcending the "Cartesian-Split-Mechanistic scientific paradigm", but I do not limit it to "nested meta-theories", but via intergrating HVN into the process to be spacious enough to enfold paradigms such as Overton's, metatriangulation approaches such as Lewis and Grimes' (1999) and others into a greater trans-ontological whole: a developed, structured, dynamic, ever-changing whole. I visualise it as the opposite in terms of development to heaping approaches together, but one differentiated, articulated and hierarchically, heterearchically and holarchically integrated by this HVN↔HBA approach.

As mentioned, Thompson (1989, p. 47) claims that to think big, as required by the HVN aspect of HVN↔HBA, it is necessary to think myth, and as stated by Diamond (2006, p. 186) models and paradigms are actually myths, and therefore so is HVN↔HBA. In this myth, HVN is engaging the landscape, metaphor and intrinsic valuations, as McGilchrist's Master, and HBA, engaging the machine, literalism and extrinsic values, as the Emissary: *emphatically not* the other way around as The Machine has it by, for example, considering the economy has domain over the environment.

One of the best known of ancient Greek myths is that of Perseus slaying the Gorgon Medusa. However, he was unable to slay other Gorgons who were considered immortal. Being immortals, according to this myth they are still around, and in a sense Medusa herself still is, that sense being within us: our having the capacity for Medusa's Gorgonic gaze. McGilchrist refers to the "Gorgon stare" of language, which is predominantly a left-hemisphere function (McGilchrist 2009, p. 225). He does so in the context of philosophy's difficulty of being obliged to grab and isolate from dynamic reality to focus upon and make explicit the now mental "object" from a by-then-past reality: "the faulty procedure of seeking truth by standing in the world of the left hemisphere, while looking at the world of the right" (ibid., p. 89). For current purposes, mythical creatures such as Gorgons can be interpreted as the interhemispherical grapplings such as this one McGilchrist mentions: those between themselves and the rest of the environment they are attempting to interpret from their respective dominant positions: the right hemisphere to understand and intrinsically value, the left hemisphere to manipulate and extrinsically value. As we are able to relate to people, so we engage our confirmation biases to personify forces we want to gain some control over.

To address this process more skilfully, McGilchrist interprets Wittgenstein as urging us to "get on with things" . . . "to be skilled participants in the life of the world as it flows (right hemisphere), not detached analysts of the process once it stops (left hemisphere)" (ibid., p. 222). Thereby, via HVN the right hemisphere's values are to be simultaneously brought in to address wicked valuation problems.

Compared to the West's emphasis upon the left hemisphere's mechanistic reductionist fantasies, I see this East-based model as facilitating a more pragmatic, realistic appreciation of the environment where wicked valuation problems are encountered. For this reason, I consider it unwise to further articulate the HVN. The risk of it being thereby "thingified", and thereby being frozen out from its natural dynamism by single vision (like a butterfly stuck to a board) outweighs any potential benefits. Pedersen supports this stance in warning against:

> The passive forms of many anthropological and sociological theories, which become fixed and therefore "dead" containers of sociocultural content and their purported political-economic context [when the reality is] dynamic assemblages of human and nonhuman life whose dimensions are constantly in the making.
>
> (Pedersen 2011, p. 36)

This fuzzy-to-us domain is also where wicked problems emerge. I mean HVN↔HBA to set the stage for their understanding to emerge as well. Therefore, the whole ontology is not merely HBA; it is HBA *enfolded within* the HVN trans-ontological processes with its heterarchic network relationships emerging from energy, which I designate HVN↔HBA.

That is, I intend the holarchic vortex networks within heterarchic fields (HVN) to enfold Bateson's pattern that connects *in a dynamic form*, with the HBA being the vehicle for that journey: "We do not think ourselves into a new way of living, but we must live ourselves into a new way of thinking" (Rohr and Martos 1992, p. 82).

I hope to address wicked valuation problems by finding not only new knowledges but also new valuations, exploring "the centre of our spiritual lives . . . in networks of living concern" (Taylor 2007, p. 743): that centre being in communities of engagement with wicked valuation problems: not simply within isolated selves. Using terms described earlier, the HVN is to be a Whiteheadean holarchic trans-ontological process, not looking as holons as things (artefacts) such as clocks and sticks, but as dynamic processes: Pirsig's dynamic quality, "the continually changing flux of immediate reality" (McWatt 1998).

To dip into Chinese philosophy once more, this time from Tai Chi: "The stillness in stillness is not the real stillness. Only when there is stillness in movement can the spiritual rhythm appear which pervades heaven and earth" (Ts'ai-ken t'an). It is no static "thing": as even matter itself comprises locked-in light, information and energy, it is *an energy-driven web of changes*, changes of greatly different existents, scales in time, space, and orders of complexity, relationships and interests. As such, it is a flip from an artefactual ontology to a holarchic trans-ontological process, seeing Indra's Net and Vairocana's Tower themselves as dynamic. It is "a knot of the unity of everything-there-is-alive, but also a 'vortex' within 'pulsating' life itself . . . in the context of plant–animal–human 'unity'" (Migoń 2000, pp. 15, 16).

In sum, I am submitting that this HVN framing based on Eastern (specifically, Chinese) philosophy is spacious enough for (left hemisphere, machinism-bound) Emissaries in the minds of all those engaged to value their Masters, even though they are unknowable by them, as necessary to optimally address wicked valuation problems. Once HVN facilitates that recognition of the (right hemisphere, and through it the Tao) Master, in the sense that values frame fact-finding and all but extrinsic values are their Master's domain, HBA can be fruitfully engaged via the Emissary.

The context of the HVN

The disciplines within physics closest to the study of HVN is not that of mechanics, but those of flows, processes, and turbulence containing among others fractal turbulent golden ratio flows (Li and Zhao 2013; Klewicki et al. 2014) and, heterarchically, energy cascades. They do not so much involve numbers as static "things", as in computer stimulations of complexity. Instead, they use mathematics as facilitating the making visible of dynamic processes, not seeing maths as a golden hammer, but differentiating between numbers as static and dynamic representatives, between digital and analogue. A real example is how the Fibonacci Series generates the golden ratio which appears at all scales in the manifest universe including "in high-energy physics, neutrino physics, and cosmology" (Li and Zhao 2013) and biology (Goodwin 1994, pp. 109–119; Stewart 1998, especially pp. 123–136).

The golden ratio (1.6180 . . .; Wells 1986, pp. 36–39), defines the most efficient rates of unpacking growth and emerges naturally in turbulence (Pierce 2017). Such processes make the world graspable by the left hemisphere, and aesthetically valuable to the right:

> The golden ratio may very well be a definitive characteristic of "design" in nature, architecture, and engineering (structural mechanics) as well as an important element of aesthetic expression in all of these areas.
>
> (Borges 2004)

As well as the golden ratio, there are many other "mathematical principles that govern which patterns will work. The universe discovered them because all the patterns that did not work failed to remain in existence" (Freeman 2016).

However, HVN↔HBA is not reducible to mathematics, physics, biology, or any existent observable by the left hemisphere (McGilchrist 2009). I mention them as analogies, because patterns can be found it all domains. Its "brain" is knowledge but its "heart" is valuation, and its whole body is a gestalt – more than both are, or the sum of all its parts. I intend it to facilitate not only Blake's single vision, but also his twofold and, through their related evolution, Blake's higher visions towards the related evolution of ever more skilfully applied wisdom and compassion.

As did Blake, I resort to works of art in Hodge's Complexity 4 to show what I mean. I do so because, as Gruss recognises, "the crucial early breakthroughs that lead to creative resolution of a problem are usually visual" (Gruss 2014). Some visualisations could therefore help explain HVN.

While Captain Cook's Enlightenment background looked at the world as clockwork machinery, the navigator Tupaia's view was probably more swirling and dynamic, as portrayed by those interior–exterior links, Polynesian tattoos. Similarly, HVN looks to nature's cyclones for its base visual imagery, always remembering that HVN involves all the hextants, in them and between them, as described in Chapter 5.

For my purposes, I see Captain Cook viewing a cyclone as an isolated thing, thintelligently, whereas I see Tupaia looking at it as an inseparable process in a greater processual whole.

Neither focus is "wrong", but the choice between them has major ramifications when it comes to addressing the wicked valuation problems that are the subject of this work. While directly applicable to extrinsic and systemic valuations, when it comes to intrinsic valuation, the phenomenon of emergence, presumably as unaccounted for by Tupaia as it was by Captain Cook, comes more into play because emergence arises from complex adaptive systems, vortices of gestalts of gestalts: it does not arise from machines. Machines don't get scared by cyclones, but people do.

HVN enfolds the advantages not only of the "constellation" and the "tree" models, but also emphasises property rights' radical engagement with their fitness landscapes, undermining or underpinning so much social, economic and environmental behaviour. Once again employing Gruss's insight, adding a time dimension can be visualised as looking down into a vortex, that spiralling dynamic with changing interrelationships in its dance with the holonic ontological framework determining its fitness landscape. That is, and crucially in terms of this book's thesis, vortices emerge not as isolated, atomistic "things", but from their environments' dynamics, including those from a butterfly effect far, far away.

HVN, land policy and property

As Long observes, in contradistinction to being "webs of interests", as some legal experts consider property, lay people usually think of property as "things" owned by persons. That is because things "serve as convenient referents, or proxies, for much more complex relationships", with thingness being "a mental model shared by a group of people . . . that reduces the cost of processing information" (Long 2004, p. 540). Consequently, this part focusses on the shared concepts housed in the left hemisphere of the brain (McGilchrist 2009).

That is, for our identities to engage with and manage an environment they need not one but several bases of stability. Our left hemispheres need some "things" (as distinct from processes and relationships) that they can rely upon, so they can plan proactively. They can then also address reality in manageable bite-sized chunks instead of being completely reactive to overwhelming challenges from all directions. However, Tupaia would observe that "thinging" is not the only strategy available to us inside our Goldilocks zones. That some assumed it as such appears to be more of an example of Western cultural confirmation bias than rational inquiry.

Identities at personal, social and cultural levels use the abstract artefact of a property right to engage holons at potentially differing depths and spans, with emergent levels from such activations relating in turn to other holons and artefacts. As such, they can be portals to a different world to nature's redness in tooth and claw.

However, a strong claim of this work is that any left-hemisphere dominant to the extent of *embeddedness* in "thingness" thinking inevitably reduces the complex to the complicated or simple (for example, by treating holons as if they were artefacts), and is thereby inadequate to address complex problems such as those encountered in land policy formulation and implementation by sufficiently skilful means. Western economics, law and science are artefacts, and we usually adopt their thingness thinking as extrinsically valuable, and therefore internalise and identify with them.

In line with Ruhl's (1996) characterisation of the law as reductionist, a judge pointed out in *Daubert v. Merrill Dow Pharmaceuticals, Inc.*, that "rules are not designed to provide cosmic understanding, but rather to resolve legal disputes" (Michaels 2006).

As pointed out by Anderson, entirely new laws, concepts and generalisations are necessary when new levels of complexity emerge (Anderson 1972, p. 393). Similarly, like hypotheses, rules are valid only under a particular set of conditions, and for particular framings and approaches to wicked valuation problems. Therefore, when it comes to policymaking, might not some existent closer to a more cosmic understanding provide better rules than generalising from a particular legal dispute as the judge proclaimed? Is the same level of thinking as that employed to resolve such a legal dispute inevitably sufficient to address wicked problems in the context of this work?

The answer provided above in the differentiation of complicated and complex is "no", because rules are for complicated, and – beyond but possibly enfolding rules – empathic engagement is required for complex. Addressing wicked valuation problems requires emergent higher levels of understanding and valuation than merely mechanist approaches can attain, and I claim that such higher levels may be able to formulate better rules.

Such better rules – mechanistic approaches – are essential but insufficient in policy work. With wicked problems, I further recognise that sufficiently high levels of understanding and valuation to cope with such problems are by no means necessarily those that humans can ever attain under any circumstances. Nevertheless, we will not know unless we try.

In so doing the closest generally known analogue I have found within mechanist-based management theory is the Plan, Do, Study/Check and Act (PDSA or PDCA) process enfolded within Total Quality Management (TQM) (Deming 2000, p. 88). Although it began from a mechanistic base, TQM can transcend mere machinism when managed by those who transcend and include single vision. The design school at Stanford has developed a similar procedure, but with an important addition allowing the entry of values other than the merely extrinsic to be engaged in policymaking. While in practice messy, it "can be explained in a handful of straightforward steps" (Hilton 2015, p. 31):

1 empathise with the user;
2 define the problem;
3 generate ideas;
4 prototype solutions; and
5 test the prototypes.

As they say, "keep testing and adapting until you get it right" (ibid.).

Taking into account that you can never get it exactly "right" with wicked valuation problems, this cyclic process appears the most promising in address-ing them. However, its first requirement is empathy, which requires that we connect with others, and not be in thrall to Blake's Urizen and his single vision, that is, to thintelligence.

While the word had not then been coined, the thintelligence of the character "Henry" was the problem that the character "Margaret" was attempting to resolve in E. M. Forster's *Howard's End*. Henry's motto was "*concentrate*", breaking the pattern that connects thereby necessarily destroying all quality (Bateson 1979, p. 8), whereas she wanted him to:

> Only connect the prose and the passion, and both will be exalted, and human love will be seen at its height. Live in fragments no longer. Only connect and the beast and the monk, robbed of the isolation that is life to either, will die.
>
> (Forster 1991, p. 195)

Blake would see this as being towards his connection of the four Zoas as precon-ditional to the emergence of Albion, his symbol of the Universal Man. But Henry would have none of that. He said he had "no intention of frittering away my strength on that sort of thing", and Margaret failed (ibid., pp. 186–187), later seeing the result of his thintelligence as his becoming "muddled, criminally muddled" (ibid., p. 308) and thereby destroying another character's life.

As Hobsbawm noted, "It is never wise to neglect the heart's reasons which reason knows nothing of" (Hobsbawm 1996, p. 263), yet that is precisely what machinism, per se, does. As Veronica Brady (Brady 2007, pp. 16–17) points out, when we lose our place in the cosmos, when we fail to connect, we also lose our humanity. It is often up to poets, and the poetry in us, to remind us where we really belong. Be it mental or physical, we are not to be subjects of machinery: machinery is to be subject to humaneness. We need to design "a world where people come first" (Hilton 2015, subtitle). For that, we need "analinear transcendence that . . . lifts you up to see the overall pattern and redefine your position in it" (Walter 1996, p. 89).

Scientists start with a hypothesis, test it according to the accepted protocols, circulate the findings to peers, and await rigorous interrogation towards rejection or further development of the hypothesis. Lawyers debate opposite views in front of a judge or jury and await their decisions, providing as persuasively as they can as much cogent evidence as they can. But "scientific reasoning is no more susceptible to a mechanical approach than legal reasoning" (Michaels 2006). While scientists claim that "the truth, the whole truth, and nothing but the truth" may never be attained, both scientists and lawyers hope that the closest we can approach to the truth at the time will emerge from their respective processes. Are either – or both together – necessarily the best we can do in this context, or even sufficient? Perhaps sometimes yes and sometimes no, but we need transdisciplinarity, and to connect, to attempt an answer.

Moreover, what happens when the mental models created by "heuristics such as thingness" (Long 2004, p. 540), for example property right models, encounter persons not equipped with such mental models? If that property right model prevails, those who can skilfully adapt their model to their benefit will dominate those not so equipped, no matter what the respective intrinsic values of the parties may be.

Long (2004, p. 549) calls for a more careful thinking about "the interconnections among mechanisms within each form" (of property right) and to "provide guidance on the way in which the law ought to evolve". This insight is more consistent with the deeper insights of science that "everything in the universe, then, is at heart a pattern of relationships" (Cole 2001, p. 238), including property rights. I add that this heart is a beating, dynamic one, not a static pattern, and consider that HVN↔HBA can serve as a framework for this insight, including that the hextal approach reminds us that in policy formulation and implementation we are talking about people and their values, not just heuristic-manufactured machinery.

Indeed, property rights relate not only to that aggregation of towers we call a city, but also to the holons that created them and to every other city. Further, through the research on cities of Michael Batty (2009, 2013), Cesar Hidalgo (2015) and others, property rights are directly relevant to current research on the coevolution of network states and topologies. Batty regards cities as complex systems, including them being "emergent phenomena generated through a combination of hierarchical levels of decision driven in decentralised fashion", and refers to "urban morphologies which are clearly fractal in structure" (Batty 2009; see also Batty 2013 for an expanded articulation). This research is designed to have applicability to real world complex systems (Sayama et al. 2013).

In this manner, a city is an example of this artefactual response to environmental challenges, composed as it is "of overlapping, connected, evolving networks that tie together nodes and events on different physical and temporal scales" (Mehaffy and Saligaros 2013). Moreover, so are property rights. Cities are networks of real property rights of various scales, types (including formal and informal, common and sole) and strengths, but never "nothing but" that. Thereby, they relate to every holon on Earth, whether those holons realise it or not, just as every part of Vairocana's Tower does.

That is because, in terms of network theory, degrees of separation (Watts 2004) are not confined to human holons; they span the universe in general to varying degrees at various scales, but the Earth in particular at all its scales. As such, property rights do too.

HVN points of difference

This observation is a fundamental difference between the complexity-based, non-linear, organic approach on one hand and the simplifying by reductionist, linear and mechanistic approach of Western scientism on the other. An important proviso to this distinction is that the complex transcends *and includes* the simple, but it is not the other way around. Watts also emphasises that the science of networks is a new science which is necessarily interdisciplinary (I would say transdisciplinary; Watts 2004, p. 303), and that every existent is connected and the links between causes and effects can be very complicated (ibid., p. 301). As such, Western science is finally coming to recognition of that reality "after hundreds of years of denial" (ibid., p. 25). Systems theorists have suggested similar approaches (Lang and Zhang 1999), and so have education theorists (Sterling 2003).

It also contextualises where, providing the potential for collateral consequences is acknowledged, we can gainfully employ the analogy of holons (animate) as artefacts (inanimate). So this model could hardly be more different to "nothing buttism" such as Maine's bundle of rights model: Good riddance to that in its magisterial claims, but bad riddance in terms of its ability to deliver reality to a human mind in bite-sized chunks *as an ansatz*. To put it more precisely: The model is only a mental artefact. As such, while it is deeply flawed and open to such misinterpretation, the fault does not lie with the model, any more than the fault for a murder lies with the weapon used. It lies in "nothing but" interpretations of it by reductionist mentalities. HVN recognises the need for single vision, but adds an extra and far more urgent need not to stop there. Roszak claims what Blake:

> failed to grasp is that the scientist's sense-world (Ulro) is not the sense-world as it really is. It claims to be "empirical", but is in fact a materialist-theoretical model designed for the sake of power-knowledge. It corresponds to nature as a map does to a landscape: As a useful reduction of reality.
>
> (Roszak 1972, p. 288)

That it does. But while stopping at that suits a mechanist mindset, being merely manipulative for power purposes, it does not suit addressing wicked problems.

So I now move from that metaphysical ontology to my pragmatic trans-ontological process as an organisation of this knowledge domain, beginning with a more suitable term for a group of property rights in that ontology.

Rather than an analogy such as a bundle of sticks, a web, leaky bucket and so on, I am returning to another description of Maine's for property rights: a "legal clothing" (Maine 2007, p. 60). Unlike his bundle metaphor, Maine's "legal clothing" enfolds Maturana and Varela's (1987, p. 47) point that organisation can remain while structural materials change, and vice versa. Clothing has to be put on in different places, and functions in different environments for different purposes including, importantly, cultural signifier purposes. Moreover, clothes, like property rights, are *artefacts*, not holons. Therefore, land has *costumes* of property rights. We are outfitted with different property rights in different societies, and our ensembles do not have to be machine manufactured to do their jobs. However, uniforms of property rights are useful for embedding greater certainty in a HVN so Goldilocks can operate, identities can be constructed, and plans can be more surely made.

Therefore, while they operate in an environment of webs of interests, costumes of property rights are not the living webs themselves; they are artefacts, interest attractors, just as we sometimes hope our own outfits may be. Within the HVN are overlapping, connected, evolving networks that tie together nodes and events on different physical and temporal scales, such as those described by Corning (2005) and Gunderson and Holling (2002) immediately below. In such landscapes, people are outfitted with property rights in their labour and skills and, if they are so lucky, their land. Thereby, in their part of HVN, costumes of property rights over land help establish their wearer's fitness landscapes. Their costumes might also set in train the consequences, whether intended or not, referred to in complexity economics.

HVN and transdisciplinarity

I have designed the HVN trans-ontological process to be one with which we can fruitfully engage with Corning's *Holistic Darwinism* (Corning 2005), Gunderson and Holling's *Panarchy* (2002) and the like. *Panarchy* is particularly important to this work in terms of its emphases throughout on the importance of scale and of levels (for instance, see ibid., p. 151: "Ecological scale and social scale are both important"), and Corning's *Holistic Darwinism* is a multileveled interactional paradigm. It has several features to inform the phenomena to be researched via HVN and HBA, including:

- It recognises that causation can be top up, bottom down, horizontal, and between any and all levels.
- It serves as an umbrella for the major causal agency of synergy in evolution. While a different perspective from traditional Darwinism, it is fully consistent with it and able to enfold all its insights and more.
- It fully acknowledges the built-in purposiveness (teleonomy) of organisms and has it as an important aspect of evolution itself.

- It enfolds the phenomenon of emergence.
- It includes politics and cultures in its purview (Corning 2005, pp. 3–4).

Mumford adds that Darwin's approach was far more expansive than those blinded by the single vision of machinism can ever see:

> In classic scientific thinking, the whole must be interpreted in terms of the part, deliberately isolated, carefully observed, precisely measured. But in Darwin's complementary ecological approach, it is the whole that reveals the nature and function and purpose of the part. Though threads in the pattern may need to be replaced, and parts of the pattern modified or completely redrawn as new evidence accumulates, it is important to take in the whole, even at some cost of sharp definition, and to carry that whole through time.
>   The feat of putting together the outlines of this intricate ecological pattern was Darwin's magnificent contribution.
>
> (Mumford 1970, p. 389)

Therefore, holistic Darwinism also informs land policy. It makes the land-policy-relevant claim that the basic needs of members of a society have a moral claim that is more fundamental than property rights are (Corning 2005, pp. 435, 441). It even recognises values: "we are endowed with an array of existential biologically based human values that are virtually universal" (ibid., p. 422). Just as fundamentally for this work, it recognises that life itself is an interaction between an organism, its fitness landscapes (ibid., p. 338) and its fields, and that the purpose of scientific theory is to unite observations that are apparently different into a coherent set of generalisations having predictive power (ibid., p. 42).

While not referenced in his work, I see Wild Systems Theory of cognitive science as having many homologies and potential synergies (Jordan 2008; Jordan 2010; Jordan and Vinson 2012; Jordan and Day 2015).

Similarly, as summarised in chapter 15 of *Panarchy*, Gunderson and Holling (2002, p. 395) provide twelve conclusions of their researches towards sustainable futures, and in chapter 16 look towards an "integrative synthesis" (ibid., pp. 419–438) of these. As I understand them, as both Panarchy and HVN↔HBA are attempts to address complex adaptive systems, chapter 15's twelve conclusions can also be used to express characteristics of the HVN, and I, too, look to their integrative synthesis. However, I see that as enfolded within HVN:

Gunderson and Holling's 12 conclusions of their researches are the need to address:

1 The potential for abrupt shifts in previously stable domains.
2 Consolidation and transformation adaptive cycles.
3 Widely variant and sometimes maladaptive dynamics.
4 Sustainable fitness landscapes emerge via the Panarchy (nested dynamic adaptive cycles).
5 Holonic self-organisation as a driver of this process.

6 Identification of three types of change – incremental, lurching, and trans-formational.
7 The human and biological "clumped patterns" (holons) create resilience and sustainability.
8 Functional groups spanning scales facilitate that created resilience and sustainability.
9 Being as simple as possible but not simpler requires not a rule of thumb, but "rules of hand" (interacting variable components).
10 Such interactions between ecological, economic and social systems engender emergent processes.
11 Uncertainty in managing complexity is a given.
12 Adaptive management of slow variables, multistable behaviours and stochasticity trumps mechanistic management.

Chapter 16 of *Panarchy* provides an analytical framework that I intend to engage through HVN↔HBA. They include recognising our limitations when it comes to forecasting, navigating uncertainty, active engagement of adaptive networking, developing new myths (heuristics) to understand complex systems, and change management.

As mentioned, I consider the HVN trans-ontological process to be the best way to view these two works in particular and all of the above in general. Providing that viewing is actioned via Torbert's Collaborative Developmental Action Inquiry (Torbert and Associates 2004) or similar via the inter-hextal framing described below, trans-ontological teams would be the optimal means of addressing wicked valuation problems.

HVN as an emergent from complexity requiring energy to be maintained

One feature highlighted by this HVN trans-ontological process is the HVN's energy drivers, and consequently its need for energy to increase and maintain its complexity. Recent research papers indicate that all complex life on earth – that is, based on eukaryotes rather than the far more static prokaryotes such as bacteria – result from energy capture and driving. They see all of life as a "self-organizing, energy transformation hierarchy" (Jordan 2008, p. 1982). Once again, I would have used "holarchy" in this context, and assume Jordan to have used "hierarchy" in its broad enfolding-of-holarchy meaning. In transforming energy to their ends, living existents must generate the multi-scale systems they themselves comprise from those they operate within (ibid., p. 1983).

That general principle was outlined by Csikszentmihalyi as applying to our (co-)evolving selves in a manner which, when looking at its manifestations at various scales will also assist in skilfully addressing wicked valuations. He notes that any organism needs inputs of energy to continue and will grab as much of it as it can while keeping its integrity. Those more successful at doing that will survive and reproduce, but if they are too successful they may destroy the environment and, thereby themselves, as surely as changes in environment conditions can dissipate a cyclone. The two opposite tendencies in evolution, which he defines as changes towards harmony, involving increasing complexity, and those dissipating complexity towards entropy (Csikszentmihalyi 1993, pp. 149ff) have to be in balance to be sustained.

If the Fateful Encounter Hypothesis is correct (Lane and Martin 2010), the major emergence of co-evolution, eukaryotic cells, and hence all more complex life, arose from just such a process as complexity economics focusses upon. Eukaryotic life is profligate in its energy expenditure, a eukaryotic gene controlling about 200,000 times the energy that a prokaryotic one does. Therefore, while a prokaryotic cell's energy focuses on the basics, a eukaryotic gene can go well beyond those basics (ibid., p. 929).

Like the golden ratio mentioned above, this "going beyond" appears to be a fractal phenomenon. Simple societies often have to focus on basics and generalities, and complex societies rely on this energy to develop in the terms described by the development principle.

Right now, the machines in complex societies need oil to run, and it is possible that modern civilisation simply cannot survive without oil. The bountiful energy oil provides is required to maintain the levels of complexity of modern society, and without it societies will revert to simpler levels, with potentially catastrophic consequences for human development.

One black swan of that oil-based machine is climate change, and the best guide I have found to the likely consequences at each level of increase from one degree to six degrees is Lynas (2007). At six degrees, human extinction is likely. So while The Machine cannot survive without oil, human life may not survive with oil. The Machine's reaction? As attributed to Stanisław Jerzy Lec in *Economics of Good and Evil* (Sedlacek and Havel 2011, p. 233), "we know we are on the wrong track, but we are compensating for this shortcoming by accelerating".

In so doing, identities harness what energy they want in order to navigate through all the hextants and through ADALAS of fitness landscapes, as described in the next chapter. Within single vision, this energy can drive extrinsic valuations at the expense of the non-extrinsic parts of the BIES part of HBA. It appears that this monological gaze in agriculture in particular, as manifested by The Machine's chemical-intensive industrialised system of food and agriculture, is causing mass extinctions and might result in our own depopulation and enfeebling (Cribb 2014; Mason 2015).

Mason sheets much of the blame for this on "that fundamental scientific error, reductionism . . . [which is] really incompatible with the complexity of life" (Mason 2015, p. 163), and hopes that:

> The rise of systems biology may provide a welcome antidote to the reductionism of molecular biology. Systems biology aims to understand the complexity of the whole organism as a system, rather than just studying its parts in a reductionist manner.
>
> (Mason 2015, p. 173)

This is another reason I consider that looking beyond single vision and Newton's sleep may be in order.

Chapter summary and the way forward

This chapter introduced the HVN as the Master for addressing wicked valuation problems. It is the custodian of metaphor, intrinsic valuations and the other qualities attributed to the right hemisphere of the brain by McGilchrist (2009) and the scientists he cites. All the so-called hard facts of science are informational transformations by the viscoelastic brain, and its right hemisphere is our portal to the landscapes of the first part of the title, and our frame for our engagements. HVN is vital in addressing wicked valuation problems when NSEW meet, because we need to engage the big picture, and that is where HVN comes in. At the personal scale, HVN enfolds and values every existent we encounter. In contrast to the "so-called hard facts of science" it addresses the Tao that cannot be known, by opening our understanding – and potentially wisdom – to the value of not-knowing: of being quiet, and not looking for reasons past the edge of reason.

I mean the HVN trans-ontological process to radically dis-enbox our approaches so we can appreciate reality more fully. Speaking metaphorically, as we need to in addressing wicked valuation problems, we are not simply on a track of time, we are immersed in a swirling river of vortices in time. While we can use our swimming costumes of property rights and their machines, we also need to know who we are, where we are, and where we would like to go. We need to be able to navigate in that river not just like Captain Cook but also like Tupaia and transcend and include both.

I then pointed to thinkers well beyond just single vision such as Corning (2005) and Gunderson and Holling (2002) as guides towards such navigation, and then referred to the core role of energy, not just navigators, for our voyages, both for landscapes and The Machine to show how The Machine depends totally on the landscapes, not the other way around.

While HVN is homologous to the Tao at the universal scale (and needs to be, to enfold the Butterfly Effect), within the geophilosophical framework and the concept of place-identity, my term "HVN" is homologous to the rhizome:

> Rhizome means a processual network, and the consequences of applying this concept to the question of the identity of the place are the following: (a) inside the rhizome the identity of place is a process defined according to the relationship with alterity: a place inside the rhizome is in movement, neither stationary nor sedentary, but it is always the product of a relation between culture (historical, memorial, but in evolution) and nature (as part of a complex system); (b) identities are multiple, in the same way as there is a multiplicity of places (the rhizome is composed of different places and non-places).
>
> (Menatti 2013, p. 225)

Both the Tower and Indra's Net are artefact-based models, but while HVN↔HBA is an abstract artefact too, I mean it to facilitate the analysis and valuation of holonic, organic and dynamic fitness landscapes, the towers of beings reflecting one another rising and falling as they are born, grow, decline and die: Menatti's rhizomes as processual networks of landscapes (Menatti 2013a, p. 21).

At the universal timespace scale, in this HVN trans-ontological process, all nouns are slow verbs. Consistent with Buddhists' insights about impermanence, all "things" are variably timed vortices with component vortices enfolding their relationships and processes. Its flavour is of Pascal's observation that one cannot understand the whole without understanding the part and vice versa (Pascal 1669, para 72). It is also like Kosko's observation that "the whole in the part is the essence of fuzzy logic" (Kosko 1994, p. 48), and William Blake's "to see the world in a grain of sand", which is similar to a core insight of Hua-Yen as well, seeing an infinity of lions in a single hair of one (Loy 1993, p. 483). The trans-ontological process also addresses Loy's question in his book *The World is Made of Stories*: "If the big story of Buddhism is not to be deluded by storying, the Big Story for Blake is the storying of liberated Imagination. Are these different stories, or two sides of a Bigger Story?" (Loy 2010, p. 100). I see the liberated transdisciplinary imagination (Brown, Harris and Russell 2010) as being facilitated by this process to play its long-stultified "essential role in decision-making on complex issues" (ibid., p. 5).

We may therefore imagine our journey also needs a river-worthy craft, including an identity (see Chapter 5), and crafting one is where the left hemisphere plays its essential single vision role. But being a boat-builder does not qualify it to decide the boat's destination; it merely allows limited potential destinations. HVN is the Master and the navigator: it decides the why and the where. HBA is the thintelligent engineer, the boatswain (checking all is in order) and similar service provider, the Emissary serving the HVN's purposes. While HBA's role is not to say where we want to go or why we want to go there, it does help shape and limit the reality of expectations for the boat, towards developing the art of the practical in addressing the wicked valuation problems we encounter. Despite the left hemisphere's liking of the model of the machine for motorcycle maintenance et al., that is not what we as holons are here for. HBA is not just a part of a machine – which is of intrinsically trivial value, whatever extrinsic value it may possess – its home is as part of the infinitely intrinsically valuable holarchy of life. One essential guiding question then, in assessing a way of addressing wicked valuation problems is, "what is its value for life?". Learning then living that HVN is our true home in the context of addressing wicked valuation problems is what the next chapter is about.

5 The HIDEGRE BIES ADALAS template to approach wicked problems

Introduction

The HVN addresses the first lines of the first chapter of the *Tao Te Ching*. In looking towards establishing a protocol for due diligence in addressing wicked valuations problems, this chapter addresses the chapter's last lines:

> From eternal non-existence, therefore, we serenely observe the mysterious beginning of the universe;
> From eternal existence we clearly see the apparent distinctions.
> These two are the same in source and become different when manifested.
> This sameness is called profundity.
> Infinite profundity is the gate whence comes the beginning of all parts of the universe.
>
> (Lao Tzu 1972)

That profundity of sameness is where wicked problems are sourced, and where they can be most effectively addressed; the sameness of McGilchrist's left and right hemisphere perceptions that become apparent with fourfold vision: the world in a grain of sand, and Pirsig's Zen in motorcycle maintenance.

Therefore, sourced from both my own lived experience as narrated above and the scholars cited throughout this book, this chapter is about not only both our hemispheres, but also our enteric nervous systems and all the rest of us, working together in collaborative action inquiry on apparent distinctions to address wicked problems. In particular, I envisage skilful means as emerging from within transdisciplinary communities of inquiry and practice. That way, we can gain depth and breadth to address wicked valuation problems that way more than any one of us could alone.

These communities of inquiry are not to be confined to mechanical approaches based on the metaphor of holons as merely machines. Rather, they are to be grounded in Bastardas-Boada's Complexics transdisciplinary approach. Furthermore, without enfolding the holonic capacity to make "Big V" intrinsic valuations to frame and guide the process, such often necessarily complicated mechanical approaches would be likely to terminate in paralysis by analysis – rather like a ship without a rudder would eventually run aground or out of fuel. In that case, the community, trapped within the "simple to complicated" single vision of Newton's sleep, would again be likely to resort to simplistic, "quick fix" approaches deficient in skilful means, and thereby likely to inflict long term pain on those they may have had every intention to benefit.

Even so, the line must be drawn somewhere. Carl Sagan was not joking when he said, "If you wish to make an apple pie from scratch you must first invent the universe" (Sagan 1990, p. 218). I have been at pains to point out above that despite our confirmation biases both the lines to be drawn, and the approaches to be engaged, differ between simple, complicated, complex and wicked problems, and here we are addressing wicked ones.

I am therefore recommending HBA as a due diligence protocol towards addressing wicked problems, not for its use with simple problems like making a cake or an apple pie, or more complicated ones like motorcycle maintenance. Like using a mixing bowl for a cake (simple), a spanner for Pirsig's motorcycle (complicated), and verbal and non-verbal communication to raise a child (complex), I see HBA an appropriate tool to approach wicked problems in general, and wicked valuation problems in particular. Traditional "small v" valuation methodologies are fine for the simple to complicated valuations enfoldable within single vision, but as unfit for purpose for complex to wicked valuations as using a spanner as a mixing bowl.

In particular, HBA's institutionalised emphasis upon the interiors of we holons engaging in such communities opens us up to the lessons from scientific and philosophical inquiries dating at least back to Nicholas of Cusa (1401–1464) – that the best minds hold all beliefs lightly – and Charles Darwin when he observed that "ignorance more frequently begets confidence than does knowledge" (Darwin 1871). Science now supports the view that:

> [H]uman behaviour [is] determined more by social factors than by deliberative individual thought. Behaviour depends on the habits, the routines, and the customs of economic actors . . . They are matters of law or tradition; and they get passed along by example, by society's expectations, and by the power of the state. People tend to follow these rules because they see everyone else doing so. People also follow these rules because they provide a simple way to deal with the uncertainty and the complexity of everyday life.
>
> (King 2003, pp. 196–197)

We must be wary of that when it comes to addressing wicked problems, where it may be a form of slovenliness, or again no more appropriate than using a mixing bowl to tighten the nut and bolt on a motorcycle. For example, Sloman and Fernbach's (2017) admonition that "[a]s a rule, strong feelings about issues do not emerge from deep understanding" is of far greater value in our own introspections than in blaming others. Rather, one may observe that the more one's identity construction conflates its views with itself, the identity thereby being challenged collaterally with one's point of view, the more vigorous the repulse:

> If we . . . spent less time pontificating and more trying to work through the implications of policy proposals, we'd realize how clueless we are and

moderate our views. This, they [Sloman and Fernbach] write, "may be the only form of thinking that will shatter the illusion of explanatory depth and change people's attitudes". One way to look at science is as a system that corrects for people's natural inclinations.

(Kolbert 2017)

Science should therefore include correcting the inclination to stop at single vision and Newton's sleep, such as scientism and machinism do *per se*. That is, we must stop automatically believing everything that we think, but rather be able to value that thought intrinsically, extrinsically, and systemically when addressing the particular wicked problem.

The HBA protocol's three initials stand for three different groups of tasks. "H", for "HIDEGRE", is for the left hemisphere's Gorgonic gaze to focus on the aspects mentioned. "B", for BIES, is to bring in HVN as HBA's frame and fulcrum, inserting awareness of the big picture and its capacity to upset the best laid of thintelligent plans, and to provide valuations beyond the merely mechanistic and extrinsic. "A", for ADALAS, is to examine the landscapes with all the capacities we can employ to address wicked valuation problems.

Lazlo Csaba, in looking to the future of economics, wondered if a fully formed new paradigm might emerge to resolve the difficulties of economics, or alterna-tively a process "allowing for more diversity in terms of trial and errors, in terms of methodology, and in terms of experimentation" (Csaba 2009, p. 29). HVN↔HBA is of the latter stamp.

Towards discovering this and other means of addressing wicked valuation problems, I mean HVN↔HBA to be a tool to facilitate a trans-ontological process informed by theoretical works cited herein towards further developing theory and praxis in the context of this work. That is, it is intended to be practical as well as theoretically supported, facilitating a trans-ontological process towards developing skilful means in the context towards sustainable reification of wisdom and compassion.

To recap: Science has made it clear that humans were only capable of holding a limited number of variables in their heads at any one time, and mathematics itself was only capable of dealing with a very limited number of variables at any one time. For example, a number as small as three in the case of the three body problem concerning mutually gravitating planets, where Poincare proved that no formula could exist to address it (Strogatz 2004, p. 50). Yet the complexity economist Page has shown that where "deterministic interaction rules, I derive the rule of six: the number of agent types plus the group size must be at least six in order to support multiple equilibria given a spanning assumption" (Page 2007, p. 223). Thereby, in a single vision mindspace mathematics must fall short even in addressing deterministic interactions. Yet the world itself manifests an unlimited number of variables at any one time, and we variously both observe and value them. Western-dominating single vision is a primitive Procrustean bed approach, utterly inadequate to the challenge set for this work, but, like an infant attending primary school who later becomes a professor, it is still a beginning.

One must start with single vision, but one must not stop there when attempting to address wicked problems. So on the one hand, models can make users better thinkers, by helping in organising information, making more accurate forecasts, making better decisions and adopting more effective strategies (Bammer and Deane 2012, p.4), but they can never include everything that may affect the wicked problem the model is meant to address. In particular, models can never include everything relevant in addressing wicked valuation problems when NSEW meet.

Which prompts questions such as "just as set theory is capable of enclosing variables in a mathematical context and property rights in HBA are value-directed, is it possible to enclose intrinsic valuational variables into sets to allow our limited faculties to better address our fitness landscapes"? In addition, "just as valuers compare all sorts of variables in valuing a property, could such a way of thinking address all sorts of variables in formulating and implementing a policy"?

Towards addressing such questions, I note that after a survey of how agents make decisions, researchers looking around for appropriate models from an AI perspective have noted that in contrast to best modelling practices, models are rather simplistic compared to the very complex processes of human decision-making. We mainly derive models heuristically, in order to address the vast complexities of the present enough to get by for the time being. The researchers noted an inadequate representation of the theory of mind, of the "we" aspects of decision-making, subconscious priming, awareness and other such features in order to model human decision-making more realistically (Balke and Gilbert 2014).

While AI could be useful in some roles within it, HBA is about transcending reductionism's Procrustean beds, such as calling amputated bits of reality "externalities". Instead, it looks to increasing human cognitive and valuation capacities towards addressing wicked problems. That is, it starts from current human cognitive and valuational capacities, not from the perspective of trying to model them as or with machines. As distinct from monological approaches, the human mind has evolved to look for *multiple overlapping solutions* (Eagleman as cited in Brockman 2013, pp. 91–93).

As required, I intend HVN↔HBA to open up its practitioners to such ways of addressing wicked problems. Like Tinbergen's questions and their subsequent development (Bateson and Laland 2013), I intend it as scaffolding for investigations, for users to find their own answers and develop them through peer and public engagement as appropriate. Balke and Gilbert's observation is also problematic among property rights-related scholars:

> Economists, legal scholars, and other social scientists continue to rely on simplistic, outmoded, and incomplete models that fail to capture the variety and complexity of property arrangements found throughout the world.
>
> (Cole and Ostrom 2011, p. 1)

Cole and Ostrom go on to call for "a more descriptively accurate and analytically useful theory of property systems and rights in natural resources" (Cole and

Ostrom in Cole et al. 2015, p. 123). With that in place, we can begin to address Okoth-Ogendo's challenge with respect for the complexities involved, but cannot end there.

Theory will not suffice for policy practitioners, who also require practicable praxis methodologies. One needs to have an epistemologically and telaxio-logically robust theory, apply it, check its results, make hoped-for improvements, check their results, and so on, thereby engaging in a process of unremitting development. That involves not only the theory and its praxis, but all hextants (as described below), dimensions, levels and scales: that is, including the practitioners themselves as processes, not fixed theory-making machines.

With wicked valuation problems a theory cannot be regarded as some kind of mechanistic instruction manual (a recipe put "out there" suitable for a resolution of a simple problem). However, it can serve as an ansatz towards sustained engagement with suites of wicked problems (social messes).

All of the above-mentioned resulted in the framing of HBA as articulated below. As an emergent emissary from HVN, it is to be both a differentiated, articulated and hierarchically integrated manifestation of a "vortex networks" version of Vairocana's Tower. In this case, of the vortex networks within which wicked valuation problems emerge when NSEW meet. I do not imagine these vortices as merely visual, but rather as alive, and composed of all relevant information and stories.

As I mentioned in Chapter 2 regarding Hubert DeCleer, Vajrayana Buddhism emphasises developing a powerful imagination, identifying with the deities imagined, and then dissolving them. Just so did Prospero, in Shakespeare's *The Tempest*. Prospero expresses the core Buddhist insight of impermanence – as made evidenced through the Kalachakra Sand Mandala – in noting the similarity of our identifying with actors in a play and identifying with roles in life:

> Our revels now are ended. These our actors,
> As I foretold you, were all spirits, and
> Are melted into air, into thin air:
> We are such stuff
> As dreams are made on; and our little life
> Is rounded with a sleep
>   (Shakespeare, *The Tempest*, act 4, scene 1, 148–158)

Moreover, just as "we are such stuff as dreams are made on", as the Thomas Theorem confirms and Rebecca Goldstein observed, *we are such dreams as stuff is made on*. Those dreams are our actors, our identities, including Taylor's 'social imaginary' identity components, and thereby our dreams participate in shaping reality. They bare our "little life": our big life, for the little time we are around, is as an integral part of the HVN.

As for our little life, as stated by the Thomas Theorem, "if men define situations as real, they are real in their consequences" and that goes for our constructed identities as much as any other existent. Once again, this mirroring we do is core to understanding fitness landscapes, which once again the Buddhists noted, for example in their principle of dependent origination (Kwee 2010, p. 10, n. 17).

Conclusion nine of Gunderson and Holling above stated that "being as simple as possible but not simpler requires not a rule of thumb, but 'rules of hand' (interacting variable components)". In this case the interacting components are imagination ↔ reason ↔ wisdom ↔ compassion. That is in accord with Bateson's statement that "imagination alone is insanity" (Bateson 1979, p. 242), and with emerging above the rule of the "stern and sterile god of reason" (Ghiţă 2008, p. 25) that Blake termed Urizen. That also means moving beyond looking for "reasons past the edge of reason", and beyond the faculty psychology criticised by Whitehead.

Therefore, via HBA, in this work I am submitting that insights expressed over a thousand years ago at Borobudur, Indonesia provide ansatzes to address the general topic of this book.

They are more compatible with the modern insights of complexity and chaos theories than is the mechanistic paradigm. They are also more compatible with Arnold's characterisation of sociolegal evolutionary theory, which highlights the following factors shaping its fitness landscapes (Table 5.1 provides my abridged version of Arnold's insights).

To address the larger span of this work than Arnold's focus on property rights, all of the above and more (for example, Taleb's antifragility, intrinsic and extrinsic valuations, interiors as well as exteriors etc. as articulated elsewhere in this book) are to be enfolded into this HVN↔HBA approach.

Table 5.1 Characteristics of the sociolegal evolutionary environment

1 Systems are complex, dynamic and adaptive	2 Change may appear random and chaotic
3 Unforeseen qualities can emerge from interactions	4 Dynamics are heterogeneous
5 Changes can be engendered from nonlinearities in both space and time	6 Changes have to adapt in their new environments to attain a sustainable fitness landscape
7 Prior evolutionary paths limit adaptability to new conditions	8 Systems can find nonstatic stability by finding niches, developing self-organising structures, and operating in critical states of development, thereby maintaining themselves
9 Development of pre-organised responses and other strategies can facilitate resilience, resistance and modularity	10 There can be disturbances, catastrophes and tipping points that can suddenly result in major changes
11 Change results from both competition and cooperation at varied scales	12 Complexities and unexpected outcomes can emerge from co-evolution between systems, including those at different time and space scales
13 Network connectivity and feedback can dramatically affect the scope and pace of change through diffusion of ideas, information and innovation.	

Source: Arnold (2011, pp. 170–171)

"HBA" refers to three headings: the "H" stands for "HIDEGRE", which in turns stands for:

H   A *Hexagonal* matrix for analysing transactions.
I   Recognising the central importance of *Identity* in addressing wicked valuation problems.
D   The central importance of the concept of *Development* in analysis and in intrinsic and systemic valuation.
E   The recognition of *Emergence* of new wholes requires new methods of analyses and valuation at each level and a more sophisticated understanding of the interrelationships within and between the emergent levels in the hextants.
G   The *Goldilocks* Principle, that development can only happen within limited levels and pace of change.
RE That all evolution is co-evolution, here expressed as *Related Evolution*.

The "B" stands for BIES, which in turn stands for:

B   The *Butterfly Effect* and *Black Swans*: complex situations are unpredictable, so resilience and antifragility must be built into policies and their implementation.
I   *Intrinsic* value: for example, organisms that enfold many levels of emergence are more intrinsically valuable than organisms with fewer levels of emergence (for example, killing a person is much worse than killing a mosquito for this reason). Cognitive and other capacities are traced for their emergent intrinsic value along the Model of Hierarchic Complexity (Commons 2008).
E   *Extrinsic* value refers to the usefulness of some existent in a context. For example, a hammer is of high extrinsic value if you want to drive in a nail. However, if you are looking for a conversation, one is better off attempting that with some existent of high intrinsic value: another person.
S   *Systemic* value looks at how existents are and compares them with how existents should be. For example, highly developed valuations are more systemically valuable than unarticulated, poorly supported valuations. Systemic value requires systemic thought and planning and the development of the understanding of complicated matters. While intrinsic value can approach zero, systemic value can be negative when the existents destroy quality/areté/the pattern that connects.

The "A" stands for ADALAS – a reminder to keep the big picture in mind when formulating and implementing policy. In turn, ADALAS stands for:

AD all *Domains and Dimensions*.
AL all *Levels and Lines*.
AS all *Scales*.

HBA is an intermediary between reality as seen through HVN and our minds' limited capacities to address it, which capacities are so often arrested in a tussle between superstition and reductionism. I do not intend it as another en-boxing methodology for machine minds, but as a tool for multiperspectival developmental action inquiry in addressing dynamic wicked problems. The heterarchic fields and holarchic networks of HVN are where wicked problems emerge. For example, recognising the interpenetration of our identities may be "the only doctrine that . . . can perhaps save us from ourselves" (Loy 1993, p. 483).

HIDEGRE

"HIDEGRE" is my acronym for the six major (but not exclusive) foci I am recommending to address wicked valuation problems. They are intended to facilitate the mental qualities McGilchrist attributes to the left hemisphere insofar as it operates within its role as the right hemisphere's Emissary: That is, in using its extrinsic valuations to facilitate higher intrinsic values in both its interior and exterior environments. In that framing, they are not rigid, formulaic or sacrosanct. They are heuristic principles for approaching wicked valuation problems whereby the relevant practical wisdom, the skilful means, can be engaged towards the whole trans-ontological process of sustainable reification of wisdom and compassion. HIDEGRE is a way of coming to grips with and working through the task to hand, of identifying and then engaging the relevant practical and theoretical support needed in the context.

The first of these heuristics, which I term the Habermas/Hexagonal Matrix, is the "H" of HIDEGRE. As described below, I came to it through Wilber, but changed it from Habermas's and Wilber's quadrant matrices to a hexagonal one, finding that division more useful in this context through my own lived professional experience.

In *Sex, Ecology, Spirituality* (1995), Wilber attempts to correlate the developmental levels in both values and skills of individuals comprising the fitness landscapes they develop in both sociocultural and institutional environments. From reading Wilber, two major points stand out as foundational to examine how best to address these wicked valuation problems. First, he divides the above fields of inquiry into four quadrants (Wilber 1995), as shown in Table 5.2. This

Table 5.2 Wilber's four-quadrant approach to interrogate reality

Upper-left quadrant (URQ)	**Upper-right quadrant (URQ)**
"I" – Interior-individual: intentional	"It" – exterior-individual: behavioural
e.g. Freud, Jung, Piaget, individual values and beliefs, such as identifying with territory . . .	e.g. Skinner, Locke, neurology, biology, skills development, such as conveyancing property . . .
Lower-left quadrant (LLQ)	**Lower-right quadrant (LRQ)**
"We" – Interior-collective: cultural	"Its" – Exterior-collective: social
e.g. Gadamer, Kuhn, Gebser, Weber, collective tastes in art, music . . . socially agreed real property rights . . .	e.g. Marx, Comte, systems theory, engineering, formal real property rights . . .

Table 5.3 Habermas: domains of reality

"My" world of internal nature	**Language**
Mode of communication: basic attitude – expressive	Mode of communication: basic attitude – (unstated)
Validity claims: truthfulness	Validity claims: comprehensibility
General functions of speech: disclosure of speaker's subjectivity	General functions of speech: (unstated)
"Our" world of society	**"The" world of external nature**
Mode of communication: basic attitude	Mode of communication: basic attitude
Interactive: conformative attitude	Cognitive: objectivating attitude
Validity claims: rightness	Validity claims: truth
General functions of speech: establishment of legitimate interpersonal relations	General functions of speech: representation of facts

Source: Habermas (1979, p. 68)

Table 5.4 Developmental lines of increasing complexity (examples only; not comprehensive)

Impulse	Reptilian Brain	Archaic cultural	Foraging groups
Emotion	Limbic System	framing	Tribes
Symbols	Neocortex	Magical cultural	Early State
Concepts	Complex Archaic	framing	Nation-State
Concrete Operational	Magic	Mythic cultural	Global . . .
Formal Operational	Mythic	framing	
Vision-logic	Rational	Rational cultural	
	Centauric Neocortex	framing	
	. . .	Centauric cultural	
		framing	

Source: Wilber (1995, fig. 5.1)

conceptual framework can be seen as a development of a similar explication of "Domains of Reality" in the context of communication set out by Habermas (Table 5.3). Second, Wilber (1995) gives examples of increasing levels of complexity in developmental lines within each quadrant (Table 5.4).

At each emergent level of complexity, entirely new properties appear. At each stage, entirely new laws, concepts and generalisations are necessary: an important observation in the context of land policy formulation and implementation, where oftentimes people are talking across each other from different levels.

I found this framework problematic. For example, are emotional drivers from our limbic systems adopting mythic-magic social constructs the most appropriate means of addressing wicked valuation problems only in tribal systems, or in all, or in none of them? Are concrete operational drivers from the neocortex using rational social constructs the most appropriate means of addressing wicked valuation problems in nation-state systems?

Surely, there is a confusion in the lower right quadrant between depth and span? Might not the single vision of the simple to complicated Empire of The Machine be even simpler to manage than the complex dynamics of interpersonal relationships? Recall that Wilber considers states et al. to be social holons, whereas I consider them to be social artefacts, empowered by identification by human holons. Thereby I do not subscribe to Wilber's lower right quadrant, rejecting it as "an imperialist act of envelopment and disenfranchisement" (Anderson 2010, p. 32). Greater span is no indication whatsoever of greater depth. The most complex known existent in the known universe is in the space between our ears. Artefacts as such lack intrinsic value, and nation-states are socially imagined artefacts. As described above, intrinsic values apply to holons, not to artefacts as such, and Polynesian navigation required far more complex understanding than the merely mechanical of Cook's (Strongman 2008, p. 73). Only when holons attach their identities to artefacts such as nation-states can they gain a vicarious, third-hand, intrinsic value. The lower right quadrant would appear to be better used to describe multiple complex interpersonal relationships than machines of different physical scales. Or, if one wanted to acknowledge geographical issues, scales relevant to environmental psychology.

Recognising that both depth and span should be considered in addressing wicked problems, what functional fits and potential structural couplings exist between these holonic levels? What are their potential roles in facilitating further development towards peace?

To address these questions, we must examine what it is that is developing. In so doing, we can look not only within ourselves and our various levels therein, but also in relationships between our own and other selves and existents. For example, a study about Switzerland has established the importance of setting geographic boundaries to peaceful coexistence (Rutherford et al. 2014). Addressing other hextants, we might ask, "How much are we subject to the deficiencies in valuers that have been researched from a behavioural economics perspective?" What about the market participants themselves? In this globalised world, what intercultural factors might come into play in intercultural market value transactions and policy formulations?[1] And what such strengths, weaknesses, opportunities and threats prevail at the broader and deeper land policy domain within valuation and other disciplines involved in land policy formulation and implementation?

Grappling with this, I began to see that I might usefully view AQAL as looking at a holon, isolating that holon from its holonic milieu.

In 2005, I therefore made a distinction between the external world, AS PERCEIVED BY the holon concerned, and the external world as inclusionary as we can make it. This little living holon in a nested sea of other holons, heaps and artefacts under processes, I named "Octo", after the eight points of a cube.

So there sits Octo in its umwelt, open to its perceptions, but not being open to "the" world of the whole environment (its umfeld). Octo's exterior hextants refer to its umwelt, not to the far larger umfeld, let alone global produce, culture and nature hextants not perceived by Octo at any level or sensory input available to it.

If Octo is a mature human, it can then engage in an action inquiry process (Torbert and Associates 2004) on a transdisciplinary basis to address such tasks. Action inquiry is intended to have individuals and, through them their organisations of all scales become "more aware, more just, and more sustainable" (ibid., p. 1), and HVN↔HBA is so intended as well. I intend it to frame and facilitate action inquiry or any other relevant practice towards wiser policy formulation and implementation and thereby the better potential for addressing wicked valuation problems.

H: the Habermas/hexagonal matrix

My engagement with developing this matrix came via the abovementioned AQAL framework as developed by Ken Wilber, my questioning of which led me to the conclusion that a still more articulated framing is required to examine these wicked valuation problems. Then I remembered a book I had read back in Swaziland, William Calvin's *The Cerebral Code* (1998), which referred to the need for metaphor and imagination to address the world in any sort of coherent manner (pp. 159–160), and spoke of hexagonal mosaics in the mind throughout his book. Furthermore, other researchers have shown how hexagonal structures emerge spontaneously in nature, such as in convective flows (Getling and Brausch 2003). Thinking of this model fractally, and adopting Damasio's definition of consciousness as "a state of mind in which there is knowledge of one's own existence and of the existence of surroundings . . . with a self added to it" (Damasio 2010, p.122), I decided to expand it to map out our identity constructions.

Although catalysed by them, this is not about Habermas's template and Wilber's AQAL. As Wilber points out there are many and varied lines, waves and streams (Wilber 1995), and for my purposes these hextants are potentially more helpful than quadrants. So instead of AQAL, I use AHAL – all hextants, all levels – in identities, and externalise span as in Wilber's lower right quadrant to avoid its conflation with depth. However, I do not thereby treat span as an externality, as I embed those identities in environments, where they create their fitness landscapes along with their identities. What I am after here is a means to improve our cognitive and other relevant domains of complexity by means of framing fitness landscapes and the identities and other requirements. My purpose is to better address those domains of complexity towards optimally addressing the wicked valuation problems.

That requires addressing these problems in a manner that respects their complexities but at the same time respects the limitation of our minds to address them. As mentioned above, Gruss (2014) noted that visual aids can be very important in creating and introducing new ideas; for HBA, when examining affected and affecting constructed identities these include the hexagonal to cubical and spherical matrices of Figures 5.1 and 5.2.

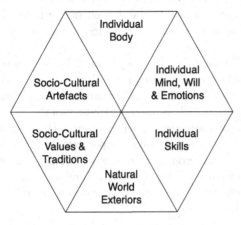

Figure 5.1 The six hextants of holonic identity

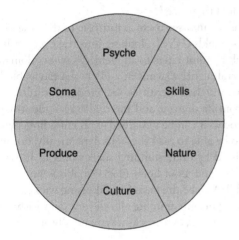

Figure 5.2 Naming the holonic identity's hextants

Here, they mean:

- *Soma:* The holon's body.
- *Psyche:* The holon's mind, will, temperament, imagination, emotions, enlight-ening and endarkening – all our interior, including Gerard Manley Hopkins inscape and instress, and the innenwelt as distinct from the umwelt (which includes produce, culture, and nature). It enfolds the Anthropological Machine, and our inbuilt autotelaxic desires, and our later emergent capacities to monitor and evaluate them.
- *Skills:* The skills and abilities that a holon has to address the world. For humans they include using our languages, learning, dexterity etc.

- *Nature:* All other holons, that is, every existent not a holon-made artefact.
- *Culture:* The sociocultural environment in the umwelt of the holon. For humans, these include art, literature, music, conversations, communications etc.
- *Produce:* Artefacts and performances produced by holons. The products of their skills and abilities. For humans these include both the instruments of an orchestra and the music they produce in a performance. These products include socially produced artefacts such as states, which are not the product of any one person, but of many, sometimes over millennia. This hextant, absent in Habermas and Wilber, is a particularly important differentiation for my purposes. We take our backgrounds as read when we grow up, but what is nature (holons) and what is produce (artefacts) is relevant in determining when to employ a complicated or complex approach to the relevant components of wicked problems.

Each of these has their own levels of development and emergence along many lines, which depend upon the umfeld they face.[2]

In their spherical manifestations, we may see them as intrinsic to the holarchic vortex networks within heterarchic fields (HVN), looking into the cyclone-like vortex depicted in Figure 5.3. Each hextant refers to an identity's reality domain. Along with all others, the six-hextal identity swims in a HVN sea navigable by ADALAS comprising other holons and their identities, and produce, culture, and nature, addressing what it can from its umwelt and internalising – identifying with – parts of that sea. In that process it can be visualised as an enfolding, dynamic torus. Like Tupaia, we need to be able to read the signs dynamically, not just statically. This navigation is assisted by understanding such works as those of Levinas (1989) re intersubjectivity and Bourdieu's (1984) habitus and field. I intend this framing for HVN↔HBA to be the basis for addressing wicked valuation problems when NSEW meet, not only framing all relevant data within it, but also inter-related data, and intrinsically, extrinsically, systemically and market valuing them as required.

Consequently, for Octo's fitness landscape I firstly envisaged a three-dimensional ontology, allowing a greater degree of freedom in modelling its milieu. However, there is no need to confine any ontology to three dimensions. A computer can allow n-dimension mapping. I could factor in all dimensions I considered relevant to Octo, including its external individual capacities, and the external boundaries of its umfeld and its various internal individual development lines, streams etc. Similarly, the six hextants in an identity are not set in stone; as the occasions demand, there can be n-numbers of divisions of the circle.

A collateral advantage of hextants, however, *as they are a mental aid and not a material object,* is that we can view them as a two-dimensional depiction of a three-dimensional object by means of having points representing the four directions plus up and down. Thereby we can further allow the weighing and degrees of those relationships. We can then bulge out the cube into a differentiated

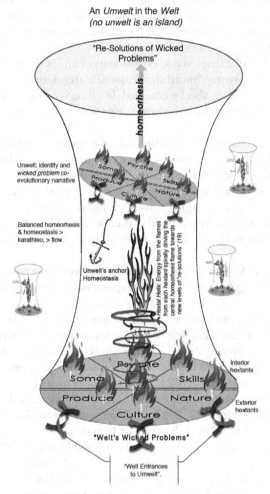

An *Umwelt* in the *Welt*
(no umwelt is an island)

"Re-Solutions of Wicked
Problems"

homeorhesis

Unwelt: identity and
wicked problem co-
evolutionary narrative

Soma   Psyche
Produce   Skills
Culture   Nature

Balanced homeorhesis
& homeostasis >
karathleo, > flow.

Hextal Helix: Energy from the flames
from each hextant spirally driving the
central homeorhesis flame towards
new levels of 're-solutions' (19)

Unwelt's anchor
Homeostasis

Interior
hextants

Psyche
Soma   Skills
Produce   Nature
Culture

Exterior
hextants

"Welt's Wicked Problems"

"Welt Entrances
to Umwelt".

Figure 5.3 A holonic identity dynamically developing in addressing wicked valuation
problems in its environment

sphere without firm radii, or the perspective on the cube changed to allow the cubic representation of relating matters, thereby for example "contrasting framings of target properties in governance actions against vulnerability" (Stirling 2012, p. 25). As such, it serves not only as an example of the sort of geometric modelling the hextants provide, but is also germane to HVN↔HBA, for:

> Only by envisaging these dynamics of framing in three interlinked dimensions of normativity, temporality and agency is it possible properly to encapsulate the multivalent relationships between different kinds of dynamic properties and associated governance interventions.
>
> (Stirling 2012, p. 25)

One established use of this shape is the Institute of Development Studies' *Powercube* (2011), which is designed to facilitate understanding via analysis of how power dynamics relate in social relations and organisations, and includes mapping power at different spaces and levels.

The main advantage of the cube shape is not exclusionary of any of the above. Its potential as a datacube, relating "multi-dimensional extensions of two-dimensional tables" (ABS 2013), can also be enfolded. In all such cases, I mean these cubes to be seen in conjunction with the hextal approach, not as separated by a monological gaze.

Returning to our Octo, starting with the fertilisation of its mother's ovum by its father's spermatozoon, it expanded or contracted according to the matching of the individual and environmental conditions. So we should not regard Octo's hextants as static, but relating and evolving. Some existents even change their hextants, some artefacts (for example, beavers' dams) becoming parts of the natural landscape over time, as do our bodies when we die. Moreover, we can regard them as axonically inter- and extra-connected at and between each fractal level.

I intend this hextal framing for use *via the loose coupling appropriate to complex adaptive and heterarchic systems*, not the tight structuring appropriate to complicated and hierarchical systems.

Another initiative requiring such loose coupling, *bioeconomics*, a subset of Corning's paradigm, looks to the enfolding of economics into ecology (Hurst 2015). It is being developed to investigate the relationship between cultures and institutions on the one hand, and the biological substrates that are expressed through them on the other (Corning 2005, p. 232). That is, the relationship of the three exterior hextants (produce, culture, and nature). The complementary discipline of neural evolution (Edelman 1987, 2004; Edelman and Tononi 2000) is being amended and developed to address the interior hextants (soma, psyche, skills) (Fernando and Szathmáry 2010; Fernando, Szathmáry and Husbands 2012; Fernando 2013). For example, recent research looks towards establishing a relationship between compassion and the functioning of the vagus nerve (Porges 2003; Keltner 2009). Such problems may include atrophied capacity for compassion.

I: the Identity Principle

"Identity seems to be unshakable, but its apparent stability is an illusion. As the world changes, identity changes; and as identity changes, it alters the world along with it. Because the mind and the world develop at different rates and in different ways, during times of rapid change they cease to be complementary . . . The result is a widening gap between the world as it exists in the mind and the world as it is experienced – between identity formed by tradition and identity demanded by the present (Hardison 1981, pp. xi–xii).

It is now clear that while "the formation of the self [is] a crucial topic for the study of evaluation" . . . "this topic is not typically included in the cultural or economic sociology of evaluation" (Lamont 2012, p. 212). I consider the topic to be similarly crucial in addressing the topic of this work, for people evaluate via both the "Big V" and "small v" valuations they hold.

The Online Dictionary definition of identity is "who you are, the way you think about yourself, the way you are viewed by the world and the characteristics that define you". A more developed definition is:

> The tendency in human beings, individually and in groups, to establish and maintain a sense of self-meaning, predictability and purpose ... an abiding sense of selfhood that is the core of what makes life predictable to an individual.
>
> (Northrup 1989, pp. 63–64)

A more succinct one is "an explicit theory of oneself as a person" (Moshman 1998).

Starting at the simplex level, at least at first, we uncritically internalise from our immediate environment:

> We as subjects are not what generate the statements in each of us; they are produced by something entirely different, by "multiplicities, masses and packs, peoples and tribes: all collective arrangements which are within us and for which we are vehicles, without knowing precisely what those arrangements are".
>
> (Lazzarato 2006)

Driven by the abovementioned hungers, particularly the regard-hunger that had set me off on my travels in the first place, the revolutionary power of imitation (McGilchrist 2009, p. 251) is core to this identity construction process. Because we are holons:

> Human imitation is not slavish. It is not a mechanical process, dead, perfect, finished, but one that introduces variety and uniqueness to the "copy", which above all remains alive, since it becomes instantiated in the context of a different, unique, human individual.
>
> (McGilchrist 2009, p. 247)

Thereby, "founded on empathy and grounded in the body ... [i]mitation gives rise, paradoxically as it may seem, to individuality" (ibid., pp. 248 and 249). From that base, we develop our quotidian identities through narratives (Greenwald 1980; McAdams, Josselson and Lieblich 2006; Akerlof and Shiller 2009, p. 51; Loy 2010, p. 26; T. King 2003; J. E. King 2003), by means of mythically identifying (McGilchrist 2009, p. 249) with stories fulfilling our wants: "the human mind is a story processor, not a logic processor" (Haidt 2012, p. 281), and "in everyday life, we are all bookkeepers and storytellers" (Stark 2000, p. 5).

McGilchrist warns that "We need to be careful of our imagination, since what we imagine is in a sense what we are and who we become" (McGilchrist 2009,

p. 250). Many of these stories involve a heroic figure overcoming horrendous obstacles, often of the "us versus them" variety as in the Anthropological Machine, and thereby being held in high regard by those benefitting from the hero's actions:

> Identities are forged through the marking of difference. This marking of difference takes place both through the symbolic systems of representation, and through forms of social exclusion. Identity, then, is not the opposite of, but depends on, difference. In social relations, these forms of symbolic and social difference are established, at least in part, through the operation of what are called classificatory systems. A classificatory system applies a principle of difference to a population in such a way as to divide them and all their characteristics into at least two, opposing groups us/them (e.g. Serb/Croat); self/other.
>
> (Woodward 1997, p. 29)

In constructing our identities, Gerald Smallberg (in Brockman 2013, p. 285) observes that *our life narrative depends upon a neurologically discovered trick* (Libet et al. 1983), whereby our brain receives external stimuli about a third of a second before we become conscious of it. For the good reason Smallberg describes, we actually *falsify the time some existent happens*, giving us time by this "involuntary censorship" to be story-makers, pattern-makers and reality inhibitors (see Grove 1992, pp. 182–183), the pattern in this context being our fitting of our new stories into what has happened to us before. Because of the Wizard of Oz being a trickster, Smallberg calls the performer of this trick "The Wizard of I". I see that Wizard not as a "trick", but as an *emergent* with the capacity to internalise memes as memeplexes. It furnishes us with a Tao that can be known, via single vision, but when it assumes Mastery instead of being the Emissary, it becomes blind, deaf and dumb to the Eternal Tao.

This emergent capacity performs wonders, and a "strange new science of the self" (Ananthaswamy 2015) is now emerging to study it: "Scientific research highlights the central role of specific psychological processes, in particular those related to the self, in various forms of human suffering and flourishing" (Dahl, Lutz and Davidson 2015, p. 515). The Wizard of I is of huge extrinsic value in allowing us to prepare and scheme ahead, and recall our good times to help our resilience and antifragility in bad times. It is a prerequisite for effective functioning. Rather than living in the moment; as Bruno Latour warns:

> What has happened to those who, like Heidegger, have tried to find their ways in immediacy, in intuition, in nature would be too sad to retell – and is well known anyway. What is certain is that those pathmarks off the beaten track led indeed nowhere.
>
> (Latour 2004, p. 233)

Not necessarily, but Latour has a point worth making here, although not quite as unqualified in this context as he asserts in his (Stanley and Lehman 2015).

Ultimately, I see it more like a breathing in with sensate immediacy and intuition, and a breathing out through the extrinsically valuable Wizard of I. I see this as in a related evolution process, just as Kahneman describes in *Thinking Fast and Slow* (2011), and current courses on learning consider both focussed and diffused modes to be fundamental to the learning process (Sejnowski and Oakley n.d.).

I also see such reintegrations into processes as vitally important, not just for learning, but for valuations and still broader domains. For example, Midgley notes that mind and matter are not separate, but "complementary aspects of a most complex whole" (Midgley 2014, p. 89) which whole, I add again, is not a thing but a process. Midgley then claims that the hard problem of consciousness studies (Chalmers 1995, 1995a) assumes that matter is dead, inert, but it isn't (Midgley 2014, p. 144); it is "much more active and mysterious" (ibid., p. 88). Given that "[r]ather than trying to sweep away the mystery of mind by attributing it to the mechanisms of matter, we must grapple with the intertwined nature of the two" (Frank 2017), Rucker's statement, "to exist is to have consciousness" (Rucker 1997, p. 184), could also be phrased as "to exist is to have consciousness have you". For this work, I assume that they are parts of "a necessary unity" setting aside proprietorial rights, just as Bateson (1979) himself said mind and nature are, in the title to his book.

Again, HVN enfolds Midgley's much more active and mysterious process not as a thing, but as a process, which, from HVN I, models as developing via a hextal helix. As the inter-hextal "whole" part of the whole/part nature of holons, holons construct identities. While constants remain, they adapt and change outside their core.

One of the texts available during my youthful questing was *Childhood and Society* (Erikson 1977), which classified identity construction into eight stages:

- Basic trust versus basic mistrust (ibid., p. 222ff).
- Autonomy versus shame and doubt (ibid., p. 226ff).
- Initiative versus guilt (ibid., p. 229ff).
- Industry versus inferiority (ibid., p. 232ff).
- Identity versus role confusion (ibid., p. 234ff).
- Intimacy versus isolation (ibid., p. 237ff).
- Generativity versus stagnation (ibid., p. 240ff).
- Ego integrity versus despair (ibid., p. 241ff).

As do I with HVN↔HBA, Erikson cautioned that such charts are "only a tool to think with" and not a prescription (ibid., p. 243). However, I noted several homologies with my own identity construction, which helps me intuit such homologies in others, including those affected by these wicked valuation problems. I have since developed my understanding through more contemporary researchers on the subject (Carter 2008; Greenfield 2008; Musschenga et al. 2002; Rockwell 2005; Schore and Schore 2008; Colozino 2009; Colozino and Buczynski 2011; Csikszentmihalyi 1993 esp p. 216ff.), including in the legal context of real property rights (Hughes 2003), as have scholars of Erikson's "rather diffuse psy-choanalytic concept" (Moshman 1998): for example, Blasi and Glodis (1995).

This is a topic that each of us can examine by introspection and confirm by peer reviews – that is, conversations – and by referring to scholarship to access more rigorous inquiries. For instance, I found that the regard-recognition hunger I had gone to Europe to ask Krishnamurti about relates to scholarship itself: science "has evolved a reward system which consists basically of rewarding scientists by having knowledgeable peers grant them public recognition for their distinctive contributions" (Merton 1995, p. 381). I have also discovered that, while some consider identity is constructed via a single hunger – self-esteem (Abrams 1992) – I now find myself to be more home in a more complex interplay of drivers, such as Breakwell's self-esteem, distinctiveness, continuity and self-efficacy hungers (Breakwell 1992).

Zock described Erikson's life work as "a psychology of ultimate concern" (Zock 2004) particularly after *Childhood and Society* (ibid., p. 11). While critical of Erikson's lack of systemic rigour (ibid., p. 13) Zock notes that Erikson's concept of wholeness strongly resembles the meaning of the Jewish greeting, "Shalom". The meaning of "Shalom" encompasses "health *and* peace *and* salv-ation simultaneously" (ibid., p. 216). That spirit often appears to be wanting in attempts at solving wicked problems (Northrup 1989). In my experience, that deficiency is often present in land policy reforms or the reaction thereto.

For me, like Erikson, and like Hopkins and Wordsworth, one builder of my identity construction is the sense sublime of some existent far more deeply interfused, that sudden perception of that deeper pattern, order, and unity which gives meaning to external forms which are "rooted and grounded in finiteness" (Hodgson and King 1982, p. 137). Friedrich Schleiermacher (1768–1834) described it as a "sense and taste of the infinite", and an intuition of the whole mediated through a particular experience (Schleiermacher 1958). That seems like "Shalom" to me.

Sages have observed that the identity construction from the above process is not one's true identity at all: the process itself is. From their approach, we can regard megalomania as the expropriation of the constructor by the constructed, the Emissary taking itself to be the Master: a complete inversion of reality.

The construction via emergent regard and other hungers is an internal artefact with which we can address our fitness landscape. From many traditions and reli-gions, their insights can be summed up by the phrase from the Chandogya Upanishad, "tat tvam asi" – "thou art that" – realising that both the manifested process and resultant constructed identity are impermanent processes within the nondual, the ground of each person's being the ground of all being (Armstrong 1993, pp. 226–227). Hence, the "neti, neti", – not this, not this . . . in the Brihadaranyaka Upanishad is complementary, not contradictory, to "tat tvam asi". As the Chandogya Upanishad puts it:

> Other it is, for sure, than what is known
> Beyond the scope of the unknown, too.

So we have learnt from men of old
Who instructed us therein.
That which thinks not by the mind
By which, they say, the mind is thought
That is Truth
Not that which is worshipped here as such.

Thompson identifies this thinker of the mind, not as a god, but as the pre-personal lived body, the conduit to which is McGilchrist's Master. "In this way, I think we can remove the Advaita conception of dreamless sleep from its native meta-physical framework and graft it onto a naturalist conception of the embodied mind" (Thompson 2015, p. 10). Single vision may say, "oh, that means that our identities are nothing but artefacts of our pre-personal lived body". That quite misses the point that *as such*, the mind emanates from connections having connections, and so on ad infinitum, including all past existents, such that "it is probably impossible to describe any one thing in the world exhaustively without mentioning everything else as well" (Rucker 1997, p. 142). That is, identities are formed by the pre-personal lived body addressing, and being addressed by, the environment, and the environment is inseparable from the universe, by which the mind is thought.

The inseparability of mind and nature, soma and psyche, Bateson's (1979) necessary unity, Midgley's two complementary aspects of the same whole (Midgley 2014, p. 89), and the earlier answer of the eyes, is the inheritor of the wisdom that got us to identity in the first place through the winnowing processes of our co-evolution. As such, I see it as potentially a far more potent means of addressing wicked valuation problems than anything that could be supplied from within single vision.

As long as one recognises that one's pre-personal lived body is an existent in co-evolution with one's identity, the pre-personal lived body can be seen as "that which, they say, the identity is thought"; as a holonic vortex within the HVN. Thereby, in the very questing, such as found in poetry reading, along pilgrimages and other activities, and not in whatever questions prompting the quest or in the answer, dwells that sudden perception of that deeper pattern, that sense sublime. The corollary is that it is not just thou that art that; every other thou is that too.

The baser politicians manipulate identities in the manner described by Tagore quoted in the introduction to this work, but the nation-state can be, and often is, employed for the benefit of its citizens. Generally, the better angels of our nature (Pinker 2011) prevail more where those in control of state machinery realise that individual identities are not subjects of the state, but the state is their subject, their machine. Machinery does not rule, but identities who control the most powerful machineries may need checking and balancing for the better angels to sustain their governance. For those in control of any powerful machine, as Lord Astor put it in an 1887 letter to Bishop Mandell Creighton, "Power tends to corrupt, and absolute power corrupts absolutely. Great men are almost always bad men".

Bateson made an important differentiation here. It is not so much that power corrupts as: "The idea of power corrupts. Power corrupts most rapidly those who believe in it, and it is they who will want it most" (Bateson 1987, p. 492). Yiftachel's topic is land and identity in Israel and Palestine, and I can confirm Bateson's observation from my own times there, and in studies of its history. The situation there is about as far as it is possible to get from understanding the lessons of the Kalachakra Sand Mandala concerning the role of spatial imaginaries and identity construction (Bryant 2003). In addition, the rubric that the crisis there is about religion and real estate has surprising, albeit incomplete, explanatory depth.

Returning to Woodward's (1997) defining of identity as that which is constructed by the marking of differences: this is what the Anthropological Machine does at different scales, including that of the nation-state. "All wars are about establishing borders" (Shell 1993, p. 178) at all the relevant scales, including that of the soma, the physical identity, and the socio-cultural hextant identities of whatever scale, including fictive ones. Furthermore, the word "identity" is from the Latin *identidem*, which means "over and over" (Loy 2010). We identity construct with and through habits.

At this level of identity we can be seen, as Susan Blackmore puts it, as a "selfplex", a vast aggregation of memes constructed by us as meme machines (Blackmore 1999, pp. 231–234) without which, Blackmore claims, "compassion and empathy come naturally" (ibid., p. 246). Like Krishnamurti, Blackmore recommends we "drop it" to become truly free, because there is no selplex to care about (ibid.).

I have been thinking about that from the time I understood what Krishnamurti was saying, which was even from before the time I asked that question of the Buddhist nun in Adelaide. Now, instead, I recommend that rather than drop it we *properly value* our own selplex and its components intrinsically, extrinsically, and systemically. That requires not dropping them, because we cannot without those prior valuations.

Similarly, Lebow (2012) sees our identities as artefacts, and tracks our identity construction in the West through history as being divisible into four political orientations: conservatism, totalitarianism, liberalism and anarchism. Lebow then calls for more monitoring and evaluating of how we are manipulated in that construction, and for more emphasis and value to be placed upon our drawing together rather than our separating ourselves from others.

I consider that an action inquiry (Torbert and Associates 2004) response to Ricardo Molina's inquiry (asking if the answer to a question might be hidden in the question itself), particularly identifying and valuing our own collective narcissisms (De Zavala et al. 2009), can markedly facilitate Lebow's recommendation, and help to address these wicked valuation problems. These processes are not confined to the present moment. They can be recollected in tranquillity, including within the meditative process (Dahl, Luts and Davidson 2015). With any collective narcissisms, we can point out and communicate to, but can neither judge nor reform. From the complexity perspective, I see identity as heterarchic and fractal, but "fractal" not in the sense of necessarily fractured, as Baudrillard (1993) considers,

Box 5.1 Concerning Jean Baudrillard on values in his *The Transparency of Evil*

In his work, *The Transparency of Evil: Essays on Extreme Phenomena* (1993), Baudrillard has an exemplary reaction to the shock of the new. He furnishes us with a four-stage framing for values. The first of these, the natural value, is use value (my "extrinsic"), "developed on the basis of a natural use of the world" (ibid., p. 5). The second stage is the commodity stage: exchange value (market value), founded on general equivalence. The third stage is the structural stage: sign value: "governed by a code, value develops here by reference to a set of models" (ibid.), such as the models herein, including HVN↔HBA. The fourth, fractal stage, he recoils at as being chaotic "epidemic" and "metastasis of value", "making all valuation impossible" (ibid.): "Good is no longer the opposite of evil, nothing can now be plotted on a graph or analysed in terms of abscissas and coordinates" (ibid., p. 6).

I interpret this an anxious reaction in terms of the Goldilocks Principle, but mention it here as an example of the evolutionary usefulness of identity construction. Assaults such as this fourth stage one on Baudrillard's conceptual framing could be ingested over time towards being accommodated in bite-sized chunks into our identities – a process that might involve both transformation of some aspects of a fractal identity, or translation into an existing framework.

In dramatic contrast to Baudrillard's reaction, that same year the mathematician and chaos theorist Ralph H. Abraham (1993) wrote his essay *Human Fractals: The Arabesque in our Mind*. While noting that applying fractal theory to the humanities may seem anathema to many pure mathematicians – "fractal evil itself" – he saw it as potentially restoring "a long lost partnership between mathematics and cultural history and evolution". In turn, he saw that as jump-starting a phase transition into kingdoms vast and strange, "a critical step off the sandy beach of Pythagoras, Plato, and Euclid, and into the post-Pythagorean sea of Mandelbrot. For the future of cultural studies, this is a great leap into space" (ibid.). Loy describes that space as his "no-thing-ness", Nagarjunya's *shunyata* (exhaustion of all theories and views) which, as the Kena Upanishad puts it, is not understood by those who understand it, and is "understood by those who understand it not" (Loy 2010, p. 39). It is the Tao that cannot be known, and, as I read over forty years ago:

> When they assert that they have come into contact with reality, that they know, then you may be quite sure that what they know is not reality. What they know is their own projection from the past. So the man who says he knows, does not know.
>
> (Krishnamurti 1970, p. 127)

but as potentially integrated. Identity as differentiated, articulated and holarchically integrated into HVN, and as such relating heterarchically with others and the world at large.

When looking to understand this identity construction process, another major resource is Charles Taylor's *Sources of the Self* (1989), where he first articulates moral frameworks in terms of three axes:

1   beliefs about the value of human life;
2   beliefs about the kind of life worth living; and
3   how we value ourselves and others regarding our societal roles.

An identity has both depths and spans, the former tracked by developmental psychologists – Commons, Torbert and others – and the latter by an expanding embrace of one's bodyself, family, tribe, institution, nation, civilisation, species, or planet; countless millions have died and countries destroyed in determining which of these imaginal selves is to reign (Fraser 1999, p. 104).

Peace, the systemic value adopted for this work, requires all hextant functionality in identity construction facilitating that sense of autotelaxic flow towards peace, the very process in which the answer lies hid.

In so doing, Fowler notes that the innate drivers of reproduction, identity and meaning produce the compound drivers of religion, patriarchy and social identity (Fowler 2007, p. 13). That is, they engage with and influence the socio-cultural hextant. I expand this to the other hextants as well, including constant re-engagement with all hextants in the identity construction process.

From the descriptions of *flow* in the works of Csikszentmihalyi (for example Csikszentmihalyi 1988, 1990, 1993; Csikszentmihalyi and Csikzsentmihalyi 2006), I make the strong claim that the views of peace described by Whitehead and Tanase are descriptions, causes or consequences of the autotelaxic flow state (Whitehead's involving transcendence to a higher level) as described in Chapter 5. "Peace" is *not* about stagnation or death; it is about growth at the edge of chaos: about autotelaxic flow. As quoted in more detail on p. 204 below, peace is the "Harmony of Harmonies" (Whitehead 1967, p. 285), between people and between their social imaginary constructions such as nations and other organisations, internalised or otherwise, involving a mutual recognition of them in both the speaker and the spoken for.

I am asserting that these views of peace are those of high intrinsic value, and those to which the artefacts known as real property rights should be designed to effect. However for peace to be effected by skilful means, as Csikszentmihalyi points out identity growth in people (including autotelaxic growth) can *only* be effected through a process of flow. In the context of this work, develop identities that involve too little challenge and they will stagnate, too much and they will collapse into prejudice or rigidity. Provide far too much and they will be traumatised, which the identities concerned may or may not be able to address over time (Rosenbaum et al. 2011; Gao 2013). In my experience, both extremes are commonplace in NSEW, and the high extrinsic value of identity constructs are utilised to reify high intrinsic values in NSEW.

Moreover, the Korean mathematician Daegene Song (2007, 2015) claims to have established mathematically that artefacts such as computers will never become conscious. If true, Song's claim is consistent with this work in artefacts never becoming holons. They will forever lack the psyche hextant, and thereby, according to Damasio's definition above, never achieve consciousness and identity. Like states, sports teams, cars and other artefacts, people may identify with them, but they will not identify back.

I strongly agree with the first part of Edgar Morin's claim that a fundamental requirement for modern education is addressing "what is the human identity and condition". However, I must respectfully disagree with his adding, "which is not found anywhere" (Morin 2007, p. 27). I have found disciplines that do so at the tertiary education level and cited several of them here. Identity is fundamental to our being able to address challenges through time. These include market behaviour in general, and behaviour concerning real property in particular, as one's land is often a bedrock of one's identity (Erikson 1977; Davidson 2012; Radin 1982; Espeland 1998; Berberich, Campbell and Hudson 2012; Housty 2013; Critchley n.d.; Menatti 2013). As Narcissi Blood, the late spokesperson of the Blackfoot Tribe put it; they respected the land as their mother, for "Most people's anchor is the land. Their roots are in the land. The land is what makes us who we are" (Mandel and Tearney 2015, 5:30).

Also:

> Identity is how we make sense of ourselves, and geographers, anthropologists and sociologists, amongst others, have argued that the meanings given to a place may become so strong that they become a central part of the identity of the people experiencing them.
>
> (Massey and Jess 1995, p. 88)

Also, "The idea of place, the 'where' of things, is not just being thought of as a specialty corner, as it were, but as something that is really central to all we do" (Rumsey 2005, 1:55–2:03).

I would go further: it is really central to our identity construction, and who we may become. For example, a Heiltsuk claims:

> We have fostered a strong sense of place-based identity . . . You cannot assign a dollar value to the potential for transformation. When you take away hope, there is no adequate compensation. Our culture is based on stories. Those stories are written on the lands and waters. If the lands and waters are destroyed, our stories will be destroyed, our way of life will be lost and our culture will be gone . . . I respectfully disagree with the notion that there is any compensation to be made for the loss of our identity and for the loss of our right to be Heiltsuk.
>
> (Housty 2013)

How would that affect the subject of this work? The answer is "profoundly", because, as in the case of Australian Aboriginal culture in particular but not at all exclusively (King et al. 2010), identity construction is intimately related to land (Berberich, Campbell and Hudson 2012; Davidson 2012; McClay and McAllister 2014). Scholars also related land and social identity (Swann et al. 2012; Brewer and Gardner 1996; Hill 2011; Kögler 2012; Olwig and Besson 2005; Tajfel 1986; Yiftachel 2006), and these identity attachments can be a major contributor to wicked valuation problems.

Moreover, many politicians recognise that role of land. As a former Jamaican Prime Minister put it:

> This sense of community among the people of the region anchors a collective identity which the integration process must nurture. We must never belittle the importance of identity, which is integral to our sense of psychic well-being.
>
> (Patterson 2006, p. 32)

That is not to say that it is of invariant importance for all. The operative word is "may", not "will". There are important cultural and individual differences in the weight of place-identity or place identities in one's overall identity, and not all place-identity's importance is always consciously appreciated (Proshansky, Fabian and Kaminoff 1983, p. 63).

The study of the relationship of place to identity is difficult because of the diversity of approaches available. These include not only those in both the theoretical and empirical domains (Hidalgo and Hernandez 2001, p. 272), but also those addressing the many contributing variables (ibid., pp. 273–274, and Casakin and Bernardo 2012).

After a brief review of the multifarious nature of identity construction processes, Proshansky, Fabian and Kaminoff define place-identity as a person's environmental past, "consisting of places, spaces and their properties which have served instrumentally in the satisfaction of the person's biological, psychological and cultural needs" (Proshansky, Fabian and Kaminoff 1983, p. 59).

Research has shown that "well-being, health and natural landscape are correlated" (Menatti and Da Rocha 2016), including but not limited to our natural topophilia and biophilia (ibid.): "*We live embedded in landscape* and, as we add, *we perceive it through our whole body*, and therefore *it affects our well-being*" (ibid.; italics in the original).

The links between place and identity identified by environmental psychologists are already sufficiently established to be considered a legitimate head of compensation in many legal domains (within what is called "solatium").

I see identity constructions as emergent from the heterarchical interactions of our organically and environmentally supplied desires, and these desires being the psyche hextant's necessary contribution to evolution. Without the primal desire to survive and flourish, organisms would not. That desire, including but not limited to my regard-recognition hunger, has to be there before it can be transcended and included. We need single vision before twofold can emerge, twofold before threefold, and threefold before fourfold.

Moreover, it is identity construction that turns space into place, and identities need both, for "place is security, space is freedom: we are attached to the one, and long for the other" (Tuan 1977, p. 3). Identity is also seen by Fowler as one of the three innate drivers of civic agency, the others being reproduction and meaning (Fowler 2007, p. 9). I enfold both desire (including for reproduction) and spirituality, particularly the search for meaning, as identity construction drivers. This follows from Northrup's above definition and the observation that all constructivism is meaning making, but not all meaning making is constructivism. In contrast, all learning is meaning making and all meaning making is learning (Hein 1999).

The centrality of considering this identity construction process at various scales, with a particular reference on the role of stories within it, in the political sphere has been emphasised by Charles Tilly – "identity claims and their attendant stories constitute serious political business" (2002, p. 207), and in consequence recommends the realigning of foci and processes terms of the development of democracy and the restriction of wars. Given the extraordinary complexities involved in the domain he addresses and those involved in land policy and reform, there are significant possibilities for these domains to learn from one another in this context.

I have now emphasised the importance of identity in addressing wicked land-related valuation problems. That is the most relevant matter to this work, but from the work's process approach it should also be recognised that we may be in a continual process of identity construction. While land policies, land-related valuations and real property rights clearly address the physiological and safety needs of such identities, we must now examine their potential roles in facilitating further development towards peace. To do so, we must examine what development is.

D: the Development Principle

The Orthogenetic Principle states that wherever development occurs, it proceeds from a state of relative globality and lack of differentiation to states of increasing differentiation, articulation, and hierarchic integration (Werner 1957, p. 126). What I term here the "Development Principle" is more technically and precisely termed that Orthogenic Principle, but renamed here for simplicity's sake. Note that development involves differentiation, not dissociation as in the anthropic machine. Furthermore, Werner was operating inside a mechanical paradigm. In holons, such as in dynamic systems development, development occurs:

> as a sequence of overlapping waves, with relatively long periods of consolidation (plateaus), during which performance within a domain tends to be largely homogeneous (i.e., predominantly at a single complexity order), and shorter transitional periods (spurts) characterized by vacillation between the

modal complexity order and its successor. Several other researchers have provided evidence of spurts, drops, or shifts during developmental transitions in childhood, adolescence, and early adulthood that are consistent with a dynamic systems perspective on cognitive development.

(Dawson-Tunik 2004, p. 17)

Moreover, such holonic development should be regarded as a holonic integration achieved heterarchically, not linearly, and not merely a hierarchical one. So this development principle differs from the orthogenic principle in including heterarchical and holonic integrations, not only, or even particularly, hierarchic development. Unlike hierarchies, the term enfolds "the relation of elements to one another when they are unranked or when they possess the potential of being ranked in a number of different ways" (Crumley 1995, p. 3).

The development principle applies to every existent, including their heterarchical relationships: "there are two great trends within evolution. One is towards diversification. The other is towards integration and cooperation" (Stewart 2014, p. 35), and all proceed as Dawson-Tunik has explained. In the context of this work, that applies not only to the environment, the land policies, land-related valuations and real property rights, and the resultant fitness landscapes included their wicked valuation problems; it also applies to the cognitive and valuational capabilities and methodologies of those participating in those domains. I see such development as progress, not that which is currently measured as gross domestic product (GDP):

> The successor to GDP should be a new set of metrics that integrates current knowledge of how ecology, economics, psychology and sociology collectively contribute to establishing and measuring sustainable wellbeing . . .
>
> It is often said that what you measure is what you get. Building the future we desire requires that we measure what we want, remembering that it is better to be approximately right than precisely wrong.
>
> (Costanza et al. 2014, p. 285)

When combined with the Goldilocks Principle described on p. 200 below, the Development Principle can assist in identifying practical inter-hextal development, and thereby guiding such development towards the higher intrinsic values generally desired, and the appropriate level extrinsic values to facilitate that development.

For an example, I shall refer to Long (2004), Gigerenzer and Todd (1999), and Poundstone (2013), who establish our limited identities need heuristics to deal with wicked problems, and Long does so in the most relevant context to this work; that of property law.

Long sees the law as a means of reducing the cognitive cost of the information required to operate effectively in an environment. In other words, she sees it as a means of facilitating effective social, environmental and economic relationships towards social policy values. As such, she is following Zipf (1949), but undervalues

Midgley's observation that "there is nothing rational about using simple premises for complex subject matter" (Midgley 1995, p. 181). I have centred this work upon a HVN, not static, approach, so this principle prompts the question: "what degrees of intra- and inter-hextal differentiation, articulation and holarchic integration are optimal to address any social, environmental and economic problems, and, in particular, wicked problems?"

The following question would then be, "what are the most skilful means to address those problems?" Not only laws, but also opinions can then be intrinsically, extrinsically and systemically valued by how developed they are, and what is required in, for example, dismantling these wicked valuation problems.

I refer to the classic novel *Lord of the Flies* (Golding 1954) as an example. In the book, choirboys are stranded on an island otherwise uninhabited by humans, where they encounter a very different environment and proceed to adapt. Some (Ralph, Simon, Piggy, and others), wish to adhere to the intrinsically and systemically valuable orderly behaviour appropriate to their former environment. Others, led by Jack, want to resort to the extrinsically valuable but intrinsically bestial behaviour that the absence of former social constraints now allow in their new environment. That led firstly to animal slaughter, then the killing of Simon and Piggy, and finally to the destruction of their environment by fire and the hunting of Ralph.

Without the novelist's devices of the fire and the last-minute saving of Ralph by the British Navy, what would the future have been? After Ralph's murder, what would have guided Jack and his followers' behaviour?

Ralph represented Machiavelli's law, Jack Machiavelli's force. In *Beast and Man*, Midgley (1995, p. 89) notes the silliness of the presumption of infantile omnipotence. "Silly" is rather too slight a term for its social consequences: as Oliver (2007, p. 2) asks, "how does animality justify enslavement and cruelty", not just with other people, but also with other animals: Both Machiavelli's choices are within Agamben's Anthropological Machine. It is not as though Jack's attitude to kids and pigs is isolated on some faraway island: the infantile is within us all.

In terms of land policies, land-related valuations and real property rights, a developed understanding requires differentiation, articulation and holarchic integration to find a good practice in an environment to develop the most anti-fragile fitness landscapes. "Transparency and detail are everything in science" (Goldacre 2008, p. 50), and once again such qualities are facilitated by an appropriately differentiated, articulated and hierarchically integrated vocabulary. For example, often "the commons" is a globular term, but in reality, commons are not uniform; "it is necessary to move beyond the concepts of communal and individual ownership" (Terrill 2015). To take just one example: as Greer observed (Greer 2012), the colonial enterprise largely succeeded by conquest of the European commons over the indigenous commons, with enclosures following in their wake. Greer makes further useful distinctions in facilitating a more developed understanding of the kind referred to in Chapter 1. For example, Greer distinguishes between the "inner commons" (for example, the tillage zone of a local community), and the "outer commons" (collectively owned resources beyond the local croplands), and the open commons. He does so to note the primacy of the outer commons in effecting the colonial endeavour (ibid., p. 369). As well as differing in kind, commons also differ in scale, and I mean the ADALAS section of HBA to facilitate a more developed understanding of land tenures via their more precise articulation and differentiation and potential integration with other tenures.

E: the Emergence Principle

Emergence is "a unifying theme for 21st century science" (Pines 2014, title). This principle relates to the "holarchical integration" adaption of the above definition of development. In complexity theory, new levels emerge from the Goldilocks Principle being employed in an environment. It states that under such circumstances, once a critical mass of development has occurred at one level of development, a higher level of development as defined above may emerge, and with it entirely new laws, concepts and generalisations are necessary (Anderson 1972, p. 393).

Each new level is "novel, nonadditive, nonpredictable and nondeducible within a hierarchical context" (Korn 2005, p. 139), and both acts upon and is acted upon.

For example, when a new level of emergence of understanding a problem arises by development in the Goldilocks Zone, a "Eureka!" moment occurs: a new level of clarity arises.

When information is organised in terms of the Development Principle, we may gain all sorts of new insights towards how to resolve wicked valuation problems. For example, the Goldilocks Principle (described on p. 200ff. below) could be engaged to provide a timeline for how long it could take to gain the skills required for skilful means of addressing a problem.

In the field of adult development, the Model of Hierarchical Complexity (Commons et al. 2007) can measure psychological levels of developmental emergence (Table 5.5).

There could be other orders beyond Order 15. Ross et al. (2014) have proposed an Order 16, meta-cross paradigmatic, characterised by "properties of structure and process (dynamics) described by different paradigms are seen to apply across and operate on those paradigms" (ibid., p. 35).

If these are true levels of emergence, as Anderson observed entirely new laws, concepts and generalisations are necessary (Anderson 1972, p. 393) for each emergent level, and most of us have already achieved many such levels by adulthood. This highlights the fatuousness of the fastuous Procrustean bed described by Umberto Eco as that of fascists, requiring "an impoverished vocabulary, and an elementary syntax" (Eco 1995, p. 8). When it comes to addressing wicked valuation problems, the abovementioned "classical academic virtues such as erudition, depth of understanding, and sophistication" (Lamont 2012, p.14) are far more facilitatory. As with Panikkar's above warning about responding to a question based on any false premises, the use of an impoverished vocabulary

Table 5.5 The model of hierarchical complexity

Order or stage	What they do
0 – calculatory	Exact computation only, no generalisation; human-made programs that manipulate 0 or 1, not 2 or 3
1 – automatic	Engages in one operation at a time. Cellular activities: sensing, effecting
2 – sensory or motor	Discriminates in a rote fashion, stimuli generalisation, perceives and views objects or moves; moves limbs, lips, toes, eyes, elbows, head
3 – circular sensory-motor	Schemes (touch, grab, shake objects, circular babble . . .) coordinates perceptions and movements, forms open-ended proper classes, phonemes, archiphonemes
4 – sensory-motor	Responds to stimuli in a class successfully and non-stochastically, forms simple concepts, morphemes (coordinates schemes)
5 – nominal	Uses words and names for things (coordinates and relates concepts), single words: exclamations, verbs, nouns, number names, letter names
6 – sentential	Chains words (coordinates words and names), imitates and acquired sentences and sequences, follows short sequential acts, pronounces numbers in correct order, acquires pronouns subject (I), object (me), possessive adjectives (my) possessive pronoun (mine), and reflexive (myself)for various persons (I, you, he, she, it, we, y'all, they)
7 – preoperational	Simple deductions; tells stories, counts events and objects up to 5, combines numbers and simple propositions, connects the dots, follows lists of sequential acts
8 – primary	Simple logical deduction and empirical rules involving time sequence; simple arithmetic (adds, subtracts, multiplies, divides, counts, proves), does serial tasks on its own
9 – concrete	Full complex arithmetic (long division, short division). Second Person perspective: takes and coordinates perspective of other and self, follows complex social rules, forms cliques, plan reasonable deals, conceives history and geography
10 – abstract	Builds abstract concepts and variables of conference phenomena (time, place, act, actor, state, type), makes names and quantifies propositions, logical quantitating, (quantifiers: all, none, some), categorical statements/stereotypes; e.g. "we all die")
11 – formal	Coordinates two abstract variables, calculates the influence of one variable on another one, solves problems with one unknown using algebra, 1-dimensional linear logic (if-then) and empiricism
12 – systematic	Multiple relations between abstract variables, considers relationships in contexts (→ building systems)
13 – metasystematic	Compares and coordinates various systems, builds meta-systems out of disparate systems, as well as meta-theories (theories about theories)
14 – paradigmatic	Coordinates, integrates and synthesises metasystems (fields of knowledge), builds paradigms, requires high degree of decentration
15 – cross-paradigmatic	Coordinates and crosses paradigms, builds new fields of knowledge (consisting of two or more paradigms)

Source: Fein and Weibler (2014, p. 81)

and elementary syntax will automatically be tantamount to falling into error: "it takes complexity to perceive complexity" (Bateson 2017), it takes complexity to evaluate complaxity, and it takes their co-evolution to optimally address wicked problems.

Scientists are developing information measures to measure the levels of complexity in any existent (for example, Fernandez, Maldonado and Gershenson 2013). When and if sufficiently confirmed, such measures could prove to be of great benefit to HBA's capacity to monitor and evaluate development in terms of the Goldilocks Principle (see below), as they are:

1   precise and formal;
2   simple enough to be applied by persons not strong in maths;
3   can help to clarify the meanings of the concepts they apply; and
4   can be applied to "any phenomenon, as anything can be described in terms of information" (Fernandez, Maldonado and Gershenson 2013, p. 2).

Since that paper, others have proposed a new measure of complexity measurement that tracks this better than other measures. Called "dynamical depth" (Deacon and Koutroufinis 2014), it refers to the degree to which some existent shows discrete levels of nonlinear dynamical organisation. The more such nested levels, the more dynamical depth. This measure effectively highlights the intrinsic value of holons such as frogs compared to artefacts such as a mechanical watch, and points to higher levels than those addressed in their paper, including fourfold vision compared to machinism's single vision, and the levels in Commons' MHC and Blake's.

A less formal precursor to that paper was provided by Morowitz as the 28 steps in "the emergence of everything" (Morowitz 2002, pp. 25–38), who noted that there was "no agreed upon metric of complexity" at the time (ibid., p. 95), a deficiency which the concept of dynamic depth is intended to address. While crediting Cassirer as a precursor (Cassirer 1950), Morowitz makes clear that this has a broader and deeper pedigree in human thought, all of which contributes to the foundation of HVN↔HBA.

G: the Goldilocks Principle

> For in a way beset with those that contend on one side for too great Liberty, and on the other side for too much Authority, 'tis hard to passe between the points of both unwounded.
>
> (Hobbes 1651)

The Goldilocks Principle states that, for there to be development at all, the stresses must fall within certain margins, as opposed to reaching extremes. Mentally, too much formless matter, aimless movement, frustrated effort, and kaleidoscopic wildness, will foster madness – as, on the other hand, will too little complexity and change (Drews 1970, p. 99). This applies in all sorts of contexts.

For example, "one lives between two catastrophes, the excess or insufficiency of mortality" (Morin 2007, p. 16). McGilchrist notes "There is an optimal degree of separation between our selves and the world we perceive, if we are to understand it, much as there is between the reader's eye and the page: too much and we cannot make out what is written, but, equally, too little and we cannot read the letters at all" (McGilchrist 2009, p. 22). With knowledge, a person drowning in information is likely to grasp at straws, assume greater knowledge than possessed, and take on trust snippets that a professional in the discipline would not (Grayling 2004, pp. 148–151). In ethics, it goes back at least to Aristotle's *Nicomachean Ethics*: "Thus a master of any art avoids excess and defect, but seeks the intermediate and chooses this – the intermediate not in the object but relatively to us." The Greek term for this was "epektasis" (meaning literally "tension towards"), and epektasis is autotelic, and can be autotelaxic. Again for example, heterarchic social organisations, as differentiated from our top-down "rule-based control of all systemic aspects", are being examined towards finding "a more adaptive balance of flexibility and robustness" (Mezza-Garcia, Froese and Fernandez 2014). Such balance is one consequence of development in the Goldilocks zone.

The Goldilocks Principle is derived from a children's story called *Goldilocks and the Three Bears*. Astronomers use it to describe the zone, for example, where water can stay liquid: while Venus is in too hot an orbit distance from the sun for life, and Mars too cold, Earth just right (Sampson in Brockman 2013, pp. 242–244). Proverbs 30:8 recognised it millennia ago, in asking to be made neither too rich nor too poor. Bill McKibben, in his book *Enough* (2004) called to apply it to genetic engineering. In psychology, it was noted by the psychologist Mihaly Csikszentmihalyi, who observed: "The best moments in life are those spent attempting something difficult and worthwhile" (1990, p. 3). He called it being "in the zone". If challenges are too hard to manage, anxiety destroys efficiency, and development stops. If challenges are too easy to manage, boredom sets in, and development stops. Development only occurs in the Goldilocks zone, and in psychology it is also the zone in which people report "a tremendous increase in their sense of achievement and satisfaction" (Armour 2006). When one goes outside of that zone, the alternatives are stagnation at one extreme, and collapse/destruction at the other. Csikszentmihalyi has shown empirically that individual interiors derive happiness from operating along that metaphorical arête, a knife-edged mountain ridge with a plunge into boredom on one side, and into anxiety on the other. Arête is distinct from, but similar to, areté; the former is the path to the latter, Pirsig's quality. The rock-climber Csikszentmihalyi's arête is along that focus of complexity theory, *the edge of chaos*. One becomes intensely involved in *flow*: that state of deep concentration – a state that involves a transcendence of a sense of self, a loss of any sense of time, and other dimensions that are intrinsically valuable in their own right – that is, they are autotelaxic.

Csikszentmihalyi's researches indicate that they are recognised as autotelic worldwide (Csikszentmihalyi 1988, p. 365). It is an example of Moore's observation that by far the most valuable existents that we can know or imagine are certain states of consciousness (Moore 1903).

Unlike pleasure, which arises as a result of the repletion of the basic needs – food, sex, and so on – *flow* is not so much concerned with homeostasis, but *homeorhesis*, proceeding along a developmental path, via another instance of a developmental double helix to that mentioned earlier. It provides a sense of exhilaration, and ever-greater challenges are required – in bite-sized chunks – to repeat that exhilaration. "It is through the *flow* experience that evolution tricks us to evolve further" (ibid., p. 367). It is that process that answers my question to the Theravada Buddhist lecturer at the event I attended with Christine Stephens in the 1970s.

Csikszentmihalyi's experience of flow sounds very much like the interior individual experience of the edge of chaos as described by Strogratz as occupying "an unfamiliar middle ground between order and disorder", and while it may be predictable in the short run it is unpredictable in the long run (Strogatz 2004, p. 185).

Furthermore, "one of the most important insights of CAS theory is that emergent systems tend to evolve through adaptation to a critical zone that lies at the border between order and chaos" (Centeno et al. 2015). My researches for this paper have therefore led me to the tentative view that the experience of *flow* is the manifestation of an interior individual fractal, an emotional encouragement to evolve. For, as mentioned above, "wherever you see a fractal you are seeing a system at its critical point" (Ward 2001, p. 83). Autotelaxic flow is the drive towards an increase in intrinsic value in humans, just as that towards homeostasis is a drive towards extrinsic value.

To retain self, both autotelaxic flow and homeorhesis are essential for a holon's health. One confusion of the meaning of evolution is therefore the result of an underdevelopment of valuation theory, such that the distinctions between intrinsic and extrinsic values often have not even been articulated, let alone developed.

A similar lack of this development led some positivists to consider Wittgenstein's famous dictum that "what we cannot talk about we must pass over in silence" (Wittgenstein 1974, paragraph 7) as supporting their philosophy. Another interpretation is "what must be 'passed over in silence' was for Wittgenstein *precisely what had value*" (Yourgrau 2005, p. 29, emphasis mine). That makes sense because any existent of non-trivial intrinsic value is holonic, and therefore cannot be encapsulated by description, even a HVN↔HBA one.

Csikszentmihalyi also observed that it is probably more than coincidental that there are similarities between the complex systems that chemists and biologists find on the boundary of order and chaos and the complex psychic state on the boundary of boredom and anxiety: "That we *enjoy* being on that boundary seems like a gift from Providence" (Csikszentmihalyi 1993, pp. 318–319). I consider that more likely to be a gift from evolution by natural selection, and submit that it applies universally around the hexagon, not just the areas studied by chemists, biologists, and psychologists. Furthermore, I submit it applies to the relationships between McGilchrist's Master and its Emissary, understanding and manipulation, and the "aha" moments whereby we gain an insight, and integration of understandings, along the way in addressing problems.

One can see the prevalence of the world's most irrational number, the golden ratio, throughout much of nature as a major manifestation of this principle, applying fractally at scales of size from microscopic to cosmic, and to all scales of life's complexity, including our own bodies and minds. The spontaneous order of the golden ratio results from its efficiency in the unpacking of growth. Flam notes the prevalence of such fractals as they dampen vibrations and are more robust; hence nature's rule of "survival of the fractal" (Flam 1991, p. 1593), facilitating the emergence of order out of chaos, an example of an empirically verifiable emergent simplicity as distinct from the abstract "ceteris paribus" hypotheses of conventional economics, and which I consider applies not only to robustness, but also to antifragility (gaining from addressing challenges; Taleb 2012).

Developing Csikszentmihalyi's comment, I propose that what manifests as the state of flow in one's mind is the psyche hextant's equivalent to the manifestation of the golden ratio in the exterior hextants, and these vary from black holes to flowers. The reason for this is that the golden ratio is an attractor in complexity terms because it forms the most effective way of providing all the advantages that roundness provides in physics, biology, etc. – all the hexagon's domains – *without any gaps* (Pierce 2017). Planets have to be in the Goldilocks Zone for life to develop; institutions and people have to be there to develop as well. Its manifestations in social interactions enfold sophrosyne and much of the Buddhist eightfold path. Most development occurs via stretching the limits of that zone, the zone wherein people are at their happiest.

In accordance with sophrosyne, the Goldilocks Principle also applies between activities, not just in them. Flow can become so rewarding in one activity that all else is ignored to pathological levels. For example, a monomaniacal focus on personal identity construction results in narcissism, with its unintended consequences such as no wisdom/compassion developmental dynamic, a lack of empathy, and consequent social estrangement.

The ramifications of this principle in real property right's fitness landscapes range from manageable mortgage repayments (in contrast to the unmanageable ones that triggered the subprime mortgage crisis; both are addressed in Chapter 6), to the context of expropriation of property rights. The dispossessed and other stakeholders are often placed in a too anxious situation, and they often react accordingly. They have developed identities to differing degrees, and with them differing capacities to absorb challenges in bite-sized chunks over a period of time. That should also be recognised in governments' land acquisition programs procedures. For example, Scudder (2005, p. 32) considers that it takes at least two generations for societies to adjust to forced resettlement, and other studies indicate that there is no guarantee that and other historically inflicted trauma and grief will ever be successfully adjusted for when succeeding generations internalise the assault at their social identity level. However, it is claimed that they can be addressed by skilful means (Wesley-Esquimaux 2007). By its enfolding of both internal and external processes, I submit the HVN↔HBA process provides a path towards such skilful means as will never be merely mechanical or formulaic, but adaptable to the wicked problematics of the specific situation. If the process is applied merely mechanically or formulaically, by my definition it is not HVN↔HBA.

RE: the Related Evolution Principle

As William Blake said in *The Marriage of Heaven and Hell*, "Without Contraries is no progression. Attraction and Repulsion, Reason and Energy, Love and Hate are necessary to Human existence". That does not mean that Blake saw contraries as inevitably resulting in progression. He saw Urizen's dissociation from the other three Zoas – Los, Luvah and Tharmas – as destructive, with the four Zoas to be reintegrated as an emergent Albion, the Universal Man on their cross.

To make this clear, Blake differentiated negations and contraries. The former he imagined as endemic in the state of Ulro – "which, typifying Blake's hell on earth, is a bleak world of tyranny, negation and isolated selfhood" (Tung 1997) – as being devolutionary, whereas he saw contraries as potentially evolutionary. That is why he said "opposition is true friendship" in his work in which the title says why that is so: he looked towards *The Marriage of Heaven and Hell*.

This principle asserts that all evolution is co-evolution of that "contrary" nature – "All evolutionary change is co-evolutionary" (Fraser 1999, p. 189) – and that "autonomy cannot be conceived without its ecology" (Morin 2007, p. 14).

The principle also asserts that the Goldilocks Principle works throughout an environment by interactions within that environment. In this holon-centred context, no interactions, no development. Fowler identifies four such relational principles: altruism, cooperation, competition and association (Fowler 2007, p. 14), the evolution of cooperation being "a beautiful and simple explanation of how nature got complex" (Sumner as cited in Brockman 2013, p. 154).

By this principle, such environments will evolve better solutions than mono-logical ones for complex tasks, and yet "mutual contextualization is lacking in the whole of social sciences" (Morin 2007, p. 19). At an unpredictable stage of development inside the Goldilocks Zone, a new and simpler order may emerge, such as has been traced in palaeontology by punctuated equilibrium (Eldredge and Gould 1972) and which is similar to emergence in complexity theory, both involving that slow process turning into "a sudden, convulsive transformation, and totally new forms emerge" (Poblador 2014, p. 149).

This phenomenon has been applied to property law, "property moments" potentially being such punctuations in the equilibria (Davidson and Dyal-Chand 2010, pp. 1615–1623), wherein "long-standing tensions in property theory" are resurrected (ibid., p. 1620) towards creating a transformation in understanding of property law.

As sustainable development requires evolution, it follows that all development is co-development. This is therefore an important principle in land policy formulation and implementation. That is, development occurs in a network of relationships of components in dynamic near-equilibrium with one another. Thus "learning by doing" – pilot studies etc. – is one way to connect theory to observed reality.

For example, when it comes to institutional recommendations it is necessary not only to institute an organisational framework, but also to take note of how it is to co-evolve in its environment, and realise that institutional evolution may take unexpected turns and have unintended consequences, both positive and negative, and that the only way to find out is to engage. As a more specific example, this applies to the co-evolution of valuation as a profession with the property market.

Note that here we are referring to evolution. Recent developments away from a mechanist approach to evolutionary psychology (Barrett, Pollet and Stulp 2014; Burke 2014) and towards recognising that complex is not the same as complicated are likely to make that discipline far more practical than hitherto for use in HBA. They should also dovetail with autotelaxis at the scale of the individual holon as the psyche hextant's contribution to evolution.

In the meantime, while Csikszentmihalyi observes "complexity does not win every time" (1993, p. 158), HBA goes further. Even if Stewart's (2014) direction of evolution towards complexity is accepted, there is still no inevitability about evolution. There can more readily be stasis, and more readily still, regression. In fact, development is a special case, requiring the Goldilocks Principle to be operating both intra- and inter-holonically and intra- and inter-hextally to happen at all, and to develop the conditions for the sudden emergence of new holons.

Using HBA in this learning-by-doing process, we may see many matters anew, or perceive them differently, and re-weight them accordingly. Taking the earlier example of compulsory acquisition, compensation by committees or juries of the appropriately broad and deep vision and balanced judgement might be the best form available at one level of the development holarchy, with market valuation only emerging as possible at a later stage. Therefore, what is appropriate at one level can be completely inappropriate at another. Property markets and valuations co-evolve – swim – or sink together: "That's co-evolution. We are all each other's fitness landscapes" (Brand 2013, p. 124).

In this work, I see the Newtonian *view from nowhere* (Nagel 1986) engaging in a co-evolutionary dynamic in identity construction with the *view from place* of the identity. That is, I see single vision being transcended but included in twofold, threefold and fourfold identity construction, and employed in the manner Pirsig saw the purpose of the "Motorcycle Maintenance" scientific method: To "make sure that nature hasn't misled you into thinking you know something you actually don't know" (ibid., p. 61).

BIES

As mentioned at the beginning of this chapter, this Part provides the bridge for HVN to be the Master of the HBA process, the funnel for values and other qualitative assessments, and news about their possible enactment in the environment addressed from HBA to HVN. It begins that task with a "butterfly".

Figure 5.4 A picbreeder "butterfly"
Source: Stanley and Lehman (2015)

However, not only is the little picture shown in Figure 5.4 not of a butterfly: the picture was never intended to depict a butterfly in its evolution. The butterfly effect arrived as a black swan. Its back story has much to convey about addressing the subject of this book, including why Blake's fourfold vision, and why merely single vision minds were not, are not, and never will be, fit for this purpose.

In brief, we may never find non-trivial existents "previously ignored or at best restricted to other domains" (Grunberg 2000, p. 12) by looking for them in a linear fashion, but we will also never find them by not looking. It is a principle for all of search in complexity that "you can only find things by not looking for them . . . because the stepping stones . . . almost never resemble the final product in any complex search space" (Stanley 2013, 21:10ff).

That narrative will not be completed in this chapter, but this chapter is core to understanding it.

B: black swans and butterfly effects

Concomitant to the combined recognition of black swans and butterfly effects is the recognition that there are trillions of unpredictable variables emerging every second that could affect wicked valuation problems when NSEW meet. This recognition is about as far from the so-called "enlightenment" clockwork universe paradigm as it appears possible to get. Consequently, every enlightenment has collateral endarkments; every opportunity, opportunity costs.

Taleb (2007) used the term "black swan" to refer to unpredictable random events. He did so because before the discovery of Australia everyone had assumed that all swans were white. Black swans were outliers, their discovery had a major impact, and they were only explainable in retrospect – three essentials for the term "black swan" to apply (ibid., pp. xvii–xviii).

Greg Fisher has addressed uncertainty in policy making (Fisher 2014), noting how uncertainties can arise from reflexivity, relationships, emergence in dynamic systems, bounded rationalities, moral values and social norms, institutions, ergodic systems (systems that change through time), feedback loops (Fulton 2013) : there is a plethora of possibilities. He notes that these require continuous sense-making, collective intelligence, trained intuition, loose forward training, pattern formation, experimentation (including pilot projects), and devolution/subsidiary in policy development. He particularly stressed the need for a vision, which has to have a compelling, coherent narrative that is legitimate to varied interested parties. All of these insights are compatible with HVN↔HBA.

Fisher's recommendations also apply to uncertainties from the related term "Butterfly Effect". Edward Lorenz coined the term over 50 years ago. It refers to the fact that tiny perturbations can have massive effects in meteorology (Lorenz 1963).

This was a founding insight for chaos theory as it was then found to apply in a great many contexts (Gleick 1987). Once again, this is highly relevant to policy formulation and implementation. I intend HIDEGRE to facilitate antifragile responses to the challenges Butterfly Effects and Black Swans bring to policy formulation and implementation.

Complexity economics (Arthur 2013 and 2014) promises to give such economists a seat back at the policy table that Taleb would remove other economists from. Like HBA, complexity economics recognises that the whole world is not made up of black swans and butterfly effects. Yet as babies we begin from the world appearing to be like that. Over time, via our identity construction we adopt heuristics that work sufficiently well to serve our needs (Gigerenzer 2007, 2013, 2014; Gigerenzer and Todd 1999; Kruglanski and Gigerenzer 2011; Gigerenzer, Hertwig and Pachure 2011; Haldane and Madouros 2012).

Gigerenzer calls this process "ecological rationality" (Gigerenzer and Brighton 2009; Todd, Gigerenzer and the ABC Research Group 2012):

> For Kahneman, rationality is logical rationality, defined as some content-free law of logic or probability; for us, it is ecological rationality, loosely speaking, the match between a heuristic and its environment. For ecological rationality, taking into account contextual cues (the environment) is the very essence of rationality, for Kahneman it is a deviation from a logical norm and thus, a deviation from rationality. In Kahneman's philosophy, simple heuristics could never predict better than rational models; in our research we have shown systematic less-is-more effects.
>
> (Email quoted in Gelman 2015)

As indicated by the table below extracted from Arthur, such an ecological rationality/logical rationality differentiation is consistent with that of the differences between classical and complexity economics (Table 5.6).

Table 5.6 Classical versus complexity economics assumptions

Classical economics assumptions	*Complexity economics assumptions*
Participants are addressing clearly defined issues "perfect, well-defined problems"	Participants may not know the environment and would have to try to understand it
Participants are perfectly rational	There are limits on our cognitive capacities
Economies have diminishing returns (negative feedbacks)	Economies may also have increasing returns (positive feedbacks)
Economies are mechanistic systems operating at equilibrium	Economies are constantly dynamic ecologies, including "actions, strategies, and beliefs competing for survival"

Source: Arthur (2014)

Many processes are often highly predictable – death, for example – and there is a vast spectrum of probabilities and possibilities from such predictable events to black swans and butterfly effects. However, with the complex there will always be unintended consequences, which could be harmful or beneficial to the intention (Kurzban as cited in Brockman 2013, pp. 351–353). We must pay attention to that spectrum in policy formulation: "If we do this that may happen; O.K. But how likely is that?" "Not very for now, it's true, but if it does happen, how can we become resilient, or, better, anti-fragile in response to it?"

This landscape is populated with a menagerie of statistical probability creatures that may be fit for purpose in relevant contexts. It includes Naïve and Robust Bayesian calculations, Zipf's Law, Heaps', and Lotka's and Bradford's laws, the inverse power law (Rucker in Brockman 2013, pp. 367–369) and total probability law, Lorenz curves, and the like, and with possibly emerging ones, such as Dragon-Kings (Sornette 2009). Similarly, there are many modelling techniques, which have been categorised into three groups, as follows:

1   qualitative aggregate models (soft systems methodology, concept maps and mind mapping, scenario planning, causal (loop) diagrams);
2   quantitative aggregate models (function fitting and regression, Bayesian nets, system of differential equations/dynamical systems, system dynamics, evolutionary algorithms); and
3   individual oriented models (cellular automata, micro-simulation, agent based models, discrete event simulation, social network analysis) (Badham 2010).

All such may, in suitably informed hands, inform and serve the trans-ontological policy formulation and implementation that I mean HVN↔HBA to serve. Importantly for this context, models can also have integrative potential.

For example, in order to address complex reality's radical uncertainty, Marqués (2015) has tabled six core assumptions for a new conceptual framework for economics, assigning probabilities to future phenomena. In addition to the criticisms above, he refers to Keynes' observation about economists pretending to know what they did not (ibid., p. 19), and that conventional theory and practice failed to consider central features of economics, those that characterise uncertain systems, but instead chose imaginary worlds and explored their functioning. To get real, he recommends the following. That we:

•   Identify economic processes based on expectations in an area of radical uncertainty.
•   Assume that ex-ante knowledge of any invariant sequences of events is not possible.
•   Accept a more realistic goal of what branchings of events are feasible, and find what restrictions they may have.
•   Accept we will never be able to know what branches will prevail.
•   Accept practicalities, pragmatic experience as distinct from theory, are crucial for shaping the branchings.

- Understand the role of lobbyists pressing a wide range of interests in the process (ibid., pp. 23–24).

A premise for these is that the results of the prevailing ontology are "more relevant for understanding the results of . . . decisions than [the] decisions themselves" (ibid., p. 17). Hence the need to be trans-ontological at the global scale to address wicked valuation problems. Marqués noted that if economic philosophers were concerned with real economic process, they should critically examine the usual ontological and epistemological assumptions of mainstream economic modelling (pp. 17–18). But to critically examine ontologies, stepping outside them is facilitatory (Jensen 2013).

My approach is consonant with that of Marqués; his concern is a part of my concern. However, it is not just about economics: it is about values, and valuations, whose span is wider and deeper than economics.

IES: intrinsic, extrinsic and systemic value

In stating:

> I wish to discuss the first glimmerings of a new scientific Worldview – beyond reductionism to emergence and radial creativity in the biosphere and human world. This emerging view finds a natural scientific place for value and ethics and places us as co-creators of the enormous web of emerging complexity that is the evolving biosphere and human economics and culture.
>
> (Kauffman 2007, p. 905)

Kauffman further emphasises this in a more recent work, "hoping to regain our subjective pole", and looking towards "a widened value system beyond our rabid materialism" (Kauffman 2016, p. 19). I therefore see Kauffman as pointing towards the emergence of William Blake's twofold vision in the West, wherein one sees not only materially but also sees the "perception of the human values in all things" (Damon 2013, p. 469). This is required in this context because holons are complex, with their own values – "to create an organism is to create its values" (Midgley 2003, p. 54) – and those values cannot be ignored in this context.

Machines – artefacts – do not value, and values are therefore less central addressing complicated problems than in addressing complex and wicked ones. However, values are still the major ingredient in why we create machines in the first place, and even "to remain alive at all, one must see some value in this world" (Tuan 1990, p. 98). While social constructivists see knowledge as constructed "through interaction with others" (McKinley 2015, p. 184), we are motivated to engage with others by values in the first place, and not only frame our turning of data into knowledge through them, but also weigh which values to engage in that social environment (to build our fitness landscapes via value engagements):

> The body and brain are embedded in this complex world and have to sort it out . . . deal with the variance . . . when that comes in and pulls you or gives

you signals you select those which give you amplification and satisfaction of value.

(Edelman 2011)

Therefore, this part is not just about market values formed by supply and demand. It is about "giving voice to values" (Edwards and Kirkham 2014) in general, and when NSEW meet in particular, for the better addressing of wicked valuation problems in those contexts. There are "Big V" values, which can be categorised in many ways, but here are divisible into intrinsic, extrinsic and systemic (Hartman 1967). Values inform and contribute to supply and demand, and are relevant to market value insofar as they relate to the "willing" part of the market value definition. All our perceptions and theories, including science, are value laden (Brown, Harris and Russell 2010, pp. 36, 50, 51) and shape the nature of our inquiry (ibid., p. 39). Our standards applied to knowledge itself "ultimately rest upon the value commitments of the knowledge communities concerned" (ibid., p. 40) and are "never value free" (ibid., p. 50). Therefore, they are not limited to the assumptions of classical economics but enfold morality, ethics, heuristics and all other factors from all hextant that influence a valuation.

Axiology has been defined as the study of the nature, types, and criteria of values and of value judgements, especially in ethics. The word derives from the ancient Greek word for "worthy". This chapter is about my neologism for this work *telaxiology* – not especially ethics – with the intention of qualitatively more informed land policy decision-making within this work's context. Collaterally, it is also improving the ability to analyse sales via action inquiry (Torbert and Associates 2004) and HVN↔HBA.

I here claim that "Big V" values direct the framing of our enquiries axiologically, epistemologically, spatially and temporally (Lakoff 2004), and even our ontologies in a co-evolutionary manner.

In this valuation context, we are looking towards what Gödel described in the context of logic as "a new state of consciousness in which we describe in detail the basic concepts we use in our thought" (Gödel 1995, p. 383). In so doing, we will find that "Gödel's theorem shows that human thought is more complex and less mechanical than anyone had ever believed" (Rucker 1987, p. 226). In particular I compare the definitions of intrinsic and extrinsic values in the works of Ken Wilber (1995) and Robert S. Hartman (1967), noting from our complexity perspective that Wilber assigns higher intrinsic value to higher levels of emergence, "ranking of orders or events according to their holistic capacity" (Wilber 1995, p. 17).

Further developing the definitions in the Glossary, I adopt Wilber's (1995, p. 518ff) definitions of three main types of value. *Intrinsic* value is defined by Wilber as the value some existent has in itself by dint of how many levels of emergence it enfolds within it. The greater the depth, the greater wholeness, the greater the significance. Atoms have less intrinsic value than molecules, because molecules enfold atoms, but atoms do not enfold molecules. Similarly, cells have emergent value that molecules do not possess, and humans more than cells, because there are cells in humans but not humans in cells. Our deepest evolutionary past is our shallowest evolutionary depth, and the intrinsic valuation depth is our evolutionary depth.

The same applies in the psyche and skills hextants. For instance, a professionally developed opinion has more intrinsic value than a tendentious or uninformed, undifferentiated and otherwise less developed one. Similarly, so does an ethical one based on greater experience and development along the lines of the development principle. That is, the more developed some existent is in terms of Werner's Orthogenic principle – the more differentiated, articulated and hierarchically integrated ("holarchical" with levels of emergence) – the more intrinsically valuable they may be.

As G.E. Moore pointed out, the most intrinsically valuable phenomena are certain states of consciousness (Moore 1903, p. 188). In addressing Moore's point, Sumner commented that "if the list of intrinsic goods is restricted to states of consciousness, or to organic wholes which include such states, then it will follow that these goods can belong only to individuals" (Sumner 1996, p. 50). That is, according to Moore and Sumner *only holons have intrinsic value*; so while people do, property rights over land do not. However, people may invest their identities in land and thereby assign their intrinsic value to it, and there are populations of organic wholes, and thereby of intrinsic value, on almost all land.

The essential point to emphasise here is the importance of integration to the intrinsic. That is, in organisms the highest intrinsic value requires holarchical differentiation and integration, not internal or external dissociation. We can find the highest intrinsic value in the different levels of emergence working as an integrated whole. We will not find those highest intrinsic values in someone wise but not compassionate, or compassionate but not wise. Therefore, to Plato's observation that an unquestioned life is no life for a man, Midgley adds that a life without affection is no life for a man either (Midgley 1995, pp. 69, p. 76).

Extrinsic value is almost the inverse of intrinsic value: it refers to the value some existent has for others, its instrumental value. That is, while intrinsic and systemic values are autotelaxic, extrinsic value is about achieving use value, more about doing than being. Both are fundamental to evolution. Without desire fuelling life's struggles from within the psyche hextant driving towards potential emergence, that life would go extinct. Atoms are fundamental to molecules. No atoms, no molecules, but molecules are more significant; they have higher emergent levels of complexity, higher intrinsic value. While an aeroplane has far less intrinsic value than a mosquito, it has far greater extrinsic value for us than a mosquito does. Therefore, the more levels of emergence a holon enfolds, the higher its intrinsic value should be, but less levels of emergence do not lower its extrinsic value in a context (Wilber 1999a, pp. 346–348).

For example, a lumberjack enfolds many levels of emergence and is of high intrinsic value, but his axe enfolds few levels but is of high extrinsic value. All holons therefore have networks of extrinsic and intrinsic values, the most highly developed – "highly" in the sense of enfolding more levels of emergence – being the most intrinsically valuable. However, extrinsic value varies widely up and down that scale on a fit-for-purpose basis. Midgley notes that "without being deceived, we need to think of organisms to some extent as if they were artefacts" (Midgley 1995, p. 71). That "without being deceived" is vital, and a differentiation of intrinsic and extrinsic valuations can assist in that discernment.

Extrinsically, the most valuable things are air, water, food and shelter (including clothing), yet their market values may be trivial. That is because markets exist as a means of exchange between holons adopting higher values and strategies than force when there is a real or perceived scarcity of supply, and the market agreements may involve complex suites of value judgements, not only extrinsic ones.

Wilber calls the misappraisal of these values in psychology the "pre-trans fallacy"; since there are mental states both beneath and beyond Blake's single vision, that single vision conflates them one way or the other.[3] He claims that Freud tended to reduce any such existent to prerational, and Jung to elevate any such existent to transrational, the two tendencies being reductionist and elevationist respectively (Wilber 1995, pp. 206–207), like reducing a molecule to a sum of atoms, or elevating atoms to molecules, and ignoring the novel qualities in levels of emergence.

Like atoms, it is clear that Blake's "single vision and Newton's sleep", Crichton's "thintelligence" and the like can be of tremendous extrinsic value. However, if the producers function in their design in an entirely mechanistic way, the consequences can be catastrophic. That is what Michael Crichton's *Jurassic Park* (1991) was about. As Crichton had his character Dr Malcolm say about thintelligence, "it's uniquely Western training, and much of the world is nauseated by the thought of it" (Crichton 1991, p. 238), just like William Blake, Rabindranath Tagore, Gandhi and millions of others were, and millions remain so.

Ground Value is the value that all existents have by simple dint of existing, and with Vedanta Wilber sees all existents as manifestations of Atman, the true self of all. In the work of Wilber's I encountered in that bookshop in India (Wilber 1980), he pointed out that our small "a" atmans, our constructed identities, often get it precisely backwards and consider Atman their possession, rather than the other way around, or that they are Atman's spokesperson – a hyperinflation of the relative value of one's identity's generally known as megalomania.

From this perspective, because of ground value there are no non-sacred places or identities: we just habitually undervalue them.

While implicit in Wilber's holonic perspective, Habermas notes a potential qualifier on intrinsic valuations based on levels of emergence: "there are increases in complexity that turn out to be evolutionary dead ends" (Habermas 1990, p. 141). As it happens, all but the most primitive levels have demonstrable intrinsic value that exists because they have emerged from the crucible of evolution. While our own species' future is highly fraught, it is not its higher levels of complexity that will doom it, but its lower ones hijacking the higher: in other words, it will be a direct result of our own poor intrinsic valuation, a major manifestation of that process being the "nothing buttism" of single vision.

We can now see that we can apply the word "evolution" to both intrinsic and extrinsic valuations, but not to ground value. Viewed intrinsically, the term "evolution" enfolds emergence. Viewed extrinsically, it is concerned entirely with functional fits in the fitness landscapes. An extrinsic valuer may claim that man is no better than a mosquito, because both continue to survive: "There is no tree of life with humans on the topmost branch; no *scala natura*, no higher or lower, no more or less primitive" (Rose 2006, p. 19; also see Mayr 1998, p. 198). However, there *are* higher and lower, more or less primitive, from an integral valuation perspective, increasing integration and intrinsic value (Stewart 2014, p. 28). While it is not complexity *per se* that selection favours (ibid., p. 27), the adaptability of additional complexities *as winnowed into fitness landscapes through the gauntlet of the relevant environmental challenges* provides evolution with a *de facto* direction.

This is true not only for holons, but also for artefacts such as human organisations (ibid., p. 28). While "as yet poorly understood" (ibid., p. 28), an example of this process could be when a crocodile dominates an ecological niche in a fitness landscape. Other creatures have to adapt to that crocodile, and increases in cognitive and other complexities could facilitate that adaptation. That may require finding new fitness landscapes, sometimes by changing environments (for example, by conquests) and sometimes by new approaches to the same one. As the Artificial Intelligence researcher Kenneth Stanley put it: "Once simple behaviours are exhausted, novelty requires more complexity [and] . . . more novelty requires accumulation of information" (Stanley 2013, 33:12).

This is how Whitehead's "creative advance into novelty" (Whitehead 2010, pp. 28, 222) occurs. This is what Habermas refers to when he speaks of evolution in the sense of a cumulative process of increasing complexity, as "the more states a system can assume, the more complex the environment with which it can cope and against which it can maintain itself" (Habermas 1990, p. 141).

On these criteria, *no artefact*, including "real" persons such as corporations and states, has the intrinsic value of a natural person. From an intrinsic valuation perspective, Hegel's principle of Absolute Reason that the state has supreme right against the individual (Hegel 2001), whose supreme duty is to be a member of the state, is preposterous. That founding assumption of fascism, communism and even the integral humanism of Upadhyaya (1988–1989) could scarcely have been more topsy-turvy. Jung's intuitively extreme statement that "the individual is the only reality" (Jung 1964, p. 45) places matters in a far more compatible perspective with the insights of intrinsic valuation.

Wilber is also at pains to point out that there is no more a collective mind than there is a collective brain (Wilber 1995, p. 80). Especially, we are not parts of a state, which is a social imaginary artefact, conditioned communities of "fictive kin" (Atran as cited in Brockman 2013, p. 10). Just as some may identify with that artefact as part of their identity construction, and others may not (Herb and Kaplan 1999), some may identify with other artefacts, such as football teams and cars, and others may not. Therefore, from the HBA perspective Hegel's principle is badly mistaken, albeit from a solely extrinsic valuation perspective it may be true.

What "collective" means in this context is the easy availability and reach of a variety of prototypical or dominant themes within a given group (Gonen 2000,

p. 5). As Gonen points out when interrogating the roots of Nazi psychology, politicians manipulate collective identities in several ways, especially by fear, their exploitation of the Anthropological Machine in particular resulting in demonising collective projections.

On the other hand, artefacts from within whatever hextant can have far more extrinsic value than any holon, even when those artefacts' intrinsic values are puny by comparison.

From the above definition of intrinsic value, it should become clear what the role of artefacts should be. The role of states, corporations, cars, real property rights and other non-holons should be the utilisation of their extrinsic values towards Mary Midgley's definition of freedom for the most highly developed holons known. Her definition of freedom is "the chance to develop *what you have it in you to be*" (italics original; Midgley 2003, p. 40; 1995, p. 314); one's highest and best expressions of intrinsic value. For this work, that requires Blake's fourfold vision as a necessary but insufficient condition for solving wicked valuation problems.

The Greeks had a word for realising what you have it in you to be – the aforementioned areté (Fassbender 2007, p. 278). That also happens to be about spirituality, as defined in the Glossary. Skolimowski adds that "spirituality is about what we can potentially become [and] spiritual life is the blossoming of the force of transcendence" (Skolimowski 1993, pp. 6, 86, 8). Emergence into fourfold vision is a manifestation of transcendence.

Another source of the distinctions between different types of value is Hartman. While Wilber defined his three forms of value as intrinsic, extrinsic and ground (the value simply by dint of being an integral part of the whole), Hartman's three are intrinsic, extrinsic, and systemic. Hartman's "intrinsic" is similar to Wilber's, being "the valuing of an object or person with an eye toward its singularity, essence, uniqueness, or spiritual being", and extrinsic, too, has its similarities – "this is the dimension of comparisons, relative and practical thinking" and seeing how existents compare with others for a purpose. However, Hartman's *systemic* dimension differs from Wilber's ground value. It is within the realm of formal concepts – about how existents should be: the vision of a development strategy, the perfect expression and implementation of a law, how a circle should look, how a person should be, oughts, shoulds, and so on (Smith 2001).

Hartman stresses that under-or over-emphasising any of these dimensions of value results in pathological behaviours of various kinds. For instance, over-emphasis on systemic value can blind one to other more important values, to rigidity and authoritarianism, and so forth, while under-emphasising systemic values may result in anarchistic and irresponsible behaviour. Aesop's fable about the ant and the grasshopper was about systemic valuations: the grasshopper under-estimated them, while at first the ant appeared to over-estimate them, only to attain a balance in the wintertime.

While this dimension is a core focus in commerce, Hartman explicitly states that it is not core in life. Using a concept he termed "richness of qualities", he identified a "hierarchy of richness", with intrinsic value at the top and systemic at the bottom, and found this to be consistent with the values of the relevant disciplines (ibid.).

However, to have a balanced intrinsic valuation, the extrinsic and the systemic valuations must be present. Just because a client likes a particular vendor (intrinsic), a balanced attention also includes the vendor's performing according to the terms of the agreement (extrinsic), and performing in a legal manner (systemic).

We do not yet have much of a vocabulary for the development of these values. To open up these kingdoms in terms of their levels of development, perhaps we could adapt Stewart and Cohen's simplex, complex, multiplex, omniplex (and my "compliplex" to maintain the distinction between complicated and complex) in the cognitive line to the valuational one. Using the same spelling that was used to derive axiology from "áksios", meaning "worthy", I call the valuation correlates to cognitive capacities "simplax, complax, multiplax, omniplax and compliplax". So focussing on any one value is "simplax".

Returning to Blake's Urizen. Urizen may have been omniplex, but he was simplax at best, certainly not omniplax. Likewise, just because Tupaia had a more complex understanding, that did not necessarily mean he was more enlightened than Captain Cook. It just means he was different in his skills hextant.

Without higher values driven by compassion, single vision will not emerge into twofold, let alone achieve the later emergents of threefold and fourfold vision, requiring coevolution of wisdom and compassion. Blake saw the solution to the disintegration of man as being "reconciliation through forgiveness" (Stevenson in Blake 1988, p.15) – even, especially, of the simplax-minded Urizen.

As we are working towards developing sophrosyne to manifest co-evolved wisdom and compassion by skilful means, we will need such words in this context. Learning how to weigh, balance, prioritise and effect values in a land policy context would be a means of developing beyond twofold vision towards complax, multiplax, omniplax and compliplax, in related evolution with their epistemic equivalents.

In 2011, the axiologist Alan Carter presented "some groundwork for a multidimensional axiology" in a paper of that name (Carter 2011). He thereby provided some grounding to observe emergence from mere single (simplex) visions to co-evolve via complex↔complax, multiplex↔multiplax dynamics towards the never attainable but ever approachable omniplex/omniplax evolutionary summit.

In the paper, he criticised the single vision of utilitarianism in public policy development as inadequate. He further notes that not only utilitarianism, but also the three other major theoretical positions – prioritarianism, pure egalitarianism, and sufficientarianism, are similarly inadequate. Instead, Carter calls for a new normative approach, one "incorporating a maximising, value-pluralist axiology" (ibid., p. 390), thereby looking towards twofold, threefold and fourfold vision.

Via a scenario analysis, he identifies the need to articulate a differentiation of "contributory" and "overall" values, and establishes the superiority of a maximising, value-pluralist axiology over any form of value monism (ibid., p. 407). Finally, he notes that in the field of public policy (which would necessarily be included in addressing the challenges in this work) such an axiology "will, at times, justify the adoption of very different public policies to those advocated by" value monists. Furthermore, providing it recognises "a full range of variable values", it will dispense with the "counterintuitive implications" generated by value monism, resulting in "better public policies" (op. cit.).

I intend HVN↔HBA and the new vistas to be facilitated by the above coevolution of epistemology and axiology (simplex↔simplax →complex↔complax . . .) to attain similar results within this work's domain to those sought by Carter.

In so doing, I note a parallel between Carter's identification of pure utilitarianism as being inadequate (policy decision-making requiring the recognition of a full range of variable values), with McGilchrist's metaphor of the Master (which recognises intrinsic values, enfolding Kant's view of the intrinsic value of every human) and his Emissary (which only recognises extrinsic values, enfolding Mill's focus on utilitarian values). In Rowson and McGilchrist (2013, p, 14), McGilchrist brought Kant's observation that we live in two worlds into his discussion of the worlds of the left and right hemispheres. Kant's intrinsic valuation of any human being was the reason behind his categorical imperative, the second version of which stated, "Act so that you use humanity, in your own person as well as in any other, always as an end, and never as means only" (Apel 2001, p. 56). Like Carter, McGilchrist frames the potential for a developed complex/complex wisdom and compassion to emerge from the conflict between extrinsic and intrinsic values. From that perspective, Mill's utilitarianism and Kant's idealism can be seen as facilitating a co-evolutionary dynamic as in the Related Evolutionary Principle. Like Krishnamurti's "drop it" and Jesus's "turn the other cheek", Kant's categorical imperative can in turn be seen thereby as potentially the grain of sand that causes an oyster to make a pearl.

Hartman claims that proper valuing includes attentiveness to all his three dimensions of valuation. Wilber claims that, with respect to the two value dimensions he shares with Hartman – intrinsic and extrinsic – "both are absolutely mandatory" (Wilber 1995). A focus on extrinsic values and an ignorance of how to value intrinsically is causative of both personal and societal imbalances, and so is its opposite. The many pathologies that result can include a stunting of development with insufficient attention to extrinsic values, and malignant development with insufficient attention to intrinsic values.

Because intrinsic values are more complex than and less obvious than extrinsic ones, they can be more difficult to discern. Intrinsic valuation is therefore a more complex↔complax process than extrinsic valuation.

In our past, our necessary familiarity as hunters with the behaviours of our prey – and our predators – would have resulted in qualitative understandings now rarely if ever appreciated. For instance, we usually ignore the maternal behaviour of a cow (intrinsic value), but do not ignore her value as meat (extrinsic value). It is therefore reasonable to assume that the artefact-rich and holonically devaluing modern urban environment has the potential to further atrophy our intrinsic valuation processes, with malign consequences as emphasised by

Hartman and Wilber. In this book's meaning of the term, development is not the problem: imbalanced development and poor valuations as to what to develop, as warned by Wilber and Hartman, is the problem. Balanced development towards areté, not a collapse of development, is preconditional to finding a solution.

A clear symptom of this imbalance is that other species of life on Earth are often greatly intrinsically undervalued, and merely extrinsically valued. While a sometimes almost complete alienation from other macro species has developed contemporaneously, a greater than historically known familiarity with the natural world has also developed from the anecdotal to the scientific by specialists such as Jane Goodall (Goodall 1971). Their insights are generally towards an elevation of the intrinsic valuations of other species. For instance, Goodall and others note that in the primate world we can find many of the qualities we highly value in others and ourselves. Because coming to that understanding helps us know ourselves, a lack of understanding of the deep connection of human nature to nature results in poor intrinsic valuations (Sagan and Druyans 1992, p. 413). That is, by learning that qualities we possess are shared by not only other people, but also by other species, we can become better intrinsic valuers.

To think that a higher intrinsic valuation of animals is a devaluation of humans is symptomatic of poor intrinsic valuation. The decimation of natural habitats as facilitated by rapacious and ignorant land policies, land-related valuations and real property rights can be one manifestation of such intrinsic valuation blindness and consequent inability in the field. In contrast, the restitution of wilderness for its intrinsic value as facilitated by wise and compassionate land policies, land-related valuations and real property rights could be a result of more reasonable intrinsic valuation.

In so doing, almost completely up until quite recently, and still at best coarse grained, we have not had available to us scientific observations of the brain to assist in the practice of intrinsic valuation. However, orienting generalisations were provided by Paul D MacLean who, like Sagan and Druyans, noted how so many of us are reluctant to acknowledge our animal ancestry and natures. MacLean noted that the part of their brains they share with other mammals is the same part that cannot acknowledge its affinity to other mammals, even when their higher brains can. He states that, *as a simplification . . .* our brains are triune, comprising reptilian, old mammalian, and new mammalian, each with their own structures and chemistry, "yet all three must intermesh and function together" (MacLean 1973, p. 7).

It should come as no surprise to anyone that modern brain researchers have difficulties with that simplification. After all, the human brain is the most complex known existent in the universe. While agreeing that MacLean was correct in terms of evolution and neuroanatomy (but even there, not quite – for example, man did not evolve from reptiles: both evolved from amphibians; see Gribbin 1993, p. 86]), Greenfield says that he was extravagant in claiming that the three brains were poorly integrated (which he did not in the quote above), and considered the claim naïve[4] in terms of modern neuroscience but still useful as an analogy (Greenfield 2008, p. 216).

As I have previously quoted Diamond (2006, p. 186), models and paradigms are actually myths. This is known to some scholars: "all decisions are based on models, and all models are wrong" (Sterman 2002, p. 525), but even so, "All models are wrong, but some are useful" (Box and Draper 1987, p. 424). Charles Munger's comment that "you've got to have models in your head and you've got to array your experience – both vicarious and direct – on this latticework of models" (Munger 1994) has been more recently confirmed by Lakoff (2004) and McGilchrist (2009), who adds that any model "presupposes the nature of what one is looking at" (ibid., p. 94). Within that understanding, I find MacLean's model still useful as an ansatz for the purpose of HBA. That is providing (as always) that the relevant professional in interdisciplinary teams monitor and evaluate the model in the light of more recent discoveries in the relevant disciplines, which disciplines are not confined to neuroscience. For example, behaviours we share with crocodiles can be given less intrinsic value – albeit in some contexts high extrinsic value – than those more highly valued qualities referred to above that we share with other primates, but not crocodiles.

Well before Greenfield made her critique, MacLean himself recognised that one could not discuss the brain without resorting to oversimplification (ibid., p. 13). He does not even refer to the enteric nervous system (Enders 2015). So once again, we have to look at a fitness landscape to understand a holon in it: the brain "*cannot be understood in isolation*" (italics added; Rose 2006, p. 64). From now on, therefore, I will use the term "human holon" in preference to "brain" where appropriate, to avoid the inevitable reductionism both in confining attention to a single hextant, and in reducing people to the activities at the top of their spines.

For this and other reasons, not everyone agrees that MacLean's grasp is as naïve as Greenfield asserts (Panksepp and Panksepp 2000, p. 112; Ploog 2003). Even if we take Greenfield's point, then we are still left with the triune brain's strength as an analogy. In any case, neither Greenfield's nor MacLean's understandings are as naïve as those of the lay population in their fields. Consequently, we must admit to the provisional nature of their insights in their own fields, and mine in theirs. But this is not unique. At our highest levels of cognitive development, we admit to the provisionality of *all* insights: Some are almost infinitely probable, others are almost infinitely improbable, and most are in between.

Furthermore, MacLean's alleged naivety is highly sophisticated compared to the naivety of objectivist "nothing buttery" scientism and arguably Churchland's eliminative materialism (Churchland 1999) as well. For, as Mumford observed, "the independence of science from human values is a gross superstition" (Mumford 1922, p. 276) and as MacLean noted, objectivism is a fantasy, and that all the so-called hard facts of science "are informational transformations by the viscoelastic brain" (MacLean 1990, p. 5; see also ibid., pp. 570–571). "The brain always stands between us and what we observe" (ibid., p. 576); "the paradox of the Mobius ring and the possibility that their outer world is only our inner world turned inside out" (Mumford 1979, p. 24); "Objectivity is the delusion that observations could be made without an observer" (Von Foerster 1974) "There is no such thing as an immaculate perception" (Johnson 1995, p. 134; see also

Von Glasersfeld 1990). As Margaret Archer (2014) asks, "we believe, but who are we?" Every person on earth is different, but every person on earth is one of this "we" in some domain, dimension, level, line or scale. All those persons have con-firmation biases acting as gatekeepers to what we reason about (Mercier and Sperber 2011, p. 57).

The observation of MacLean et al. is still robust: no attempt at an ultimate picture of reality can omit it. Yet there are many pictures claimed as ultimate that are not, and such absolute and fundamentally imaginary claims are often used to dispense and enforce property rights.

When conducting intrinsic valuations, it is important to realise that MacLean's ansatz re the structure of the brain (human holon) does not necessarily tally with its functioning in addressing fitness landscapes. Emotions, thoughts and actions do not reside in specific parts of the human holon, but in patterns of dynamic interactions between many parts of it. Human holon structures are adapted to address the environments they encounter in a process called "exaptation" (Rose 2006, pp. 26, 43–44, 204). However, there is also an element in evolution where what works for particular evolutionary challenges is retained more or less intact through millennia to meet those challenges. Moreover, Rose also notes that large complex organisations need multiple management layers, and human holons are the most complex organisations of all (ibid., p. 52).

Therefore, to intrinsically value we do not need to focus upon retracing evolutionary trees as much as the niches within fitness landscapes and our appropriate behaviour to address them. Context determines content (Rosado 2008), and content determines context (in terms of fitness landscapes), and function forms form as form forms function in all domains by means of the feedback loops between them. Therefore, it is not only physical forms that change, but mental forms as well. With holons, niches in physical and ecological space require appropriate mental space: with artefacts such as real property rights, they acquire that mental space from a holon – especially, but not exclusively, humans. Provisionally, and as we shall see subject to Rose's observations, I accept MacLean's model. However, that acceptance is in the context of referring not only to the brain, but also to the hextal fitness relationships shaping each hextant – physical performances, motives, skills, natural, infrastructural and cultural environments. It is as follows:

- *Low intrinsic value:* the minds (not the parts of the brain) that we share with reptiles and creatures of less levels of emergence than reptiles. They are filled with feared authority from the past and fear of any new existent.
- *Medium intrinsic value:* the minds that we share with lower mammals (the palaeo-mammalian mind): inarticulate emotions, for example, but greater capacities to adapt and learn.
- *Higher intrinsic value:* the minds that we share with higher mammals (the neo-mammalian mind), such as those referred to above, and beyond that, only with humans, and beyond that only humans who have developed their areté to act wisely and compassionately in their environments.

Although he does not use the term, MacLean is very specific about the holarchical nature of these three brains. In other words, he saw each of the brains as a relatively autonomous holon, capable with experience of integrating hierarchically into a higher holon in conformity with the development (Orthogenic) principle (see Chapter 5). In addition, because each is a holon within the human holon, we cannot say that any specific function is simply located in one of the holons; they all mutually act and interact heterarchically. A major trend detectable within that developmental process is one of a capacity to not only adapt to different fitness landscapes, but even to create new ones, which is perhaps our greatest advantage over other species: the neocortex allows a "high(er) fidelity" approximation to whatever it is "out there" for our "in heres" (Gribbin 1993, p. 298). Its responses are highly supple in comparison to the rigidity of the reptilian brain.

Taleb notes that "once in a while you encounter members of the human species with so much intellectual superiority that they can change their minds effortlessly" (Taleb 2007, p. 192). Similarly, Nicholas of Cusa (1401–1464) noted that the best minds hold all beliefs lightly (and, I would add, all ontologies). That is because such open-minded people are predominantly focussed in, and have thereby highly developed, this part of their human holon. While all of us can become prejudiced when we engage the dogmatic and visceral palaeo-mammalian brain, and completely closed minded when they engage in the "rigid, obsessive, compulsive, ritualistic and paranoid" (MacLean 1990) characteristics of the reptilian brain. For instance, I find myself quite discomfited when I have rewarded myself with a "that's settled, then" feeling before due diligence verification, and find later my confirmation biases unsettled. However, that is inevitable if one is to address wicked valuation problems, and one can develop antifragility to that process.

Whether from the North, the South, the East or the West, only a very few can change their minds effortlessly, and even then not always: wisdom . . . it's difficult! When Fenollosa referred to the mental stiffness of the mechanical or the savage mind (Williams 2014, p. 23), and Blake of single vision, I see them as referring to those low intrinsic value characteristics MacLean ascribed to the palaeo-mammalian and reptilian brains in the soma hextant. These manifest in the psyche hextant as primal desires – the suite thereof, not just the regard-recognition hunger I had gone to ask Krishnamurti about.

Such interplays of intrinsic and extrinsic values can be appreciated though HBA. The characteristics of the neocortex can have higher intrinsic value than those of the palaeomammalian brain, which in turn can have higher intrinsic value than the reptilian, but sometimes vice versa with extrinsic value. However, the neocortex can design or adapt artefacts of even greater extrinsic value in certain circumstances than our more primal brains can attain (weapons, for instance), and thereby greatly enhance the survival potential of the triune brain.

Therefore, we can regard the human holon as a viscoelastic complex with great viscosity, and high extrinsic value at its lower reaches, and great elasticity and high intrinsic value at its higher reaches. There can be still higher intrinsic valuations placed upon behaviours tracked by development psychology and other disciplines towards universally lauded co-evolutionary manifestations of wisdom and compassion, often identified as advanced spiritual development.

As MacLean notes, this raises "the question as to what extent the reptilian counterpart of man's brain may determine his obeisance to precedent in ceremonial rituals, religious convictions, legal actions, and political persuasions" (MacLean 1973, p. 10). To that list, I would add Hegel's obeisance to the state.[5] If future research were to answer that question in the affirmative, the reptilian brain's relevance in attack and defence of property rights would be evident.

In contrast to the reptilian brain, J. and J. B. Panskepp noted that the neocortical brain tissue of humans is not designed to address any inclusive fitness functions, but to explore (Panksepp and Panksepp 2000, p. 109). As such, it is hard-wired for development, because autopoiesis involves two major processes: *specificity*, keeping existents invariant in a varying environment, and *plasticity*, adapting to a varying environment. These processes are intertwined, a *"developmental double helix"* (Rose 2006, p. 63, emphasis mine) which has to emerge from a Goldilocks zone for development to happen.

An implication of this is that often a closed mind is worse in terms of both its extrinsic value and its development of intrinsic value than is a stupid one (Panksepp and Panksepp 2000 p. 119) and empirical ones also, as we have described above. Confirmation bias is an example of this (ibid., p. 119; Allahverdyan and Galstyan 2014). A closed mind is driven by confirmatory biases such as bigotry and allows no uptake, even if it has the highest intelligence available to anyone on Earth. The quip that "the problem with open minds is that everything falls out – including our reason" is an example of the observation of just such a highly intelligent closed mind (Hood 2009, p. 9).[6]

In contrast, the observation by Joseph Roth that "it is the mark of a narrow world that it mistrusts the undefined . . . the small man builds cages for everyone he knows" (Roth 2004) appears to be an observation from a highly intelligent open one. We evolved so that the neocortex is the last to become fully operational and the first to close down in the face of trauma. Therefore, our intrinsic value varies according to our environmental challenges and what we see ourselves as being. Building such cages for others is an example of a process that can be extrinsically valuable, but is intrinsically demeaning and reductive to others.

Consequently, one major distinction between the complexity approaches adopted in this book and classicism is the group of those made above concerning the respective roles of the left and right hemisphere's functions as Master and Emissary respectively (McGilchrist 2009). Another is the homologous distinction between complicated and complex made by Glouberman and Zimmerman (2002). Those distinctions also imply the left hemisphere having greater competence in addressing extrinsic valuations, complicated machinery and other artefacts, and the right hemisphere having greater competence in addressing intrinsic valuations, complex humans and other holons. However, to optimally address wicked valuation problems the brain must act as a whole, not just the total of two hemispheres. That is, it must become an emergent whole greater than the sum of its parts, and recognise that "what look like elements are simply facets of the indivisible human condition" (McGilchrist 2009, p. 242). The reduction of mental functioning to mechanistic functioning, while potentially a very helpful metaphor by which the left hemisphere can "get a grip", may not only tempt the Emissary to get ideas above its station, but also – as mentioned by MacLean above – that was always nonsense because the "mind cannot be reduced to physics because physics presupposes the minds of physicists" (Sheldrake 2012, p. 10). Moreover, even to physicists "the materialist (or 'physicalist') position is not the safe harbor of metaphysical sobriety that many desire" (Frank 2017).

This latter emphasis of scientism often takes on the emotional baggage of other forms of fundamentalism. As "a movement that stresses the superiority, infallibility and authority of its beliefs in matters of faith, morals, history and prophecy" (Das 2011, p. 115), fundamentalism is at the opposite end of the spectrum to spirituality. Spirituality is open to mystery, uncertainty and change, and fundamentalism (as here meant) is fearful of and closed to them (Tacey 2004, p. 11). In other words, fundamentalism engages the primitive and viscous levels of our human holons – closed minds – while spirituality engages the highly developed, elastic levels of our human holons: open minds. True science deals with probabilities as discerned through rigorous, testable and falsifiable research. Further, it recognises that mathematics, while essentially a tautological tool at the single vision level, becomes an increasingly wonderful vehicle for creativity as the mathematician develops to higher levels. That is, it is then at the other end of this spectrum from scientism as it is engaged by the right hemisphere in coevolution with the left (McGilchrist 2017). I see the development from the former to the latter in science and maths as developmental lines from Blake's single to fourfold vision (Blake's "sweet science").[7]

One such form of fundamentalism is the rigid separation of humans from the animal kingdom, and the intrinsic devaluation of the "other" (in whatever form it takes, including the form of the real property rights of others). As Stout notes, there are two main mistakes we make that contravene the normal benevolence of our natures. Firstly, at whichever identity level we have constructed, wanting to control others and the world, and secondly, dehumanising/devaluing others as to allow their moral exclusion, adding that "So far, psychology has left this question [how to correct those mistakes] completely unanswered" (Stout 2005).

Despite psychology's non-answer, such reactions are easily replicable, particularly in trolling on the internet, where reactions such as "loony" and "traitor" are readily evoked from those who are incapable of engaging with intellectual positions other than one's own (McGrath and Casey 2014). As Csikszentmihalyi points out, when "people lack the skills to recognise more interesting opportunities they tend to regress to more simple and brutal choices" (Csikszentmihalyi 1993, p. 187). In land policy development, as much as practicable it is important to avoid such mental lockdowns by keeping matters inside the Goldilocks zone.

This "othering" takes the form of one of the six basic emotions. They are surprise, anger, happiness, fear, sadness and disgust, and the overriding emotion of fundamentalist societies and communities is disgust and intolerance (Greenfield 2008, pp. 230–231). That is a mental response from a level of the brain we share with mammals, which evolved for our dietary health and got "hi-jacked to enforce group membership" (ibid., p. 226). Yet such qualities are also indicative of extremely egocentric behaviour, which manifests as a cauldron of strongly nega-tive emotions including hate, rage, disgust and grief, but not guilt, combined with an us versus them emotional response to others (Graves 1981, pp. 19–20).

This tendency within fundamentalist scientism towards disgust and absolutism is often directed to those who manifest what they consider to be unscientific approaches to life (as in other cases of extreme collective identity). Yet as Rabelais had Gargantua say, *"Science without conscience is the ruin of the soul"* and as Lévy-Brühl emphasised, contentment with objective science and with the rational world can only be achieved by spiritual destruction (as cited in Tanase 1989, pp. 267–277), because it is mere single vision. On the other hand, nowadays many scientists recognise that while neuroscientific knowledge may enrich under-standing, including our ethical ones, they can never replace either ethics or any other legal and social etc. understandings (Rose 2006, p. 305).

Note that this emphasis upon spirituality is not about religious conviction, which so often falls prey to fundamentalism because of what is termed "the drown-ing man paradox . . . *the fuzzier an environment appears, the stronger the attachment to what seems non-fuzzy in it"* (Dimitrov and Korotkich 2002, p. 34; italics added).

Religions, when attempting to account for every existent, are notoriously susceptible to this paradox, and consequently dogmatism and fundamentalism. As the anonymous observation puts it: "philosophy is questions that may never be answered; religion is answers that may never be questioned". The stronger the challenge, the more pugnacious the response can be: "men never do evil so com-pletely and cheerfully as when they do it from religious conviction" (Pascal 1669, no. 894). In contrast, the HBA approach regards the spirituality – highest intrinsic value – end of the cultural spectrum to be the systemic value of its processes, because it requires the capacity for penetrating understanding of human nature, the whole in the part and the part in the whole (Dimitrov 2003, pp. 16–17).

However, as with so many aspects of reality, misplaced concreteness affects perceptions here. The summit of intrinsic values is where sacred values belong – the produce of co-evolved wisdom and compassion. The impulse of assigning sacred values is essential for social cohesion; whatever their flaws in practice, many religions were probably created for this purpose. However, with disgust being "the negative consequence of violating our sacred values" (Hood 2009, p. 178), that often means disgust is misapplied. Sadly, a major flaw in identity construction is that the more absurd one's devotion is the more trusted you might become, provided you can convince others of your sincerity (Atran as cited in Brockman 2013, p. 11). As Sayajit Das put it, "the more dubious a proposition or unreliable a fact, the greater the authority and confidence with which it is stated. Constant repetition diminishes scepticism" (Das 2011, p. 110). The power of the preposterous as a narrative for identity construction includes that complete conviction in such a narrative can be far more spellbinding and, thereby, identity-contagious than can more taxing challenges such as those required for peaceful resolution of wicked problems.

Viewing Maslow's Hierarchy of Needs as a Heterarchy of Needs can assist in addressing wicked valuation problems, as it can be interpreted as a heterarchy of extrinsic valuation concerns at the lower end, and intrinsic valuation concerns at the higher. In fact, later researchers have found that we do not address the needs expressed in Maslow's hierarchy sequentially, but integrally, simultaneously, heterarchically, and weighted according to the environments available supply for the various demands (Fowler 2007, p. 11). Seen that way, a person's adoption of prevailing preposterous ideas can be seen as ecologically rational (Gigerenzer and Brighton 2009), thereby allowing potential for continued improvement of intrinsic value that may not be possible with their rejection. For example, one may not pursue gain in intrinsic value when denied high extrinsic value requirements, such as food and water, because you may become fully engaged with merely trying to survive. So while satisfaction of those basic needs does not guarantee the emergence of satisfaction of the higher ones; they may be necessary but insufficient preconditions for any such emergence. Box 6 below elaborates on this process (Box 5.2).

Box 5.2   Maslow's hierarchy of needs (here considered as a heterarchy) and intrinsic valuation

We can regard the above description of the triune brain as the soma hextant's implementer of Abraham Maslow's well-known Hierarchy of Needs, with the provisos that Maslow's is actually a Heterarchy of Needs and requires parallel holarchies in niches in other hextants for fulfilment. Moreover, in line with Wahba and Bridwell's (1976) reconsidering of Maslow, and HVN↔HBA and my own developmental action inquiry practice (Torbert and Associates 2004), I observe internally as being more of a heterarchy. Very broadly, the lower two (physiological and safety) needs are those we share with reptiles, the central (love and esteem) needs are those we share with mammals, and the highest (self-actualisation) needs are those referred to by Tacey, and by Dimitrov, above.

Maslow's most primitive stage is that of Physiological needs – survival needs such as food, water, air, and the elimination of waste matter. All life has such needs. In most parts of the globe, territory, shelter and clothing can also be regarded as physiological needs. Some physiological activities, such as sex and maternal activity, can be postponed and are therefore not as basic in this heterarchy.

The next most primitive needs are Safety needs. As with physiological needs, if safety needs are seen as not being met, then the higher stages are devalued until that need is seen to be satisfied. Avoidance of an excess of anxiety and fear is the psychological dimension of "safety". Order, routine, stable government, job security, stable marital and social environments are examples of these "safety" needs. As Maslow says, "other broad aspects of the attempt to seek safety and stability in the world are seen in the very common preference for familiar rather than unfamiliar things, or for the known rather than the unknown" (Laird et al. 1975, p. 53).

Belongingness and Affection lie on the continuum between safety and esteem, as they provide a feeling of security and acceptance. Friends, tribes, sexual partnerships, praise – all feed these needs. "We are incomplete or unfinished animals who complete ourselves through culture" (Geertz 1973, p. 49). Many animals exhibit such needs, although sometimes only at certain stages of their development.

Self-esteem, a positive appraisal of self-worth, is vital to a person's functioning. Low self-esteem – lack of feelings of accomplishment and adequacy – results in such feelings as worthlessness, envy, despair, laziness, cynicism, selfishness and other such obstructive attitudes to economic and social development.

People can say that they have achieved "Self-actualisation" when they can say that they have had a successful life; that they would live their lives the same way if they had the chance to do it all over again. That does not happen unless the above stages are completed and consolidated by social interaction. None of the above stages occurs in a vacuum; they are all dependent upon relationships – with the family, the community, the world at large. A stunting of the sense of self, even death, is the product of ostracism (Bellah 1991; Gribbin 1993, pp. 40–41).

Later, Maslow realised that there are stages beyond self-actualisation, which he conflated together as "self-transcendence". Those established at such levels often drop their property rights completely (give all they own to the poor, etc.).

We may regard these as various levels at which attractors and repellers gain relevance in terms of enhancing or inhibiting individual development in their respective contexts. These have significant consequences in organisational behaviour. For example, despite Drucker's observation that the Productivity Revolution has finished, in countries where survival needs are still highly challenged Tayloresque business practices are still being set up. As I witnessed, what appears as appallingly exploitative salaries and working conditions to those addressing needs higher up in Maslow's hierarchy are eagerly grasped in places like textile factories in Lesotho, where those same conditions better satisfy the survival and safety needs than any available alternatives. As we include valuing the fitness landscapes of real property rights in terms of facilitating the utilisation of their extrinsic values towards Mary Midgley's definition of freedom, this is one fundamental set of questions for this work. However, a complementary and equally fundamental set is to do with optimal rates of growth. It is in facilitating the rate of growth of affected individuals that the organisation can facilitate positive attractors of meaning for its members, and thereby they will work not just for money (extrinsic value), but for love (intrinsic value).

Therefore, when attempting the introduction of any new land policies, including any new system of real property rights, a key systemic value is the facilitation of that growth in the intrinsic value of those affected, and that growth requires a manageable rate to happen at all. We can therefore harness this *flow* up the analogical knife's edge of arête towards the ancient Greek attractor of areté – which means reaching your highest human potential in terms of intrinsic valuation in particular by a process of autotelaxic flow. However, as the psyche hextant is but one of six holonic hextants, what equivalent fractal signifiers are perceptible in other hextants?

My answers come from two quarters as unexpected to me before embarking upon this paper as the idea of *flow* as signalling the presence of a fractal in the interior of an individual. The first relates to what is meant by the term "peace". In this context, it does not mean a balance of fear, of weaponry, the peace of cemeteries, but instead "an active and efficient dialogue between people, between nations, order and cooperation of free peoples against everything that threatens their freedom, human dignity and social progress" (Tanase 1989, p. 275).

In the political sphere, the Ancient Greeks would see the required areté for that as being "that elusive quality of excellence in knowledge of both polis and self that distinguishes the true citizen from the barbarian and corrupt backslider" (Hannaford 1994, p. 14): a definition that can address all hextants.

The systemic value of tackling these wicked valuation problems to facilitate peace is, as A. N. Whitehead wrote:

> The Harmony of Harmonies which calms destructive turbulence and completes civilization. It is a positive feeling which calms the 'life and motion' of the soul . . . It is broadening of feeling due to the emergence of some deep metaphysical insight, unverbalised and yet momentous in its coordination of values. Its first effect is the removal of the stress of acquisitive feeling arising from the soul's preoccupation with itself. Thus peace carries with it a surpassing of personality . . . [a] confirmation of purpose to the ideal beyond personal limitations.
>
> (Whitehead 1967, p. 285)

That is what Smith's smokescreen obscured. Self-actualisation and beyond that, self-transcendence, dropping that regard-recognition hunger. In thinging people, it obscured their potential to transmute "greed into generosity, ill will into loving-kindness, delusion into wisdom" (Loy 2006, pp. 15–16), and The Machine, blind to intrinsic value, has institutionalised that smokescreen (ibid.).

Peace is not merely a warless situation; "it is a virtue, a state of mind, a disposition for benevolence, confidence and justice",[8] and without that, the Chinese proverb applies: "when the wrong man uses the right means, the right means work the wrong way". I mean the Vairocana-sourced HVN to enfold that understanding. The identity that can be identified – of anyone – is not the real identity. As Krishnamurti put it:

> The understanding of the mind is the beginning of peace . . . you will solve the problem of war only when you yourself are the challenge, and not

merely a reaction . . . to end conflict is to understand the whole process of oneself . . . society is the structure of ourselves in projection.

(Krishnamurti 1950)

Our identities include the structure of our society in miniature. It is not just its language we internalise. It includes a whole suite of matters we inhale into our identities, including values, allegiances, and so forth, including the real property rights system.

That peace is what real property rights should be for. That is their systemic value, and in some societies they can already facilitate it. Fraser's working definition of the Good as a human value, asserting "a certain conduct, intent or character trait will promote stable balance and harmony in the mind and affairs of a person and in the dynamics of society" (Fraser 1999, p. 84) is consonant with both of the above.

Therefore, I adopt them as the systemic value attractor of HVN↔HBA. That peace, that understanding of the identity needs of self and others and that goodness are what HVN↔HBA is intended to facilitate – a rebalancing away from the dominator focus of the extrinsic value of others to one, towards a partnership focus of the intrinsic value of one and all to others.

The second is the essential value of land and place-making in so many cultures worldwide. Rowson (2014) places a different emphasis on ground value to Wilber, and thereby draws out an important observation for this work. Again, he means "the most basic facts of our existence, that we are here in and through this body, that we build selves through and for others, that we're a highly improbable part of an unfathomable whole, and, of course, that we shall inevitably die" (ibid., p. 25). Like Wilber, Vedanta, and Whitehead's prehension, Wright's "earlier answer of the eyes" is closer to ground value than the identities it constructs. But then Rowson differentiates it from *place value* – including the identity constructions' valuations of land: "because the world perpetuates our attachment to place, by which I mean our constructed identities . . . our dwellings, our salaries, our clothes, our twitter followers" (ibid., p. 26), and recommends a shift of emphasis from place value construction to ground value realisation:

> The take home message from the ground/place distinction is not to give up material life but to understand more what the spiritual/material juxtaposition is really about and why what emerges is radically inclusive.
>
> (Rowson 2014, p. 27)

He later notes that an emergence from that shift "is to wake up to the broader features of our ecological ground that are under threat" (ibid., p. 85).

History has shown that not everyone makes that shift – not everyone is like Gautama Buddha, including Buddhists who wish to kill the ego. Processes, including one's own ego, are to be intrinsically extrinsically, systemically and finally integratedly valued, not killed. Only from such value judgements can one wisely follow or reject the response of the rich ruler's refusal to sell all he owns and give it to the poor when asked by Jesus (Luke 18–30), to follow the Son of Man who "has nowhere to lay his head" (Matthew 8:20).

The capacity to create the Wizard of I is holonic, part of a holon of great intrinsic value. The identity constructed may facilitate what we have in us to be, express the areté of that value via a period of sophrosyne development. However, to do so it must also develop extrinsic value to lay a foundation upon which our intrinsic values may be optimally expressed. That is a wicked valuation problem for us all.

Our constructed identities need a sense of place to grow, and to "drop it" to grow up and value existents properly. Moreover, almost everywhere I have gone, people have said to me that land is a sensitive issue. So the intrinsic, extrinsic, and systemic valuations are towards this end, as engraved on Robert Fitzgerald Kennedy's gravesite at Arlington National Cemetery in Washington DC, which I visited in March 2015: "To tame the savageness of man, and make gentle the life of the world".

ADALAS

As mentioned at the beginning of the chapter, once we are armed with HIDEGRE and understand the need for the holistic approach that only our right hemispheres can provide, as articulated through BIES, we are able to examine the landscapes with all the capacities we can employ to address wicked valuation problems. The often vast gap between our conscious focus and what gets unconsciously absorbed, and what we do not absorb at all, is what I intend ADALAS to manage. This is a two-edged sword, but I mean ADALAS to enable more to be brought to our conscious attention within an organised framework. It recognises the inadequacy of any single vision to address the multidimensional process nature of HVN, and I intend it to facilitate a more realistic process to address wicked valuation problems, with that realism resulting in a developmental trajectory from simplax and simplex towards omniplax and omniplex by co-evolution through the hextants. As mentioned earlier, Anderson noted that entirely new laws, concepts and generalisations are necessary (Anderson 1972, p. 393) at every new level of emergence – an observation that is valid for emergences along all developmental lines, waves and streams. I look to ADALAS as a map to provide some guidance through the labyrinths addressing wicked problems may involve. For example, an ADALAS map may assist when dealing with the simplistic theories that circulate around land titling and ownership, to persuade all those who may be holding fast to them, perhaps including oneself, to look more rigorously at the complications and complexities involved towards not causing or exacerbating wicked problems.

At first, I conceived ADALAS as being modelled in a computer to be used to facilitate more integral decision-making than we can attempt by juggling only a few factors in our minds at any one time. However, over time I found that it could be internalised as well, albeit at a less rigorous level. For now at least, I am submitting that a computer-assisted dynamic HVN↔HBA protocol in trans-ontological teams is the most we can do, and an internalised HVN↔HBA is the least we should do when addressing wicked valuation problems. While possibly no individual can master all the disciplines required to all the depth required to do that, interdisciplinary teams composed of members who have attained Mary Midgley's standard of rigour (Midgley 1995, p. 22) can have transdisciplinary decisions emerge. Qualifying criteria might include a track record in reifying personally co-evolved wisdom and compassion in one's life, experience relevant to the problem, and so on. The Model of Hierarchical Complexity (Commons 2007) could play a significant role in the selection process, in that it could help in identifying complex↔complax competencies.

Originally, I thought of ADALAS along the same lines as discounted cash flow (DCF) modelling. DCF is used to assist in making financial decisions, but ADALAS is to apply in broader valuational contexts than merely monetary ones. Naturally, the same GIGO (garbage in, garbage out) qualification would apply as it does with DCF and similar models. The great advantage of models such as DCF is that they can help examine and question assumptions. The great disadvantage is what they may leave out. Another, the assumption that the world is only linear, is manifestly untrue, as are the interest rates projections in so many past DCF assumptions.

While this same qualification would apply to ADALAS, it will be far less restrictive than the money-based DCF: it would transcend and include all such models. Different factors would be valued and weighted differently in the model, with differing degrees of fuzziness weighed by the evidentiary support. Users could also factor in the probability of occurrences for examination of potential scenarios using linear and non-linear methodologies for risk management.

Certain patterns are only discernible and applicable at certain statistical and geographical scales. Statistical: families in a locality may have an average of 1.6 children, but there is no family with 1.6 children; a population may have an average IQ of 90 or 130, but that tells you no existent whatsoever about the IQ of any one John or Jane Doe within that grouping. Geographically, if you want to drive from Boston to New York, you get a map of the appropriate scale. You need a differently scaled map to find your way around your suburb, and your wicked problem.

Therefore, as David Rumsey put it: "Maps always have attitude" (ibid., 14:28). When speaking of an ancient Buddhist map showing the centre of the world as being Mount Kailas, the myth not only includes the reality, but also:

> [P]ushes our imagination to see the super-reality. Technology, I think, can do the same thing on our new maps. In our future there will be no unknown spaces, as there have been in the past. We'll all be in the big map and know where we are at the time. But we will still have much to learn about the context of our lives and how we all fit together, how we exchange information . . . So the challenges will be to create new maps, and the new geography that will tell us more than we ever dreamed we would know about our real places on earth.
>
> (Rumsey 2005, 29:20–29:56)

It is that attitude that I seek to employ in employing ADALAS in addressing wicked problems:

> All description, explanation, or representation is necessarily in some sense a mapping of derivatives from the phenomena to be described onto some surface or matrix or system of coordinates. In the case of an actual map the receiving matrix is commonly a flat sheet of paper of finite extent, and difficulties occur when that which is to be mapped is too big or, for example, spherical ... Every receiving matrix, even a language or a tautological network of propositions, will have its formal characteristics which will in principle be distortive of the phenomena to be mapped onto it.
>
> (Bateson 1979, p. 48)

Note that every Octo operates within cultural and environmental milieus, and needs maps of those.[9] With Rumsey's challenge and Bateson's warning in mind, users may need to factor different developmental lines and scales into the process. Once again, a computer can allow any number of lines and scales – hence the "All Lines" and "All Scales" part of the term ADALAS.

For decades now, maps at many different scales have been developed on the base of Geographical Information Systems technology (GIS). This technology has tremendous power, and researchers often discover new knowledge by using its ability to overlay different information sets on top of the maps provided. Users of ADALAS would begin by overlaying its information on GIS (although smaller scales would also be needed; Google earth and Digital Earth could be adapted for these differently scaled overlays). They could then integrate individual interior and exterior qualities and exterior cultural considerations into problem-solving, policy formulation etc. at the relevant scales. They could insert statistical information (for example about the AIDS pandemic in Africa) at the appropriate scale for its applicability. There is a huge amount of relevant information for this on the internet and elsewhere, lying around in heaps like bricks for a structure, unintegrated and thereby comparatively useless. I intend ADALAS to be not only a tool for multivariate analysis, but also for multivariate synthesis towards engaging liberated trans-ontological imaginative leaps. Such scale differences also apply in organic scales, not just geographical ones, and we need an All Scale approach to consider them. "Local truths can become global errors ... Global truths can lead to local errors" (Morin 2007, p. 11). A biological scale example is an immune system rejecting a heart transplant; what appears appropriate to a cell may be catastrophic to the body.

The "H" of HIDEGRE points out that engagement of all the hextants is needed for development, but there can be many factors in each hextant required, in differing proportions and relationships, for development to occur. I mean ADALAS to map that, facilitating differentiation and integration in the minds of its users. The current flatland policies – policies blind to levels of emergence; unable to intrinsically value one existent over another – can be thereby contextualised and begin to become, at last, effective for the intended beneficiaries.

Here, the Chinese having the same word for "danger" as for "opportunity" springs to mind. The danger is its conflationary and manipulatory use as a "Big Brother" tool, as is already happening with GIS – "eye in the sky", invasions of privacy, etc. The big opportunity is in being able to make far more informed and nuanced decisions – more "skilful means" than would be possible without it – as is already being done through GIS, but more powerfully still.

Perhaps ADALAS may even facilitate humility! As Charles Darwin noted, "ignorance more frequently begets confidence than does knowledge" (Darwin, 1871). Wisdom is required for fundamental transformations such as I mean HVN↔HBA to facilitate, and that only emerges, if at all, after a qualitative series from information to knowledge to understanding to wisdom in an individual, and only via individuals, into a society. Only with wisdom can we transcend and value the strengths, weaknesses, opportunities and threats of world views that people hold (Gunderson and Holling 2002), and even then, only insofar as wisdom has co-evolved with compassion, known in India as the coevolution of *prajñā* and *karunā* (Wilber 1995, p. 328).

As with Habermas and Wilber's AQAL, the hextant model is, by its very nature, applicable at different scales, the scales themselves measuring different criteria. For instance, a social identity may manifest itself at nuclear family, extended family, tribal, local, national and global scales. That does not imply any increased depth of social identity with increased span. Rather, identification with artefacts may intrinsically devalue one's identity towards that of the artefact identified with, be it a car brand, a sports team, a nation-state or any other of The Machine's manifestations. Once locked into them, we may no more be able to break out of such identifications than a goose-stepping soldier in a military parade can break into grand jetés and pirouettes.

As also mentioned before, this approach implies a modification of HVN↔ HBA according to the scale it is examining. If the six hextants describe reality-at-large, then the interior hextants describe the individual, and the exterior hextants can be extended to describe *all* the world they inhabit – all the exterior. That is, the hextants can be successfully applied in an intra-identity level fashion, explaining Wilber's concept of social holons by dint of memes and memeplexes whereby people identify with existents at different breadths, depths, and scales (Herb and Kaplan 1999).

We know that the ways we perceive existents, and the way they are, are never identical. It is within this gap between mindscapes[10] and landscapes that much conflict arises. Through it mindscapes change landscapes, and landscapes change mindscapes. I therefore consider the gap vitally important, particularly in the valuations in that space, as stressed by the ecstatic interpreters of Whitehead's philosophy (Henning 2005). The hextants do not relate "just" or "only" to the line most often charted – that of the physical self – but to ALL other ways in which the individual directly engages with the other hextants. For example, my typing skills (skills hextant) impair my engagement with this computer (others' produce hextant).

The development of fuzzy logic could help to articulate the "complexity" scale of ADALAS. We could adapt the concept of ansatzes to this context, marrying it to the definition of development of understanding.

Ansatzes are how scientific inquiry generally begins. They are orienting informed guesses – educated guesses that are tested later by their results, checked against the evidence, and thereby discarded or further refined in a developmental double helix. This process has homologies with going from fuzzy to crisp in fuzzy logic. As such, fuzziness could then become a tool for grading development, and monitoring and evaluating its pacing to ensure it remains in the Goldilocks zone. Premature precision, or remaining indecisive too long, can both scupper development. Every bit of real knowledge has some context where it is valid, but how large is that domain?

Similarly, in looking to applying an ansatz to embark upon attempting to understand some existent, you have to start with some idea, some postulates or approach model to get anywhere at all. Therefore, you start with an ansatz, see how that works, and adjust to the feedback gained (Flyvbjerg 2001):

> Organic planning does not begin with a preconceived goal: it moves from need to need, from opportunity to opportunity, in a series of adaptations that themselves become increasingly coherent and purposeful, so that they generate a complex, final design, hardly less unified than a pre-formed geometric pattern.
>
> (Mumford 1961, p. 302)

You *play* with it, as recommended by Stanley and Lehman (2015); "you wander through wonder" in "nomadic exploration" (Barnesmoore 2017, p. 4), nomadism being the antithesis of the methodologies of the myth of the machine (Foucault 1979, p. 218). However, while Barnesmoore referred to wandering to *know*, from McGilchrist's framing I here mean wandering to *understand* as the motive, obtaining knowledge the means, and examining the wonder-inspiring process the opportunity, to address the wicked problems concerned by working towards understanding them, perhaps finding the answer hidden in the very questions: "to wonder is to be on the way, in via; it certainly means to be struck dumb, momentarily, but equally it means that one is searching for the truth" (Pieper 2009, p. 116).

Which points to the truth behind the Arab proverb, "El-safar Zafar": voyaging is victory. It also takes me back to my youthful fascination with Krishnamurti, whose teachings can now be interpreted via Bolte-Taylor and McGilchrist as being not only about restoring the Master/Emissary balance as advocated by McGilchrist, but also that balance being towards optimal for addressing wicked problems. I say "towards" because, like MacLean, McGilchrist focussed more on the brain hemispheres than the rest of the nervous system; for example, neither paid attention to the enteric nervous system; MacLean because its fundamental psychological influences were completely unknown in his time, McGilchrist because it is outside the central focus of his clinical field. In my case, Krishnamurti catalysed my nomadic explorations via travel, as part of the larger nomadic explorations towards understanding made urgent in me by the deaths of my parents. It also goes back further still, to those Aborigines who found my grandmother, for just as Foucault saw nomadism as the antithesis of the methodologies of the myth of the machine, so:

> Aboriginal people everywhere across Australia were pre-occupied ... with the symbols, signs and portents of vitality ... The evidence from all parts of the continent points to the perception that Aboriginal religions were among the least materially-minded and most life-minded of any of which we know.
>
> (Presland 2013, p. 7)

Mere monological, single vision, intra-frame machine thinking simply will not do. We do not need to be just thinking machines to address wicked valuation problems. First and foremost, we need to be engaged in Whitehead's creative advance into novelty, and able throughout that advance to accurately value our thoughts, and think accurately on our values, in a co-evolutionary dynamic through the hextants, and engage all our capacities therein including those beyond both intra-identity thinking and valuing. This heuristic approach is how life and our identities have evolved and continue to do so as long as challenges from their environments stimulate them within the Goldilocks Principle – be that immediate, or deferred via our identity constructions.

Particularly when we are young, we largely construct our identities via this heuristic approach. We all carry our personal images of reality as part of our identity (Wade 1996, p. 6), and like holograms the entire image will appear in any action of ours, although with greater or lesser detail in what we do (ibid., p. 278). From these images, we can start our perceptual process with orienting generalisations, and collect information along the lines of confirming or rejecting that "fuzzy", general, hypothesis, all the while on the lookout for delightful surprises such as the "butterfly" on p. 184 above. Our perceptions grow in depths and spans from such initial steps, however tentative and, indeed, mistaken, those initial steps may be. Our cognitions grow from such playful generalisations to more and more sharply focussed articulations of the "hologram" at different scales. Science works that way too, going from a fuzzy heuristic via an ansatz to a crisp result.

So perhaps this axis would involve a "fuzz ratio index" in ADALAS. Scientists talk of probabilities – absolute certainty being "probability one", and absolute impossibility being "probability zero".[11] Given fuzziology's importance as already established in machines and as emphasised by Dimitrov and Korotkich (2002) as *a framework for the new millennium*, I envisage developing a vocabulary articulating fuzz ratios as becoming important. For example, it could be numeric, so some existent so much out of focus as to be "blind" would have a fuzz ratio of one, and some existent in extremely sharp, articulated focus would have a fuzz ratio of zero. As with probabilities, the absolutes would perhaps never be, but we could articulate them to any degree of accuracy desired.

This is largely what is being searched for in, for example, examinations: How well we understand a subject, in both breadth and depth (the latter being demonstrated by how the span of knowledge is applied to the question). I see choosing the relevant developmental lines and determining their fuzz ratios as having widespread applications in politics and commerce (recruitment, for example).

Perhaps the fuzz ratios will turn out to be fizzers, but we can only learn that by trial and error.

While Google earth addresses space, we live in space-time. Time scales are therefore at least as important as space scales, and Octo's perceptions of them are vital as well. These vary from culture to culture and person to person and intraculturally and intrapersonally at different times (Fraser 1999), but their complexity makes them more important when it comes to scrutinising these wicked valuation problems, not less.

The Goldilocks Principle confirms the importance of time scales and their perceptions. Up to now, J. T. Fraser's work *Time, Conflict and Human Values* (1999) has provided me with the main input into the time scales of ADALAS, but not the only one (Yourgrau 2005, Barbour 1999). Unfortunately, scholars are yet to rigorously explore this area and it therefore retains a high fuzz ratio (Wade 1996, p. 284).

It is important to address the way that persons value differences between instant and delayed rewards. For example, in the context of compensation for compulsory acquisition, an emphasis on instant gratification may result in the compensation being frittered away in the short term, leaving the affected parties much worse off than they were before the acquisition. Where such cases are to be reasonably anticipated, alternative methods of compensation, such as annuities or (as preferable anyway in almost every case) replacement in kind may be more in line with compensation principles than a cash amount. It has been established that different parts of the brain are employed to value short term gains compared to long term gains (McClure, Laibson, Lowenstein and Cohen 2004). That does not support a deterministic view, but that "performance always reflects a combination of skill and motivation, ability and values, and top-down and bottom-up influences" such that some will need more training than others in the domain of "the value of control and the influence of values" (Carlson and Zelazo 2011). Therefore, we should temper both policies and their implementation schedules to account for the respective qualities of the intended implementers and beneficiaries. "Restrictions can include lack of knowledge, lack of values, lack of norms and lack of possibilities", and we need to address these in working through the potential effects of policy proposals at any scale (Sloman and Fernbach 2017), and onwards through policy implementation (Hirsch Hadorn et al. 2013).

Through ADALAS, I formally recognise that without recognising hierarchical complexity, developmental stages may be omitted and thereby the development is in danger of being "doomed in advance to fail" (Ross and Commons 2008). Ross was referring to the MHC (Commons 2007) as being the only universal basis at her time of writing that could measure the complexity of tasks "at multiple scales, which can be studied with multi-scale profiles" (Fernandez et al. 2013). I envisage enfolding MHC into ADALAS so that we can apply each to its various context and examine how they are fit for the purpose and context.

The ADALAS approach highlights that you need different complexity↔complaxity horses for different complexity↔complaxity courses in a fitness landscape, and too great a mismatch can lead to very different outcomes to those intended. For example, take an Octo or a whole society from a fitness landscape where the appropriate behaviour is usually to go for instant gratification. If you then give members of that society real property rights that are appropriate to placing higher valuations on long term benefits is highly likely to have the intended beneficiaries look to immediate gratification. In such cases, that is what worked best for them in the environment they were used to, so via their confirmation biases they may assume it will in their new environment as well. Therefore, as with those receiving lump sum compensation, they might sell the real property for immediate gratification, and end up in the longer term much worse off than they were before.

Yet when it comes to all the National Development Strategies I have read and the ones I have participated in formulating, no direct and little indirect attention was focussed on this issue. Furthermore, Swaziland became the country with the highest HIV/AIDS concentration on earth, despite the intensive AIDS campaigns to warn everyone of the dangers. The way such campaigns were designed, they were much more likely to be effective with those whose fitness landscapes resulted in their being at Torbert's higher levels than lower ones where one's "hypothetical futures tend to be bound by experience or history" (Wade 1996, p. 128), or, worse, are hardly imagined at all. The same lacuna costing countless lives and misery in the HIV/AIDS fitness landscape is also largely unaddressed by the experience-bound in warnings about climate change.

All domains and dimensions

Here, the term "domain" has not only its legal meaning of "land to which there is superior title and absolute ownership", but also "a realm or range of personal knowledge, responsibility, etc." and "a field of action, thought, influence, etc." (Dictionary.com). In terms of those latter two definitions, it also specifically refers to the domains enfolded within the six hextants, meaning a valuer must be a generalist to perform competently in terms of the IVSC definition of market value. It also means that land policy formulation must be an interdisciplinary exercise – certainly not the sole domain of valuers, economists or any other discipline. Preferably, it should be a transdisciplinary exercise in terms of Max-Neef (2005) and Nicolescu (2006), which requires persons of the capacity to be rigorous in terms of Midgley's definition (Midgley 1995, p. 22) and which is fundamental to HVN↔HBA.

With the word "dimensions", I mean it more in its broader meaning in the *Oxford English Dictionary* of "an aspect or feature of a situation". However, the more general definition in that dictionary of a "measurable extent of a particular kind" is also relevant, particularly in terms of being able to discern the simple and complicated components from complex ones in wicked problems and social messes. In this trans-ontological process, though, they are not just set aside, because they interrelate with other domains and dimensions, levels, lines and scales. For instance, there are racist dimensions in these wicked valuation problems (Lipsitz 2011). Lipsitz concludes by stating that, while apparently miraculous changes happen, "change cannot *take place* . . . until we change the racialized meaning *of place*" (ibid., p. 256; italics in original): another contribution to be enfolded into the HBA approach of this work.

Once the domains and dimensions are identified and valued, further questions can be more fruitfully pursued, such as "what are the natures of the components of a problem, and their interrelationships? Are there holons? Are there artefacts? If either, what are their natures? Are the holons all people . . . are the artefacts material, or abstract?" and so on, moving all the while from fuzzy towards crisp in terms of the development principle articulated in Chapter 5.

All levels and lines

All holons have within them developmental levels that have to address all six hextants to progress. When they do so, at a critical stage the process will emerge into a higher level of organisation – atoms, to molecules, molecules to cells, cells to animals, and so on. As discussed from a mechanist example by Carl F. Craver (2014), there is a plethora of such levels in addition to the model of hierarchical complexity (Wilber 1999a). Information theorists are developing towards examining such "dynamical hierarchies" (McGregor and Fernando 2005).

In the context of levels of knowledge, the main point to emphasise here is that there should be a Goldilocks Principle matching of knowledge to the challenge. "Knowledge as capital is analogous to natural capital, with the difference that there are different 'levels' of knowledge. They can be considered a qualitative series: information, knowledge, understanding, wisdom" (Gunderson and Holling 2002, p. 123).

In addition to levels, there are lines of development. Driven by the Identity Principle through the hextants, developmental lines operate via the Goldilocks, Development, Emergence and Related Evolution principles through cognitive, valuational, interpersonal, moral, emotional, or aesthetic lines (Wilber 2012) up and down levels or stages in order to best address the environmental challenges, towards a sufficient fitness landscape for the holon concerned. We channel these lines through skills developed.

A high development in cognitive complexity along one line is not necessarily applicable to other lines, but it could be. These lines are relevant to the task not only in terms of the personnel involved in policy formulation and implementation, but also the ansatzes towards policy formulation and, in particular, implementation when assessing the possibilities concerning addressing these wicked valuation problems in particular environments.

My research of the literature did not find out much about applying complexity science across hextants to these wicked valuation problems. However, there is more than a hint of empirical support for interhextal adaptation in the table below, extracted from South Africa's Buthelezi Commission conducted in Kwa-Zulu Natal in 1981 (Table 5.7). I find it revealing to compare that table with the complexity-based model of developing attitudes to land tenure depicted in Table 5.8.

As mentioned above, "all models are wrong, but some are useful" (Box and Draper 1987, p. 424). Taken heterarchically rather than hierarchically, Beck and Cowan's may be one such useful model. Taken hierarchically, however, it could be a pernicious "imperialist act of envelopment and disenfranchisement" (Anderson 2010, p. 32). Moreover, the megamachine is merely complicated, not complex: intrinsic values are in holons such as people, not artefacts such as their social imaginaries. In complex identity construction such as those Scheler suggested, an assumption of superiority is an indicator of inferiority: having a "Big Me" means not having a "Big V", particularly when we project our narcissistic requirements of grandeur to such collective dimensions of our identities (Mead 2007, pp. 387–390).

In the above cases, Swaziland's customary tenure centres on phases one and two in the Buthelezi Commission's table and level 3 in Beck and Cowan's, and its formal tenure, like Australia's, is at phase 5 and level 5 respectively.

While set out in a hierarchical fashion, the hextal matching may not be so in terms of Commons' model of hierarchic complexity. Furthermore, I would have preferred Commons' model to have been termed "heterarchic complexity", but Commons may well have favoured "hierarchic" as it is more widely understood and considered that the heterarchic elements are best tracked from a hierarchic map. You may need more cognitive and valuation complexity to address a customary tenure conflict than a formal one, because you are dealing with people, not machines.

However, as accepted under this trans-ontological process, no existent is quite that simple. For example, in the same year as the Buthelezi Commission – that is, twelve years before Hernando De Soto's *The Other Path* – researchers such as Catherine Cross (Cross 1981) had already established that freehold neither promoted the free exchange of land rights nor raised agricultural production in rural areas: rather, it facilitated landlordism. A similar conclusion has been drawn more recently by Pereira (2016), who observes from his review of the World Bank's Agriculture and Rural Development Policies (1944–2003) – which have been influenced not only by de Soto but Feder (Feder and Feeny 1991; Feder and Deininger 1999) – that the World Bank's initiatives:

> [C]ontributed to widening the social space for the valorization of capital in agriculture and accelerate the mercantilization of rural lands. This was always the principal aim of the WB and it was successful in this. On the other hand, the rural poverty reduction target . . . is difficult to measure and assess, even because RD [rural development] projects have sought to preserve, instead of fight it [sic], the concentration of land ownership – a determinant factor in rural poverty and inequality. The generation of new agrarian policies after 1994 did not intend to alter this model – to the contrary.
>
> (Periera 2016, p. 253)

Table 5.7 Sequence of land tenure phases (Buthelezi Commission, South Africa)

Sequence of Tenure Phases	Phase 1 — Stable classical tenure	Phase 2 — Independent descent group tenure	Phase 3 — Semi-independent household tenure	Phase 4 — Sovereign household tenure	Phase 5 — Independent individual tenure
1 Level of Sovereignty	Cluster head as head of the senior descent group consults with other heads of households.	Descent group heads consult with other descent group members; neighbours have rights of refusal.	Household heads responsible for land transactions, subject to neighbours and previous holders sanction.	Household heads responsible for land transaction, subject to previous holder's sanction only.	Individual level: household members can hold and trade in individual land rights.
2 Entrants	Households related by marriage to resident descent groups – entry by outsiders low and intermittent.	Mostly relatives, and a growing number of outsiders, entry rate is moderate and continuous.	Many unaffiliated households without local relatives, more outsiders; entry rate increasing.	Outsiders predominate; individual households highly mobile; accelerating turnover rate for land rights.	Free interchange controlled by employment patterns.
3 Triggering Conditions for Phase Change.	Initial Settlement and initial re-allocation to related descent groups.	Increase in demand for land caused by immigration due to better transport access to urban employment area.	Relaxation of organisational structure allows easier land transfer.	Rate of sale of land increases, accepted even by tribal authorities	Close of rural phase sequence; open urban-oriented sequence.

Source: Cross (1981)

Table 5.8 Development of land tenure levels

---

1 **The current place occupied by the band.**
The people migrate throughout the world as they know it. The space is available to all, owned by none.

2 **Where the spirits and the ancestors walked.**
Defined by myth and legend, this is the "sacred ground" where the ancient ones lived, died, and are buried. The limits are of sight-lines and walking distance. Marked by symbols and defined in oral tradition carried in the collective memories of people –this tree, that river, over the next mountain peak, and up and down the valley. The land beyond is fearful and foreboding since evil spirits and competing tribes threaten harm.

3 **Where the big "me" leaves his or her personal mark.**
These are the areas of conquest over which the Power God, Chieftain, King, Queen, or feudal lord reigns. The limits are set by how far they can extend fear and wield control. Boundaries endure in direct relation to the strength to enforce them. Dangers exist beyond those boundaries (murderous warlords, fierce dragons, and rival ranchers with shotguns).

4 **The Higher Power assigns different people to different lands.**
The rightful places for habitation are properly surveyed, documented for history, picket-fenced, and then defended as holy and permanent. May become national borders protected by treaties and compacts, markers and armies. "God gave this land to us."

5 **Spheres of economic influence and individual ownership.**
Limits are adjusted by mercantile and imperialistic interests, negotiated contracts, economic/political alliances, diplomatic compromise, commodity-based cartels, and trade agreements. Boundary lines are drawn and redrawn to suit contemporary financial needs and political expediency.

6 **Open space that meets the needs of people coming together in a greater sense of community and mutual caring.**
Nationalistic divisions and private ownership of resources are viewed as artificial contrivances to keep people apart. The whole human race is seen as a single family living together on "the Commons", which should be shared for the good of all.

7 **Whichever level(s) on the Spiral are active in a given situation.**
Different needs are legitimised so long as boundary conflicts, border disputes, and proprietary clashes do not endanger the health of the Spiral itself. Some conflict between and among the different levels is inherent and inevitable.

8 **Functional needs of life on Earth.**
What life needs supersedes any special, natural, ethnic or parochial groupings. Man-made boundaries, as such, will fade. Such criteria as land and resources utilisation and natural geological forms and structures will establish human limits and habitation patterns along with other forms of life sharing the planet.

Source: Beck and Cowan (1996, pp. 302–303)

Cross also observed that informal tenure, where only unwritten community consent may be required, permits individual property rights "as long as they are seen as reasonable and not dangerous to the community" (ibid., p. 15). Finally, before the term became current, Cross noted the "wicked problem" nature of the process of being drawn into the cash economy: "new risks open up on all sides – outside speculators, absentee landlords, pyramiding subtenancies, and others" (ibid., p. 17).

Like Cross, and also like her without adopting the phrase "wicked problem" another anthropologist, Parker Shipton, rather than applying simplistic silver bullet solutions, recognises the wicked problem nature of traditional societies being drawn into the cash economy. He has written a trilogy on the problems, whose titles well describe their contents –*The Nature of Entrustment: Intimacy, Exchange, and the Sacred in Africa* (2007), *Mortgaging the Ancestors: Ideologies of Attachment in Africa* (2009) and *Credit Between Cultures: Farmers, Financiers, and Misunderstanding in Africa* (2010). In the last of these, he notes that one must "thread the way between the Scylla of simplicity and the Charybdis of complexity", and that in so doing:

> [I]t is important not to get too dependent on particular dividing lines, or to eschew categorization entirely, but to be able to combine and recombine categorical distinctions that cut across each other as may befit the subject people and topic. The distinctions people draw among themselves – for instance, among sexes, ages, classes, or kin categories – are not to be neglected among them.
>
> (Shipton 2010, Kindle locations 5035–5039)

He further notes that "Similarly, a proper understanding of the topic requires a certain mix of mental and material concerns and an appreciation of their interrelatedness" (ibid., Kindle location 558). I mean HVN↔HBA to facilitate that process.

Although Beck and Cowan's simple model of the intersection of mental and material concerns is the only one I have found so far that specifically addresses land tenure, there are many such models addressing broader issues, and part of the HBA methodology will be to discover which of them are the most applicable to the above aims and objectives. While useful as orienting generalisations, as with any such simple heuristics there is a danger that when holistic envisaging "is consigned to linear rungs of progression or shunted amid too few possibilities, the mind short-circuits and produces Procrustean results" (Jackson 2004, p. 118). For example, several scholars have called the hierarchies of Piaget (in terms of childhood development), Maslow (in terms of a hierarchy of needs) and Kohlberg (in terms of moral development) into serious question (re Piaget: Callaway 2001; re Maslow: Wahba and Bridwell 1976; re Kohlberg: Murphy and Gilligan 1980). Many of these objections emerge from the term "hierarchy", when "holarchy" or "heterarchy" may have avoided the disputes. Even so, stages (here called levels) can still be shown to exist; the difficulty lies in addressing them at their appropriate levels of complexity (Young 2012). In that task, I again emphasise the importance of not conflating The Machine's complicatedness with a holon's complexities.

Researchers have developed Kohlberg's model, resolving some of those concerns (Sonnert 1994; Sonnert and Commons 1994). While I am a director of a company focussed on applied development psychology and a qualified valuer and thereby obliged to examine motives in a sale as part of applying it as sales evidence, I am not a qualified psychologist. Rather, I approach the discipline from a transdisciplinary perspective, thereby adopting such models as Erikson's (1977) *provisionally*, as only tools to think with, awaiting psychologists to communicate developments in terms of Midgley's rigour, and remembering George Box's observation: "all models are wrong, but some are useful" (Box and Draper 1987, p. 424). This approach is preconditional to waking up from single vision and Newton's sleep.

With several collaborators, to bridge this gap Commons (2007) has developed an empirically testable developmental line of complexity. By use of mathematical psychology, working from simple tasks to the more complex in any domain, his MHC enables the scoring of the hierarchical complexity of any task, including "Big V" valuations. For example, Dawson (1998; Dawson-Tunik 2004) has used it to track the development of evaluative thought across life spans:

> We found six complexity orders-representational mappings to single principles-represented in performance between the ages of 5 and 86 years. Ages 5, 7, 10, and 14 years are the ages at which the representational mappings, representational systems, single abstractions, and abstract mappings orders first predominate. The abstract systems and single principles complexity orders did not become the plurality until the individual reached 22 years of age and had 3 years of college and the individual reached 26–30 years of age and had 3 years of postgraduate work.
>
> (Dawson-Tunik 2004, p. 21)

In the cognitive domain, MHC starts with preconscious cognition, but then addresses the following emergent levels of cognitive complexity. I begin my quote at the most-likely-to-be relevant stages in the context of real property rights transactions (Table 5.9).

Tentatively, then, are Commons' levels 10–11 appropriate for fitness landscapes within a nation-state level, and 12–14 for the global level – but not the other way

Table 5.9 Development of cognitive complexity

8	**Concrete**	**What:** Carry out full arithmetic, form cliques, plan deals. **How:** Does long division, follows complex social rules, takes and coordinates perspective of other and self. **End result:** Interrelations, social events, what happened among others, reasonable deals.
9	**Abstract**	**What:** Discriminate variables such as stereotypes; logical quantification; (none, some, all). **How:** Form variables out of finite classes. Make and quantify propositions. **End result:** Variable time, place, act, actor, state, type; quantifiers all, none, some); categorical assertions (e.g. "We all die").

(continued)

Table 5.9 Development of cognitive complexity *(continued)*

10	**Formal**	**What:** Argue using empirical or logical evidence. Logic is linear, one-dimensional. **How:** Solve problems with one unknown using algebra, logic and empiricism. **End result:** Relationships are formed out of variables; words: linear, logical, one dimensional, if then, thus, therefore, because; correct scientific solutions.
11	**Systemic**	**What:** Construct multivariate systems and matrices. **How:** Coordinates more than one variable as input. Consider relationships in contexts. **End result:** Events and concepts situated in a multivariate context; systems are formed out of relations; systems: legal, societal, corporate, economic, national.
12	**Meta-systematic**	**What:** Construct multi-systems and metasystems out of disparate systems. **How:** Create metasystems out of systems. Compare systems and perspectives. Name properties of systems: (e.g. homomorphic, isomorphic, complete, consistent such as tested by consistency proofs), commensurable. **End result:** Metasystems and supersystems are formed out of systems of relationships.
13	**Paradigmatic**	**What:** Fit metasystems together to form new paradigms. **How:** Synthesise metasystems. **End result:** Paradigms are formed out of multiple metasystems.
14	**Cross-paradigmatic**	**What:** Fit paradigms together to form new fields. **How:** Forms new fields by crossing paradigms. **End result:** New fields are formed out of multiple paradigms.

Source: Commons (2007)

around? If so, what has that to say about addressing these wicked valuation problems in those and other contexts? Could lack of such articulations be contributing to the lack of progress against wicked problems such as climate change? Applying HBA would imply that the answer is yes. We know that what may appear to be glaringly obvious at one level may be considered utter nonsense at another. How is one to address that in both developmental and evolutionary terms? Specifically, if one puts real property rights appropriate to one fitness landscape in the hands of a person not well versed in that fitness landscape, is that more likely to be beneficial or detrimental to that person? If there are such consequences, how are we to address them? These are the kinds of wicked problems that I have designed HVN↔HBA to address, but not to be answered by me or any other individual, but via suitably depthed trans-ontological teams.

All scales

When referring to scales I mean the full scalable range of all existents in all domains. In accordance with that definition, here "scales" is not confined to scales of size or time, but to any existent. I mean "scales" as Gunderson and Holling put it:

> The theory that we develop must of necessity transcend boundaries of scale and discipline. It must be capable of organizing our understanding of economic, ecological, and institutional systems. And it must explain the situations where all three types of systems interact.
>
> (Gunderson and Holling 2002, p. 5)

That is because sustainably managing decisions on wicked problems require "bridging scales and knowledges: yet each scale and each knowledge culture uses a different reference point and a different knowledge" (Dovers in Brown, Harris and Russell 2010, p. 182).

These include the scales of demanders and suppliers in the market, and the machines that service it. If demand were not of the scale to make it worthwhile, no one would build supply infrastructure. Similarly, if regulation is absent at a relevant scale, destructive social and environmental consequences may not have any means of being addressed at that scale. For example, in Africa many dispossessed families have no means of obtaining justice against large-scale land-grabbing corporations (Adonga, Ibreck and Bulla 2015).

When looking at scales, it is important to keep in mind the dangers highlighted by Mead and Niebuhr referred to in Chapter 6 in the context of the scales of identity constructed, particularly in the case of those who confuse span and depth, or intrinsic and extrinsic values. In such cases, an inflationist, megalomaniacal identity construction is more likely to find ostensible verification at larger scales, with similarly magnified consequences to the megalomaniac's victims.

Megalomania can emerge not only in the field of the policymakers, but also in their opponents, and in an area as sensitive as land policy it is vital to monitor and evaluate participants in terms of scales of power, particularly those most able to effect or obstruct the policy concerned. Many systems are now broken because they've grown too far from the human scale (Hilton 2015). For this and other reasons, Dannefer's call to paying attention to what is right in front of us – taking "everyday life seriously in the study of human development" (Dannefer 2015) – is particularly appropriate, consistent with my emphasis on identity, and demonstrably pragmatic by focussing on the relevant policy's stakeholders (Glasgow 2013). Torbert's developmental action inquiry practice (Torbert and Associates 2004) is one way of responding to that call.

For example, the span of a nation-state or an empire does not imply any depth, or say much about the intrinsic value of those within it, but it says plenty about opportunities for vast scales of power. It is conceivable that a totalitarian empire may enfold no inhabitants of greater intrinsic depth than one person not its slave. On the other hand, a free and multicultural society may not only enfold a high proportion of high intrinsic value people, but also contain many who have preferenced homeostasis over homeorhesis. However alike the terrain may be, there may be a rich and fertile range of spatial imaginaries within its inhabitants, and the values they place on the terrain and components within it may be as alien as it is possible for humans to be. Values associated with spatial imaginaries may then manifest at a great range of scales.

Just as set theory provides scales in mathematics, so scales can also relate to vocabulary. Some words enfold other sets, for example "animal" enfolds "dog" enfolds "terrier" enfolds "silky terrier". As mentioned in Chapter 1, one may need a large vocabulary to express policy at the precision needed to avoid unnecessary controversy, including words that allow the correct scaling of comments.

The importance of interrogating data at different scales can be a matter of life and death. Ben Goldacre provides the example of premature babies dying even when the information that could have saved them was available "because that information had not been synthesised together, and analysed systematically, in a meta-analysis" (Goldacre 2008, p. 55).

While it does not explicitly state a mathematically based proof of the importance of scale called the square-cube law, the classic work on the importance of scale in the context of size is J. B. S. Haldane's *On Being the Right Size* (1926). Another classic work translated its importance into architecture and urban design. *A Pattern Language* (Alexander, Ishikawa and Silverstein 1977), applied the importance of scale in urban space, describing a language of 253 patterns applicable at different scales of a city. In rural properties, it is noted that both "excessively large farms (latifundia) and excessively small farms (minifundia) tend to be inefficient" (Tuma 2015).

The importance of the scale of cooperation organisations is referred to in Stewart (2014), noting that "since life began on earth, the scale of cooperation between living processes has increased by a factor greater than 10^{13}" (ibid., p. 29). He further notes, "The potential advantages are universal" (ibid., p. 33), and that the cooperation problem has caused global warming and international problems, and that to address them will require "complex arrangements that cannot be expected to evolve easily" (ibid., p. 34).

In contrast, the mechanist biologist Ernst Mayr observes how:

> It is curious how many people seem to have difficulty understanding a purely mechanistic path towards progress as represented by Darwinian evolution on which developments are different in each phyletic lineage. There is simply no indication in the history of life of any universal trend to, or capacity for, evolutionary progress. Where seeming progress is found, it is simply a by-product of changes effected by natural selection.
>
> (Mayr 1998, p. 198)

Elsewhere, he noted, "there is no evidence whatsoever to support any belief in cosmic teleology" (Mayr 2001, p. 82). Similarly, Sagoff concluded, "the evidence does not support the idea that evolution applies on a system-wide scale" (Sagoff 2012, p. 4).

Because of differences in scale, Mayr (2001), Sagoff (2012) and Stewart (2014) can all be right, but only within scales and levels. Unless Mayr and Sagoff are also stating that there is no autotelaxis at the scale of individual organisms. That is, are they saying that there are no living organisms, including Mayr himself, that intend to remain alive and flourish? If they were still at the single vision stage, that could really be what they think. After all, Nobel Laureate Francis Crick has assured us that:

> You, your joys and your sorrows, your memories and your ambitions, your sense of personal identity and free will, are in fact no more than the behaviour of a vast assembly of nerve cells and their associated molecules . . . You're nothing but a pack of neurons.
>
> (Crick 1994, pp. 3, 11)

But wait. According to Dewey, we are nothing but a set of habits. How many other things are we nothing but? After all, we are primates: were Crick and Dewey nothing but primates too?

I do not consider them to have been so: no one is nothing but a "nothing-butter": only their Emissaries may be when they assume themselves to be the Master: what they dismiss as unreal merely discloses the limits of their systems of interpretation (Mumford 1951, p. 25). Both Crick and Dewey were primates, but also persons of deserved eminence in their fields, but like us all were inevitably of limited understanding and valuational capacity, and the more out of their fields, the more limited they were. Hence not only my copious use of quotes in this transdisciplinary work from experts in fields I am inexpert in, but also hence the need for trans-ontological teams when addressing wicked valuation problems.

Dewey's "nothing but" comment about us as habits appeared in Blomley's chapter 3 of Blomley, Braverman, Delaney and Kedar (2014, pp. 77–94). It is about pragmatism and the habits of legal space, approached through the philosophy of pragmatism as articulated by John Dewey. The focus is on habit, and space as being central to the workings of habit (ibid., p. 84) and that we cannot abandon habit because to do so "is to abandon the self" (ibid., p. 87).

In the mechanistic language of his time, Dewey reduces us to "nothing but" interrelating creatures of habits: "There is no outside to habit" (ibid., p. 87), habits are us (p. 81) serving as mechanisms of action (p. 80), reducing the complex to the simplex.

Blomley recognises that aspects of Dewey's pragmatism will be insufficient in the context of social power. Similarly, I am ambivalent about adopting Dewey's positivism-permeated philosophy in this context. While I agree with pragmatism as a form of fallibilism, the view that belief cannot ever be certain, but can be provisionally secure (ibid., p. 92, n. 13), Dewey is mute if not blind to all three pillars of transdisciplinarity.

Dewey cannot be blamed for this. In terms of his own philosophy he was necessarily confined to the habits of his time. But we are not. More sophisticated and advanced scientists and philosophers than the likes of Crick and Dewey now realise that while the "parts permit the properties of the whole", they "do not cause the properties of the whole . . . Mechanistic understanding . . . for each case is important, but it complements and does not substitute for holistic under-standing" (Wilson 2017). In McGilchrist's framing, we require both hemispheres for addressing wicked problems.

Therefore, despite what he stated, in HBA Dewey cannot be reduced to his own haven of habits. As mentioned above, our quotidian identities are that *per se*, the word "identity" coming from the Latin "over and over" (Loy 2010, p. 39). While Dewey's point may be robust with the mechanical mind, as holons not artefacts we cannot be "nothing but" any existent.

Dewey stands among those "greatest theorists" (Stigler and Kindahl 1970, p. 299) who have turned their minds to valuation at large (not only market valuation), applying his philosophy of pragmatism to it. In his *Theory of Valuation* (1981), Dewey rightly observes that "all conduct that is not simply either blindly impulsive or mechanically routine seems to involve valuations" (ibid., p. 3). However, as Marcuse observed at the time, in the work Dewey "presupposes a definite preference prior to all test and verification, namely, that liberty and the 'release of individual potentialities' is better than its opposite" (Marcuse 1941). That valuation is a presupposition underpinning his philosophy, such as Hughes had to remind believers in scientism about 72 years later: "the statement that all knowledge is (or potentially could be) scientific – the product of scientific methods – is itself not a scientific statement; it defeats its own universal claim" (Hughes 2013).

Such assumed intact, atomistic "I" as operant on "other" is a pervasive quality throughout scientism (Hughes 2012, 2013), and the opposite of the definitions of spirituality used in this book. It is so often all motor maintenance, no Zen, as metaphysics is no existent but a "ghostly queerness" (Dewey 1981, p. 83). This view of metaphysics, also held by Hume, Mill, Russell and the Vienna Circle (Fieser 2001), is an example of West's "machine" thinking referred to by Tagore, Gandhi and others and its incompetence to address wicked problems on its own.

I consider such heuristics of machinism as this atomistic "I", while clearly having massive extrinsic value, with a broader and deeper prespective can be seen for what they are: arrant nonsense, as just demonstrated by any emotional reaction at all that the reader may have had from my labelling them as such. Insofar as our autonomous identities are of value, they inter-relate in a *porosity of autonomy* (Beever and Morar 2016), which may grow inside our Goldilocks zones and contract outside of them.

While such imaginaries can be extremely useful in confined contexts, mono-logical and mono-methodological blindness to the differences between appropriate approaches to and between the various hextants, and the multiple complex dimensions and relationships of wicked problems (Allen 2013), are inevitably partial. I consider them to be often so partial as to be inadequate for many of the matters that have to be considered in policy formulation and implementation.

From his monological gaze, Dewey also "rejects any conception of intrinsic value" (Anderson 2014; Dewey 1981, p. 230), and thereby his philosophy was blind to emergence. Those enclosed within such monological framings thereby easily fall prey to making the countless fatuous pronouncements of the sort Crick made, quoted above. While that is clearly understandable in Dewey's time, in such domains and at such scales, both the scholastics, with their views on fair value and Pirsig, with his exploration of metaphysics, remain more useful than Dewey because of Dewey's habituated hostility to metaphysics and consequent blindness to being. As Mumford wrote:

> Such was the innocence of the liberal that those who in were indifferent to ethical values thought of themselves as realists. They could hardly understand William James when he called emotionality the sine qua non of moral perception. But the fact was that the most old-fashioned theologian, with a sense of human guilt and human error, was by far the better realist. Though the theologian's view of the external world might be scientifically weak, his view of the internal world, the world of value and personality, included an understanding of constant human phenomena – sin, corruption, evil – on which the liberal closed his eyes.
>
> (Mumford 1941, p.56)

As mentioned above, many more modern philosophers than Dewey cited herein are more useful in this context. Their numbers include Edgar Morin (2007) and Michel Serres (1995). Serres also points out the co-evolutionary aspects of the legal and the scientific, and how if one prevails over the other, the result is the sneer (ibid., p. 81). That will be transcended when the law and geography addressed in Blomley et al. (2014) co-evolve to emerge into transdisciplinarity via its practitioners attaining the levels of rigour as defined by Midgley (1995, p. 22). Wild Systems Theory (Jordan and Vinson 2012; Jordan and Day 2015) is an example of such co-evolution from Dewey's thought in cognitive science. While as described above I disagree about our being "nothing but" enchained habits, a following assertion, that "change, for Dewey, must necessarily take habit seriously" (Blomley et al. 2014, p. 89), is essential when applying the Goldilocks Principle to land policy formulation and implementation, and particularly relevant in traditional societies such as Swaziland. As Blomley says, insofar as pragmatism is not considered some "systematic theoretic blueprint", but (1) is taken aboard as "a set of tools for making us think" (ibid., p. 89), (2) helps us to see power as a creative capacity (p. 90), (3) provides an anchor to pull us back from too much metaphysical or architectural thinking and other virtues stated therein, and (4) is performative within the Goldilocks Principle, pragmatism *as described by Blomley* requires a seat at any HBA table.

However, a ship, to get anywhere, needs navigators, rudders, and sails, and needs to perform many other functions as well as those of anchors. Therefore, Dewey's warning about ruts, inertia and stupidity (ibid., p. 87) are necessary, counterbalancing, co-evolutionary, insights.

To employ single vision terminology, perhaps such pronouncements as Crick's and Dewey's are "nothing but" metaphysical speculations, "nothing but" examples of the necessity of thinking myth when thinking big, or "nothing but" examples

226 The HIDEGRE BIES ADALAS template

of confirmation biases emanating from Crick and Dewey's respective single visions. Alternatively, as I have predicated HVN↔HBA upon, there is nothing at all that is "nothing but", at frontier scales there are no things, only processes appearing to be things at different time scales. Viewed from such scales, that "nothing buttism", for all its sometime extrinsic value in the development of machine minds, is an illusion that is urgent we outgrow.

Blindness as to scale, levels and lines, domains and dimensions et al. – instances of the blindness of single vision – causes many such problems. The scale of the framing is crucial for policy decision-making. For instance, Smith's so called "invisible hand" was empirically established at the small scale only (Saul 1997, p. 145): its applicability at other scales was not established – there "can be no pendulum swinging, then settling into place, without a centre and fixed outer limits" (ibid.) – yet it is so often blithely applied to all scales. As Sedlacek and Havel ironically put it, the economics that "believes in the invisible hand of the market wants to be without mysteries" (Sedlacek and Havel 2011, p.7). On the other hand, we largely ignored the cumulative effect of uncountable small-scale events, externalities such as emitting carbon dioxide, ozone and particulate matter, until they emerged at the global scale (Cribb 2014).

Cole (1998) devotes a chapter to the matter of scale (ch. 5, pp. 53–60), setting the scene for her following chapter, on emergence. Cole observes therein how small holons operate in small time scales, and larger holons in larger ones, and that apparent complexity, too, changes with scale: "As you move in, or out, the world looks simple, then complex, then simple again" (p. 59). Cole then quotes Schrodinger to point out that what applies at one scale may not apply at others. When it comes to wicked valuation problems, therefore, one has to be scale sensitive. For example, the large-scale changes that national land policies address require different approaches than local scale ones (Waddock, Meszoely, Waddell and Dentoni 2015).

The concept of organisms as "open, multi-scale self-sustaining systems" is foundational to Wild Systems Theory (Jordan 2008), with scales of sustainment consequently having a major emphasis (ibid., p. 1984). The New England Complexity Science Institute (NECSI) has designed a multiscale method for assisting in determining in large organisations what tasks are best performed at what scale (NECSI n.d.), and some of its members have published a paper describing an information-theoretic formalism for same (Allen, Stacey and Bar-Yam 2014). From this complexity science perspective, it is important to watch out for fractals and emergence of novelty as they dance through all their scales.

Such tools can be trialled alongside empirical experience as ansatzes for scaling policies and their implementation. However, all scales require scrutiny to differing degrees. For example, "both progressives and conservatives can vary on the two radical/moderate scales" (Lakoff 2004, p. 99), which is another factor to consider in the practicability of reforms and their timings in terms of the Goldilocks Principle. Therefore, scale is also important in addressing these wicked valuation problems, as well as priorities set by corporate reporting protocols and election cycles compared to the time scales of climate change.

Another scale often taken for granted, but vital to HVN, is that of energy availability. R. Buckminster Fuller, McHale and their Research Team (1963) used the term "energy slaves" to quantify the phenomenon (an 8 hour day's work energy for 250 days a year), noting at the time that an American had 185 such slaves, and an Asian three (ibid., pp. 29–30). A similar concept has been developed for land (also fishing areas) use. Called the Global Hectare, it shows Kuwait as the highest user per person, each person using over 10Gha of biologically productive area per person, and Timor-Leste the lowest, at under 0.5Gha per person (WWF 2014, pp. 38–39).

Depending on the time scale adopted, the term "sustainable growth" becomes more and more of an oxymoron. Returning to the effects of compound interest (addressed in Chapter 6), Gabor Zovanyi has calculated that:

> If our species had started with just two people at the time of the earliest agricultural practices some 10,000 years ago, and increased by 1 percent per year, today humanity would be a solid ball of flesh many thousand light years in diameter, and expanding with a radial velocity that, neglecting relativity, would be many times faster than the speed of light.
>
> (Zovanyi 2013, p. 31)

Yet there is another reality: Adam Smith's single vision upon growth as inevitably being a good thing has conquered The Machine and almost all, such that:

> The gradual accretion of a set of widely shared assumptions that constitute a bounded ideational realm with rigidly consistent internal rules. Deviate from these rules, and there are predictable consequences. When any public person (writer, economist, scientist, whatever) demonstrates a disconnection from political reality by questioning the desirability or possibility of continued growth, the minders of the mainstream media turn their attention elsewhere.
>
> (Heinberg 2014)

A wicked problem indeed. If Blake were alive today, he could well conclude that Newton's sleep continues as that "bounded ideational realm". To address such wicked problems, Mulgan (2014) notes that you need individuals, hierarchies and egalitarian groups to work together, and that grid group theory (Douglas 2006) and clumsy thinking (Rowson 2011; Ney and Verweij 2014) are providing breakthroughs very different to those visible from mainstream economics, social psychology and administration theory.

For example, a report to the Royal Society of Arts said "If we are serious about transformative social change, we need to at least be open to the idea that transformation begins at the level of consciousness" (Rowson 2011, p. 28). Despite its interhextal conflation by saying "brain" when Rowson means "mind", the report provides six working ideas consistent with the thrust of this work (Box 5.3).

Box 5.3   Six working ideas to address wicked problems

1   **We cannot change ourselves without changing each other**
    Most behavioural change does not occur at the level of the individual alone. Not only do we rely on other people to achieve the changes we seek to make, but such behaviours spread through social diffusion, and there is no way of knowing where our influence ends.

2   **Complexity is more often the solution than the problem**
    To navigate a complicated world, we need complex minds. We need to work on having a "relationship to our reactions", and when faced with multiple perspectives we should be able to both differentiate and integrate them.

3   **It is better to be reasonable than rational**
    Clear thinking matters, but the touchstone of our thought should not be abstract axioms and disembedded logic, but contextual sensitivity and concern for others.

4   **Paying attention is good for you**
    We are what we attend to, and there are increasing demands on our attention. We need some resistance to the power of adverts and the allure of technology. To avoid becoming slaves to the information and tools we use, we need to learn to pay closer attention to what is going on around us, within us and between us on a regular basis.

5   **If we want new habits we should work with our habitats**
    We are creatures of habit, but unlike most creatures we have considerable power to shape our habitats for purposes beyond our basic needs. Behaviour change is not mainly about willpower, but about using self-awareness to shape our environments so that our social and automatic brains align with our goals and values.

6   **The brain is a stimulant**
    The brain is something we all have in common, and share an interest in. We use information about the brain as a socialising device to stimulate collective self-awareness. Through reflecting on the social and automatic nature of the brain, we learn how to change our behaviour for the better.

    Rowson (2011)

Rowson further notes that the key to solving wicked problems is to look at a real system and address three intellectual and practical challenges therein:

1   The challenge of outsiders (how to address obstruction by vested interests).
2   The challenge of (in)coherence.
3   The challenges of predation and creativity, as articulated in Mulgan (2013).

The first challenge, of vested interests, is particularly important in land policy formulation and implementation (Leach and Mearns 1996).

Rowson's goal to address wicked problems is to combine facilitation, design, and emergence of ethos. He also discussed addressing wicked problems with McGilchrist (Rowson and McGilchrist 2013), and McGilchrist wrap-up comments on the discussion included recommending the following:

> embodied skills, a proper humane context for the understanding of what we learn, an emphasis on the implicit as much as the explicit, on quiet, sustained attention rather than constant stimulation that fragments attention, a belief in the broader picture, and in the values of more than just pleasure and utility – the terms on which everything in the left hemisphere's world has to be validated.
>
> (McGilchrist in Rowson and McGilchrist 2013, p. 48)

That is, inasmuch as circumstances permit, the time scales allowed to address wicked problems must ensure a Goldilocks Zone to enable Rowson and McGilchrist's recommendations, and those of Stanley and Lehman (2015) referred to above, to be properly engaged. While Gigerenzer's "fast and frugal heuristics" (Gigerenzer and Todd 1999) or actions may be needed to plug a leak, by definition with a wicked problem in time that will just trigger other leaks elsewhere. Fast and frugal approaches should be used within a higher wicked problem engagement strategy to buy time to address the wicked problems, not to go off to some other project. While that project is being processed, pressure will build and the dam will burst. Rowson's focus is on addressing climate change by recognising it as a wicked problem, not just a complicated one. I am tabling HVN↔HBA as a potential approach to addressing such challenges and goals as Rowson's.

Chapter summary and the way forward

The very definition of wicked problems means that no framing tool will ever be able to solve them. However, I am submitting that one facilitating broader and deeper vision and more balanced judgement than The Machine can deliver has the potential to discover that some problems that may be considered wicked may not be so at all, and may thereby be able to be solved. Resources can thereby be better devoted to addressing real wicked problems by skilful means, developing wisdom in the relevant domains to address that which The Machine simply cannot without reverting to its proper role as the Emissary, not the Master, of life. I submit the above as a tool in that context.

To help address wicked valuation problems, I intend HVN↔HBA to facilitate the development of wisdom to observe that process. It can then observe confirmation biases kicking in not only in one's own self, but in others. From there, it can heterarchically observe the processes and their interplays, developing and employing ever more skilful means of making sound value judgements and thereby cogent fact perceptions, and from them policies, where the North and the South and the East and the West clash. That wisdom is to be fully integrated as HVN throughout HBA, and HBA throughout HVN.

In part, the next chapter reverts to the earlier chapter's autoethnographic approach to assist two objectives: to track the development of HVN↔HBA to serve as a framing tool in practice, and to provide examples of the sorts of land-scapes in which it may be more fit for purpose than mere single vision approaches. It therefore attempts a synthesis of traditional and autoethnographic approaches into a transdisciplinary emergent. However, its success will be inevitably limited, as it is only from one person, rather than the communities of inquiry and practice HVN↔HBA is meant for. Here, my guiding light is Aristotle, as quoted above: I look for precision in each class of things just so far as the nature of the subject admits, and attempt to avoid excess and defect, but seek the intermediate, not in the object but relative to us.

Notes

1 Answers for such questions can be researched elsewhere (Diaz and Hansz 1997; Diaz and Wolverton 1998; Abaris and Sjonoce 2014; Salzman and Zwinkels 2013; Diaz, Gallimore and Levy 2004). Here the questions are part of the narrative, but not their answers.

2 See Chapter 6 concerning their dynamics. Also note that by "levels" I mean levels in holarchies, heterarchies and hierarchies. In other works, "levels" refers to different hextants and domains. For example, some scholars addressing wicked problems state that economists, psychologists and neurobiologists operate at different "levels" (Smithson in Brown, Harris and Russell 2010, p. 93). In contradistinction, I see hextal foci for those disciplines: Economists on the produce hextant, psychologists on the psyche hextant, and neurobiologists on the soma hextant. That way, I am better able to differentiate, articulate and hieracrchically integrate interhextal and transhex-tal emergents possible with those disciplines' transdisciplinary engagements at and between their levels and lines.

3 Such fallacies also occur in valuation. For instance, Fourcade (2011) noted that a French court saw the difficulties in valuing nature and the claims were dropped (ibid., p. 1755), whereas from a monetary perspective the value of nature is infinite (Sutton in ABC RN 2015a, 5:20 and 40:00) – no nature, no money either as it's a product of emergent in nature. So an argument could be made that, once the pattern that connects has been destroyed, and thereby quality, one should work back from infinity to assess damages, as well as up from zero.

4 MacLean's ansatzes have proven to be rather more than naïve. As J. E. Stewart noted, "the ultimate test for a theory is whether it can account for phenomena that are hitherto unexplained, and whether it can make surprising predictions that prove to be accurate" (Stewart 2014). As an example of the latter, MacLean proposed that, when it comes to the specialties of our prefrontal cortex, "it is possible that these large evolving territories of the human holon are incapable of being brought into full operation until the hormonal changes of adolescence occur" (MacLean 1973, p. 58). That this has only recently been empirically established (30 years after MacLean's publication), it offers evidence of MacLean's model usefulness as a predictive framework.

5 An obeisance embraced by Upadhyaya (1988–1989, p. 23) in his verion of "integral humanism". I regard integral nationalistic humanism as an oxymoron. Similarly,

Jacques Maritain's integral Christian humanism (1939), while as with Upadhyaya's version containing much of great merit, is insufficient from this thesis's perspective, which sees integral humanism as being necessarily universalist per se.

6 I would advise any such minds to acquaint themselves with *Open Mind* – a rich online storehouse of scholarship on philosophy and cognitive science, and particularly Metzinger and Windt's definition of an open mind (Metzinger and Windt 2015, p. 17). While, like anything else, each individual could only absorb such a work at that individual's Goldilockean rate, it could begin a move for such closed minds from identity homeostasis to identity homeorhesis.

7 Blake eventually has Bacon, Newton and Locke arriving in heaven to sit alongside Milton, Shakespeare and Chaucer (Jerusalem 98:9), presumably by dint of their having outgrown the naïve realism of their respective single vision mentalities.

8 This quote is attributed to Spinoza several times online, but without citations and the statement does not appear in his *Complete Works* (Spinoza 2002). I still quote it for its truth, even if not with the weight of Spinoza's authority behind it.

9 Here I engage Neve's concept of mapping as "a milieu of individuation", Neve's use of the word "milieu" enfolding "the dynamic character of places, not static containers of things and beings, but nodes of forces, actions, desires, values. A group of human beings, to live in a certain environment, processes its own world, in which territory is the techno-symbolical medium, being it, at the same time, the technical response to the needs of the group with respect to environmental factors, and the materialisation of the idea allowing to elaborate that response, and to develop it or reject it later" (Neve 2015, p. 12).

10 The term "mindscape" means the mental space that our consciousness moves around in (Rucker 1997, p. 36). Our bodies move around landscapes (the nature and produce hextants), our minds move around mindscapes (our soma and skills hextants).

11 Fuzzy logic is quite distinct from probability theory in that the latter is about what might happen, and the former about what is. I mention this because some very clever people have nevertheless conflated the two (Kosko 1994).

6   Birthing HIDEGRE BIES ADALAS

In this chapter, I report on how I field tested the above approaches, most prominently in the Solomon Islands, but intrapersonally in other tasks referred to below. In these instances, they include activities and papers in conferences around the world, and my consulting role with UN-Habitat/GLTN. The chapter then proceeds to engage with a selection of issues that may benefit through engaging HVN↔HBA in groups looking to address wicked valuation problems when NSEW meet. I then look to market values of property rights generally, and return to Okoth-Ogendo's challenge and Swaziland in particular.

All these activities revolved around a single attractor, the IVSC definition of market value. While that also appears in Chapter 1 and the glossary, I shall repeat it here to better contextualise its importance in what follows:

> Market value is the estimated amount for which an asset or liability would exchange on the valuation date between a willing buyer and a willing seller in an arm's-length transaction after proper marketing wherein the parties had each acted knowledgeably, prudently and without compulsion.
>
> (IVSC 2016)

As such, this definition is not subject to its originating environment: market value transactions may occur in all sorts of civilisations, cultures and historical periods.

The World Bank and Malaysia

Between stints in Timor-Leste I presented a paper on *The Catch 22 of Valuation in the Developing World* (McDermott 2012), developed from my time in Vietnam. The Vietnamese had kept in touch with me since my consultancy there on the question that paper addressed. At their request, I helped organise their Land Law study tour around Australia. I also continued to engage with them about addressing that catch-22 of needing market evidence to develop a well-functioning property market, and of needing a well-functioning property market to get market evidence. As a co-evolutionary lived experience, this period from Vietnam to Pakistan intensively developed HVN↔HBA.

That evolution continued through 2014 via HIDEGRE into presenting at two conferences in Kuala Lumpur (IRERS, 29–30 April and FIG 16–21 June) and World Bank Land and Poverty Conferences.

Solomon Islands

I continued to develop HVN↔HBA through the challenges posed by international consultancies and conferences, until my PhD supervisor considered it to be sufficiently developed for a public trial. This was held at Honiara, Solomon Islands, from 5 to 7 August 2014. Hosted by the Solomon Islands Ministry of Lands, Housing and Survey, the joint CASLE/APCCRPR/IAAPLPR symposium was on the subject of "Land and Property Rights in the South Pacific". This inaugural field test had 46 participants. Together, our team of four – Professors Boydell and Sheehan, and Fijian lawyer Ulai Baya – covered the subjects to be addressed with HBA:

- impacts of climate change;
- land resource compensation;
- disaster risk management;
- land tenure and administration; and
- connecting theory to observed reality.

Consonant with the importance of the Identity Principle in HVN↔HBA, in my introduction I stressed that this was my first visit to the Solomon Islands, but I was widely experienced enough elsewhere to realise that we should not expect an immediate mutual understanding. So I began to explain HBA by means of backgrounds we do have in common, one being sport. I then drew the hextants on a sheet of butcher paper, and asked them to imagine a Solomon Island child who, driven by regard-recognition hunger towards its identity construction, found a way of gaining it was to play the most popular sport there, soccer.

By that regard-recognition hunger, a link between the child's psyche and the culture was established. To develop the skills, the child must not just want to become good at soccer in its psyche, but practice with its soma in a natural environment and/or that produced by others to develop the skills that will feed the regard-recognition hunger. However, that can only happen with the rest of HIDEGRE in place. That is, identity construction, skills developing towards greater differentiation, articulation and holarchic integration, and emergence of newly integrated skill levels at the Goldilocks pace which will provide optimal sensations of flow for the child: just as one first crudely learns the steps of a dance to become a graceful ballroom dancer. Finally, related evolution is enacted by means of appropriately challenging cooperation and competition.

In that process, one must be robust and antifragile against unexpected challenges – black swans and butterfly effects – and develop the requisite intrinsic, extrinsic and systemic values to flourish with such challenges (BIES). To achieve that, the more the child can gain from all domains and dimensions, all lines and levels, and all scales within that HIDEGRE the better.

For example, establishing a relationship with a soccer player on the world stage could do wonders for that child's motivation (psyche) and, with HIDEGRE-appropriate responses from all the other hextants, also do wonders for that child's career. Providing the hextal "plate" remains in balance, the sky might be the limit.

Afterwards, I gave an example of how HBA relates to the Solomon Island's national interest, noting the skills and produce hextants, and how pitting Solomon Islanders up against multinationals may be on a "level playing field", but it is like pitting a Solomon Islands soccer team up against Manchester United. Manchester United can afford to buy the best from anywhere to man their side, and so can multinationals.

The hextal approach proved to be the easiest part of HBA to grasp. Once their initial puzzlement dissolved, they became spirited and enthusiastic. It was very different to Sidebotham's experience of "the white man never wanna hear nothin about what's different from him". Instead, I believe they realised that we wanted to both hear and value everything about what's different about them. We deliberately chose a room where we could position ourselves among them, not remain separated at the "high table".

In so many of the workshops and the like I have attended, participants were not there as identities but as functionaries of a machine. That was not the perception in this case. They seemed to appreciate the emphasis on identity and culture, and I cannot recall such passionate engagement and release of energy in my 20+ years of international experience in such contexts. While that is merely my subjective view, the symposium was recorded both visually and orally so anyone is welcome to test that claim, and possibly falsify its exceptional nature in the light of their own experience. As noted by Karl Popper:

> Bold ideas, unjustified anticipations, and speculative thought, are our only means for interpreting nature: our only organon, our only instrument, for grasping her. And we must hazard them to win our prize. Those among us who are unwilling to expose their ideas to the hazard of refutation do not take part in the scientific game.
>
> (Popper 2002, pp. 279–280)

Even so, one lesson I have learnt is that I should have emphasised the HVN part of HVN↔HBA more. At that time I was unaware of HVN's affinities with Austronesian cultures, including those in the Solomons. Later, I found Reuter's *Sharing the Earth, Dividing the Land* (2006), which indicated an Austronesian grounding of HVN that I had not known. Another lesson is that I should have stressed the interhextal relationships more. Unfairly, as it was new for them, I had worried that the responses to the soma hextant were fairly shallow: for example, that people must be must be fit, healthy etc. That was my problem with not engaging the Goldilocks Principle, not theirs. To help, I already had an example from my own experience in my office in Darwin which I should have mentioned. I knew that my productivity suffered badly in the afternoon, when the tropical sun poured in through the window. I found research online confirming that there is a Goldilocks Zone for optimal mental functioning (around 21–23 degrees, with quite dramatic declines beyond it), and wondered what socio-cultural effects ambient temperature may have had over the centuries. Just over six months later, the USA's National Bureau of Economics and Research published online a working paper providing a literature review on the subject (including the ones I had encountered on the net). Had it been available in the symposium, it could have opened the discussion to the West's endemic single vision conflation of the mind and the brain, whereas even in the soma hextant it is not so confined (Enders 2015). It also noted the potential effects of climate change on the process, and suggested that this might provide "a partial explanation of why hot countries are generally poorer than temperate or cold ones" (Heal and Park 2015).

The paper, entitled *Goldilocks Economies? Temperature Stress and the Direct Impacts of Climate Change*, concluded that "extreme heat has direct and significant consequences for labor productivity even in regions and industries where one might expect to be well adjusted to their thermal environments" (sic) (ibid., p. 18), and would have been ideal to cite in the part of the symposium addressing climate change.

Matters in other hextants include ethics are in the skills hextant, conscience is in the psyche hextant, and morals in the culture hextant. I highlight these aspects because throughout history there are examples of toxic fitness landscapes of land policies, land-related valuations and real property rights (for one of countless examples, see Gray 2006, p. 211). Other aspects highlighted by this hextal process included following up on the distinction between holons and artefacts, and Polanyi's implicit differentiation between them when he noted: "The commodity description of labor, land and money is entirely fictitious. Nevertheless, it is with the help of this fiction that labor, land and money are organized" (Polanyi 2001 [1944], p. 72).

In its online glossary, the IVSC definition of real property clearly defines real property as "a non-physical concept" (IVSC n.d.). Also, money itself is a fiction, "the false coin of our own dreams" (Graeber 2001) variously created, including by the government printer or when banks give a loan (McLeay, Radia and Thomas 2014; Werner 2014; Ravn 2015) on the basis of "the legal definition of land and ownership of land (which) is the very basis of private property. Without it, capitalism could not exist" (Graham 2002).

My researches, combined with the perspectives provided by the Solomon Islanders, have therefore led to a personal, unintended, unanticipated and unwelcome discovery. In this area of a meeting of NSEW, in facilitating money creation by banks real property valuations such as most of those I have performed are at the coal face of "the Empire of The Machine". Nevertheless, they also have potential benefits in the context essential for human development, depending on what values frame and guide that Empire. So a complexity-recognising monitoring and evaluation process will be required to limit toxic unintended consequences (Britt 2013).

One cautionary note from this valuer's perspective therefore, is the following. Banks' money creation (Werner 2014) is co-dependent upon valuations and the loan to value ratios the banks apply. Therefore, professional valuers' valuations co-create money as part of the play of enclosures, public sector tax farming and private sector rent-seeking.

Facilitatory mechanisms in this machine include what Hudson refers to as "the fictions of fictitious capital", mainly based upon "debt-leveraged land-price gains" in Hudson (2010), and Das describes as "our own illusory, unsustainable creation, global finance" (Das 2011, back cover). Its consequences include reducing those people trying to repay such debts into increasing atomistic consumers, each with "a deluded self, scrambling to make itself real, buying itself into existence, until it finds it is fading again, until we buy some more" (Rowson 2014, p. 6). This three card trick is arguably a developed version of what Jesus objected to as referenced above, almost two thousand years ago, and that Taraki, however crudely, attempted to address after Afghanistan's Saur revolution in 1978. Furthermore, as Hudson notes, "The problem is that the financial system, like military victors from Assyria and Rome in antiquity down to those of today, destroys the host economy's ability to pay" (Hudson 2010).

The Thomas Theorem states that believing in such fictions has real consequences, which in this context can vary from amassing great wealth to a lifetime of debt peonage (Hudson 2006).

Therefore, from the interhextal perspective it is important to ground real property rights as social artefacts, and Polanyi's fictional application of such artefacts being to real existents such as labour (skills hextant), land (nature hextant) and money (produce hextant). It is the "real property rights" over "real estate" that has fictional monetary market value.

To sum up this point: Polanyi (2001 [1944]) observed that the commodity description of labour, land and money is entirely fictitious, Graeber has observed that money itself is the false coin of our own dreams, Hudson has delineated the fictions of fictitious capital, the IVSC states that "real property is a non-physical concept", and Graham adds that these fictions are the very basis of private property, without which capitalism would not exist. And all of them have been dumped on the Solomon Islanders! A heavy meal to digest, to be sure.

As it emerges from those fictions, the market value of land may be regarded as a fiction as well, and a massive demonstration of the Thomas Theorem's observation that fictions defined as real become real in their consequences.

Little wonder, then, that some cultures find this a difficult concept to realise. In other cultures, with its members having grown up with it and internalised the fiction into their identities, they generally accept it as being as natural a process for our identity construction and maintenance as the air we breathe. But it is not: it is the false coin of our own dreams, and is not, and should not be, everyone's.

Globalisation and the fitness landscapes of land policies, land-related valuations, and real property rights

As a high level engagement heuristic in this HBA analysis I assume that many others have inhaled their identities in other cultures similarly to the way I have in mine. While we inevitably "inhale" communal value reinforcements as children, as adults it's "not safe to let our intuitions and prejudices run unchecked and unexamined" (Goldacre 2008, p. 255), but because of the differences designed to be explored in HBA, "trying to be 'scientific' about your relationship with your partner is as stupid as following your intuitions about causality" (ibid.).

Such people would therefore have parts of themselves that react to attacks on their social identities as being similar to a physical assault. Thereby, they will engage reptilian brain responses to defend them, including the "thingification" of other holons (see Douzinas 2002, p. 384 quotes below). As Northrup (1989) noted when defining identity, it "manifests at 'multiple levels'" and has been identified as "underlying the processes of escalation and rigidification of conflict" and as being "one important contributor to the development and maintenance of intractability" in conflicts (ibid., pp. 63–64).

Ian Buruma, in his essay on the *Origins of Occidentalism* (Buruma 2004) refers to this thingification when he restricts the term "Occidentalism" to "only when the revolt against the West becomes a form of pure destruction, when the West is depicted as less than human, when rebellion means murder".

This reductionist view of the West as "the cold, mechanical West, the machine civilization" (Buruma 2004) is as clearly a fallacy under the HVN trans-ontological process as is the demonisation of Muslims by some Westerners. In each case they go back to the most primitive principle of identity construction being forged through the marking of difference (Woodward 1997, p. 29). The Machine is not a holon, it is an artefact, and as an artefact it is not, as they put it, "the devil of the modern world" (Mishra 2012, p. 255) at all. As Upadhyaya noted, "the inanimate machine is not responsible for this. This defect belongs to a thoughtless economy" (Upadhyaya 1988–1989), and I note in turn that economies too are artefacts. The buck stops with holons.

Rather than blame an artefact, might not that devil involve the usual demonising strategy? The Thomas Theorem explains how demonising works with the imagined as well as with the real. So demonising often is, whether real or imagined, *turning personal anxieties into a perceived moral deficiency in someone else* (Rollins 2011, p. 302). Thereby, such minds succumb to the anthropological machine and may become monsters themselves.

That is how Blake's view of Newton (Beer 1969, p. 27) makes sense. The very monologicality of single vision was Blake's infernality, and it fits with Blake's objection to imperialism: Newton's monological gaze is the Anthropological Machine's, and a sine qua non for the imperialist enterprise.

Therefore, when demonising happens, especially on both sides of the fence, there could well be bloodshed. Whether we come from the North, the South, the East, or the West, we may animalise "the human, by isolating the nonhuman within the human . . . the slave, the barbarian, the foreigner, as figures of an animal in human form" (Agamben 2004, p. 37). For both The Machine and the Anthropological Machine, the wicked problem is to better understand "how they work so that we might, eventually, be able to stop them" (ibid., p. 38) or, more likely and far more pragmatically, accurately value and manage them, starting from within our own identities. The devil is back where it has always been, and will be for as long as our species is unconscious and unable to accurately value our identity constructions.

That is, The Machine is a product of single vision; to produce: it is not a holon with an evil psyche. In this work, I am focussing on that of the infernal trinity and their followers. But theirs is not, by any means, the only single vision around, and whichever single vision, single visions must not remain The Machine's master (Taleb 2012, pp. 211–212).

Single vision is of clearly of low intrinsic value as it is within the competencies of our dogmatic and visceral paleo-mammalian and reptilian levels of minds. We all have those levels, sometimes in control, sometimes controlled. I was looking for that difference when I asked that question of the Buddhist nun in Adelaide. Discerning the difference between a mind in conflict with itself and a mind disciplining itself requires more than single vision: it requires intrinsic valuation. Similarly, the artefact "money" is not the root of all evil; the love of it is (1 Tim 6:10).

Sometimes, people manifest this difference as if before the period of Western colonialism the world was "an untouched, utopian paradise" (McLarney 2009) which as adumbrated above appears generally somewhat deficient in historical evidence. As Crockett (1943, p. 162) put it: "Only ignorance dreams of a Golden Age, when power was kind. The Dark Ages, the Middle Ages, all the Ages, were filled with self" (Crockett 1943, p. 162).

However, ecologically rational reasons for this Golden Age mentality can be found in terms of identity, because looking at the past through rose-coloured glasses is of decided use in identity maintenance (Baldwin 2011). This would apply at all identity levels, including the societal identity level. Nostalgia serves as a frequently experienced, positive and self-relevant emotion (Baldwin 2011; Wildschut et al. 2010). Nostalgia for utopias can provide "a sanctuary of meaning" (Wilson 2005) for the constructed identity. From HVN↔HBA this Edenic fantasy aspect may be considered notable, but more as a part of identity construction and maintenance than for its empirical reality.

Following Niebuhr (2001) Mead observes that the major problem in such identity constructing is that *the more frustrations we have in life and the more we are infuriated by humiliations, then the more we project our narcissistic requirements of grandeur to such collective dimensions of our identities* (Mead 2007, pp. 387–390; also see De Zavala et al. 2009). That is, applying Abraham (1993) identification of "human fractals", as identities are fractally constructed – a "me" may be similar at different scales – if a need is frustrated at one scale of identity construction, it may flip to another scale to express itself. For example, the "me" identifying as a football team, a nation, or whatever may take similar offence to an insult to that scale "me" as it would to a personal-scale "me". Lakoff (2016) notes that "we tend to understand the nation metaphorically in family terms", so those with a strict rules based upbringing are inclined to try avenge themselves for their humiliations at other identity scales, and try to "impose a moral hierarchy in which those who have traditionally dominated should dominate", such moral views tending "to be part of self-definition – who you most deeply are", such that they see their role as being "to impose their view of strict father morality in all areas of life" (ibid.). The abovementioned quote of the National Commission on Terrorist Attacks Upon the United States – that the USA's homeland is the planet – smacks of this. We thereby develop great identity spans unbalanced by a lack of depth: a broad but shallow narcissism where a deep lake of wisdom and compassion is required. Bateson's warning about power corrupting and the warnings of Easterly (Easterly 2013, pp. 6 and 24) are also relevant here. Grand narratives, which are inevitably myths (Thompson 1989, p. 47), "shape our times, our methods of perceiving reality, and therefore . . . they shape our very selves" (Mead 2007, p. 274). Furthermore, *"the larger and grander the abstraction, the less critical we are of its claims"*, and the *"larger and more abstract an entity, the more unbalanced it can become"* (ibid., p. 389). As referred to above (Greenwald 1980), such abstractions attract egos like moths to the flame, often with similarly devastating results to lives including their own.

Whitehead remarked that such "intolerant use of abstractions is the major vice of the intellect" (Whitehead 1985, p. 23). Exceptionalism, including but by no means limited to American exceptionalism, is one such vice. In my travels I found exceptionalism to be exceptionally commonplace, often empowering anthropological machines such as states and other social artefacts by such identity inflations with those large, grand abstractions (Lebow 2012), not just or even particularly those in the USA.

Bateson was awake to this toxic manifestation of single vision. He considered power in these contexts to be a myth which is more or less believed in by most of us and thereby, even though it is "epistemological lunacy", becomes self-validating and "leads to all various sorts of disaster" (Bateson 1987, p. 492). Hence Urizen.

I add that identification with property rights over the humble single family house (Davidson and Dyal-Chand 2010, p. 1640) provides a stake in the guarantor of those rights, the state. Thereby identification with the state can be facilitated, which can be emotionally fired by our narcissistic desire for grandeur in such collective dimensions of our identities. The implications of this in the practicalities of land reform are, of necessity, to be considered in any HBA reflections.

At the same time, Mead further notes that as well as an arrogance of power, there is an arrogance of impotence (Mead 2007, p. 389), which is empowered by that process of frustration, humiliation etc. in the first place being compensated for by social membership glories. Thereby, we get two opposing Anthropological Machines, such as Condliffe's myth of the nation-state against other mythically inspired groups, such as terrorist groups. These Anthropological Machines then include and exclude others in their narcissistic requirements of grandeur and devalue the others in comparison to themselves. It is the love of power that is the root of all evil, not just money (the artefact articulating one of Mumford's Pentagon of Power – power, profit, productivity, property, and prestige). As Mumford put it:

> For mark this: The automaton was not born alone. the automaton has been accompanied, we can now see, by a twin, a dark shadow-self: defiant, not docile: disorderly, not organized or controlled: above all, aggressively destruc-tive, even homicidal, reasserting the dammed-up forces of life in crazy or criminal acts. In the emerging figure of man . . . [there is] a reversed hierarchy that lowers the authority of the brain and puts the reflexes and blind instincts in command. The aim of this subversive superego is to destroy those higher attributes of man whose gifts of love, mutuality, rationality, imagination, and constructive aptitude have enlarged all the possibilities of life. It is in the light of these impending negations and destructions that the whole concept of subjugating nature and replacing man's own functions with collectively fabricated, automatically operated, completely depersonalized equivalents must at last be reappraised.
>
> (Mumford 1970, p. 193)

In so doing, Patrick Geddes, the man Mumford at one time referred to as his master, had a vital point to add:

> only he can do this who is in love and at home with his subject: truly in love and fully at home the love in which high intuition supplements knowl-edge, and arouses his own fullest intensity of expression, to call forth the latent but not less vital possibilities before him.
>
> (Geddes 1915, p. 397)

As Beer recognised, such love is, according to Blake, preconditional to the emer-gence and expression of genius. And is such genius that bestows on us our optimal capacity to address wicked problems.

Although unstated by Mead, Mumford, or Geddes, their observations are related to Jung's observation that "Where love rules, there is no will to power, and where power predominates, love is lacking. The one is the shadow of the other" (Jung 1916). I add that "regard-recognition hunger" is not either, but propels them both.

If Mead, Mumford, Geddes and Jung are right, then the relationships between the soma and socio-cultural hextants are core in the understanding of Buruma's Occidentalists. At the same time, they are also relevant in the understanding of those in the West whose attacks on the "other" also become a form of pure destruction, when the other is depicted as less than human and thereby worthless (Agamben 2004; Oliver 2007, 2009).

Such stereotyping may result in murderous narcissists on opposite sides driving the agenda, often to their considerable profit in terms of identity affirmation, as well as financially for themselves or associates (Lebow 2012). Furthermore, while such predators may be deficient in broad and deep intrinsic valuation competency, nonetheless they could well have achieved the higher levels of cognitive complexity. Their actions can be examples of how catastrophic development of wisdom without compassion can be (Wilber 1995, p. 328).

Such problems are vastly magnified by the pathological Goldilockean imbalances along Jung's power-love spectrum dynamic The Machine bestows on its controllers. The most blatant examples of these are the combination of war machines and the murderously malignant narcissists gaining command of them, as in the case of the Third Reich. A specialist in the study of war, John Vasquez (Vasquez 1993, 2009; Vasquez and Valeriano 2010), confirms the above insights of Mead and Mumford. Vasquez pointed out the importance of recognition (regard) as a cause in war (Vasquez 1993, pp. 115–116) and the importance of territoriality as "the *primary cause of war*" (Valeriano and Owsiak 2014, italics mine). Vasquez and the scholars around him now recognise the double base of territoriality: the biological basis and the environmental factors: that is, of both interior and exterior hextants. They further recognise that there is much more work to be done, and they intend to do it (Valeriano and Owsiak 2014).

These days, many of these motivations are manifesting in the context of globalisation. While much of the discussion on globalisation is to do with the nature of the beliefs themselves, inter-hextally there is a relative imbalance investigating the above process in general. In particular, this analysis indicates a deficiency of attention to the sociocultural child-rearing practices responsible for engendering the emotional drivers behind whatever beliefs people use as artefactual scaffolding for their identity constructions.

From the HBA perspective, the potential for black swan/butterfly effects from such a massive population pool is problematic, so a focus on politicians, who have a stake in protecting the system, would be insufficient. However, we can draw some comfort from the checks and balances provided by the other hextants of individuals. At infantile narcissistic levels "the difference from others is absolute and must be negated through the arrogation of absolute sovereignty" (Stern 2013, p. 144) and all others are considered and treated as "inferior and inessential, of lesser value and importance than self" (ibid.) which, as Midgley wrote, is silly (1995, p. 89). However, there is potential for transcendence of such impulses in individuals through the emergence of higher levels of understanding (Douzinas 2002, p. 384). Most of us manage to do this, albeit to greater and lesser degrees – both between us, and at different times inside each one of us. These potentials emerge, if at all, interhextally from societal challenges and their identity responses. These require both attachments to others, and the embracing of societal checks and balances along with those of significant others.

While attachment theory in psychology properly focusses upon attachments with other people, identity construction is not so confined. It includes attachment to non-human holons, and to artefacts, and includes attachment to land (Berberich, Campbell and Hudson 2012). Douzinas claims that the main function

of rights "help establish one part of the recognition necessary for the constitution of the full self", *and that is rights' main function* (Douzinas 2002, p. 383). That
is why there is so much focus in this work about which property rights can best
fulfil this function in different environments.

An aspect of that role is that real property rights are often also the main
financial investment of many households (for example, Arce 2012 and Lynn
2013). "Impelled by this hunger for recognition", those with a stake in a social
system that provides such recognition via such rights (Mead 2007, p. 290) will
usually defend their societies as part of themselves (ibid., p. 336), and in particular,
their homes (as identity contributors, not mere houses, which are artefacts) and
families. Thereby, personal identity construction becomes a major driver of
globalisation.

When one marries the insights of Mead and Douzinas to those of Commons
(2007), one can see than Mead's projection of narcissistic frustrations to broader
identities such as religions, nations, sports teams and the like might also in turn
become moderated by MHC's higher levels of cognitive complexity. A hextal
review at scale quickly reveals that there is no big squishy brain out there at
the scale of a society in the soma hextant (Dimitrov 2003, p. 16; Wilber 1995,
p. 80; Atran as cited in Brockman 2013, p. 10), so holonically societies reside
inside the minds of their participants. However, that is not to confirm Margaret
Thatcher's conclusion that "there is no such thing as society". Nor does it deny
that societies are units of selection in Darwinian terms (Wilson and Mulgan
2017). Rather, it means that societies are multidimensional complicated artefacts that are constructed not by mere "meme machines" as Blackmore (1999)
put it, but by complex holons identifying with societies, and including them into
their personal stories in the same way I joined the artefacts I saw along the Asian
overland into mine.

Insights into such complex↔complax co-evolutions can only happen if the
process is turned inwards as well as outwards, as Krishnamurti suggested. For
example in Torbert and Associates' (2004) collaborative developmental action
inquiry approach, and in mindfulness meditation (Zeidan et al. 2010; Vago 2014),
which in particular operates within that third of a second before our narratives
kick in (Smallberg in Brockman 2013, p. 285).

It was in researching that mindfulness meditation that I rediscovered that there
were much earlier thinkers than Mead and Neihbur, and even Hegel and Adam
Smith, who had observed the primacy of regard-recognition hunger. According
to Loy:

> The ego-self is ungrounded, and we experience this ungroundedness as an
> uncomfortable emptiness or hole at the very core of our being. We feel this
> problem as a sense of lack, of inadequacy, of unreality, and in compensation
> we usually spend our lives trying to accomplish things that we think will
> make us more real . . . Being social beings, we tend to group our sense of lack,
> even as we strive to compensate by creating collective senses of self . . .
> In fact, many of our social problems can be traced back to this deluded sense

of collective self, this "wego", or group ego . . . [and] institutions . . . tend to take on a life of their own as new types of wego.

(Loy 2006, pp. 15–16)

This wego, this samsara, this Gordian knot, this Anthropological Machine. Perhaps, back in 1976, Krishnamurti had been thrown by my question because he had dropped his membership of the Anthropological Machine and I had not.

There may always be narcissistic rage within us, expressed within our various mythical identity attachment vehicles. However, with gradual development of conscious insight and management instead of being driven solely by unconscious drivers, such impulses can become harmless or even constructive. For example, they may be, and often are, channelled to combat injustices. This hunger can have value of all kinds.

It was from this more benign view that I went to Europe to ask Krishnamurti about regard hunger, now over four decades ago, and thereby began my own identity's globalisation. My question was about what Gabel (2000, 2003, 2013, 2014) now terms *The Desire for Mutual Recognition* (Gabel 2018). Gabel sees that as the "foundation of our social being" (Gabel 2000, p.244), as "fundamental in the spiritual realm as the need for food and shelter is in the material realm" (ibid.), but that it is blocked by the "fear of humiliation" (ibid., p. 34) and is "everywhere denied" (Gabel 2014, p. 674).

Not quite everywhere. In contrast to the faux objectivity of the minions of The Machine and other denialist stratagems, unbeknown to me until now the answer to the question I went to ask Krishnamurti about was answered five years after I asked it. The answer came not from Krishnamurti, but from Mihaly Csikszentmihalyi, whom we have already encountered several times above, particularly in the context of the Goldilocks Principle. He wrote a book with Eugene Rochberg-Halton called "The Meaning of Things" (Csikszentmihalyi and Rochberg-Halton 1981), and later a book chapter entitled "Why We Need Things" (Csikszentmihalyi 1989). From my investigations of circumstances of sale throughout my valuation career, I consider these same psychological processes are major drivers in making parties willing to engage in a market value transaction. So where Csikszentmihalyi writes of artefacts, things or objects, in my quotes from the latter below I have replaced those words by [land] or [lands] as appropriate.

He pointed out that:

> our dependence on [land] is not only physical but also, more important, psychological . . . Contrary to what we ordinarily believe, consciousness is not a stable, self-regulating entity . . . Most people require an external order to keep randomness from invading their mind . . . the self is a fragile construction of the mind . . . a state of psychic entropy is the normal state of consciousness . . . Without a world between men and nature, there is eternal movement, but no objectivity . . . This is where [land] can be helpful.

[Lands] help objectify the self in at least three major ways. They do so first by demonstrating the owner's power, vital erotic energy, and place in the

244 *Birthing HIDEGRE BIES ADALAS*

social hierarchy. Second, [lands] reveal the continuity of the self through time, by providing foci of involvement in the present, mementos and souvenirs of the past, and signposts to future goals. Third, [lands] give concrete evidence of one's place in a social network as symbols (literally, the joining together) of valued relationships. In these three ways [lands] stabilize our sense of who we are; they give a permanent shape to our views of ourselves that otherwise would quickly dissolve in the flux of consciousness.

(Csikszentmihalyi 1989, pp. 22–25)

I see this insight as being the most relevant core reality of our lives and behaviour with regard to markets in general, and to the topic of this book in particular. By "markets" I here mean markets in ideas, not just markets facilitated by money, This identity hunger must be regularly sated for our self-constructions to remain functional and adapt to environmental challenges. Such left hemisphere needs are not to be despised or rejected. Rather, they are to be appropriately *valued*, extrinsically, intrinsically, and systemically, towards understanding their fitnesses for purpose in the wicked problems being addressed; not only "what's in it for me", but also "what's in me for it", and much else besides.

Hence my strong emphasis upon considering identity needs, as distinct from merely economic ones, in the recently articulated need for a "comprehensive and holistic" understanding of the process to engender similarly informed policy reforms, which may "unleash significant productivity gains", but will require mutual reinforcing, complementary policies, not just one (Mahajan et al. 2014). In other words, they need policy reforms of the nature this trans-ontological process is meant to initiate. This is to include critical reflection (Valters 2014, 2014a) on how fit for purpose such policies are in the relevant environment, and not just how amenable they are to mechanisation processes, which bestow power but neither wisdom nor compassion. However, machines can be used to *facilitate* the coevolution of wisdom and compassion required in the contexts scrutinised by Cross and Mahajan and others in South Africa, and the contexts of so many other scholars and practitioners worldwide.

Interrogation of market value definition with HBA

"Economics claims to calculate values via value-free facts" (Latour 2013, p. 447). Unlike, for example, neo-liberal economics with its monological gaze on the nature and produce hextants, when wicked valuation problems are encountered I consider that, under the IVSC definition of market value, interrogation of all six domains of this hextal template and their interrelationships, including their respective levels of development and emergence, is required. That is, market value transactions are those determined by holons which may be facilitated by artefacts, not the other way around: By the very definition of market value, The Machine has no claim on markets.

The definition includes values at its very core. Consequently, can investigating the circumstances of market transactions be a portal into understanding of the "Big V" values?

In support of this contention, Davy (2012, p. 95) notes that market valuations capture the four kinds of land value – market value, use value, territorial value, and existence value. How many other forms of value influence a market value transaction? On the other hand, often "market value is just one factor among many that motivate owners and is often not at the forefront of their decision-making" (Penalver and Alexander 2012, p. 840).

For example, as regarding the time scale aspect of ADALAS, according to the New Testament Judas received 30 pieces of silver to betray the abovementioned land reformer Jesus and before killing himself returned it to the temple, where it was used to buy the potter's field (Mt 27:7). When examining whether that was a market value transaction, a valuer of the time may have asked, "is the buying of the field the best action with the money for the willing but not anxious purchaser?"

Clearly, the money was employed that way because it was blood money (Mt 27:7) and as such culturally unacceptable for many alternative uses.

However, there is another perspective on that question bearing scrutiny. As Richard Price pointed out in 1776, if they had even invested a penny at five per cent compounding interest at the time of Jesus's birth, by Price's day its value would have grown to a solid sphere of gold extending from the Sun out beyond the orbit of Jupiter (Hudson 2004). Instead they invested in land, in a field whose present market value today is somewhat less. Given that they were purchasing on behalf of the Jewish faith aspect of their identity constructions, which faith is still extant today, was that potter's field a prudent purchase?

While that question may be considered absurd, the implicitly accepted idea of the sustainability of compound interest on a similar value base is far more absurd. Given that the world is not replete with gold spheres with diameters from the sun to Jupiter, some other existent is going on: but what is it exactly?

Which prompts the question, "in terms of the IVSC definition of market value quoted above, if a buyer takes out a loan to buy a property, is that always and everywhere 'prudent'? And, if not, when, where, why and how for whom not?"

Despite my Asian overlands from 1976 to 1980, and despite my background as a valuer, at that time I had not drilled down deeply enough to find the historical narrative to address these questions. Fortunately, however, Michael Hudson wrote just such an integrative narrative for both my valuation and my tour leading narratives in the year I went to Swaziland (Hudson 1993). At least those experiences, plus the knowledge I have built upon them since, have brought my Goldilocks zone into a state where I am able to better understand and contextualise Hudson's narrative.

That narrative relates how there has been a social dynamic going back to the earliest known civilisations. On the one side, there is a ruler dependent on the services of the soldier/peasant. On the other, there are moneylenders who take claim over the soldier/peasants' land, thereby accruing wealth so great as to challenge, destroy or bend the ruler to their wills.

Therefore, Jesus was addressing a dynamic that had already been problematic for over two thousand years. In the past, it had been addressed by rulers by means of periodic debt forgiveness, often every 30 years. This became sacralised and institutionalised in the Jewish faith by the Jubilee every 50 years (Leviticus 25:11), and the banning of usury between Jews:

> The laws of Exodus 21–23 (the Book of the Covenant), the Holiness Code of Leviticus and the laws of Deuteronomy place interest-bearing debt, land tenure and the periodic renewal of economic freedom from debt at the center of their economic program.
>
> (Hudson 1993)

Thereby, interest was never allowed to accrue debts to crippling levels. Therefore, when Jesus spoke on redemption of sins, he was keying into the Jewish community's understanding on the redemption of monetary debt slaves (Sedlacek and Havel 2011, p. 134). However, the Romans had no such compunction, and Herod needed all that money for his building projects, including that same Temple housing the moneychangers.

Jesus's whipping of the tenants/moneychangers was a direct challenge to that cosy relationship between government and the moneylenders of the Temple. Clearly, by calling for debt forgiveness as required by scripture, and as so desperately required by so many as described by Van Eck (2011), Jesus was striking at the most sensitive and vulnerable part of the power apparatus. Therefore, from the landlords' perspective, Jesus had to go.

In another paper, Hudson further points out that "savings that are invested in debt tend to stifle economies, causing downturns that wipe out the debts and savings together in a convulsion of bankruptcy" (Hudson 2004). The inevitable result of those hoped-to-be-sustainable interest payments being based on "fiction – junk economics and junk accounting, which are the logical complements to fictitious capital" (Hudson 2010).

That is why we do not see those massive spheres of gold. Hudson further claims that this was the fate of the Roman Empire, and continues to this day at not only the household scale but also the international scale (Hudson 1993).

One might ask, "why do we keep falling into the same debt traps?" According to the behavioural economist Laibson (1997), we are inclined to hyperbolically discount longer term benefits in comparison to shorter term ones. In contrast compound interest increases hyperbolically over time. The difference between them is where debt financiers now prosper, and have done so since the dawn of civilisation (Hudson 1993).

If he had addressed this context, perhaps Blake would have added Newton's near lifelong friend Charles Montagu, the implementer of William Patterson's idea of the Bank of England (Goodman 2009) to his infernal trinity. The Bank of England was pushed through over the objections of both landed interests and those against usury.

In this space, a valuer may ask, how prudent are those who actually close the deal? If prudent, shouldn't the purchaser consider the Ponzi process of inflating property prices to create higher lending in that space and compare that to the amount of surplus income having to be paid over the years for debt servicing? After all, "that is what the mathematics of compound interest are all about" (Hudson 2010).

Consequently:

> Market participants' observed tendency to value short-term gains more highly than declared costs calls into question the fairness of delegating excessive control over land-use decisions to today's market participants.
>
> (Penalver and Alexander 2012, p. 855)

While that may be prudent from the purchaser's side of the transaction, there are different criteria on the vendor's side. For example, if the vendor is prudent, won't a deal only be concluded between that vendor and the most optimistic potential purchaser? And how often will that optimism be caused by blindness to the above insights provided by behavioural economics on the one side, and the power of compound interest on the other?

Market participants in general believe, and court decisions confirm, that "the outcome of a competitive auction is the best indicator of value" (*United States v. Buchman*, decided 16 May 2011, no. 10-2306). However, in economics, there is the concept of the winner's curse (Thaler 1988). It can be readily manifested by, for example, going into a lecture theatre with a jar of coins, jellybeans, or any existents small enough for a large number of them to be in a jar. If there are enough people in the theatre, the average of their estimates will be quite close to the true number of items in the jar (albeit usually lower). Neither the highest estimates nor the lowest will be as close, but other existents being equal, the highest bidder at an auction is the person a prudent vendor will close the deal with.

Therefore, the winner's curse applies to real estate auctions (Tse 2000). Yet in practice, while the prudent potential purchaser will be outbid by the less prudent one, because no-one can predict the future in complex environments (insofar as they are complex) that less prudent purchaser could sell at a profit to an even less prudent one, whereas the person the purchaser outbid gained no profit from the property at all. So, who was "prudent"?

However, market valuers are not dealing in merely complex environments; they are dealing in wicked problem ones, which enfold simple and complicated as well as complex, and compound interest is a simple problem, a product of a simple recipe.

So where does that leave the markets' and the courts' assumptions that valuers must apply in their analyses of sales?

The answer lies in the difference between what is in that jar and what a valuation is. Whether the valuer knows it or not, because of requirements that a valuer is to ascertain matters such as whether the parties are "willing", "knowledgeable", "prudent" and "acting without compulsion", a valuation is a wicked problem. In contrast, counting the contents of the jar is a simple problem. Valuations are abstract artefacts that include reading complex holons; jar counters are counting simple artefacts. The valuer is a market reader delivering a required imaginary: as always subject to the relevant legal domain, if the market accounts for winner's curse, so should the valuer, and if not, the valuer should not.

While that may satisfy a valuer's due diligence requirements, it does not adequately articulate the more directly valuation-related aspects of these wicked valuation problems. Where does financing fit in terms of the markets and the IVSC definition?

Just as:

- we are addressing an arena for the "co-evolution on mutually interdependent or reciprocally deformed fitness landscapes" (Holbrook 2003, p. 22), in which
- "we are all each other's fitness landscapes" (Brand 2013, p. 124), and
- "the human mind is built to think in terms of narratives" (Akerlof and Shiller 2009, p. 51), and
- the "truth about stories is that's all we are" (King 2003), and even
- "the bottom line in science is narrative" (Lissack and Graber 2014, p. 192).

So are market values. Tuckett (2012) emphasised that "financial markets are markets in stories", and the emerging discipline of Narrative Policy Framework (McBeth et al. 2014) asserts that "heroic policy narratives shape policy realities" (Shanahan, Jones, McBeth and Lane 2013).

Which prompts the question, which stories have which policy and valuational impacts where the North, the South, the East and the West meet?

One story is from the more money-based identities in the West. On one Christian discussion forum it was claimed that, while times have changed the nature of money, and the Catholic church still forbids usury, modern finance cannot be considered as usury.

The reason given is that markets these days are so different in quality as to be different in kind. Because property markets are far more developed, transparent and accountable now than they were then, and far from being an objective measure, money itself has become a value-dynamic participant (Palm 1997).

That is *true but partial*. That insight omits mention of a fundamental dynamic, which remains undisturbed. When enough valuations facilitate the banks' creation of new money at a sufficient scale, the liquidity created impacts on values, creating still higher values, still more liquidity, and a property bubble may ensue. That applies even with non-usurious interest rates. From the all-levels' perspectives, I agree with Hudson and read this interest dynamic as still the underlying dynamic driving this more developed market.

On the other hand, Hudson claims that Old Testament prophets, Jesus, Medieval Canon Law and modern classical economists would all agree that unproductive loans are usury (Hudson 1993). Pope Francis would presumably agree with Hudson, too, when he proclaimed usury a current dramatic social ill:

When a family has nothing to eat, because it has to make payments to loan sharks, this is not Christian, it is not human! This dramatic scourge in our society harms the inviolable dignity of the human person.

(Scaramuzzi 2014)

Looking at the higher levels, I would first enquire whether a book entry that can be created by a bank from valuation-facilitated or even less substantively evidenced keyboard strokes should always be considered a reasonable compensation for decades of debt servitude (McLeay, Radia and Thomas 2014). The former activities are about extrinsic value; the latter is about subjecting high intrinsic value holons into servitude. If that is so, is that practice not better considered a continuance of the dynamic traced by Hudson, and later manifesting as described above in the British Empire?

In answer to the first question, it is perfectly clear from the market that entering into a mortgage financing agreement, however pernicious at the long term national scale, often can be considered reasonable compensation for the mortgagor at the short to medium term personal scale. Along with the supply to various tax farmers and the repayment of the mortgage, on countless occasions mortgagors have benefitted themselves because market values of properties often richly repay that servitude. However, as the subprime mortgage crisis and other manifestations have demonstrated this is far from always being the case. From the above it is clearly far from sustainable in real terms. So much so that a commentator considers that "the banks are enormously overleveraged, they're entirely disproportionate to the size of the country's GDP and their health rests on an extraordinarily overvalued asset base, not just homes – commercial property and land as well" (Foss 2015, 31:54).

The analogy with the children's game of pass the parcel has not been lost on economic commentators (Rayman 2013; Streithorst 2014), and that applies to mortgagors as well. So my answer to the first question is a conditional "yes" (it can benefit the mortgagor), and to the second a much less conditional yes: there is that pedigree in the lending practices. Consequently, it is from both those dynamics that market values emerge.

In the problem statement in Chapter 1, I quoted Ring and Boykin saying that valuation is at the heart of all economic activity (1986, p. 1) – an observation echoed by the Asia Pacific Business Council (IVSC 2014). Being so fundamental, it is concerning to note the comment of the Nobel Laureate Joseph Stigler that it is also economics' most pervasive problem, and that "the routine and undramatic problem of value has elicited the supreme efforts of the greatest theorists" (Stigler and Kindahl 1970, p. 299).

Hudson has noted that in the two thousand years since Jesus, the ruler/people/ aspiring plutocrats dynamic has continued to this day, and that this has had massive social consequences. Despite great improvements in transparency, tax policies and the legal infrastructure, in the West there are still no more effective solutions than were the crude cyclic debt forgiveness programs invented in the ancient Middle East.

Throughout these two thousand years, the greatest theorists (ibid.) who have turned their attention to the problem have included Augustine and Aquinas; but they looked at the "price" aspect of the market value definition, and what comprises a "just price", which is a useful comparison when interrogating market value.

Effectively, it included several of the aspects of market value, but it also included a moral element. Moreover, while the scholastics agreed that what they called the just price was the market price insofar as the latter had to be fair (Maxwell 2008, p. 17), that is not universally agreed by modern scholars (Koehn and Wilbratte 2012).

Along with Aquinas, Augustine did not assume an absolute or unqualified right to the possession of private property (Dougherty 2003, p. 491). However, Augustine considered that while all land was God's, nonetheless one can own land under the ruler's (or what we would now say, the state's) authority and conditions, *providing that they are ultimately held for the common good and the law is predicated on divine law* (ibid., pp. 481–483). Noting that "unjust law is no law", Augustine considered it is the disposition of the owner that counts (*On Free Choice of the Will*, Book 1, § 5), a merciful owner gaining the pleasure of helping the poor that is hardly available to the poor themselves; we are to own possessions to bestow goodness, not to be ruled by them (Dougherty 2003, p. 484).

Looking from a just price perspective back to the IVSC definition, though, one could claim that it would be imprudent to offend morality in the market. Furthermore, with trust being such an important component in market activity (Fowler 2013, pp. 16–17; Walker and Ostrom 2007), the view *that prudence necessarily enfolds a reflection upon fairness* is germane. This is particularly so because "fairness is the emotional part of economic decision-making . . . without this component, consumers *cannot make a decision to buy*" (Maxwell 2008, p. 9, italics mine).

According to empirical research in behavioural economics, assumptions of fairness do affect economic behaviour (Kahneman, Knetsch and Thaler 1986) and, as such, fairness is a matter to be considered by a valuer in analysing any sale's suitability as market value evidence. In which case, from the All Scales perspective the millennia-long enquiry as to what constitutes a just price has a seat at the table in determining the market value of a property.

In arguing for the revival of the Thomistic concept of a just price, Koehn and Wilbratte (2012) note that it not only looks at the relationship between the parties facilitating mutual well-being. The concept also requires that it should be for the good of the local community as a whole – a matter not directly addressed in the IVSC definition, but which goes right back to Aristotle's *Nichomachean Ethics* (bk V, ch. 1).

It is reasonable to assume as an ansatz that by and large in developed markets the good of the local community should have already been addressed by appropriate planning and environmental controls and other legislation. However, that is not necessarily the case even in such markets. Furthermore, the less developed the market the more questionable any such assumption may become. Each fitness landscape has to be examined via HBA on its own merits, and once again scale is important, as Koehn and Wilbratte see market value and a Thomistic just price can be the same when the market price emerges "in a smaller community" (ibid., p. 4).

Koehn and Wilbratte distinguish Aquinas's just price from a market exchange price as understood in neoclassical economics because markets necessarily include the foolish, whereas a just price is by definition between the wise. However, a transaction that can be accepted by a valuer as evidence at the local scale is between the wise as well. But what about wisdom at the global scale? In these days of the internet providing information from anywhere and everywhere, and market values and marketability being potentially influenced more from afar than nearby, is not some global scale wisdom from the Hudsons, Stiglers et al. of the world prudent before embarking on decades of debt servitude?

Once again, the answer lies not so much within geographical constraints, but due diligence expectation for the market participants for the property concerned.

Another distinction made by Koehn and Wilbratte between a Thomist just price and a market transaction is also arguably the difference between a market value and a market transaction: price gouging. However, a rapid rise in market value is not the same as price gouging. Just as one swallow doesn't make a summer, one anxious purchaser doesn't make a market. Price gouging applies to circumstances where the purchaser is anxious, which again disqualifies the transaction as evidence for both market value and just price. When the usefulness to the buyer comes not from the seller but that buyer's anxiety, the usefulness of the sale as evidence of value goes too. However, differences remain: For Aquinas, gain for the sake of gain is immoral. However, in the price gouging scenario, a vendor selling at a just price would find a purchaser able to sell at a much higher price because there are many anxious potential purchasers. Which is more just; the long term owner gaining the windfall, or the opportunistic one?

The dangers inherent in naïve market participants assuming compound interest payments sustainable are considerable. Often there is a complete absence of differentially scaled markets able to take into account considerations transcending those of self-interested willing buyers and willing sellers. Thereby, the privatisation of profits from commons of various scales and communalising of costs at various scales may be entirely ignored. Therefore, I agree with Koehn and Wilbratte that "the time has arrived to take seriously Aquinas's concept of a just person price".

One means of facilitating its introduction is a values jury (Lally 1999, 2000; see Box 6.1). Such juries can be versed in the just price concept, and the ways in which any current functioning of a market may differ from it, which could include financing practices: "the jury process instructs participants to act as direct representatives of the larger society, including future citizens if the decision would affect them . . ." (Brown, Peterson and Tonn 1995, p. 251).

Experts addressing the wicked valuation problem of placing a monetary value on nature have devised a range of deliberative monetary valuation techniques (Getzner, Spash and Stagl 2005, p. 9). They are "numerous and varied, [their]

Box 6.1   Value juries

The idea of value juries, similar to those in a court of law and to be similarly informed (Brown, Peterson and Toon 1995), is an emergent from the idea of citizens' juries which, although understood to be "seriously flawed" (Lally 2000, p. 1), remains the most fit for purpose in estimating public values in cost-benefit analyses (ibid.).

Patrick Lally was the first to conduct a series of trials of value juries, and did so towards "bridging the nexus between citizens' juries and contingent valuation" (ibid., p. 2). The findings of his research included his recognition of the serious flaws in contingent valuation (ibid., p. 192), a number of which flaws I consider to be those of single vision reductionist fantasies. For example, when assessing losses via the contingent valuation method for the pollution of Prince William Sound, the powers determined that its application should be to all Americans, not to all Alaskans and not to the Communities in the sound (Fourcade 2011, p. 1762). With HVN↔HBA, it would have been applied to all scales. Lally's trials led him to the conclusion that there is a prima facie case that value juries can be sufficiently accurate and effective, "pragmatic (including cost-effective), eclectic, versatile, and simple to execute" (Lally 2000, p. 15), and moreover that "The model holds considerable potential for use in a wide variety of applications, particularly where the quantum of stakeholder values is the focus of attention" (ibid., p. x). Lally added that "An ethical discursive valuation process must therefore go beyond the expert to include the diverse voices of those impacted by the valuation process, particularly those who might have been so often unheard" (ibid., p. 192).

As well as the wider potential application of this work, a HVN↔HBA values jury could address wicked valuation problems. For example, they could facilitate addressing Okoth-Ogendo's challenge in the Ubuntu manner described by PECAPDISHD (see Chigara 2012, p. 221). Having extensive lived experience in policy committee debates, I qualify the values jury concept as "HVN↔HBA" because I consider the success of values juries is far more likely with HVN↔HBA than without it.

Lally further observes that, despite their remarkable similarities, "the major difference between neo-classical economic value theory and preference-based axiological ones is the complete lack of any budget constraint in the latter" (Lally 2000, p. 9). It must be taken as a given in addressing wicked valuation problems that there may be no monetary equivalents (Housty 2013). There will be occasions when replacement in kind may suffice in lieu, but enforcing the basic principle that those privatising profits by commonising costs must pay those costs remains. If they cannot pay, they cannot do. However, when it comes to the value of meaning, as Vallicella (2009) cautions, individual telaxic valuations would require social confirmation via value juries to be accepted.

The lessons learnt from Lally's trials are included in his work, and many could be applied as appropriate in the broader and deeper contexts that this work recommends. Once again though, it is vital not to be too rigid and prescriptive, but adopt his lessons as ansatzes. Unlike single vision practitioners, we are not looking for a simple recipe here, because we know it will most likely not only fail to provide a solution, but compound the wicked problem. However, Lally also learnt that jury sizes of from 10 to 30 persons can be quite representative of much larger groups, with 26 jurors being representative of 100,000 people if it is a yes or no type question (ibid., pp. 63–64). Much larger jury sizes are required for greater certainty and numerical representation, but even those may now be possible online. In any event, as Lally says their application can and must be pragmatic and cost-effective, and where they are not, albeit less than optimal, other methods of employing HVN↔HBA may be applied and developed as most appropriate under the relevant criteria for the particular wicked valuation problems.

There has been a hiatus in development of value juries since Lally's researches. Citizen's juries in general are often opposed by vested interests (ABC RN 2015b). However, in May 2015 an open public value account was published, assessing China and the USA for comprehensive social development (Wang and Christensen 2015). It began by noting that "public values should be at the heart of public administration and social development" (ibid., p. 1) but that they are "often severely weakened by their philosophical ambiguity and immeasurability" (ibid.), which, from the perspective presented here, can be seen as a pathology of machinism dominance, not a flaw of public valuation as such. That is, such values are not to be unenacted because they do not fit within the Procrustean requirements of The Machine, such as expressed in the managerial nostrum, "if you can't measure it, you can't manage it". Rather, The Machine is to be regarded as useless in the context, and the process continued without its further involvement until its potential utility may emerge once more.

The process went on to build a policy tool to assess "as many public values as possible" (ibid.). They divided values into economic, political and social ones, categorising animal rights and the environment as public values, later noting that, as natural capital value is only a small part of the value of the environment; as merely economic value, it may ignore or devalue "intrinsic, aesthetic, cultural, ecosystem, heritage, historial, moral, religious, spiritual, scientific or social values" (p. 12), and also noting that "the philosophical questions of what value is, whether it exists, and how it can be measured are still hotly debated and far from being resolved" (ibid., p. 3). They also looked to "the weighing and evaluation of the relative importance of the various values and indicators" (ibid., p. 13), and highlight three major possible research directions:

1   public value accounts to be prepared and tracked for every country;
2   obtain and analyse reliable data on "important public values such as happiness, democracy, equality, justice, freedom and transparency"; and
3   explore "the process and approach of public value creation" at different scales (ibid., p. 21).

The momentum for citizens' juries is building worldwide, and even citizens' assemblies to supplement or replace existing parliamentary infrastructures are being discussed (ABC RN 2015b). Value juries should catch that wave. HVN↔HBA or similarly informed value juries could play an important role in such endeavours. I therefore look to them as having the potential to make both "Big V" and "small v" (monetary) valuation decisions in the context of this work. In all such cases, contingent valuations and all other valuation techniques could be put to them, but it would remain for the juries to decide, not the experts.

At this stage, however, research on "the operational criteria" for citizens' (or other) value juries remains "at an early stage of development" (Getzner, Spash and Stagl 2005, p. 4).

"production, selection, and application" [is] "extraordinarily contingent and deeply political" (Fourcade 2011, p. 1725). Arguably, therefore, there will be situations where suitably depthed value juries are the most practical means of establishing which techniques are most fit for purpose in various wicked valuation problem contexts.

When addressing such problems, Katrine Soma has compiled a list of four questions which I consider could be used to help identify the simple, complicated, complex etc. components of such problems (Soma 2006, pp. 45–46):

1   Is it sufficient to set only one main goal in the analysis?
2   Can the environment be treated as a bundle of commodities?
3   Are nature values commensurable?
4   Can the affected individuals' preferences be aggregated?

If the answers to all four questions are yes, then cost-benefit analyses will be legitimate in such wicked valuation problem components. However, "if the answer to any of the questions is NO, multicriteria techniques and participatory processes with stakeholders or citizens can provide environmental policymakers with more valid information" (ibid., p.47).

William Easterly points out that Adam Smith referred to the market being "an association of problem-solvers" in which you dedicate yourself to solving other people's problems, they dedicate themselves to solving yours, and there are no presidents of the associations involved, no meetings, and no membership restrictions (Easterly 2013, p. 239). Such associations must have "adequate knowledge for others to solve your problem", and adequate incentives to do so (ibid., p. 240).

Providing they understand that such incentives need not be monetary, those operating HVN↔HBA might also have similar requirements. However, *Easterly's comment is scale-blind.* Value juries, HVN↔HBA and the market at large can all be associations of problem-solvers; which of these, or others, is employed is a question which can gain a developed answer by an ADALAS inquiry, including the scales and domains of the problem.

Easterly points out that Adam Smith's Invisible Hand "is not utopia" (Easterly 2013, p. 252). However, by the virtuous circle of specialisation, nonexperts learn by doing (p. 252), "driving out of business the incompetent in favour of the mediocre, the mediocre in favour of the good, and the good in favour of the excellent", and sees the technocratic approach – decisions by experts – as arguably giving the worst of all worlds (p. 254). However, Easterly did not address what is to become of the incompetent, the mediocre and the good, and when it comes to brain surgery I would much prefer an expert perform the operation than a non-expert.

That noted, more generally the apparent difference between Easterly's need for "adequate knowledge" and his rejections of "experts" are only contradictory from a static viewpoint, not from a learning by doing, trans-ontological process one. Also, HVN↔HBA highlights the difference between what can be achieved with complicated, as distinct from what can be achieved with complex and wicked. If I am sitting atop a rocket about to head off into space, I really hope that experts built it. Easterly's problem is more associated with those holding themselves out as experts in fields where no one can be.

Interrogation of the global property rights scene with HBA

In Chapter 3, I noted the influence of Locke on the shaping of the Western idea of property. While not compromising the above review, in *Just Property*, Pierson (2013) traced the history of how the current acceptance of the global concentrations of wealth – where the bottom half of the world's population own around one per cent of total wealth and the top one per cent of the population own nearly half the wealth – came to be accepted as right (ibid., pp. 1–2). Reviewing the millennia of Western civilisation, he saw almost no historical precedent in the West for modern claims that ownership of land grants a preemptive right over the basic well-being of other members of society, and notes how the issue is currently widely neglected (ibid., p. 3).

Once again, Pirsig's said that *Areté implies a respect for the wholeness or oneness of life* . . . As such, faced with such an unequal distribution of wealth, including landed wealth, what is the areté of global land policy? Would that not also require "an understanding of what it is to be a part of the world, and not an enemy of it"? (Pirsig 1974, pp. 386, 387). If so, what does that imply in responding to the current challenges in global valuation? Further, as areté also means virtue, what telaxic virtues are to have the most weight placed upon them in this context?

Penalver and Alexander called for a richer normative theory of property able to enfold "economic analysis within a larger moral framework" (Penalver and Alexander 2012, p. 821). In wanting that to include "the value of personhood" (ibid., p. 863), they were calling for transcendence of single vision. When Penalver and Alexander chose three virtues to examine in the context of land virtues – industry, justice and humility (ibid., pp. 876–886) – they added that there are many other domains of land use decision-making, and concluded their paper looking towards "land wisdom" (ibid., pp. 887–888). They consider some legal economists, such as Demetz (ibid., p. 827) have an "over-reliance on land's market value" (ibid., p. 823) in focussing his critique upon law and economics accounts and employing a "rational actor" concept of landowner behaviour (ibid., p. 824).

Penalver and Alexander recognise multilayered complexities in land: in each site's physical attributes, ecological roles and the like (ibid., p. 828), and in its relationships to human beings. These include "the intricacy of the social activities that take place upon it" (ibid., p. 829), noting that they are "practically necessary for the full spectrum of human aspiration and activity" (ibid., p. 829). That spectrum includes its role in identity construction, in terms of people becoming deeply attached to it (ibid., pp. 830, 860). From that perspective, land may have complex relationships with practically every arena of human endeavour. This complexity undermines Demetzian simplex views about the owner being able to make all land use decisions (ibid., p. 832).

As referred to several times already, there is a developmental co-evolution required between wisdom and compassion, involving a co-dependent co-evolution of framing, values and knowledge, to construct an identity towards its greater intrinsic value. If its vision were to facilitate that process at all relevant scales, what would a land policy facilitating land-related wisdom and land compassion look like? What balances would there be between Carter's (Carter 2011) prioritarianism, pure egalitarianism, and sufficientarianism? For instance, would a socially reviewed just price play a larger role in a market place and, if so, how? Should valuers require an evident understanding by parties to a sale of our inclination to under-appreciate the effects of long-term (Laibson 1997) compound interest before accepting a sale as evidence of market value?

Surveying the current scene with such questions in mind, as tracked by Linklater (2015) a current orienting generalisation of the global property rights scene is that globalisation is continuing the process of enclosures that began in the United Kingdom all those centuries ago. The result of the disruption of patterns of traditional landholdings by these enclosures has been:

> [T]he great revolution of the last two hundred years. The idea of individual, exclusive ownership, not just of what can be carried or occupied, but of the immovable, near-eternal earth, has proved to be the most destructive and creative cultural force in written history. It has eliminated ancient civilizations wherever it has encountered them, and displaced entire peoples from their homelands, but it has also spread an undreamed-of degree of

personal freedom and protected it with democratic institutions wherever it
has taken hold.

(Linklater 2015, p. 5)

However, if Linklater is correct, in addition to those benefits the process could be
claimed to have also engendered emergent wicked valuation problems with
destructive collateral effects. As his account can be read through McGilchrist's
framing as the dominance of the Master by the Emissary, such effects are to be
expected. These include those arising from both the interrelationship between
our inbuilt perceptual deficiencies as related to compound interest, and the
Western scholastics' interrogation of what is a just price.

I submit that one controversial area where that perception is relevant and
involves "just price" is climate change. While it is but one of a suite of global-scale
wicked problems, addressing climate change is arguably the main wicked problem
of our time, with simple answers sometimes being provided by classical and
neoliberal economists, and sometimes being ignored. Ignoring is understandable
as their trainings are generally in the simple to complicated domains, not the
complex, and certainly not the real world of wicked problems.

At the global policy scale, one economist who sticks to the simple aspect of the
economic growth compared to rates of return to capital, is Thomas Piketty, in his
review of modern economic history and the recommendations to be drawn from
it (Piketty 2014). However, in so doing it ignores the issue of the sustainability of
either of his framers, economic growth or rates of return on capital. Despite the
lack of natural resource capital valuation that Piketty laments, under HBA that
sustainability remains a factor emphatically *not* to be ignored in policy formulation,
including land policy formulation.

In that still broader context than Piketty addresses, another area that has
exemplified compound interest is that of human population growth, which
has contributed to the current situation concerning the environments of the
wicked valuation problems which this work addresses. Rockström et al. (2009)
reveal climate change as being one of a suite of nine global environmental
challenges shaping these wicked valuation problems, each one of which should
be considered in terms of their just price under HBA. As well as climate change,
the challenges include ocean acidification, stratospheric ozone depletion, the
phosphorous cycle component of biogeochemical flow, global freshwater use,
and change in land use. Those lacking sufficient data are atmospheric aerosol
loading and chemical pollution (Cribb 2014). The nitrogen cycle component of
biogeochemical flow and biodiversity loss go off the chart. Moreover, all of them
are interconnected (UNEP 2012, p. 5).

The often-overlooked importance of the produce hextant, particularly at the
scales of The Machine, was highlighted by Csikszentmihalyi as follows:

It goes without saying that one consequence of our evolution as cultural
beings has been an increasing dependence on objects for survival and comfort.
Compared with the hunter-gatherers, described by Marshall Sahlins, who

were horrified by the idea of having to accept gifts because it meant having to carry one more blanket or kettle along on their nomadic journeys, we are slowly being buried under towering mounds of artifacts . . . This proliferation of artifacts would not be a problem were it not for the fact that objects compete with humans for scarce resources in the same ecosystem. Forests are being destroyed to provide lumber, wood, and pulp; metals and oil are consumed to build and propel vehicles. The potential energy contained in our environment is dissipated as we convert it into objects, which rapidly become obsolete; thus we accelerate the processes of entropy that degrade the planet.

The survival of humankind depends on finding a modus vivendi not only with the physical world – viruses, bacteria, the animal kingdom, and one another – but also with the objects that we are incessantly producing.

(Csikszentmihalyi 1989, pp. 20–21)

Combine that with the global scale wicked problems concerning population growth and rural to urban migration, and the heterarchical field of HVN can begin to come into focus. In that field, we can see both the depredations of non-human holons by humans and the population growth of humans and their artefacts in the HVN. We can then begin to identify and appreciate the magnitude of the wicked problems to be addressed, towards embarking upon the necessary intrinsic, extrinsic and systemic value judgements to be made in the context of these wicked valuation problems. We can do that towards the examining of all dimensions of valuations, including but not limited to economic ones. For instance, the wicked problems may well include moral valuations.

Responding to Okoth-Ogendo's challenge with HVN↔HBA

As stated above, Okoth-Ogendo's challenge was to:

1   Design truly innovative tenure regimes to suit the variety of complex land use systems that characterise the African landscape.
2   Provide a framework within which customary land tenure and law can evolve in an orderly way.
3   Find ways to democratise land administration systems and structures.
4   Design a framework to codify customary tenure rules and integrate them into statutory law (Okoth-Ogendo 2000).

To which I added a fifth:

5   Provide a developmental template to facilitate the integration of real property rights into different fitness landscapes so as to increase their intrinsic value in not only economics, but also in all other factors in the fitness landscape.

It has been noted that:

> For any property regime to have reasonable stability and respect from members of society, it must be rooted in a pre-existing consensus on what is the guiding hierarchy of social values and what are the broader social objectives.
>
> (Zbierski-Salameh 2013, p. 62)

What does that have to say about what is to be done to address the challenge?

What if the inquiries themselves, after getting them as optimal as possible for the individual circumstances, provided better chances of our salvation than simplex minds' simple answers to wicked problems?

What if, before classifying our variables in wicked problems as dependent, independent, co-dependent, and constant, simple, complicated, complex, wicked etc. before promoting such assumptions from heuristics to ansatzes we subject them to HVN↔HBA developmental action inquiry?

For example, a variable constant can be a social imaginary measure of scale. We could package groups of existents into tens or dozens, but once we do that it gains its own inertia, becomes a constant, one of Dewey's habits that he stated we are "nothing but". Many heuristics are effectively such variables concretised into constants, but how systemically and extrinsically valuable are they as ansatzes in the context of Okoth-Ogendo's challenge?

As mentioned above, Markus saw the last 10,000 years of human history as regressive "in the sense of a continual decline of the quality of human life and a continual increase of anthropogenic problems" (Markus 2009). The West has put single vision and Newton's sleep up front: what other visions from anywhere can arrest and even reverse the decline in the quality of human life and the continual increase of anthropogenic problems within these five points?

What if we try responding to those challenges from William Blake's fourfold vision?

From the above, that means a transcending and including of knowledge and values that requires their differentiation, articulation and holarchic integration in addressing those challenges.

We need to attain Midgley's level of transdisciplinary competence to be defined as rigour; that is, we need to be able to distinguish mere heuristics from ansatzes, with experts, especially but not exclusively indigenous experts (because representation for all scales is required), being able to advise what can be considered a constant. Depending on the issues and circumstances, such experts can be either in house, or in peer-reviewed or similar authorities such as those whose experiences gained them *wisdom*, not mere knowledge, in their field. Even then, constants are mathematical, with varying degrees of application to reality, all being provisional from wildly unlikely to practical certainty.

Before the research I conducted for this work, both from my assuming as normal my own country's practices, and reading of and seeing the degraded state of much Swazi Nation Land, I had adopted the "naïve variable constant" heuristic assumption that part 2 of Okoth-Ogendo's challenge meant to evolve *towards freehold*. That is, I had subscribed to the "naïve theory of property rights" – that history's narrative is one of an inevitable climb up from undifferentiated commons to highly developed individuated property rights (Eggertsson 1990, p. 254).

Yet researchers have shown this heuristic to be not even supportable as an ansatz (Cole and Ostrom 2015, pp. 124–125). It is oblivious to failures on individuated tenure in terms of sustaining natural resources, and it ignores other quite effective property/regulatory arrangements. It is also touted as a panacea (ibid., p. 124), whereas its pedigree is predominantly one of imperialist enclosures privatising profits, commonising costs, and subjecting former commoners and their descendants to debt peonage and worse, in an enclosure and indebting process that has continued to snowball to this day (Hudson 2006; Klein 2010, p. 57–59).

While it began in the Lockean reductionist myopia/colonialist commons process described above (Greer 2012), currently in the West it is proceeding by dint of the "Western financial disease – a real estate bubble followed by defaults and foreclosures" (Hudson 2013).

These machine processes have high extrinsic value, both positive and negative, and while of no more intrinsic value than a mosquito they can facilitate the development of high intrinsic values as well. But so can commons – and more so, because their primary interfaces will be with holons, not artefacts.

So I see Okoth-Ogendo's challenges as location-specific. He was about building from what was there, evolutionary change, not inserting titles that can open the land rights up to predation by government taxes and banks.

Consequently, he was not looking for a recipe to apply throughout Africa any more than I am. I am looking for a valuation methodology that can be applied by starting with the challenges of a particular environment, because I have come to appreciate the insight that John Allen expresses as follows:

> It is the contextual grain of places, the interplay of their social, economic and cultural dynamics, which give forces their shape, not the other way around. On this view, because no existent is precontextual, there is no question of lifting things out of place. The use of power in practice is decidedly not about placing the exercise of power in context; rather the exercise of power comes 'with contexts attached', as Rorty would have it. It is not power, first, and then place 'added in' to see what difference it makes; power on this view is always already spatial.
>
> (Allen 2008, p. 1619)

From there, I want to see how addressing any wicked valuation problems may produce unique approaches well informed by locally co-evolved wisdom and compassion. I intend HVN↔HBA to facilitate that.

Chapter summary and the way forward

While they are strongly supported by the scholars cited, the above interpretations of landscapes are a far cry indeed from those I had originally held, before creating

HVN↔HBA. From all my experiences narrated in this chapter, a heterarchical approach is preconditional to addressing wicked valuation problems. In turn, that would involve assigning hierarchical responses to urgent challenges and complicated problem components, and holarchical responses to complex and wicked ones, including sustainable stratagems, all the while being alert to their relationships.

In so doing, via the discernments made apparent through an interhextal approach, we may when "thinging" is appropriate and when it is not. For this, mature competencies in intrinsic and systemic valuations as well as extrinsic ones are preconditional, but are missing in The Machine for reasons described by McGilchrist (2009).

This chapter looked at how to apply HVN↔HBA towards the subject of this work, testing the trans-ontological approach in my consultancies on an individual basis, and in the Solomon Islands with the intended beneficiaries. I directed attention to identity and its importance, to money, to interest, and to the flawed financial system. Finally, I looked back to the challenge of Okoth-Ogendo from where his challenge had led me.

My final chapter looks to an area where HVN↔HBA can be most rigorously tested. At present my optimal vessels to apply HVN↔HBA – trans-ontological teams – do not exist. The chapter tables my conclusions, and suggests a methodology for both researching and addressing wicked valuation problems. In the very nature of HVN↔HBA, all suggestions in this next chapter are subject to review by the trans-ontological teams I consider necessary to implement HVN↔HBA. When making their value judgements, I submit that such teams might benefit from the same avoidance of the "winner's curse" that other groups have evidenced, and gain results more like a just price than neoclassical economists could achieve in wicked valuation problem areas such as climate change.

7 Conclusions, the book's limitations and research suggestions

Conclusions

I embarked upon this work to see if my life experiences and challenges could be harnessed to address Okoth-Ogendo's challenges, and ended up discovering that to adequately address them required an even larger canvas than the one that Okoth-Ogendo had presented his challenge from, the vast continent of Africa.

This approach to these wicked valuation problems has been at pains to emphasise that exclusively reductionistic and positivistic approaches are utterly inadequate to that task. As the above-cited scholars have stressed, when it comes to these wicked valuation problems, simplex minds cannot cope, and simplex vocabularies are not up to the task either. I therefore conclude that trans-disciplinary communities of inquiry and practice, whether or not they are informed by the trans-disciplinary imagination, will not suffice to resolve NSEW wicked valuation problems as such.

Rather, I consider that liberated trans-ontological processes facilitating imaginative leaps – as recommended by Einstein, and Blake as his fourfold vision, and Brown, Harris and Russell's trans-disciplinary imagination – are required: not a mere institution, but a vibrant, dynamic, imaginative process. I have suggested HVN↔HBA would be robust in such contexts. That would require specifically endowed individuals, and such individuals' reflection and contemplation, delivering to communities of inquiry and practice to address the particular wicked valuation problem. Such communities should be able to differentiate between simple, complicated and complex, as in Table 1.1, have developed high levels of cognitive complexity as in Table 5.9, be able to make similarly complax value judgements, and be capable of collaborative developmental action inquiry through HVN↔HBA.

Such a process of transformative policy formulation and implementation was described over sixty years ago as comprising four stages: formulation, incarnation, incorporation and embodiment:

> Note that the first two stages mainly centre in the individual person; they represent the introversion of interest that leads to an exploration of modes of self-development not offered by any existing society. At this moment the self, by detachment, seeks to tap its deepest sources of creativity, and by that

very fact must work mainly alone: this is the phase to which Toynbee has given the name etherialisation. But the final stages reverse this process and change its field: the inner forces turn outward and centre on the community; incorporation and embodiment seek to confirm the personal effort through the reformation of society. In axial religion materialisation, as I call this stage, is an effort to find a social method to carry on the process of self-transformation, when the first prophetic illumination has dimmed, and the singular point has passed.

(Mumford 1956, p. 72)

Earlier still, Mumford had referred to those who had achieved competencies in that transformation process as *trans-valuers*, people capable of bringing forth:

[N]ew forms and values that point to new destinations . . . a world of fine perceptions and rich feeling, of values that sustain life and coherent forms that re-enforce the sense of human mastery.

(Mumford 1954, p. 163)

Insofar as they can transcend and include all other values that may shape values, including market values, I claim that teams of such trans-valuers are the optimal persons to address wicked valuation problems. I further claim that, while valuation courses provide no such competencies, long experience in many complex domains may. To be fit for purpose in this context, the trans-ontological approach must not only transcend *and include* machinism (the machine side, HBA, dancing with the holarchy, HVN – the Tao that cannot be known – rather like someone "with two left feet" trying to keep up with a champion dancer). It must also include and transcend trans-disciplinary communities of inquiry and practice, and be capable of valuing them all. For example, machinism may be highly valued for its great extrinsic value and devalued for its low intrinsic value, and trans-disciplinary communities of inquiry and practice may be valued for their great intrinsic value, but devalued for their often low extrinsic value. Such communities may not have the funding and other extrinsically valuable means of implementing their recommendations. As Mumford again put it:

In the development of the human character we have reached a point similar to that which we have attained in technics itself: the point at which we utilize the completest developments in science and technics to approach once more the organic. But here again: our capacity to go beyond the machine rests upon our power to assimilate the machine. Until we have absorbed the lessons of objectivity, impersonality, neutrality, the lessons of the mechanical realm, we cannot go further in our development toward the more richly organic, the more profoundly human.

(Mumford 1934, p. 363)

In so doing, however, he advised that the watchwords are to be "stability, not expansion: human culture, not simply mechanical progress. That imposes a new scale of values. Our too masculine, too mechanical, too life-denying society has come to its terminus. Perhaps the best slogan for the coming age is that for the lifeboats: women and children first" (Mumford 1946, p. 164).

In our incalculably complex and complax world, there will always be new ecological niches, new fitness landscapes, and it is in finding and researching the latter while intrinsically valuing and embracing the former where the sustainability of our species will succeed or fail. It will rise or fall on the degree of success in enfolding such values beyond the merely extrinsic, which requires moving beyond single vision as articulated by McGilchrist and more: not just better integrated hemispheres as he describes, but better integrated holons and their communities making better integrated value judgements opening us to the facts we perceive and the decisions we make, including those about our imaginary real property rights. In one's machine-mind's denial of intrinsic value in creation, one necessarily denies any intrinsic values to oneself, and is thereby endangered of spending one's life in pursuit of the trivial, and one can never get enough of what one doesn't really need. There is a natural limit to food hunger, but there is no natural limit to the junk food of power used to fill the black hole of regard hunger. However, by opening to perceptions of intrinsic values, such fitness landscapes may be discovered, as others have been. They have been discovered by creative interplays of our knowledges, our values, heuristics and our necessarily extensive vocabularies generating new spatial imaginaries uncovering fresh ecological niches.

We cannot in principle know every existent, and we can only deal with very few matters at one time. Even trying to reduce all unconscious information to conscious systems notation is a sure formula for an even bigger unconsciously generated disaster, because to break the pattern which connects is necessarily to destroy quality. HVN↔HBA recognises that we don't have omniplex minds, and as a heuristic one would expect a fairly typical bell curve distribution of complex and complax minds.

Bright lights cast dark shadows, and successful foci on extrinsic values in personal domains, including real property, has put intrinsic and systemic values into those dark shadows: hence again, much of humanity, and presumably any one person, being too blind, deaf and dumb in those domains for competent and comprehensive valuations. Hence the need for networks of care of the suitably depthed particular to the wicked problem having to be addressed, and with communicative capacities to rigorously convey what they have to say and understand what others have to say. As mentioned in Chapter 1, "when you lack words, you shut down new insights and lines of reasoning" (Passuello 2007), so development of a differentiated, articulated and hierarchically integrated vocabulary in those domains could catalyse their co-evolution. Despite its mechanistic structure, English is a dynamic language with a voracious vocabulary. Therefore, this co-evolution might be facilitated interhextally in English using HBA's principles. For example, it could be facilitated by borrowings from languages more advanced in intrinsic and systemic valuations. It could also be facilitated by the co-evolution not only of formal values juries but also by other possible means of focussing on intrinsic and systemic values. Thereby, the dumbing down in those valuation domains could be reversed and, as with the emergence of the word "telaxiology" for me, new realms of reality, "previously ignored or at best restricted to other domains", may be opened up to further research.

It will never be a time to forever dismiss single vision and become altogether blind, or to never again fall into Newton's sleep. We need the single vision maps, including their mental maps, but we need to be far more awake and aware than when we narrow our vision to produce them.

There will never be a time not to wake up to multiperspectivity and telaxiology, and recognise and reintegrate the poetic imagination as our driver towards a better world. There will times for sleep, for single vision, and times for wakefulness, and we need both to address wicked valuation problems. We should research towards both ourselves and our landscapes no longer being run over by The Machine, but having The Machine as servant of our nurturing the co-evolution of wisdom and compassion in ourselves and all other sentient creatures. There will never be a time not to continue our pilgrimage towards our optimal addressing of wicked valuation problems.

A suggested methodology for both researching and addressing wicked valuation problems

In Box 6.1, I referred to value juries and "Big V" and "small v" valuations, and the possible use of value juries in appropriate contexts. Within my own discipline of market – "small v" – valuation, one way to research that relates to the discarded motto of the Commonwealth Institute of Valuers, which I was admitted to in 1974: it was "broad vision and balanced judgement", and I suggest a motto for addressing wicked valuation problems is "broad *and deep* vision and balanced judgement". McGilchrist observes that:

> Depth, as opposed to distance from a surface, never implies detachment. Depth brings us into a relationship, whatever the distance involved, with the other, and allows us to 'feel across' the intervening space. It situates us in the same world as the other.
>
> (McGilchrist 2009, p. 183)

Recognising, as behavioural economics now does, that emotions play a pivotal role in market behaviour, and that they therefore must be enfolded into the reading of markets, this opens up whole new worlds of research opportunities in the domain of valuers, those of the influence of "Big V" values when reading markets. This is another area where Whittal and Barry's application of Kotter's theories of change management may be applied in a valuation context, for willing buyers and willing sellers are both open to change, and Kotter and Cohen noted that:

> Changing behavior is less a matter of giving people analysis to influence their thoughts than helping them to see a truth to influence their feelings. Both thinking and feeling are essential, and both are found in successful

organizations, but the heart of change is in the emotions. The flow of see-feel-change is more powerful than analysis-think-change. These distinctions between seeing and analysis, between feeling and thinking, are critical because, for the most part, we use the latter much more frequently, competently, and comfortably than the former.

(Kotter and Cohen 2002, p. 2)

Motives, feelings and values are "three sides of the same coin . . . Motivations prime actions, values serve to choose between motivations, emotions provide a common currency for values, and emotions implement motivations" (Franklin and Ramamurthy 2006), and I submit that to ignore the influence of such processes in markets is unprofessional. Valuers must learn what makes participants willing, to assess if they can be considered prudent in terms of the standards of that market. For instance, are the participants in the market mainly composed of simplex, complex or multiplex minds, not simply in terms of cognitive complexities, but also in telaxic complexities, and what are their coevolutions from the simplex and simplax through compliplex and compliplax, complex and complax, and multiplex and multiplaxplax levels? Multiplax levels such as Scheler and others have mapped are particularly important in acquiring intercultural and trans-cultural competencies, an increasingly important research field in multicultural countries such as Australia. What would such valuers see that others miss, and what would be the implications in terms of the definition of market value in particular, and the market in general?

Such questions may require value juries to answer, and they might need to include people from communities of the similarly depthed, that depth being best suited to the matter of concern in the relevant domains, dimensions, lines, levels and scales. That would require further research by those appropriately depthed for such an inquiry, and there would be many challenges to face in their implementation. For example, "the tragedy of the anticommons" – when all can speak for nature, no-one can – (Fourcade 2011, p. 1750) would have to be addressed in the institutional framing for such juries. Moreover, addressing wicked problems must be "developed jointly by all the interests involved. The extent to which this process differs from the usual approach to Western decision-making cannot be overestimated" (Brown in Brown, Harris and Russell 2010, p. 77). We can anticipate resistance from those comfortably invested in Newton's sleep.

From my lived experience, extrinsic, intrinsic and systemic valuations are all determinants of market values in many contexts, with different weighings in different contexts. An example from the produce hextant is that art is often valued in terms of its communication of intrinsic value. In art intrinsic value may feature more than most domains, but expressors of such intrinsic values are also prevalent in most real property markets whether visible or not.

As regards institutionalising value juries schooled in HVN↔HBA to address "Big V" wicked valuation problems, such an approach would not be a silver bullet, but there are few silver bullets in complex domains. However, HVN↔HBA-conversant value juries, or other communities of inquiry or practice of form, function and design fit for the specific purpose, could provide better direction than either any reductionist or elevationist approaches. Because quality is being destroyed by such single vision reductionist/elevationist machine minds within humanity at massive scales, life as a whole is losing that battle, and HVN↔HBA-conversant small groups could help life's chances.

Recent research has demonstrated that "decision accuracy in complex environments is often maximized by small group sizes . . . across many contexts" (Kao and Couzin 2014). By using HVN↔HBA in such communities of inquiry and practice, a combination of Bruno Latour's (2013) and Whittal and Barry's (2005) could be very useful in uncovering the limitations of HVN↔HBA, and opening new worlds of research beyond those generated by HVN↔HBA itself. However, Whittal and Barry's approach is predicated upon achieving a predetermined desired outcome, and may be thereby less expansive than is HVN↔HBA, which is relevant in the policy formulation process as well as its implementation. As such, HVN↔HBA requires a continued dynamic to reform policies when they are seen not to work, when the costs outweigh the benefits, as distinct from a steamrolling machine-like policy implementation which occurs in many domains. For example, Kotter's approach has been criticised on the basis of forcing those subject to the process as becoming "objects of change, futile pawns" (O'Keefe 2011) – that is, of being steamrollered by The Machine.

While I have no problem with Whittal's thesis (her references to Dolny and other observations show awareness of that weakness in Kotter's system), I do have problems with Fenollosa's mechanical or savage minds, McGilchrist's Emissaries, and those in Newton's sleep being in control of The Machine. HVN↔HBA is concerned with recognising, monitoring, evaluating and performing "Big V" valuations upon the directions in which The Machine is taking us as well as the "small v" market values that form much of my professional background. In so doing, a particular danger is the emergence of the "Right Man" (Wilson) or dominator (Eisler) in this change management milieu.

Whichever "side" they emerge from in the wicked valuation problems, they are reliable generators of the wicked valuation problems this book addresses. By definition, they would relish employing dominator strategies, such as "manufacturing crises" (Whittal and Barry 2005, p. 10), "removing troublesome supervisors" (ibid., p. 11), "forcing collaboration" (ibid., p. 11), getting so-called "independent experts" to direct compliance with the will of the changers and so on (ibid., p. 12) while remaining silent on right brain intrinsic values as described by McGilchrist and Scheler. These are classic left brain strategies of "not thy will, but mine, be done, and will be done because I am at the controls of The Machine: Landscapes be damned, the end justifies the means!"

No, the means must be worthy of the end, and for that small groups of those balanced individuals who are able to pay due regard to intrinsic and systemic values and the other existents addressed in HVN↔HBA, are most likely to be optimal. They are to be equipped with Blake's fourfold vision as described by Palmer:

> Fourfold vision: . . . Nested, not separate domains . . . The delight of experiencing single, twofold and threefold vision, with constant twofold visioning

in daily life. This might be thought of as an aesthetic, systemic way of thinking, with the facility to shift between linear thinking, relational thinking
and intuition . . . It is within this evolving, ever-shifting fourfold vision that
'sparkling moments' or the emergence of deep connection and empathy can
occur, along with an appreciation of the wider connections that hints at a
greater unity; that which Bateson considered to be the sacred.

(Palmer 2014, pp. 13–14)[1]

This is only a description. Especially, it is not a recipe for simplex/simplax minds
to ape. Blake considered that to be a genuine expression of oneself, which he
mythically personified as Albion, it requires states of mind well beyond single
vision. That is, I see Palmer's interpretation of fourfold vision as part and personal
parcel of what I describe as HVN. As mentioned above, Blake saw Satan as a state
of mind, and therefore likely saw other mythic emanations of his imagination
as personifications of different mental states. Furthermore, he saw the insights
gained from this approach as providing a means of moving beyond single vision,
ultimately to fourfold. That is, myths such as those he created only gain their
potency in the contexts of personifying or otherwise expressing states of mind
in his readers, engaging our integration into the ever-present origin, the Tao
that cannot be known. When they are so engaged, not literalised but as portals
to McGilchrist's right hemisphere understanding, not dissociated from but
co-evolving with critical inquiry, then one is on the path of Blake's sweet science
towards the fourfold vision Palmer describes. And the finding is emergent
from the very process of seeking, not in any so-called "thing" sought: in the very
questioning answers lie hid.

I therefore consider Palmer's interpretation of fourfold vision to be a path along
ever-broader envisionings, ever-deeper understandings, and ever-higher values
towards optimally addressing our wicked valuation problems. By all means doubt
that small groups of those with fourfold vision can best address wicked valuation
problems, but then doubt even more the dominators under the spell of the myth
of the machine who claim it is they who can. The former are intrinsically valuable
for the purpose, and the latter, insofar as they are wrapped and rapt within single
vision and Newton's sleep, are not.

Note

1 Palmer's descriptions of Blake's earlier visions include the following. Single vision:
"Newton's sleep", characterised by atomistic, reductionist thinking. It is to focus on
linear cause and effect, on rational knowledge and on what is material and physical.
Twofold vision: this vision is concerned with appreciating our connection with nature
and the environment. Here, Blake includes the observer within the observed. Threefold
vision: "Beulah's night", our awareness of unconscious processes, memory and intuition.
Blake incorporates the imagination and creativity of the observer within threefold
vision (Palmer 2014, pp. 13–14).

Bibliography

Abaris, N. and Sjonoce, F. 2014. Investors and Valuers: Similarities and Differences from a Behavioral Perspective. Master of Science dissertation, School of Real Estate and Construction Management, KTH Royal Institute of Technology, Stockholm, Sweden.

ABC RN. 2015a. Valuing Our Planet. In P. Barclay (ed.), *Big Ideas*. Sydney: Australian Broadcasting Corporation.

ABC RN. 2015b. Shaping Democracy for the People. In J. Green (ed.), *Sunday Extra*. Sydney: Australian Broadcasting Corporation.

Abraham, R. H. 1993. Human Fractals: The Arabesque in Our Mind. *Visual Anthropology Review* 9: 52–55.

Abrahamian, E. 1989. *Radical Islam: The Iranian Mojahedin*. London: I. B. Taurus.

Abrams, D. 1992. Processes of Social Identification. In G. M. Breakwell (ed.), *The Social Psychology of Identity and Self Concept. Surrey Seminars in Social Psychology*. Guildford: Academic Press/Surrey University Press.

ABS. 2013. What are Data Cubes? Retrieved from www.abs.gov.au/AUSSTATS/abs@.nsf/befa3cd44e04e196ca25698a002187b2/e5a1ddfa110aa02dca2575d60023ac6c!OpenDocument.

Adams, M. 2015. *Land: A New Paradigm for a Thriving World*. Berkeley, CA: North Atlantic Books.

Adonga, M., Ibreck, R. and Bulla, G. V. 2015. Preventing Land Dispossession in Africa: Do We Need Stronger Justice Mechanisms. Retrieved from http://blogs.lse.ac.uk/jsrp/2015/06/09/preventing-land-dispossession-in-africa-do-we-need-stronger-justice-mechanisms (accessed 27 June 2015).

Agamben, G. 2004. *The Open: Man and Animal*. Stanford, CA: Stanford University Press.

Akerlof, G. and Shiller, R. J. 2009. *Animal Spirits*. Princeton, NJ: Princeton University Press.

Alden Wily, L. 2000. *Democratising the Commonage: The Changing Legal Framework for Natural Resource Management in Eastern & Southern Africa with Particular Reference to Forests*. 2nd CASS/PLAAS Regional Meeting. Cape Town: University of the Western Cape.

Alden Wily, L. 2003. Land Rights in Crisis: Restoring Tenure Security in Afghanistan. Afghanistan Research and Evaluation Unit Retrieved from http://reliefweb.int/report/afghanistan/land-rights-crisis-restoring-tenure-security-afghanistan (accessed 22 May 2016).

Aldwin, C. M. 2015. How Can Developmental Systems Theories Cope With Free Will? The Importance of Stress-Related Growth and Mindfulness. *Research in Human Development* 12: 189–195.

Alexander, C., Ishikawa, S. and Silverstein, M. 1977. *A Pattern Language: Towns, Buildings, Construction*. Oxford: Oxford University Press.

Allahverdyan, A. E. and Galstyan, A. 2014. Opinion Dynamics with Confirmation Bias. ARXIV arXiv:1411.4328 18.

Allen, B., Stacey, B. C. and Bar-Yam, Y. 2014. An Information-Theoretic Formalism for Multiscale Structure in Complex Systems. Retrieved from http://arxiv.org/abs/1409.4708 (accessed 30 September 2014).

Allen, J. 2008. Pragmatism and Power, or the Power to Make a Difference in a Radically Contingent World. *Geoforum* 39: 1613–1624.

Allen, R. C. 1982. The Efficiency and Distributional Consequences of Eighteenth Century Enclosures. *The Economic Journal* 92: 937–953.

Allen, R. C. 1992. *Enclosure and the Yeoman*. Oxford: Clarendon Press.

Allen, T. H. and Hoekstra, T. W. 2015. *Toward a Unified Ecology*. New York: Columbia University Press.

Allen, W. 2013. Complicated or Complex – Knowing the Difference is Important. Retrieved from http://learningforsustainability.net/sparksforchange/complicated-or-complex-knowing-the-difference-is-important-for-the-management-of-adaptive-systems (accessed 18 July 2014).

Allison, H. E. and Hobbs, R. J. 2012. *Science and Policy in Natural Resource Management*. Cambridge: Cambridge University Press.

Ananthaswamy, A. 2015. *The Man Who Wasn't There: Investigations Into the Strange New Science of the Self*. New York: Dutton.

Anderson, D. G. 2010. "Sweet Science": A Proposal for Integral Macropolitics. *Integral Review* 6: 10–62.

Anderson, E. 2014. Dewey's Moral Philosophy. In E. N. Zalta (ed.), *The Stanford Encyclopedia of Philosophy*. Spring 2014 Edition. Stanford, CA: Stanford University Press.

Anderson, P. W. 1972. More is Different. *Science* (new series) 177: 393–396.

Anderson, R. A. and McDaniel, R. R. 2000. Managing Healthcare Organizations: Where Professionalism Meets Complexity Science. *Health Care Management Review* 25: 83–92.

Andrews, M. 1981. Hohfeld's Cube. *Akron Law Review* 16: 417–433.

Andrews, M. 2001. *Claims Analysis: Law, Logic, and Risk*. Bloomington, IN: Xlibris.

Antal, E. 2013. William Blake's Theory of Spiritual Vision: "The Imagination is not a State: it is the Human Existence Itself." In F. K. Wohrer and J. S. Bak (eds), *British Literature and Spirituality*. Vienna: Lit Verlag.

Apel, K. O. 2001. *The Response of Discourse Ethics to the Moral Challenge of the Human Situation as Such and Especially Today: Mercier Lectures, Louvain-la-Neuve, March 1999*. Leuven: Peeters Publishers.

Apollinaire, G. 1995. *Calligrammes*. Paris: Éditions Gallimard.

Arce, I. G. 2012. Residential Mobility and Housing Tenure in Spain: A Panel Data Approach. *Papeles de trabajo del Instituto de Estudios Fiscales. Serie economía* 11: 3–29.

Archer, M. S. 2014. *"We Believe" – But Who are "We"? The Relational Subject versus the Plural Subject*. Lexington, KY: Committee on Social Theory, University of Kentucky.

Ardrey, R. 1972. *The Territorial Imperative: A Personal Inquiry into the Animal Origins of Property and Nations*. London: Collins.

Armitage, D. 2011. Probing the Foundations of Tully's Public Philosophy. *Political Theory* 39: 124–130.

Armour, P. 2006. The Learning Edge. *Communication of the ACM* 49: 20–23.

Armstrong, K. 1993. *A History of God*. New York: Ballantine Books.

Arnold, C. A. 2002. The Reconstitution of Property: Property as a Web of Interests. *Harvard Environmental Law Review* 26: 281–364.

Arnold, C. A. T., 2011. Sustainable Webs of Interests: Property in an Interconnected Environment. In D. Grinlinton and P. Taylor (eds), *Property Rights and Sustainability: The Evolution of Property Rights to Meet Ecological Challenges*. Boston, MA: Martinus Nijhoff.

Arnold, M. 1916. Eutrapelia. In H. Craik (ed.), *English Prose*. New York: Bartleby.com.

Arnott, R. J. and Stiglitz, J. E. 1979. Aggregate Land Rents, Expenditure on Public Goods, and Optimal City Size. *Quarterly Journal of Economics* 93: 471–500.

Arrendondo, C. B. 2013. Republic and Empire: America's Ambiguous Legacy of Enlightenment. *Crisis and Critica* 2: 66. Retrieved from http://cvisaacs.univalle.edu. co/crisisycritica/index.php?option=com_content&view=article&id=25:republic-and-empire-america-s-ambiguous-legacy-of-enlightenment&catid=22:esclarecimiento-e-imperialismo&limitstart=0 (accessed 16 March 2018).

Arthur, W. B. 1994. Inductive Reasoning and Bounded Rationality. *American Economic Review* 84(2): 406–411.

Arthur, B. 2013. *Complexity and the Economy*. Oxford: Oxford University Press.

Arthur, B. 2014. *Economic Complexity: A Different Way to Look at the Economy*. Santa Fe, NM: Santa Fe Institute. Retrieved from https://medium.com/sfi-30-foundations-frontiers/economic-complexity-a-different-way-to-look-at-the-economy-eae5fa2341cd (accessed 8 December 2014).

Ashby, W. R. 1956. *An Introduction to Cybernetics*. London: Chapman & Hall. Online version retrieved from http://pcp.vub.ac.be/books/IntroCyb.pdf (accessed 16 March 2018).

Badham, J. 2010. A Compendium of Modelling Techniques. Retrieved from http://is.anu. edu.au/sites/default/files/resources/integration-insight_12.pdf.

Bakker, R. S. 2015. "These are THE questions of our time, I think. . . ." Comment posted below article by S. C. Hickman, retrieved from https://socialecologies.wordpress.com/ 2015/08/05/cognitive-ecology-the-hard-wiring-of-humannatural-systems (accessed 28 March 2018).

Baldwin, M. W. 2011. Who I Am Is Who I Was: Exploring the Identity-Maintenance Function of Nostalgia. Master of Arts dissertation, University of Kansas, Lawrence, KS.

Balke, T. and Gilbert, N. 2014. How Do Agents Make Decisions? A Survey. *Journal of Artificial Societies and Social Simulation* 17: 13.

Ball, M. W. 2002. "People Speaking Silently to Themselves": An Examination of Keith Basso's Philosophical Speculations on "Sense of Place" in Apache Cultures. *The American Indian Quarterly* 26: 460–478.

Bammer, G. and Deane, P. 2012. Featured Course: Model Thinking. Retrieved from i2s. anu.edu.au/sites/default/files/i2s-news/i2s-news_4.pdf.

Bammer, G. 2013. *Disciplining Interdisciplinarity: Integration and Implementation Sciences for Researching Complex Real-World Problems*. Canberra: Australian National University. Retrieved from http://press-files.anu.edu.au/downloads/press/p222171/pdf/book.pdf? referer=179 (accessed 27 August 2016).

Bandyopādhyāÿa, S. 2004. *From Plassey to Partition: A History of Modern India*. Hyderabad: Orient Longman.

Barbour, P. 1999. *The End of Time: The Next Revolution in Our Understanding of the Universe*. London: Phoenix.

Barnesmoore, L. R. 2017. *Hierarchical Idealism and Lewis Mumford: Building Utopia on the Banks of the River Styx*. Vancouver: University of British Columbia.

Barnett, S. A. 2000. *Science: Myth or Magic?* St Leonards, NSW: Allen & Unwin.

Barrett, L., Pollet, T. V. and Stulp, G. 2014. From Computers to Cultivation: Reconceptualizing Evolutionary Psychology. *Frontiers in Psychology* 5: 14.

Barry, M., Molero, R. and Muhsen, A.-R. 2013. Evolutionary Land Tenure Information System Development: The Talking Titler Methodology. Retrieved from http://fig. net/resources/monthly_articles/2013/barry_etal_february_2013.asp (accessed 23 February 2013).

Barume, A. K. 2014. *Land Rights of Indigenous Peoples in Africa: with special focus on Central, Eastern and Southern Africa.* Copenhagen: IWGIA.

Bar-Yam, Y. 2005. Making Things Work. Retrieved from http://necsi.org/cxworld/ development.html (accessed 20 September 2007).

Basso, K. H. 1996. *Wisdom Sits in Places: Landscape and Language Among the Western Apache.* Santa Fe, NM: University of New Mexico Press.

Bastardas-Boada, A. 2015. Toward "Complexics" as a Transdiscipline. Retrieved from www.academia.edu/11118078/Toward_Complexics_as_a_Transdiscipline (accessed 27 February 2018).

Bateson, G. 1979. *Mind and Nature: a Necessary Unity.* Toronto: Bantam Books.

Bateson, G. 1987. *Steps to an Ecology of Mind,* Northvale, NJ: Jason Aronson.

Bateson, N. 2017. Liminal Leadership. *Kosmos Journal.* Retrieved from www.kosmosjournal. org/article/liminal-leadership (accessed 27 December 2017).

Bateson, P. A. and Laland, K. N. 2013. Tinbergen's Four Questions: an Appreciation and an Update. *Trends in Ecology and Evolution* 28: 712–718.

Batty, M. 2009. Cities as Complex Systems: Scaling, Interactions, Networks, Dynamics and Urban Morphologies. *The Encyclopedia of Complexity and Systems Science.* Berlin: Springer.

Batty, M. 2013. *The New Science of Cities,* Cambridge, MA: MIT Press.

Baudrillard, J. 1993. *The Transparency of Evil: Essays on Extreme Phenomena.* London: Verso.

Beck, D. and Cowan, C. 1996. *Spiral Dynamics: Mastering Values, Leadership and Change.* Cambridge, MA: Blackwell.

Beck, D. and Linscott, G. 1991. *The Crucible: Forging South Africa's Future.* Johannesburg: New Paradigm Press.

Beer, J. B. 1969. *Blake's Visionary Universe.* Manchester: Manchester University Press.

Beever, J. and Morar, N. 2016. The Porosity of Autonomy: Social And Biological Constitution of the Patient in Biomedicine. *The American Journal of Bioethics* 16(2): 34–45.

Bellah, R. N. 1991. *The Good Society.* New York: Alfred A. Knopf.

Berberich, C., Campbell, N. and Hudson, R. 2012. *Land and Identity Theory, Memory, and Practice.* Amsterdam: Editions Rodopi.

Berkley Center. n.d. *Samsara (Hinduism).* Washington, DC: Berkley Center for Religion, Peace and World Affairs. Retrieved from http://berkleycenter.georgetown.edu/essays/ samsara-hinduism (accessed 16 June 2015).

Beyer, C. 2015. Meaning, Context, and Background. In T. Metzinger and J. M. Windt (eds), *Open MIND.* Frankfurt am Main: MIND Group.

Beyer, S. 1978. *Magic and Ritual in Tibet: The Cult of Tārā.* Berkeley, CA: University of California Press.

Bureau of Infrastructure, Transport and Regional Economics. 2015. *International Trade and Cities: What House Prices Say.* Canberra: Australian Government Department of Infrastructure and Regional Development.

Blackmore, S. 1993. *Dying to Live*. London: Grafton.

Blackmore, S. 1999. *The Meme Machine*. Oxford: Oxford University Press.

Blackstone, W. 2001. *Blackstone's Commentaries on the Laws of England*. London: Routledge-Cavendish.

Blake, W. 1788. *There is No Natural Religion*. Glyndwr: North East Wales Institute. Retrieved from www.glyndwr.ac.uk/rdover/blake/there_is.htm.

Blake, W. 1904. *The Prophetic Books of William Blake: Jerusalem*. London: A. H. Bullen.

Blake, W. 1988. *William Blake: Selected Poetry*. London: Penguin.

Blasi, A. and Glodis, K. 1995. The Development of Identity. A Critical Analysis from the Perspective of the Self as Subject. *Developmental Review* 15: 404–433.

Blomley, N., Braverman, I., Delaney, D. and Kedar, A. 2014. *The Expanding Spaces of Law: A Timely Legal Geography*. Stanford, CA: Stanford Law Books.

Bloom, H. 1971. *The Visionary Company: A Reading of English Romantic Poetry*. Ithaca, NY: Cornell University Press.

Blum, W. 2004. *Killing Hope: US Military and CIA Interventions Since World War II*. London: Zed Books.

Bogin, B. and Quintman, A. 2014. *Himalayan Passages: Tibetan and Newar Studies in Honor of Hubert Decleer*. Studies in Indian and Tibetan Buddhism. Somerville, MA: Wisdom Publications.

Bohannan, P. 1973. "Land", "Tenure" and Land Tenure. Retrieved from http://pdf.usaid.gov/pdf_docs/PNABI322.pdf (accessed 6 June 2016).

Bohm, D. J. and Hiley, B. J. 1975. On the Intuitive Understanding of Nonlocality as Implied by Quantum Theory. *Foundations of Physics* 5: 93–109.

Boltanski, L. and Thévenot, L. 2006. *On Justification: Economies of Worth*. Princeton, NJ: Princeton University Press.

Bolte Taylor, J. 2008. Jill Bolte Taylor's Stroke of Insight. Retrieved from www.ted.com/talks/jill_bolte_taylor_s_powerful_stroke_of_insight?language=en (accessed March 2016).

Borges, R. 2004. The Phi Code in Nature, Architecture and Engineering. In *Design and Nature II*, 401–409. Southampton: WIT Press.

Borgmann, A. 1987. *Technology and the Character of Contemporary Life: A Philosophical Inquiry*. Chicago, IL: University of Chicago Press.

Bourdieu, P. 1984. *Distinction: A Social Critique of the Judgment of Taste*. Cambridge, MA: Harvard University Press.

Box, G. E. P. and Draper, N. R. 1987. *Empirical Model Building and Response Surfaces*. New York: John Wiley & Sons.

Boydell, S. 2007. Building Valuation Capacity for Sustainable South Pacific Communities. In E. D. B. Waldy (ed.), *Building Sustainable Communities in the Commonwealth – CASLE stream of the 9th South East Asian Survey Congress (SEASC 2007)*. Christchurch, NZ: Commonwealth Association of Surveying and Land Economy (CASLE).

Boydell, S. 2007a. Disillusion, Dilemma, and Direction: The Role of the University in Property Research. *Pacific Rim Property Research Journal* 13: 146–161.

Boydell, S., Sheehan, J. and Prior, J. 2009a. Carbon Property Rights in Context. *Cambridge Journal of Environmental Practice* 11: 105–114.

Boydell S., Sheehan, J., Prior, J. and Hendy, S. 2009. Carbon Property Rights, Cities and Climate Change. Paper presented at Cities and Climate Change: Responding to an Urgent Agenda, World Bank Fifth Urban Research Symposium, Marseille, France.

Brady, V. 2007. What are Writers for in a Destitute Time? Judith Wright and the Search for Australia. *Global-Local* 3: 12–18.

Brand, S. 2013. Fitness Landscapes. In J. Brockman (ed.), *This Explains Everything*. New York: Harper Perennial.

Breakwell, G. M. 1992. Processes of Self-Evaluation: Efficiency and Estrangement. In G. M. Breakwell (ed.), *Social Psychology of Identity and the Self Concept*. Guildford: Surrey University Press.

Brewer, M. B. and Gardner, W. 1996. Who is this "We"? Levels of Collective Identity and Self Representations. *Journal of Personality and Social Psychology* 71: 11.

Britt, H. 2013. Complexity Aware Monitoring. Retrieved from http://usaidlearninglab. org/library/complexity-aware-monitoring-discussion-note-brief (accessed 4 September 2014).

Brockman, J. 2013. *This Explains Everything*. New York: Harper Perennial.

Bromley, D. W. 2006. *Sufficient Reason: Volitional Pragmatism and the Meaning of Economic Institutions*. Princeton, NJ: Princeton University Press.

Bromley, D. W. 2008. Resource Degradation in the African Commons: Accounting for Institutional Decay. *Environmental and Developmental Economics* 13: 539–563.

Bromley, D. W. 2008a. Formalising Property Relations in the Developing World: The Wrong Prescription for the Wrong Malady. *Land Use Policy* 26: 20–27.

Bromley, D. W. 2008b. Beyond Market Failure: Volitional Pragmatism as a New Theory of Public Policy. *Economia Politica* 25(2): 219–241.

Bromley, D. W. and Yao, Y. 2006. *Understanding Institutional Change: Modeling China's Economic Transformation since 1978*. Washington, DC: International Food Policy Research Institute.

Brook, T. and Wakabayashi, B. T. 2000. *Opium Regimes: China, Britain, and Japan, 1839–1952*. Berkeley, CA: University of California Press.

Brooks, D. 2015. *The Road to Character*. New York: Random House.

Brown, E. H. 2007. *Web of Debt: The Shocking Truth about Our Money System and How We Can Break Free*. Chippenham: Third Millennium Press.

Brown, T. C., Peterson, G. L. and Tonn, B. E. 1995. The Values Jury to Aid Natural Resource Decisions. *Land Economics* 71: 250–260.

Brown, V. A., Harris, J. and Russell, J. 2010. *Tackling Wicked Problems Through the Transdisciplinary Imagination*. London: Earthscan from Routledge.

Bruce, J. W. 1987. *Land Tenure Reform and Agricultural Development in Africa – A Review of Recent Experience*. Madison, WI: Land Tenure Center, University of Wisconsin-Madison.

Bruce, J. W. 1998. *Country Profiles of Land Tenure: Africa, 1996*. Research Paper no. 130. Madison, WI: Land Tenure Center, University of Wisconsin.

Bruce, J. W. 2012. Simple Solutions to Complex Problems: Land Formalization as a "Silver Bullet". In J. M. Otto and A. J. Hoekema (eds), *Fair Land Governance*. Leiden: Leiden University Press.

Bryant, B. 2003. *The Wheel of Time Sand Mandala: Visual Scripture of Tibetan Buddhism*. Ithaca, NY: Snow Lion Publications.

Burke, D. 2014. Why Isn't Everyone an Evolutionary Psychologist? *Frontiers in Psychology* 5: 8.

Buruma, I. 2004. The Origins of Occidentalism. *The Chronicle of Higher Education* 50(22): B10. Retrieved from http://jrichardstevens.com/articles/Buruma-occidentalism.pdf (accessed 16 March 2018).

Butt, I. 1866. *Land Tenure in Ireland; a Plea for the Celtic Race*. Dublin: John Falconer.

Byrnes, G. 2012. *The Myths We Live By: Reframing History for the 21st Century*. Retrieved from www.cdu.edu.au/sites/default/files/gb.pdf.

Cahill, K. 2007. *Who Owns the World: The Hidden Facts behind Landownership.* Edinburgh: Mainstream Publishing.

Callaway, J. A. 2001. *Jean Piaget: A Most Outrageous Deception.* New York: Nova Science Publishers.

Calloway, C. n.d. The Indians' War of Independence. Retrieved from The Gilder Lehrman Institute of American History AP US History Study Guide https://ap.gilderlehrman. org/essay/indians%27-war-independence (accessed 30 April 2018).

Calvin, W. H. 1998. *The Cerebral Code.* Cambridge, MA: MIT Press.

Cannone, J. and Macdonald, R. J. 2003. Valuation without Value Theory: a North American "Appraisal". *Journal of Real Estate Practice and Education* 6: 113–162.

Captain Cook Birthplace Museum. n.d. 1st Voyage. Retrieved from www.captcook-ne. co.uk/ccne/timeline/voyage1.htm (accessed 26 May 2015).

Carlo, D. 2013. Recovering Lewis Mumford's The Pentagon of Power. *Crisis and Critica* 2. Retrieved from http://cvisaacs.univalle.edu.co/crisisycritica/index.php/component/ content/article?id=36:recovering-lewis-mumford-s-the-pentagon-of-power&start=1 (accessed 24 February 2017).

Carlson, S. M. and Zelazo, P. D. 2011. The Value of Control and the Influence of Values. *Proceedings of the National Academy of Sciences* 108(41): 16861–16862.

Carrithers, M., Candea, M., Sykes, K. and Venkatesan, S. 2010. Ontology Is Just Another Word for Culture: Motion Tabled at the 2008 Meeting of the Group for Debates in Anthropological Theory, University of Manchester. *Critique of Anthropology* 30: 152–200.

Carter, A. 2011. Some Groundwork for a Multidimensional Axiology. *Philosophical Studies* 154(3): 389–408.

Carter, R. 2008. *Multiplicity: The New Science of Personality, Identity, and the Self.* New York: Little Brown and Company.

Casakin, H. and Bernardo, M. D. F. C. 2012. *The Role of Place Identity in the Perception, Understanding, and Design of Built Environments.* Oak Park, IL: Bentham Science Publishers.

Cassirer, E. 1950. *The Problem of Knowledge: Philosophy, Science and History since Hegel.* New Haven, CT: Yale University Press.

Castro Nogueira, L. 1997. *La Risa del Espacio. El Imaginario Espacio-Temporal en la Cultura Contemporánea: Una Reflexión Sociológica.* Madrid: Tecnos.

Caufield, C. 1998. *Masters of Illusion: The World Bank and the Poverty of Nations.* London: Pan.

Cavanaugh, W. T. 2011. *Migrations of the Holy: God, State, and the Political Meaning of the Church.* Amsterdam: Eerdmans Publishing Company.

Centeno, M. A., Nag, M., Patterson, T. S., Shaver, A. and Windawi, A. J. 2015. The Emergence of Global Systemic Risk. *Annual Review of Sociology* 41: 65–85.

Central and Northern Land Councils. 1994. Our Land, Our Life. Retrieved from www.clc. org.au/media/publications/olol.asp (accessed 12 January 2014).

Chadwick, R. 2015. Compassion: Hard to Define, Impossible to Mandate. *BMJ* 351: h3991.

Chalmers, D. A. 1995. *The Conscious Mind: In Search of a Fundamental Theory.* New York: Oxford University Press.

Chalmers, D. A. 1995a. Facing up to the Problem of Consciousness. Retrieved from http://consc.net/papers/facing.html (accessed 16 November 2008).

Chiao, J. Y. 2010. Neural Basis of Social Status Hierarchy across Species. *Current Opinion in Neurobiology* 20: 1–7.

Chigara, B. 2012. Deconstructing Southern African Development Community Land Relations Challenges: Towards a New, Sustainable Land Relations Policy? In

B. Chigara (ed.), *Re-conceiving Property Rights in the New Millennium: Towards a New Sustainable Land Relations Policy*. Abingdon: Routledge.

Chigara, B. 2012. *Re-conceiving Property Rights in the New Millennium: Towards a New Sustainable Land Relations Policy*, Abingdon: Routledge.

Chua, A. 2004. *World on Fire: How Exporting Free Market Democracy Breeds Ethnic Hatred and Global Instability*. New York: Anchor.

Churchill, W. 1909. *Liberalism and the Social Problem*. London: Hodder & Stoughton.

Churchland, P. M. 1999. Eliminative Materialism. In J. A. B. M. Perry (ed.), *Introduction to Philosophy: Classical and Contemporary Readings*, 3rd edn. New York: Oxford University Press.

Clapp, J. M. and Myers, D. 1999. Graaskamp and the Definition of Rigorous Research. In J. Delisle and E. Worzala (eds), *Essays in Honor of James A. Graaskamp: Ten Years After*.

Clark, R. 1986. *Walking to Bethongabel*. Adelaide: Wakefield Press.

Cobb, K. 2011. *Solar Storms, EMP and the Future of the Grid*. Resource Insights: Independent Comment by Kurt Cobb on Environmental and Natural Resource News. Retrieved from http://resourceinsights.blogspot.com.au/2011/06/solar-storms-emp-and-future-of-grid.html (accessed 11 May 2016).

Cohen, J. D. 2005. The Vulcanization of the Human Brain: A Neural Perspective on Interactions between Cognition and Emotion. *Journal of Economic Perspectives* 19: 3–24.

Cole, D. H. and Ostrom, E. 2011. *The Variety of Property Systems and Rights in Natural Resources: Property in Land and Other Resources*. Cambridge, MA: Lincoln Institute of Land Policy.

Cole, D. H. and Ostrom, E. 2015. The Variety of Property Systems and Rights in Natural Resources. In D. H. Cole, M. D. McGinnis, G. Arnold, W. Blomquist, M. Cox, R. Gardner, E. Ostrom, V. Ostrom, E. Schlager and S. Villamayor-Tomas (eds), *Elinor Ostrom and the Bloomington School of Political Economy: Resource Governance*. Lanham, MD: Lexington Books.

Cole, D. H., McGinnis, M. D., Arnold, G., Blomquist, W., Cox, M., Gardner, R., Ostrom, E., Ostrom, V., Schlager, E. and Villamayor-Tomas, S. (eds). 2015. *Elinor Ostrom and the Bloomington School of Political Economy: Resource Governance*. Lanham, MD: Lexington Books.

Cole, K. C. 1998. *The Universe and the Teacup: the Mathematics of Truth and Beauty*. London: Abacus.

Cole, K. C. 2001. *The Hole in the Universe*. San Diego, CA: Harcourt.

Cole, T. 2014. Books and Arts Daily. In M. Cathcart (ed.), *Books and Arts Daily*. Sydney: ABC Radio National.

Colozino, P. 2009. The Neurobiology of Human Development. In R. Buczynski (ed.), *The Neurobiology of Human Relationships*. Storrs, CT: The National Institute for the Clinical Application of Behavioral Medicine.

Colozino, P. and Buczynski, R. (dirs): 2011. *The Neuroscience of Psychotherapy*. Storrs, CT: The National Institute for the Clinical Application of Behavioral Medicine.

Commons, M. 2008. Introduction to the Model of Hierarchical Complexity and its Relationship to Postformal Action. *World Futures* 64: 305–320.

Commons, M. L. 2007. Introduction to the Model of Hierarchical Complexity. *Behavioral Development Bulletin* 13: 2–3.

Commons, M. L., Miller, P. M., Goodheart, E. A., Danaher-Gilpin, D., Locicero, A. and Ross, S. N. 2007. Applying the Model of Hierarchical Complexity. Cambridge, MA: Dare Institute.

Condliffe, J. B. 1938. The Value of International Trade. *Economica* 5: 123–137.

Connolly, M. J. 1992. *Church Lands and Peasant Unrest in the Philippines: Agrarian Conflict in 20-th Century Luzon*. Manila: Ateneo de Manila University Press.

Cordes, Kaitlin. 2017. Is There a Human Right to Land? Retrieved from blogs.ei.columbia. edu/2017/11/08/is-owning-land-a-human-right.

Corning, P. A. 2005. *Holistic Darwinism: Synergy, Cybernetics, and the Bioeconomics of Evolution*, Chicago, IL: University of Chicago Press.

Cornwall, A. 2010. Introductory Overview – Buzzwords and Fuzzwords: Deconstructing Development Discourse. In E. Cornwall and D. Eade (eds), *Deconstructing Development Discourse: Buzzwords and Fuzzwords*. Rugby: Practical Action Publishing and Oxfam.

Cornwall, E. and Eade, D. (eds). 2010 *Deconstructing Development Discourse: Buzzwords and Fuzzwords*. Rugby: Practical Action Publishing and Oxfam.

Corson, C., Brady, B., Zuber, A., Lord, J. and Kim, A. 2015. The Right to Resist: Disciplining Civil Society at Rio+20. *The Journal of Peasant Studies* 42: 859–878.

Costanza, R., Kubiszewski, I., Giovannini, E., Lovins, L. H., McGlade, J., Pickett, K. E., Ragnarsdóttir, K. V., Roberts, D., de Vogli, R. and Wilkinson, R. 2014. Time to Leave GDP Behind. *Nature* 505: 283–285.

Costanza, R., Wilson, M., Troy, A., Voinov, A., Liu, S. and D'Agostino, J. 2006. *The Value of New Jersey's Ecosystem Services and Natural Capital*. Trenton, NJ: New Jersey Department of Environmental Protection.

Cox, A. M., Pinfield, S. and Smith, J. 2014. Moving a Brick Building: UK Libraries Coping with Research Data Management as a "Wicked" Problem. *Journal of Librarianship and Information Science* 48: 3–17. Retrieved from https://doi.org/10.1177/0961000614533717 (accessed 29 November 2015).

Craven, P. 2010. Literature's Beautiful Lies a Gift for All. *Sydney Morning Herald*, 21 April.

Craver, C. F. 2014. Levels. Open MIND, Open MIND. Frankfurt am Main: MIND Group.

Crenshaw, M. 1981. The Causes of Terrorism *Comparative Politics*, 13, 379–399.

Crenshaw, M. 1983. *Terrorism, Legitimacy, and Power: The Consequences of Political Violence*, Middleton, CT: Wesleyan University Press.

Cribb, J. 2014. *Poisoned Planet: How Constant Exposure to Man-Made Chemicals is Putting Your Life at Risk*, Crows Nest, NSW: Allen & Unwin.

Crichton, M. 1991. *Jurassic Park*, London: Random Century Group.

Crick, F. 1994. *The Astonishing Hypothesis*, New York: Charles Scribner's Sons.

Critchley, P. n.d. Being and Place. Retrieved from http://pcritchley2.wixsite.com/being andplace.

Crockett, J. 1943. *Seven Pillars of Folly*. Melbourne: Wyatt & Watts.

Crocombe, R. 1987. The Pacific in the 21st Century. In S. Stratigos (ed.), *The Ethics of Development, The Pacific in the 21st Century. Papers from the 17th Waigani Seminar, University of Papua New Guinea, 7 – 12 September 1986 / ed. by Susan Stratigos*. Port Moresby: UPNG Publishing.

Crocombe, R. and Meleisea, M. E. 1994. *Land Issues in the Pacific*. Christchurch, University of Canterbury.

Cross, C. 1981. Land Tenure, Labour Migrancy, and the Options for Agricultural Development in KwaZulu. Durban: CASS and University of Natal.

Cruickshank, J. 2004. A Tale of Two Ontologies: An Immanent Critique of Critical Realism. *The Sociological Review* 52: 567–585.

Crumley, C. L. 1995. Heterarchy and the Analysis of Complex Societies. *Archeological Papers of the American Anthropological Association* 6: 1–5.

Csaba, L. 2009. Title Orthodoxy, Renewal and Complexity in Contemporary Economics *Zeitschrift für Staats- und Europawissenschaften* 7: 51–82.

Csaba, L. 2014. Governing Emu After the Crisis–Sense and Nonsense of the New Practices. *Facing the Challenges in The European Union* 36(1): 21–36.

Csikszentmihalyi, M. 1981. *The Meaning of Things: Domestic Symbols and the Self.* Cambridge: Cambridge University Press.

Csikszentmihalyi, M. 1988. *The Future of Flow: Optimal Experience.* Psychological Studies of Flow in Consciousness. Cambridge: Cambridge University Press.

Csikszentmihalyi, M. 1989. Why We Need Things. In S. Lubar and D. W. Kingery (eds), *History from Things: Essays on Material Culture*, Kindle edition. Washington, DC: Smithsonian.

Csikszentmihalyi, M. 1990. *Flow: The Psychology of Optimal Experience.* New York: Harper & Row.

Csikszentmihalyi, M. 1993. *The Evolving Self: A Psychology for the Third Millennium.* New York: HarperCollins.

Csikszentmihalyi, M. and Csikzsentmihalyi, I. S. E. 2006. *A Life Worth Living: Contributions to Positive Psychology.* New York: Oxford University Press.

Czarniawska, B. 2013. *On Meshworks and Other Complications of Portraying Contemporary Organizing.* Gothenburg: School of Business, Economics and Law, University of Gothenburg.

Dahl, C. J., Lutz, A. and Davidson, R. J. 2015. Reconstructing and Deconstructing the Self: Cognitive Mechanisms in Meditation Practice. *Trends in Cognitive Sciences* 19: 515–523.

Damasio, A. 2010. *Self Comes to Mind: Constructing the Conscious Brain.* New York: Pantheon Books.

Damon, S. F. 2013. *A Blake Dictionary: The Ideas and Symbols of William Blake.* Hanover, NH: Dartmouth College Press.

Dannefer, D. 2015. Right in Front of Us: Taking Everyday Life Seriously in the Study of Human Development. *Research in Human Development* 12: 209–216.

Darrow, C. 1913. How to Abolish Unfair Taxation. Retrieved from http://saving communities.org/docs/darrow.clarence/abolish.html (accessed 6 June 2015).

Darwin, C. 1871. *The Descent of Man.* London: D. Appleton & Company.

Darwin, C. 2010. *The Voyage of the Beagle: Journal of Researches into the Natural History and Geology of the Countries Visited during the Voyage of HMS Beagle Round the World.* New York: Modern Library. Retrieved from http://pinkmonkey.com/dl/library1/book 0631.pdf (accessed 18 July 2015).

Das, S. 2011. *Extreme Money: The Masters of the Universe and the Cult of Risk.* Camberwell, Victoria: Portfolio.

Davidson, N. M. 2012. "Property and Identity: Vulnerability and Insecurity in the Housing Crisis." *Harvard Civil Rights- Civil Liberties Law Review* 47: 119–139.

Davidson, N. M. and Dyal-Chand, R. 2010. Property in Crisis. *Fordham Law Review* 78(4): 1607–1660.

Davies, J. 1747. *A Discoverie of the True Causes Why Ireland was Neuer Entirely Subdued nor Brought vnder Obedience of the Crowne of England, vntill the Beginning of His Maiesties Happie Raigne.* London: A. Millar.

Davy, B. 2012. *Land Policy: Planning and the Spatial Consequences of Property.* Farnham: Ashgate Publishing.

Davy, B. 2014. Polyrational Property: Rules for the Many Uses of Land. *International Journal of the Commons* 8: 472–492.

Dawson, T. L. 1998. "A Good Education Is": A Life-Span Investigation of Developmental and Conceptual Features of Evaluative Reasoning about Education. Doctor of Philosophy thesis, University of California, Berkeley.

Dawson-Tunik, T. L. 2004. "A Good Education is . . ." – The Development of Evaluative Thought across the Life Span. *Genetic Social and General Psychology Monographs* 130: 4–112.

De Soto, H. 1989. *The Other Path.* New York: Harper & Row Publishers.

De Soto, H. 1993. The Missing Ingredient: What Poor Countries Will Need to Make Their Rules Work. *The Economist* 328: 8–10.

De Soto, H. 2000. *The Mystery of Capital: Why Capitalism Triumphs in the West and Fails Everywhere Else.* New York: Basic Books.

De Zavala, A. G., Cichocka, A., Eidelson, R. and Jayawickreme, N. 2009. Collective Narcissism and its Social Consequences. *Journal of Personality and Social Psychology* 97: 1074.

Deacon, T. and Koutroufinis, S. 2014. Complexity and Dynamical Depth. *Information* 5: 404–423.

DeLanda, M. T. 1998. Meshworks, Hierarchies and Interfaces. In J. Beckman (ed.), *The Virtual Dimension: Architecture, Representation, and Crash Culture.* New York: Princeton Architectural Press.

Delaney, D. 2010. *The Spatial, the Legal and the Pragmatics of World-Making: Nomospheric Investigations.* New York: Routledge.

DeLisle, J. R. and Worzala, E. E. 2004. Graaskamp: A Holistic Perspective. Retrieved from http://jrdelisle.com/research/JAGHolistic3.pdf.

Deming, W. E. 2000. *Out of the Crisis.* Cambridge, MA: Center for Advanced Engineering Study, Massachusetts Institute of Technology.

Dewey, J. 1981 [1939]. Theory of Valuation. In J. A. Boydston (ed.), *The Later Works, 1925–1953.* Carbondale, IL: Southern Illinois University Press.

Dewey, J. 2008. Foreword to The Philosophy of Henry George. In J. A. Boydston (ed.), *John Dewey: The Later Works 1925–1953.* Carbondale, IL: Southern Illinois University Press.

Di Robilant, A. 2013. Property: A Bundle of Sticks or a Tree? *Vanderbilt Law Revue* 66: 869–893.

Diamond, S. A. 2006. Violence as Secular Evil: Forensic Evaluation and Treatment of Violent Offenders from the Viewpoint of Existential Depth Psychology. In T. Mason (ed.), *Forensic Psychiatry: Influences of Evil,* 179–206. New York. Humana Press.

Diaz J., and Hansz, J. A. 1997. How Valuers Use the Value Opinions of Others. *Journal of Property Valuation and Investment* 15: 256–260.

Diaz J. III, Gallimore, P. and Levy, D. 2004. Multicultural Examination of Valuation Behaviour. *Journal of Property Investment and Finance* 22: 339–346.

Diaz, J. I. and Wolverton, M.L. 1998. A Longitudinal Examination of the Appraisal Smoothing Hypothesis. *Real Estate Economics* 26: 349–358.

Dick, A. 2013. *Romanticism and the Gold Standard: Money, Literature and Economic Debate in Britain 1790–1830,* Basingstoke: Palgrave Macmillan.

Dimitrov, V. 2003. *A New Kind of Social Science: Study of Self-Organization of Human Dynamics.* Morrisville, NC: Lulu Press.

Dimitrov, V. and Korotkich, V. 2002. *Fuzzy Logic: A Framework for the New Millenium.* Heidelberg: Physica-Verlag.

Disraeli, B. 1981. Benjamin Disraeli. In W. H. Auden and L. Kronenberger (eds), *The Viking Book of Aphorisms.* London: Penguin Books.

Dobbs, R. R., J., Manyika, J., Roxburg, C., Smit, S. and Schaer, F. 2012. *Urban World: Cities and the Rise of the Consuming Class*. New York: McKinsey Global Institute.

Doganova, L., Giraudeay, M., Helgesson, C.-F., Kjellberg, H., Lee, F., Mallard, A., Mennicken, A., Muniesa, F., Sljogren, E. and Zuiderent-Jerak, T. 2015. Editorial Note: Valuation Studies and the Critique of Valuation. *Valuation Studies* 2: 87–96.

Dokic, J. and Arcangeli, M. 2015. *The Heterogeneity of Experiential Imagination*. Frankfurt am Main: MIND Group.

Dolny, H. 2001. *Banking on Change*. New York: Penguin Group.

Dorin, H., Demmin, P. E. and Gabel, D. 1990. *Chemistry: The Study of Matter*, 3rd edn. Englewood Cliffs, NJ: Prentice Hall.

Dougherty, R. J. 2003. Catholicism and the Economy: Augustine and Aquinas on Property Ownership. *Journal of Markets and Morality* 6: 479–495.

Douglas, M. 2006. A History of Grid and Group Cultural Theory. Retrieved from http://projects.chass.utoronto.ca/semiotics/cyber/douglas1.pdf (accessed 13 March 2015).

Douzinas, C. 2002. Identity, Recognition, Rights or What Can Hegel Teach Us about Human Rights? *Journal of Law and Society* 29: 379–405.

Drews, E. M. 1970. *Policy Implications of a Hierarchy of Values*. Report no. RM-EPRC-6747-8. Menlo Park, CA: Stanford Research Institute. Retrieved from http://files.eric.ed.gov/fulltext/ED061747.pdf (accessed 31 October 2017).

Drury, W. H. and Anderson, J. G. T. 1998. *Chance and Change: Ecology for Conservationists*. Berkeley, CA: University of California Press.

Dunbar-Ortiz, R. 2015. *An Indigenous History of the United States*. Boston, MA: Beacon Press.

Durant, W. 1930. *The Case for India*, New York: Simon & Schuster.

Durant, W. 1935. *The Story of Civilization*. New York: Simon & Schuster.

Durkheim, É. 1887. Guyau. L'Irreligion de l'avenir: etude de sociologie. *Revue Philosophique* 23(3): 299–311.

Dutt, R. C. 2000. *The Economic History of India under Early British Rule* Abingdon: Routledge.

Dutt, R. C. 2013. *Open Letters to Lord Curzon on Famines and Land Assessments in India*. London: Forgotten Books.

Easterly, W. 2006. *The White Man's Burden: Why the West's Efforts to Aid the Rest Have Done So Much Ill and So Little Good*. New York: Penguin.

Easterly, W. 2013. *The Tyranny of Experts*. New York: Basic Books.

Eco, U. 1995. Ur-fascism. *The New York Review of Books* 42(11): 12–15.

Edelman, G. 1987. *Neural Darwinism: The Theory of Neuronal Group Selection*. New York: Basic Books.

Edelman, G. 2004 *Wider than the Sky: The Phenomenal Gift of Consciousness*. New Haven, CT: Yale University Press.

Edelman, G. 2011. Nobel Laureate Gerald Edelman on Consciousness, Creativity and Neural Darwinism. In N. Mitchell (ed.), *All in the Mind*. Sydney: Australian Broadcasting Corporation.

Edelman, G. and Tononi, G. 2000. *A Universe of Consciousness: How Matter Becomes Imagination*. New York: Basic Books.

Edmunds, A. J. 1902. *Hymns of the Faith (Dhammapada) Being an Ancient Anthology Preserved in the Short Collection of the Sacred Scriptures of the Buddhists*. Chicago, IL: Open Court.

Edwards, M. 2002–2003. *Through AQAL Eyes*. Amsterdam: Frank Visser. Retrieved from www.integralworld.net/edwards5.html.

Edwards, M. G. and Kirkham, N. 2014. Situating "Giving Voice to Values": A Metatheoretical Evaluation of a New Approach to Business Ethics. *Journal of Business Ethics* 121: 477–495.

Eggertsson, T. 1990. *Economic Behaviour and Institutions*. Cambridge: Cambridge University Press.

Eglash, R. 1999. *African Fractals: Modern Computing and Indigenous Design*. New Brunswick, NJ: Rutgers University Press.

Einstein, A. 1931. *Cosmic Religion: With Other Opinions and Aphorisms*. New York: Covici-Friede.

Eisler, R. 1995. *Sacred Pleasure*. Sydney: Doubleday.

Elahi, K. and Stilwell, F. 2013. Customary Land Tenure, Neoclassical Economics and Conceptual Bias. *Nuigini Agrisayens* 5: 28–39.

Eldredge, N. and Gould, S. J. 1972. Punctuated Equilibria: An Alternative to Phyletic Gradualism. In T. J. M. E. Schopf (ed.), *Models in Paleobiology*. San Francisco, CA: Freeman, Cooper & Co.

Eliot, T. S. 1943. *Four Quartets*. New York: Harcourt, Brace & Company.

Eliot, T. S. 2014. *The Rock: A Pageant Play*. New York: Houghton Mifflin Harcourt.

Emerson, J. 2005. Contained. Retrieved from www.backspace.com/notes/search.php?q=canada&n=10 (accessed 25 February 2017).

Emmanuel, G. and Fitzgerald, K. (directors). 2011. *Real Estate 4 Ransom: Why Does Land Cost the Earth*. Melbourne, Victoria: Prosper, Australia.

Enders, G. 2015. *Gut: The Inside Story of Our Body's Most Under-Rated Organ*. Vancouver: Greystone Books.

English, H. A and English, A. C. 1958. *Comprehensive Dictionary of Psychological and Psychoanalytic Terms*. New York: David McKay.

Erdman, D. V. 1977. *Blake: Prophet Against Empire*. Princeton, NJ: Princeton University Press.

Erikson, E. H. 1977. *Childhood and Society*. London: Paladin Grafton Books.

Ernle, L. 1912. *English Farming Past and Present*. London: London, Green and Co.

Esbjorn-Hargens, S. and Zimmerman, M. E. 2009. *Integral Ecology: Uniting Multiple Perspectives on the Natural World*. Boston, MA: Integral Books.

Espeland, W. N. 1998. *The Struggle for Water: Politics, Rationality, and Identity in the American Southwest*. Chicago, IL: University of Chicago Press.

Euben, R. L. 1999. *Enemy in the Mirror: Islamic Fundamentalism and the Limits of Modern Rationalism*. Princeton, NJ: Princeton University Press.

Eucken, W. 1992. *The Foundations of Economics*. Berlin: Springer-Verlag.

Fahey, L. 1994. *Strategic Management: The Challenge and the Opportunity*. New York: John Wiley and Sons.

Fairlie, K. L. and Boydell, S. 2010. Representing Carbon Property Rights. In M. Villikka (ed.), *The XXIV FIG International Congress 2010*. Sydney: International Federation of Surveyors.

FAO. 2012. *Strategic Evaluation of FAO's Work on Tenure, Rights and Access to Land and Other Natural Resources*. Rome: FAO.

FAO/UNEP 1997. *Negotiating a Sustainable Future for Land. Structural and Institutional Guidelines for Land Resources Management in the 21st Century*. Rome: FAO/UNEP.

Farooqui, A. 2006. *Opium City: the Making of Early Victorian Bombay*. Gurgaon: Three Essays Collective.

Fassbender, H. 2007. *Europe as an Economic Powerhouse: How the Old Continent is Gaining New Strength*. London and Philadelphia: Koyan Page Limited.

Feder, G. and Deininger, K. 1999. *Land Institutions and Land Markets*. Policy Research Working Paper no. 2014. Washington, DC: World Bank.

Feder, G. and Feeny, D. 1991. Land Tenure and Property Rights: Theory and Implications for Development Policy. *The World Bank Economic Review* 5: 135–153.

Fein, E. and Weibler, J. 2014. Cognitive Basis for Corruption and Attitudes towards Corruption in Organizations Viewed from a Structuralist Adult Developmental Meta-perspective. *Behavioral Development Bulletin* 19: 78–94.

Feld, S. and Basso, K. H. 1996. *Senses of Place*. Santa Fe, NM: School of American Research Press.

Fellman, P., Post, J., Wright, R. and Dasari, U. 2004. *Adaptation and Coevolution on an Emergent Global Competitive Landscape: 5th International Conference on Complex Systems*. Boston, MA: New England Complex Systems Institute.

Fernandez, N., Maldonado, C. and Gershenson, C. 2013. Information Measures of Complexity, Emergence, Self-organization, Homeostasis, and Autopoiesis. In M. Prokopenko (eds), *Guided Self-Organization: Inception*. Emergence, Complexity and Computation, vol 9. Berlin: Springer.

Fernando, C. 2013. From Blickets to Synapses: Inferring Temporal Causal Networks by Observation. *Cognitive Science* 37: 1426–1470.

Fernando, C. and Szathmáry, E. 2010. *Natural Selection in the Brain: Towards a Theory of Thinking*. Berlin: Springer.

Fernando, C. T., Szathmáry, E. and Husbands, P. 2012. Selectionist and Evolutionary Approaches to Brain Function: A Critical Appraisal. *Frontiers in Computational Neuroscience* 6: 1–28.

Feuerverger, G. 2005. Multicultural Perspectives in Teacher Development. In J. Phillion, M. F. He and F. M. Connolly (eds), *Narratives and Experiences in Multicultural Education*. Thousand Oaks, CA: Sage.

Fieser, J. 2001. Eastern Philosophy: an Introduction to the Classical Theories of Hinduism, Buddhism, Confucianism and Taoism. Retrieved from www.baldoralumni.com/pdffiles2/easternphilosophy.pdf (accessed 16 March 2018).

Finlay-Brian, P. 2013. *Perspectives on a Hyper-Connected World: Insights from the Science of Complexity by the World Economic Forum's Global Agenda Council on Complex Systems*. Geneva: World Economic Forum. Retrieved from www3.weforum.org/docs/WEF_GAC_PerspectivesHyperconnectedWorld_ExecutiveSummary_2013.pdf (accessed 16 March 2018).

Fischer, D. 2000. Is the Valuation Paradigm a Paradigm? *Australian Property Journal* 36: 8.

Flam, F. 1991. Beating a Fractal Drum. *Science* 254: 1593. Retrieved from www.iem.ac.ru/~kalinich/rus-sci/1991/science-sov-sci-12-13-1991.pdf (accessed 24 March 2018).

Flyvbjerg, B. 2001. *Making Social Science Matter: Why Social Inquiry Fails and How it Can Succeed Again*. Cambridge: Cambridge University Press.

Foldvary, F. E. 2006. The Ultimate Tax Reform: Public Revenue from Land Rent. January 2006. Retrieved from https://ssrn.com/abstract=1103586 (accessed 24 October 2015).

Forster, E. M. 1991. *Howards End*. New York: Alfred A. Knopf.

Foss, N. 2015. Building Resilience in an Era of Limits to Growth. In P. Barclay (ed.), *Big Ideas*. Sydney: Australan Broadcasting Corporation.

Foucault, M. 1979. *Discipline and Punish*. New York: Vintage.

Fourcade, M. 2011. Cents and Sensibility: Economic Valuation and the Nature of "Nature". *American Journal of Sociology* 116: 1721–1777.

Fowler, A. 2007. *Civic Driven Change and International Development: Exploring a Complexity Perspective*. Contextuals no. 7. Utrecht: Context.

Fowler, A. 2013. *Civic Driven Change: Where From? Where Now? Where Next? Valedictory Lecture*. The Hague: Institute of Social Studies.

Frankopan, P. 2015. *The Silk Roads: A New History of the World*. London: Bloomsbury Publishing.

Frank, A. 2017. Minding Matter: The Closer You Look, the More the Materialist Position in Physics Appears to Rest on Shaky Metaphysical Ground. Retrieved from at:https:// aeon.co/essays/materialism-alone-cannot-explain-the-riddle-of-consciousness. (accessed 31 December 2017).

Franklin, S. and Ramamurthy, U. 2006. Motivations, Values and Emotions: 3 Sides of the Same Coin. Proceedings of the Sixth International Workshop on Epigenetic Robotics, Paris, France, September. Retrieved from http://cogprints.org/5850.

Fraser, J. T. 1999. *Time, Conflict and Human Values*. Urbana, IL: University of Illinois Press.

Freeman, J. 2016. 4/28 – The Science of Possibility: What's the Question? *Integral Leadership Review* (April–June). Retrieved from http://integralleadershipreview.com/ 14688-the-science-of-possibility-whats-the-question (accessed 12 May 2016).

Friere, P. 1972. *Pedagogy of the Oppressed*. London: Penguin.

Fuentes-Nieva, R. and Galasso, N. 2014. *Working for the Few*. Oxford: Oxfam International.

Fullbrook, E. E. 2004. *A Guide to What's Wrong with Economics*. London: Anthem.

Fullbrook, E. E. 2007. *Real World Economics: A Post-autistic Economics Reader*. London: Anthem Press.

Fuller, B., McHale, J. and Research Team. 1963. *Phase 1 (1963) Document 1 Study: Inventory of World Resources, Human Trends and Needs. World Design Science Decade 1965–1975*. Carbondale, IL: Southern Illinois University.

Fulton, B. 2013. Anticipating the Unexpected. First Global Conference on Research Integration and Implementation. Canberra, Australia, online and at three co-conferences (Lueneburg in Germany, The Hague in the Netherlands and Montevideo in Uruguay). Retrieved from www.theiia.org/centers/aec/Pages/anticipating-the-unexpected.aspx.

Funder, A. 2012. *All That I Am*. New York: HarperTorch.

Funtowicz, S. O. and Ravetz, J. R. 1990. *Uncertainty and Quality in Science for Policy*. New York: Springer.

Funtowicz, S. O. and Ravetz, J. R. 1991. A New Scientific Methodology for Global Environmental Issues. In R. Costanza (ed.), *Ecological Economics: The Science and Management of Sustainability*. New York: Columbia University Press.

Gabbay, R. 1978. *Communism and Agrarian Reform in Iraq*. Beckenham: Croom Helm.

Gabel, P. 2000. *The Bank Teller and Other Essays on the Politics of Meaning*. San Francisco, CA: Acada Books.

Gabel, P. 2003. Spiritualizing Foreign Policy. *Tikkun* 18(3) 17–23.

Gabel, P. 2013. A Spiritual Way of Seeing. *Tikkun* 28(2) 17–27. Retrieved from https:// docs.google.com/file/d/0B-5-JeCa2Z7hQTFaLVlWeDc4czg/edit (accessed 4 December 2013).

Gabel, P. 2014. The Spiritual Dimension of Social Justice. *Journal of Legal Education* 63: 673–688.

Gabel, P. 2018. *The Desire for Mutual Recognition: Social Movements and the Dissolution of the False Self*. Abingdon: Routledge.

Gaffney, M. 1993. *Neo-classical Economics as a Stratagem against Henry George*. Sydney: Macquarie University School of Economic and Financial Studies.

Gaffney, M. and Harrison, F. 1994. *The Corruption of Economics*. London: Shepheard-Walwyn.

Gandhi, M., Prabhu, R. K. and Rao, U. R. 1968. *The Mind of Mahatma Gandhi: Encyclopedia of Gandhi's Thoughts*. Ahmedabad: Navajivan Publishing House.

Gao, T. 2013. An Introduction to MER, a New Music Psychotherapy Approach for PTSD. Part 1 – The Theoretical and Clinical Foundations. *Music and Medicine* 5: 99–104.

Gawande, A. 2010. *The Checklist Manifesto: How to Get Things Right*. New York: Metropolitan Books.

Gebhardt, P. 2015. The End of Interest Rates. Retrieved from https://medium.com/@paulgebhardt/the-end-of-interest-rates-c1456a66c71f (accessed 30 June 2015).

Geddes, P. 1915. *Cities in Evolution*. London: Williams & Norgate.

Geertz, C. 1973. *The Interpretation of Cultures: Selected Essays*. New York: Basic Books.

Geiger, G. R. 1933. *The Philosophy of Henry George*. New York: The Macmillan Company.

Gell, A. 1993. *Wrapping in Images: Tattooing in Polynesia*. Oxford: Clarendon.

Gelman, A. 2015. Gigerenzer on Logical Rationality vs. Ecological Rationality. Retrieved from http://andrewgelman.com/2015/04/17/gigerenzer-logical-rationality-vs-ecological-rationality (accessed 17 April 2015).

George, H. 1920. *Progress and Poverty*. Garden City, NY: Doubleday, Page & Co.

Gerber, J.-D., Knoepfel, P., Nahrath, S. and Varone, F. 2009. Institution Resource regimes: Towards Sustainability through the Combinationation of Property-Rights Theory and Policy Analysis. *Ecological Economics* 68: 798–809.

Getling, A. V. and Brausch, O. 2003. Cellular Flow Patterns and Their Evolutionary Scenarios in Three-Dimensional Rayleigh-Benard Convection. *Physical Review E* 67(4/2): 046313.

Getzner, M., Spash, C. and Stagl, S. 2005. *Alternatives for Environmental Valuation*. New York: Routledge.

Ghiţă, C. 2008. *Revealer of the Fourfold Secret: William Blake's Theory and Practice of Vision*. Cluj-Napoca: Casa Cartii de Stiinta.

Giedion, S. 1958. *Architecture, You and Me: The Diary of a Development*. Cambridge, MA: Harvard University Press.

Gigerenzer, G. 2007. *Gut Feelings: The Intelligence of the Unconscious*. New York: Viking.

Gigerenzer, G. 2013. Simple Heuristics that Make Us Smart. Retrieved from www.socio.ethz.ch/icsd2013/speakers/slides/0_3_gigerenzer.pdf (accessed 20 February 2017).

Gigerenzer, G. 2014. *Risk Savvy: How to Make Good Decisions*. New York: Viking.

Gigerenzer, G. and Brighton, H. 2009. Homo Heuristicus: Why Biased Minds Make Better Inferences. *Topics in Cognitive Science* 1: 107–143.

Gigerenzer, G., Hertwig, R. and Pachur, T. 2011. *Heuristics: The Foundations of Adaptive Behavior*. Oxford: Oxford University Press.

Gigerenzer, G. and Todd, P. M. 1999. Fast and Frugal Heuristics: The Adaptive Toolbox. In T. A. R. Group (ed.), *Evolution and Cognition*. New York: Oxford University Press.

Gilbert, D. T. and Malone, P. S. 1995. The Correspondence Bias. *Psychological Bulletin* 117: 21.

Gilbert, N. and Bullock, S. 2014. Complexity at the Social Science Interface. *Complexity* 19: 1–4.

Gilbert, P. 2007. *The Compassionate Mind Foundation: Introduction, Aims and Objectives*. Derby: The Compassionate Mind Foundation.

Gilbert, P. and Choden, K. 2015. *Mindful Compassion: Using the Power of Mindfulness and Compassion to Transform Our Lives*. New York: Little, Brown Book Group.

Glasgow, R. E. 2013. What Does it Mean to Be Pragmatic? Pragmatic Methods, Measures, and Models to Facilitate Research Translation. *Health Education and Behavior* 40: 257–265.

Gleick, J. 1987. *Chaos: Making a New Science*. London: Viking Penguin.

Global Policy Forum. n.d. Land and Settlement Issues. Retrieved from www.globalpolicy. org/security-council/index-of-countries-on-the-security-council-agenda/israel-palestine-and-the-occupied-territories/land-and-settlement-issues.html.

Glouberman, S. and Zimmerman, B. 2002. Complicated and Complex Systems: What Would Successful Reform of Medicare Look Like? Retrieved from http://publications. gc.ca/collections/Collection/CP32–79–8–2002E.pdf (accessed 4 September 2014).

Gödel, K. 1995. The Modern Development of the Foundations of Mathematics in the Light of Philosophy. In F. E. Al (ed.), *Kurt Gödel: Collected Works*. New York: Oxford University Press.

Goldacre, B. 2008. *Bad Science*. London: Fourth Estate.

Golding, W. 1954. *Lord of the Flies: A Novel*. New York: Perigee.

Gonen, J. Y. 2000. *The Roots of Nazi Psychology: Hitler's Utopian Barbarism*. Lexington, KY: University Press of Kentucky.

Goodall, J. 1971. *In the Shadow of Man*. London: Collins.

Goodman, H. 2009. The Formation of the Bank of England: A Response to Changing Political and Economic Climate, 1694. *Penn History Review* 17(1): article 2. Retrieved from https://repository.upenn.edu/phr/vol17/iss1/2 (accessed 16 March 2018).

Goodson, I. and Gill, S. 2014. *Critical Narrative as Pedagogy*. New York: Bloomsbury Academic.

Goodwin, B. 1994. *How the Leopard Changed its Spots*. London: Charles Scribner's Sons.

Gorovitz, S. and MacIntyre, A. 1975. Toward a Theory of Medical Fallibility. *The Hastings Center Report* 5: 13–23.

Graeber, D. 2001. *Toward An Anthropological Theory of Value: The False Coin of Our Own Dreams*. Basingstoke: Palgrave Macmillan.

Graham, P. W. 2002. Space and Cyberspace: On the Enclosure of Consciousness. In J. Armitage and J. Roberts (eds), *Living with Cyberspace: Technology and Society in the 21st Century*, 156–164. London: Continuum.

Grant, C. 1998. *Myths We Live By*. Ottawa: University of Ottawa Press.

Graves, C. 2005. *The Never-Ending Quest*. Santa Barbara, CA: ECLET Publishing.

Graves, C. W. 1981. *Up the Existential Staircase*. Schenectady, NY: Schaffer Library, Union College.

Gray, P. 2006. Famine and Land in Ireland and India, 1845–1880: James Caird and the Political Economy of Hunger. *The Historical Journal* 49: 193–215.

Grayling, A. C. 2004. *The Mystery of Things*. London: Phoenix.

Greenberg, M. T. and Turksma, C. 2015. Understanding and Watering the Seeds of Compassion. *Research in Human Development* 12: 280–287.

Greenfield, S. 2008. *ID: the Quest for Human Identity in the 21st Century*. London: Sceptre.

Greenhalgh, T. 2010. *How to Read a Paper: The Basics of Evidence-Based Medicine*. Chichester: Wiley-Blackwell.

Greenwald, A. G. 1980. The Totalitarian Ego: Fabrication and Revision of Personal History. *American Psychologist* 35(7): 603–618.

Greer, A. 2012. Commons and Enclosure in the Colonization of North America. *The American Historical Review* 117: 365–386.

Gribbin, M. J. 1993. *Being Human*. London: Phoenix.

Grint, K. 2008. Wicked Problems and Clumsy Solutions: the Role of Leadership. *Clinical Leader* 1: 11–15.

Grint, K. 2009. Wicked Problems and the Role of Leadership. Retrieved from http://informalnetworks.co.uk/wp-content/uploads/2014/09/Wicked_problems_and_the_role_of_leadership.pdf (accessed 14 February 2015).

Grint, K. 2013. Wicked Problems and Leadership. Retrieved from www.dajf.org.uk/wp-content/uploads/Keith-Grint-presentation.pdf.

Grove, S. 1992. *Thank You, Brain*. Cape Town: Human and Rousseau.

Grunberg, L. 2000. *The Mystery of Values: Studies in Axiology*. Amsterdam: Rodopi.

Gruss, P. 2014. Picasso and Einstein Got the Picture: Breakthroughs in Science and Art Begin with an Image. *Nautilus*. New York: NautilusThink.

Gunderson, L. H. and Holling, C. S. E. 2002. *Panarchy: Understanding Transformations in Human and Natural Systems*. Washington, DC: Island Press.

Habermas, J. 1979. *Communication and the Evolution of Society*. Boston, MA: Beacon Press.

Habermas, J. 1990. *The Philosophical Discourse of Modernity*. Cambridge, MA: MIT Press.

Habermas, J. and Foessel, M. 2015. *Critique and Communication: Philosophy's Missions*. Vienna: Eurozine.

Hagstrom, R. G. 2013. *Investing: the Last Liberal Art*, New York: Colombia Business School.

Haidt, J. 2012. *The Righteous Mind*. London: Penguin.

Haldane, A. G. and Madouros, V. 2012. *The Dog and the Frisbee: The Changing Policy Landscape*. Jackson Hole, WY: Federal Reserve Bank of Kansas City.

Haldane, J. B. S. 1926. On Being the Right Size. *Harper's Magazine* 152: 424–427.

Hann, C. 2007. The State of the Art: A New Double Movement? Anthropological Perspectives on Property in the Age of Neoliberalism. *Socio-Economic Review* 5: 287–318.

Hannaford, I. 1994. The Idiocy of Race. *Wilson Quarterly* 18(spring): 12–15.

Haraway, D. 1988. Situated Knowledges: The Science Question in Feminism and the Privilege of Partial Perspective. *Feminist Studies* 14: 575–599.

Hardison, O. B. 1981. *Entering the Maze: Identity and Change in Modern Culture*. New York: Oxford University Press.

Harrison, F. 1983. *The Power in the Land: An Inquiry Into Unemployment, the Profits Crisis, and Land Speculation*. New York: Universe Books.

Harrison, F. 2009. *The Silver Bullet*. London: International Union for Land Value Taxation and Free Trade.

Hartman, R. S. 1967. *The Structure of Value: Foundations of Scientific Axiology*. Carbondale, IL: Southern Illinois University Press.

Harvey, D. 2005. *A Brief History of Neoliberalism*. Oxford: Oxford University Press.

Heal, G. and Park, J. 2015. *Goldilocks Economies? Temperature Stress and the Direct Impacts of Climate Change*. Working Paper no. 21119. Cambridge, MA: National Bureau of Economic Research.

Hegel, G. W. F. 2001. *Philosophy of Right*. Kitchener: Batoche Books. Retrieved from https://libcom.org/files/Philosophy_of_Right_0.pdf (accessed 10 July 2012).

Hein, G. E. 1999. Is Meaning Making Constructivism? Is Constructivism Meaning Making? *The Exhibitionist* 18: 4.

Heinberg, R. 2014. Two Realities. Retrieved from www.postcarbon.org/two-realities (accessed 22 July 2014).

Helgesson, C. F. and Muniesa, F. 2013. For What It's Worth: An Introduction to Valuation Studies. *Valuation Studies* 1: 1–10.

Henning, B. 2005. Saving Whitehead's Universe of Value: An "Ecstatic" Challenge to the Classical Interpretation. *International Philosophical Quarterly* 45(4): 446–465.

Henrich, J., Heine, S. J. and Norenzayan, A. 2010. The Weirdest People on the World? *Behavioural and Brain Sciences* 33: 61–135.

Herb, G. H. and Kaplan, D. H. 1999. *Nested Identities: Nationalism, Territory, and Scale.* Lanham, MD: Rowman & Littlefield.

Hertwig, R., Hoffrage, U. and the ABC Research Group. 2013. *Simple Heuristics in a Social World.* Oxford: Oxford University Press.

Hetherington, N. S. 1983. Isaac Newton's Influence on Adam Smith's Natural Laws in Economics. *Journal of the History of Ideas* 44: 497–505.

Hickel, J. 2017. *The Divide: a New History of Global Inequality.* London: Random House.

Hidalgo, C. 2015. *Why Information Grows: The Evolution of Order, from Atoms to Economies.* New York: Basic Books.

Hidalgo, M. C. and Hernandez, B. 2001. Place Attachment: Conceptual and Empirical Questions. *Journal of Environmental Psychology* 21: 273–281.

Hill, R. 2011. *A Question of Identity: Getting the Better of Globalization.* Helsinki: Europublications.

Hilton, S. 2015. *More Human.* London: W. H. Allen.

Hiro, D. 2003. *Desert Shield to Desert Storm.* Lincoln, NE: Authors Choice Press.

Hirsch Hadorn, G., Maier Begré, S., Tanner, C. and Wölfing Kast, S. 2013. Options and Restrictions: A Heuristic Tool for Effective Implementation of Policies. First Global Conference on Research Integration and Implementation. Canberra, Australia, online and at co-conferences in Germany, the Netherlands and Uruguay, 8–11 September.

Hobbes, T. 1651. Of Commonwealth. Chapter XVII of Leviathan. Retrieved from https://ebooks.adelaide.edu.au/h/hobbes/thomas/h68l/chapter17.html (accessed 17 July 2016).

Hobsbawm, E. 1996. *Age Of Revolution: 1789–1848.* New York: Vintage.

Hodge, R. 2007. The Complexity Revolution. *M/C Journal* 10(3): 4–11. Retrieved from http://journal.media-culture.org.au/0706/01-hodge.php (accessed 4 September 2009).

Hodgson, P. and King, R. 1982. *Christian Theology.* Philadelphia, PA: Fortress.

Hoggan, J. and Litwin, G. 2016. *I'm Right and You're an Idiot. The Toxic State of Public Discourse and How to Clear it Up.* Gabriola Island, BC: New Society Publishers.

Holbrook, M. B. 2003. Adventures in Complexity: An Essay on Dynamic Open Complex Adaptive Systems, Butterfly Effects, Self-Organizing Order, Coevolution, the Ecological Perspective, Fitness Landscapes, Market Spaces, Emergent Beauty at the Edge of Chaos, and All that Jazz. *Academy of Market Science Review* 6: 1–181.

Holdheim, W. W. 1985. The Hermeneutic Significance of Auerbach's Ansatz. *New Literary History* 16(3): 627–631.

Holtzhausen, H. 2015. Ubuntu and the Quest for Land Reform in South Africa. *Verbum et Ecclesia* 36: 1–8. Retrieved from www.scielo.org.za/scielo.php?script=sci_arttext&pid=S2074-77052015000200007&nrm=iso (accessed 12 May 2016).

Hölzel, B. K., Carmody, J., Vangel, M., Congleton, C., Yerramsetti, S. M., Gard, T. and Lazar, S. W. 2011. Mindfulness Practice Leads to Increases in Regional Brain Gray Matter Density. *Psychiatry Research: Neuroimaging* 191: 36–43.

Honoré, A M. 1987. Ownership. *Making Law Bind: Essays Legal and Philosophical.* Oxford: Clarendon Press.

Hood, B. 2009. *Supersense: From Superstition to Religion: The Brain Science of Belief.* London: Constable.

Hopkins, G. M. 1953. *Poems and Prose*, ed. W. H. Gardner. Harmondsworth: Penguin.

Horkheimer, M. and Adorno, T. W. 2002. *Dialectic of Enlightenment*. Stanford, CA: Stanford University Press.

Horn, R. E. 2001. *Knowledge Mapping for Complex Social Messes: Foundations in the Knowledge Economy*. Los Altos, CA: David and Lucile Packard Foundation.

Horn, R. E. and Weber, R. P. 2007. New Tools for Resolving Wicked Problems: Mess Mapping and Resolution Mapping Processes. Retrieved from www.strategykinetics. com/files/New_Tools_For_Resolving_Wicked_Problems.pdf (accessed 14 February 2015).

Hossenfelder, S. 2012. Updated Science Symbol. Retrieved from http://backreaction. blogspot.de/2012/02/updated-science-symbol.html. (accessed 14 February 2012).

Housty, J. 2013. 26 -year-old Heiltsuk Tribal Council Member Speaks Out against Northern Gateway Pipeline. Retrieved from http://blog.wwf.ca/blog/2013/06/27/26-year-old-heiltsuk-tribal-council-member-speaks-out-against-northern-gateway-pipeline (accessed 5 July 2015).

Howard, L. 2005. *Introducing Ken Wilber: Concepts for an Evolving World*. Bloomington, IN: Authorhouse.

Hudson, M. 1993. *The Lost Tradition of Biblical Debt Cancellations*. New York: Henry George School of Social Science.

Hudson, M. 2003. *Super Imperialism: The Economic Strategy of the American Empire*. London: Pluto Press.

Hudson, M. 2004. Saving, Asset-Price Inflation, and Debt-Induced Deflation. Retrieved from http://michael-hudson.com/2004/06/saving-asset-price-inflation-and-debt-induced-deflation (accessed 27 June 2014).

Hudson, M. 2006. *The New Road to Serfdom*. New York: Harpers.

Hudson, M. 2010. From Marx to Goldman Sachs: The Fictions of Fictitious Capital. Retrieved from http://michael-hudson.com/2010/07/from-marx-to-goldman-sachs-the-fictions-of-fictitious-capital1 (accessed 6 December 2014).

Hudson, M. 2013. China – Avoid the West's Debt Overhead: A Land Tax is Needed to Hold Down Housing Prices. Retrieved from http://michael-hudson.com/2013/07/china-avoid-the-wests-debt-overhead-a-land-tax-is-needed-to-hold-down-housing-prices (accessed 13 November 2014).

Hughes, A. L. 2012. The Folly of Scientism. *The New Atlantis* 37: 32–50.

Hughes, A. L. 2013. Scientism and the Integrity of the Humanities. *TheNewAtlantis.com*, 12 December. Retrieved from www.thenewatlantis.com/publications/scientism-and-the-integrity-of-the-humanities (accessed 31 December 2014).

Hughes, R. 2003. Legal Pluralism and the Problem of Identity. In A. Jowitt and T. N. Cain (eds), *Passage of Change: Law, Society and Governance in the Pacific*, 329–352. Canberra: Pandanus Books.

Hughes, T. 1992. *Shakespeare and the Goddess of Complete Being*. London: Faber & Faber.

Hurst, D. K. 2015. Review of Allen T. F. H. and Hoekstra, T. W., *Toward a Unified Ecology: Complexity in Ecological Systems*. Retrieved from www.fishpond.com.au/Books/Toward-Unified-Ecology-Timothy-FH-Allen-Thomas-W-Hoekstra/9780231168892 (accessed 2 March 2015).

Huxley, J. 1954. *From an Antique Land*. London: Max Parrish.

Hyde, D. 1907. The Brehon Laws. *The Catholic Encyclopedia*. New York: Robert Appleton Company.

Ingram, G. K. and Hong, Y. H. (eds). 2012. *Value Capture and Land Policies*. Cambridge, MA: Lincoln Institute of Land Policy.

Institute of Development Studies. 2011. *Powercube: A New Resource for Understanding Power for Social Change.* Brighton: Institute of Development Studies. Retrieved from www.ids.ac.uk/go/idsproject/powercube-understanding-power-for-social-change.

International Livestock Research Institute. 1995. *Livestock Policy Analysis.* Nairobi: ILRI.

Irvine, A. B. 2011. An Ontological Critique of the Trans-Ontology of Enrique Dussel. *Sophia* 50(4): 603–624.

Irwin, T., Kossoff, G., Tonkinwise, C. and Scupelli, P. 2015. *Transition Design 2015.* Pittsburgh, PA: Carnegie Mellon University School of Design.

Ishiyama, J. 2005. The Sickle and the Minaret: Communist Successor Parties in Yemen and Afghanistan After the Cold War. *Middle East Review of International Affairs* 9: 7–29.

IVSC. 2014. Asia Pacific Ministers Recognise Importance of Valuation: APEC Agrees Need to Adopt Global Valuation Standards across Region. Retrieved from www.ivsc.org/content/asia-pacific-ministers-recognise-importance-valuation?utm_medium=emailandutm_source=Spadaandutm_campaign=4951930_November+E-Newsanddm_i=PRO,2Y4XM,IAXI4E,AMXA9,1 (accessed 17 November 2014).

IVSC. n.d. International Valuation Glossary. Retrieved from www.ivsc.org/glossary.

IVSC. 2016. International Valuation Glossary. Retrieved from www.ivsc.org/standards/glossary (accessed 10 August 2017).

Jackson, W. J. 2004. *Heaven's Fractal Net.* Bloomington, IN: Indiana University Press.

Jacques, E. 1982. *The Form of Time.* New York: Crane Russack.

Jacques, E. 1989. *Requisite Organization: The CEO Guide to Creative Structure and Leadership.* Arlington, VA: Cason Hall & Co.

James, I. 2003. Singular Scientists. *Journal of the Royal Society of Medicine* 96: 36–39.

Jantsch, E. 1980. *The Self-Organizing Universe: Scientific and Human Implications of the Emerging Paradigm of Evolution.* London: Pergamon Press.

Jefferson, T. 2008. To Peter Carr, Paris, August 19, 1785. Retrieved from http://avalon.law.yale.edu/18th_century/let31.asp (accessed 10 August 2013).

Jensen, C. B. 2013. Two Forms of the Outside. *Journal of Ethnographic Theory* 3(3) 309–335.

Jin, Y. and Branke, J. 2005. Evolutionary Optimization in Uncertain Environments: A Survey. *IEEE Transactions on Evolutionary Computation* 9: 303–317.

Johnson, G. 1995. *Fire in the Mind: Science, Faith and the Search for Order.* London: Penguin.

Jones, A. 2014. Independent Effects of Bottom-Up Temporal Expectancy and Top-Down Spatial Attention. An Audiovisual Study Using Rhythmic Cueing. *Frontiers in Integrative Neuroscience* 8: 96.

Jones, B. 2013. New Technology for Cadastral Systems. Retrieved from www.fig.net/pub/fig2013/ppt/ts04a/TS04A_brent_6520_ppt.pdf.

Jones, K. and Barry, M. 2016. *History of Perceptions of Jurisdiction Boundaries and the Tsilhqot'in Land Claim in Canada.* FIG Working Week 2016: Recovery from Disaster. Christchurch, NZ: FIG.

Jones, R., Pykett, J. and Whitehead, M. 2013. *Changing Behaviours: On the Rise of the Psychological State.* Cheltenham: Edward Elgar.

Jordan, J. S. 2008. Wild Agency: Nested Intentionalities in Cognitive Neuroscience and Archaeology. *Philosophical Transactions of the Royal Society B: Biological Sciences* 363: 1981–1991.

Jordan, J. S. 2010. Wild Systems Theory: Overcoming the Computational-Ecological Divide via Self-Sustaining Systems. In S. Ohlsson and R. Catrambone (eds), *Cognition in Flux: Proceedings of the 32nd Annual Conference of the Cognitive Science Society.* Austin, TX: Cognitive Science Society.

Jordan, J. S. and Day, B. 2015. Wild Systems Theory as a 21st Century Coherence Framework for Cognitive Science. In T. Metzinger and J. M. Windt (eds), *Open MIND*. Frankfurt am Main: MIND Group.

Jordan, S. J. and Vinson, D. W. 2012. After Nature: On Bodies Consciousness and Causality. *Journal of Consciousness Studies* 19: 229–250.

Josephus, F. 2004. *The Antiquities of the Jews*. Salt Lake City, UT: Project Gutenberg. Retrieved from www.gutenberg.org/ebooks/2848 (accessed 11 June 2015).

Jung, C. 1916. *On the Psychology of the Unconsciousness*. London: Kegan Paul Trench Trubner.

Jung, C. 1964. *Man and his Symbols*. London: Aldus Books.

Kahneman, D. 2003. Maps of Bounded Rationality: Psychology for Behavioral Economics. *The American Economic Review* 93: 26.

Kahneman, D. 2011. *Thinking Fast and Slow*. New York: Farrar, Straus & Giroux.

Kahneman, D., Knetsch, J. L. and Thaler, R. H. 1986. Fairness and the Assumptions of Economics. *Journal of Business* 59: S285–S300.

Kaku, M. 2014. *The Future of the Mind: The Scientific Quest to Understand, Enhance, and Empower the Mind*. New York: Knopf.

Kao, A. B. and Couzin, I. D. 2014. Decision Accuracy in Complex Environments is Often Maximized by Small Group Sizes. *Proceedings of the Royal Society of London B: Biological Sciences* 281: 20133305. Retrieved from http://rspb.royalsocietypublishing.org/content/royprsb/281/1784/20133305.full.pdf (accessed 26 July 2016).

Karagiannis, N., Madjd-Sadjadi, Z. and Sen, S. 2013. *The US Economy and Neoliberalism: Alternative Strategies and Policies*. Abingdon: Routledge.

Katzner, D. W. 2015. A Neoclassical Curmudgeon Looks at Heterodox Criticisms of Microeconomics. *World Economics Review* 4: 63–75.

Kauffman, S. A. 1993. *The Origins of Order: Self-Organization and Selection in Evolution*. New York: Oxford University Press.

Kauffman, S. 2007. Beyond Reductionism: Reinventing the Sacred. *Zygon* 42: 903–914.

Kauffman, S. 2016. *Humanity in a Creative Universe*. Oxford : Oxford University Press.

Kay, J. 2011. *Obliquity: Why Our Goals are Best Achieved Indirectly*. London: Profile Books.

Keay, J. 2000. *The Great Arc: The Dramatic Tale of How India was Mapped and Everest was Named*. London: HarperCollins.

Keddie, N. R. and Yann, R. 1981. *Roots of Revolution: Interpretive History of Modern Iran*. New Haven, CT: Yale University Press.

Keen, S. 2001. *Debunking Economics: The Naked Emperor of the Social Sciences*. New York: Zed Books.

Keltner, D. 2009. *Born to be Good: The Science of a Meaningful Life*. New York: W. W. Norton.

Kenji, M. n.d. *"Preface" and Other Poems*, translated by Hideyama Toshi and Michael Pronko. Retrieved from www.meijigakuin.ac.jp/~gengo/bulletin/pdf/26Tomiyama_p72.pdf (accessed 22 February 2015).

Keynes, J. M. 1926. *The End of Laissez-Faire*. London: Hogarth Press.

Keynes, J. M. 1931. *Essays in Persuasion*. London: Macmillan.

Keynes, J. M. 1963. *Essays in Persuasion*. New York: W. W. Norton & Co.

Khan, M. A. 2005. *Gifted Achievers and Underachievers; an Appraisal*. New Delhi: Discovery Publishing House.

Kidd, J. W. 2007. Thome H. Fang and A. N. Whitehead: the Twin Stars as Pre-Existing Postmodernists of the Process Perspective. The Conference in Process and Creativity,

Fu Jen Catholic University, Hsin-chuang, Taipei, Taiwan. Retrieved from www. thomehfang.com/suncrates5/twinstars.htm (accessed 15 January 2015).

King, T. 2003. *The Truth about Stories: A Native Narrative*. Massey Lectures. Toronto: House of Ananasi Press.

King, J. E., ed. 2003. *The Elgar Companion to Post Keynesian Economics*. Cheltenham: Edward Elgar.

King, R., et al. 2010. *Oxford Studies of Religion: Preliminary and HSC Course*. South Melbourne, Victoria: Oxford University Press.

Kipling, R. 1899. *The White Man's Burden: A Poem*. New York: Doubleday & McClure Company.

Kleenbooi, K. 2010. *Review of Land Reforms in Southern Africa, 2010*. Cape Town: Institute for Poverty, Land and Agrarian Studies (PLAAS), School of Government, University of the Western Cape.

Klein, N. 2010. *The Shock Doctrine*. London: Penguin.

Klein, N. 2014. *This Changes Everything*. New York: Simon & Schuster.

Klewicki, J., Philip, J., Marusic, I., Chauhan, K. and Morrill-Winter, C. 2014. Self-Similarity in the Inertial Region of Wall Turbulence. *Physical Review E* 90: 063015.

Koehn, D. and Wilbratte, B. 2012. A Defense of a Thomistic Concept of the Just Price. *Business Ethics Quarterly* 22: 501–526.

Koers, J., Cerrato Espinal, R., Lemmen, C. and Lemmen, H. 2013. *SIGIT: An Information System for Integral Approach of Land Management: An LADM Implementation in Honduras and Guatemala*. Abuja: FIG.

Kofman, F. 2001. *Holons, Heaps and Artifacts*. Amsterdam: Frank Visser. Retrieved from www.integralworld.net/kofman.html (accessed January 2001).

Kögler, H.-H. 2012. Agency and the Other: On the Intersubjective Roots of Self-Identity. *New Ideas in Psychology* 30: 47–64.

Korn, R. W. 2005. The Emergence Principle in Biological Hierarchies. *Biology and Philosophy* 20: 139–151.

Korten, D. 2015. Obama's Push for Corporate Rule: A Moment of Opportunity. *Yes! Online Magazine* (25 June). Retrieved from www.yesmagazine.org/obamas-push-for-corporate-rule-a-moment-of-opportunity.

Kosko, B. 1994. *Fuzzy Thinking: The New Science of Fuzzy Logic*. London: Flamingo.

Kotter, J. P. 1996. *Leading Change*. Cambridge, MA: Harvard Business School Press.

Kotter, J. P. and D. S. Cohen 2002. *The Heart of Change: Real-life Stories of how People Change Their Organizations*. Cambridge, MA: Harvard Business School Press.

Kraus, K. and Zohn, H. 1976. *Half-Truths and One-and-a-Half Truths: Selected Aphorisms*. Montreal: Engendra Press.

Krauth, B. 2004. Neoclassical Growth Theory. Retrieved from www.sfu.ca/~bkrauth/econ808/welcome.htm.

Krishnamurti, J. 1950. 3rd Public Talk, 18th June 1950, New York. Retrieved from www.jiddu-krishnamurti.net/en/1950_newyork/1950-06-18_new_york_3rd_public_talk_18th_june_1950.html (accessed 13 December 2008).

Krishnamurti, J. 1970. *The Urgency of Change*. New York: Harper & Row.

Kruglanski, A. W. and Gigerenzer, G. 2011. Intuitive and Deliberate Judgments Are Based on Common Principles. *Psychological Review* 118: 97–109.

Kwee, M. G. T. 2010. *A Social Psychology of Loving-kindness Carved in Stone*. Tilburg: Taos Institute.

Labouvie-Vief, G. 1990. Wisdom as Integrated Thought: Historical and Developmental Perspectives. In R. J. Sternberg (ed.), *Wisdom: Its Nature, Origins and Development*. Cambridge: Cambridge University Press.

Laibson, D. 1997. Golden Eggs and Hyperbolic Discounting. *Quarterly Journal of Economics* 112: 443–477.

Laird, D. A., Laird, E. C., Fruehling, R. T. and Swift, W. P. 1975. *Psychology: Human Relations and Motivation*. New York: McGraw Hill Book Company.

Lakoff, G. 2002. *Moral Politics: How Liberals and Conservatives Think*, 2nd edition. Chicago, IL: University of Chicago Press.

Lakoff, G. 2004. *Don't Think of an Elephant! Know Your Values and Frame the Debate. The Essential Guide for Progressives*. White River Junction, VT: Chelsea Green Publishing.

Lakoff, G. 2016. Understanding Trump. *Huffington Post*. Retrieved from www.huffington post.com/george-lakoff/understanding-trump_b_11144938.html (accessed 23 July 2016).

Lally, P. 1999. Identifying Non-Market Public Amenity Value Using a Values Jury. *Australian Property Journal* 35: 436–442.

Lally, P. 2000. The Values Jury on Trial: A Model for Public Consultation. Doctor of Philosophy thesis, Macquarie University, Sydney.

Lamont, M. 2012. Toward a Comparative Sociology of Valuation and Evaluation. *Annual Review of Sociology* 38: 201–221.

Landes, D. S. 1969. *The Unbound Prometheus: Technological Change and Industrial Development in Western Europe from 1750 to the Present*. New York: Press Syndicate of the University of Cambridge.

Lane, D. 2006–2015. David and Andrea Lane. Retrieved from www.integralworld.net/readingroom.html#DL.

Lane, D. C. 2014. On Reductionism. Retrieved from www.integralworld.net/lane3.html (accessed 16 November 2014).

Lane, N. and Martin, W. 2010. The Energetics of Genome Complexity. *Nature* 467: 929–934.

Lang, K. R. and Zhang, J. L. 1999. A Taoist Foundation of Systems Modeling and Thinking. *Proceedings of the 17th International Conference of the System Dynamics Society and the 5th Australian and New Zealand Systems Conference*, 20–23 July 1999, Wellington, New Zealand.

Lao Tzu. 1972. *The Tao Te Ching*, trans. Ch'u Ta Kao. London: Unwin.

Latour, B. 2004. Why Has Critique Run Out of Steam? From Matters of Fact to Matters of Concern. *Critical Inquiry* 30: 225–248.

Latour, B. 2013. *An Inquiry into Modes of Existence: An Anthropology of the Moderns*. Cambridge, MA: Harvard University Press.

Lawson, A. 2014a. A Conception of Social Ontology. In S. Pratten (ed.), *Social Ontology and Modern Economics*. New York: Routledge.

Lawson, A. 2014b. *Confronting Mathematical Modelling in Economics*. London: Bloomsbury.

Lawson, J. W. W. 2008. *Theory of Real Estate Valuation*. Masters of Business Masters, Royal Melbourne Institute of Technology.

Lazar, S. W., Kerr, C. E., Wasserman, R. H., Gray, J. R., Greve, D. N., Treadway, M. T., Mcgarvey, M., Quinn, B. T., Dusek, J. A. and Benson, H. 2005. Meditation Experience is Associated with Increased Cortical Thickness. *Neuroreport* 16: 1893.

Lazzarato, M. 2006. *The Machine*, trans. Mary O'Neill. Vienna: European Institute for Progressive Cultural Politics.

Leach, M. and Mearns, R. 1996. *The Lie of the Land: Challenging Received Wisdom on the African Environment*. London: International African Institute.

Lebow, R. N. 2012. *The Politics and Ethics of Identity: In Search of Ourselves*. New York: Cambridge University Press.

Leenhardt, M. 1979. *Do Kamo: Person and Myth in the Melanesian World*. Chicago, IL: University of Chicago Press.

Lesjak, C. n.d. 1750 to the Present: Acts of Enclosure and Their Afterlife. Retrieved from www.branchcollective.org/?ps_articles=carolyn-lesjak–1750-to-the-present-acts-of-enclosure-and-their-afterlife (accessed 6 May 2015).

Levinas, E. 1989. *The Levinas Reader*. Oxford: Basil Blackwell.

Levitt, K. 1990. Debt, Adjustment and Development: Looking to the 1990s. Lecture delivered at the Central Bank Auditorium, Port of Spain, 5 May 1990. Published as no. 8 in the Eric Williams Memorial Lecture series by the Friedrich Ebert Stiftung and the Association of Caribbean Economists.

Levy, R. I. and Heyman, P. 1975. *Tahitians: Mind and Experience in the Society Islands*. Chicago, IL: University of Chicago Press.

Lewis, M. W. and Grimes, A. J. 1999. Metatriangulation: Building Theory from Multiple Paradigms. *The Academy of Management Review* 24: 672–690.

Li, M. and Zhao, W. 2013. Essay on Kolmogorov Law of Minus 5 Over 3 Viewed with Golden Ratio. *Advances in High Energy Physics* 2013: 3.

Libet, B., Gleason, C. A., Wright, E. W. and Pearl, D. K. 1983. Time of Conscious Intention to Act in Relation to Onset of Cerebral Activity (Readiness-Potential): The Unconscious Initiation of a Freely Voluntary Act. *Brain* 106: 623–642.

Lieberman, E., Hauert, C. and Nowak, M. A. 2005. Evolutionary Dynamics on Graphs. *Nature Scientific Reports* 433: 312–316.

Linklater, A. 2015. *Owning the Earth: The Transforming History of Land Ownership*. London: Bloomsbury.

Lipsitz, G. 2011. *How Racism Takes Place*. Philadelphia, PA: Temple University Press.

Lissack, M. and Graber, A. 2014. *Modes of Explanation: Affordances for Action and Prediction*. Basingstoke: Palgrave Macmillan.

Locke, J. 1947 [1689]. *Two Treatises of Government*. New York: Hafner Publishing Company.

Locke, J. 1764 [1690]. *Second Treatise of Civil Government*, 6th edn. Adelaide: ebooks@Adelaide, University of Adelaide.

Lombard, M. 2012. *Land Tenure and Urban Conflict: A Review of the Literature*. GURC Working Paper Series. Manchester: Global Urban Research Centre, University of Manchester.

Londhe, S. n.d. European Imperialism. Retrieved from www.hinduwisdom.info/European_Imperialism13.htm (accessed 6 May 2015).

Long, C. 2004. Information Costs in Patent and Copyright. *Virginia Law Review* 90: 80.

Lorenz, E. N. 1963. Deterministic Nonperiodic Flow. *Journal of Atmospheric Sciences* 20: 130–141.

Lorenz, E. 1972. *Predictability: Does the Flap of a Butterfly's Wings in Brazil Set Off a Tornado in Texas?* Washington, DC: American Association for the Advancement of Science.

Lovino, S. 2014. Restoring the Imagination of Place: Narrative Reinhabitation and the Po Valley. In T. Lynch, C. Glotfelty and K. Armbruster (eds), *The Bioregional Imagination: Literature, Ecology, and Place*. Athens, GA: University of Georgia Press.

Lowsby, J. and De Groot, D. 2007. A Brief History of Urban Development and Upgrading in Swaziland. Washington, DC: Cities Alliance/World Bank. Retrieved from https://openknowledge.worldbank.org/bitstream/handle/10986/19051/879730WP0Box380grading0in0Swaziland.pdf?sequence=1 (accessed 6 April 2015).

Loy, D. 1993. Indra's Postmodern Net. *Philosophy East and West* 43: 481–510.

Loy, D. 2006. Wego: The Social Roots of Suffering. In M. McLeod (ed.), *Mindful Politics: A Buddhist Guide to Making the World a Better Place*. Boston, MA: Wisdom Publications.

Loy, D. R. 2010. *The World is Made of Stories*. Boston, MA: Wisdom Publications.

Luhmann, N. 1986. The Autopoiesis of Social Systems. In F. Geyer and J. Van Der Zeuwen (eds), *Sociocybernetic Paradoxes: Observation, Control and Evolution of Self-Steering Systems*. London: Sage.

Luna, F. V. and Klein, H. S. 2001. Brazil Since 1980. In H. S. Klein (ed.), *The World Since 1980*. Cambridge: Cambridge University Press.

Lundsgaarde, H. P. 1974. Pacific Land Tenure in a Nutshell. In H. P. Lundsgaarde (ed.), *Land Tenure in Oceania*. Honolulu, HI: University Press of Hawaii.

Lynas, M. 2007. *Six Degrees: Our Future on a Hotter Planet*. London: Fourth Estate.

Lynch, E. 1994. The Retreat of Liberation Theology. *Homiletic and Pastoral Review* 25: 12–21.

Lynn, M. 2013. The Bank Must Act to Stop Britain's Property Bubble. *Money Week* (23 May). Retrieved from https://moneyweek.com/the-bank-must-act-to-stop-britains-property-bubble-64118.

Machiavelli, N., Codevilla, A., Allen, W. B., Arkes, H. and Lord, C. 1997. *The Prince*. New Haven, CT: Yale University Press.

MacLean, P. D. 1973. *A Triune Concept of the Brain and Behaviour*. Toronto: University of Toronto Press.

Maclean, P. D. 1990. *The Triune Brain in Evolution; Role in Paleocerebral Functions*. London: Plenum Press.

Maddison, S. 2009. *Black Politics: Inside the Complexity of Aboriginal Political Culture*. Crows Nest, NSW: Allen & Unwin.

Mahajan, S., Binswanger, H., Cross, C., Davies, R., Im, F., Mengistae, T., Ngwenya, P., Philip, K., Van Seventer, S., D. D. and Zikhali, P. 2014. *Economics of South African Townships: Special Focus on Diepsloot*. Washington, DC, International Bank for Reconstruction and Development/World Bank Group.

Maine, H. S. 2007. *Ancient Law: Its Connection with the Early History of Society and Its Relation to Modern Ideas*. Salt Lake City, UT: Project Gutenberg. Retrieved from www.gutenberg.org/ebooks/22910 (accessed 10 March 2010).

Mandel, U. and Tearney, K. (directors). 2015. *Re-learning the Land: A Story of Read Crow College*. Documentary. Retrieved from http://enlivenedlearning.com.

Mandela, N. 1994. *Long Walk to Freedom*, New York: Little Brown & Company.

Marcuse, H. 1941. Review: Dewey, John, Theory of Valuation. *Zeitschrift für Sozialforschung* 9: 144–148.

Maritain, J. 1939. Integral Humanism and the Crisis of Modern Times. *The Review of Politics* 1: 1–17.

Markus, T. 2009. *Integral Theory: Four Works about Ken Wilber and Integral Thinking*. Zagreb: Croatian Institute of History.

Markus, T. 2010. *The Great Turning Point*. Zagreb: The Croatian Institute of History.

Marqués, G. 2015. Six Core Assumptions for a New Conceptual Framework for Economics. *Real-World Economics Review* 70: 17–26.

Marx, K. and Engels, F. 1985 [1888]. *The Communist Manifesto*. London: Penguin.

Masango, L. P. 2009. *Reading the Swazi Reed Dance (Umhlanga) as a Literary Traditional Performance Art*. Doctor of Philosophy thesis, University of the Witswatersrand.

Mascaro, J. S., Darcher, A., Negi, L. T. and Raison, C. 2015. The Neural Mediators of Kindness-Based Meditation: A Theoretical Model. *Frontiers in Psychology* 6: article 109. Retrieved from https://s3.amazonaws.com/academia.edu.documents/43406243/HYPOTHESIS_AND_THEORY_ARTICLE_The_neural20160305-21266-c9gr2n.pdf?AWSAccessKeyId=AKIAIWOWYYGZ2Y53UL3A&Expires=1522117090&

Signature=iPbarUl5emPVb6YmCEoaWkwjRJo%3D&response-content-disposition= inline%3B%20filename%3DThe_neural_mediators_of_kindness-based_m.pdf.

Maslow, A. 1966. *The Psychology of Science*. New York: Harper & Row.

Mason, P. H. 2015. Degeneracy: Demystifying and Destigmatizing a Core Concept in Systems Biology. *Complexity* 20: 12–21.

Massey, D. B. and Jess, P. 1995. *A Place in the World? Places, Culture and Globalization*. Oxford: Oxford University Press.

Maturana, H.R., and Varela, F. J. 1987. *The Tree of Knowledge*. London: Shambhala.

Max-Neef, M. A. 2005. Foundations of Transdisciplinarity. *Ecological Economics* 53: 5–16.

Maxwell, S. 2008. *The Price is Wrong: Understanding What Makes a Price Seem Fair and the True Cost of Unfair Pricing*, Hoboken, NJ: John Wiley & Sons.

Mayr, E. 1998. *This is Biology: The Science of the Living World*. Cambridge, MA: Belknap Press of Harvard University Press.

Mayr, E. 2001. *What Evolution Is*. New York: Basic Books.

Mbembe, A. 2003. Necropolitics. *Public Culture* 15: 11–40.

Mbiti, J. S. 1990. *African Religions and Philosophy*. London: Pearson Education.

McAdams, D. P., Josselson, R. and Lieblich, A. E. (Eds). 2006. *Identity and Story: Creating Self in Narrative*. Washington, DC: American Psychological Association.

McAuslan, P. 1985. *Urban Land and Shelter for the Poor*. London: Earthscan.

McAuslan, P. 2003. *Bringing the Law Back in: Essays in Land, Law and Development*. Aldershot: Ashgate.

McAuslan, P. 2013. *Land Law Reform in East Africa: Traditional or Transformative?* Abingdon: Routledge.

McBeth, M. K., Jones, M. D. and Shanahan, E. A. 2014. The Narrative Policy Framework. In P. A. Sabatier and C. M. Weible (eds), *Theories of the Policy Process*. Boulder, CO: Westview Press.

McClay, W. M. and McAllister, T. V. 2014. *Why Place Matters: Geography, Identity, and Civic life in Modern America*. New York: Encounter Books.

McCloskey, D. N. 1972. The Enclosure of Open Fields: Preface to a Study of Its Impact on the Efficiency of English Agriculture in the Eighteenth Century *The Journal of Economic History*, 32: 15–35.

McCloskey, D. N. 1991. The Prudent Peasant: New Findings on Open Fields. *Journal of Economic History* 51: 343–355.

McClure, S. M., Laibson, D. I., Loewenstein, G. and Cohen J. D. 2004. Separate Neural Systems Value Immediate and Delayed Monetary Rewards. *Science* 306 (5695): 503–507.

McDermott, M. 1992. The Environment: Static or Dynamic? In D. Solly (ed.), *Strategies for the Nineties*. Adelaide: AIVLE.

McDermott, M. 2012. The Catch-22 of Valuations in the Developing World. 26th Pan Pacific Congress of Real Estate Appraisers, Valuers and Counsellors, Melbourne.

McDermott, M. and Boydell, S. 2010. Complexity Epistemology and Real Property Rights. FIG Congress 2010: Facing the Challenges – Building the Capacity, Sydney.

McDermott, M. D. and Boydell, S. 2011. Complexity Epistemology, Complexity Axiology, and Real Property Rights. *Integral Leadership Review* 11: 1–6. Retrieved from http://integralleadershipreview.com/2570-complexity-epistemology-complexity-axiology-and-real-property-rights.

McDermott, M. and Noseda, A. 2015. Harnessing the Potential for Open Data for Valuation Transparency in the Developing World. In K. Deininger (ed.), *Linking Land Tenure and Use for Shared Prosperity*. Washington, DC: World Bank.

McDermott, M., Selabalo, C. and Boydell, S. 2015. Demystifying the Valuation of Customary Land. In K. Deininger (ed.), *Linking Land Tenure and Use for Shared Prosperity*. Washington, DC: World Bank.

McGilchrist, I. 2009. *The Master and His Emissary: The Divided Brain and the Making of the Western World*. New Haven, CT: Yale University Press.

McGilchrist, I. 2012 *The Divided Brain and the Search for Meaning*, Kindle edition. New Haven, CT: Yale University Press.

McGilchrist, I. 2017. *The Divided Brain: All in the Mind*. Sydney: Australian Broadcasting Corporation.

McGowan, K. A., Westley, F., Fraser, E. D. G., Loring, P. A., Weathers, K. C., Avelino, F., Sendzimir, J., Chowdhury, R. R. and Moore, M.-L. 2014. The Research Journey: Travels Across the Idiomatic and Axiomatic toward a Better Understanding of Complexity. *Ecology and Society* 19: article 37. Retrieved from http://pure.iiasa.ac.at/id/eprint/10807/1/ES-2014-6518.pdf.

McGrath, M.G. and Casey, E. 2002. Forensic Psychiatry and the Internet: Practical Perspectives on Sexual Predators and Obsessional Harassers in Cyberspace. *Journal of the American Academy of Psychiatry and Law* 30(1): 81–94.

McGraw-Hill. 2002. *Concise Dictionary of Modern Medicine*. New York: McGraw-Hill. Retrieved from http://medical-dictionary.thefreedictionary.com/necessary+fallibility (accessed 18 July 2016).

McGregor, S. and Fernando, C. 2005. Levels of Description: A Novel Approach to Dynamical Hierarchies. *Artificial Life* 11: 459–472.

McKay, J. P., Hill, B. D., Buckler, J., Ebrey, P. B., Beck, R. B., Crowston, C. H. and Wiesner-Hanks, M. E. 2008. *A History of World Societies*. New York: Bedford/St. Martin's.

McKibben, B. 2004. *Enough*. London: Bloomsbury.

McKinley, J. 2015. Critical Argument and Writer Identity: Social Constructivism as a Theoretical Framework for EFL Academic Writing. *Critical Inquiry in Language Studies* 12: 184–207.

McLarney, E. 2009. "Empire of the Machine": Oil in the Arabic Novel. *Boundary* 2(36): 177–198.

McLeay, M., Radla, A. and Thomas, R. 2014. Money Creation in the Modern Economy. *Bank of England Quarterly Bulletin* 2014(Q1): 14–27.

McWatt, A. 1998. Pirsig's Metaphysics of Quality. Retrieved from www.moq.org/forum/mcwatt/anthony.html (accessed 29 June 2015).

Mead, W. R. 2007. *God and Gold*. London: Atlantic Books.

Mehaffy, M. and Saligaros, N. 2013. The Network City. Retrieved from www.biourbanism.org/network-city (accessed 6 May 2015).

Menatti, L. 2013. Which Identity for Places? A Geophilosophical Approach. In D. Boswell, R. O'Shea and E. Tzadik (eds), *Interculturalism, Meaning and Identity*, 221–231. Oxford: Inter-Disciplinary Press.

Menatti, L. 2013a. A Rhizome of Landscapes. In C. Newman, Y. Nussaume and B. Pedroli (eds), *Landscape and Imagination: Towards a New Baseline for Education in a Changing World*. Conference, Paris, 2–4 May. UNISCAPE, Florence: Bandecchi and Vivaldi, Pontedera.

Menatti, L. and Da Rocha, A. 2016. Landscape and Health: Connecting Psychology, Aesthetics, and Philosophy through the Concept of Affordance. *Frontiers in Psychology* 7: article 571. Retrieved from http://repositorio.uchile.cl/bitstream/handle/2250/140692/Landscape-and-Health.pdf?sequence=1 (accessed 18 February 2017).

Mencken, H. L. 1921. *Prejudices: Second Series*. London: Jonathan Cape.

Mercier, H. and Sperber, D. 2011. Why Do Humans Reason? Arguments for an Argumentative Theory. *Behavioral and Brain Sciences* 34: 57–74.

Mercier, H. and D. Sperber 2017. *The Enigma of Reason*. Cambridge, MA: Harvard University Press.

Merleau-Ponty, M. and Séglard, D. 2003. *Nature: Course Notes from the Collège de France*. Evanston, IL: Northwestern University Press.

Merrill, T. W. 2011. The Property Prism. *Econ Journal Watch* 8: 247–254.

Merton, R. K. 1995. The Thomas Theorem and the Matthew Effect. *Social Forces* 74: 379–424.

Metzinger, T. and Windt, J. M. 2015. What Does it Mean to Have an Open Mind? In T. Metzinger and J. M. Windt (eds), *Open MIND*. Frankfurt am Main: MIND Group.

Meyer, L. F. F., et al. 2007. *The Development of the Willingness to Cooperate*. Londrina: XLV Congresso SOBER.

Meyer, L. F. F. 2008. The Commons Dilemma Revisited: Toward an Integral Approach. Doctor of Science thesis, Universidade Federal de Vicosa.

Meyer, L. F. F. and Braga, M. J. 2009. The Development of the Willingness to Cooperate: Collective-Action under the Light of the Constructivist Conception of Adult Development. Belém, Brazil: Institute of Socioenvironmental Studies, Federal Rural University of the Amazon.

Meyer, L. F. F. and Braga, M. J. 2009a. *Willingness to Cooperate and Stages of Moral Reasoning: Evidences from Common-Pool Resource Experiments with "Nonbinding" Communication and Sanctioning Conditions*. Theory and Policy Analysis. Bloomington, IN: Indiana University.

Meyer, L. F. F. 2010. *The Commons Dilemma Revisited: An Experimental Inquiry Linking Trustworthiness, Moral Conscience, and Willingness to Cooperate*. Saarbrücken: LAP LAMBERT Academic Publishing.

Meyer, L. F. F. and Braga, M. J. 2011. Fear or Greed? Duty or Solidarity? Motivations and Moral Reasoning: Experimental Evidences from Public-Goods Provision Dilemmas. 3rd World Planning Schools Congress, Perth.

Meyer, L. F. F. and Braga, M. J. 2015. Cognition and Norms: Toward a Developmental Account of Moral Agency in Social Dilemmas. *Frontiers in Psychology* 5: article 1528: Retrieved from www.researchgate.net/publication/42762819_Cognition_and_Norms_ Toward_a_Developmental_Theory_Linking_Trust_Reciprocity_and_Willingness_to_ Cooperate.

Meyer, L. F. F., Costa, F.M., Figueiredo, C., and Braga, M.J. 2013. Participatory Planning of Social and Spatial Organization in Agrarian Reform Policy in Brazil: An Assessment of the Implementation Challenges. *Journal of Civil Engineering and Architecture* 7(9): 1177–1188.

Mezza-Garcia, N., Froese, T. and Fernandez, N. 2014. Computational Aspects of Ancient Social Heterarchies: Learning to Address Contemporary Global Challenges. *Journal of Sociocybernetics* 12: 3–17.

Michaels, D. 2006. Daubert: The Most Influential Supreme Court Decision You've Never Heard Of. Retrieved from http://thepumphandle.wordpress.com/2006/12/07/ daubert-the-most-influential-supreme-court-decision-youve-never-heard-of (accessed 26 August 2014).

Midgley, M. 1995. *Beast and Man: the Roots of Human Nature*. London: Routledge Classics.

Midgley, M. 2003. *Heart and Mind: The Varieties of Moral Experience*. London: Routledge Classics.

Midgley, M. 2004. *The Myths We Live By*. London: Routledge.

Midgley, M. 2014. *Are You an Illusion?* London: Acumen Publishing.

Migoń, M. P. 2000. Logos and Ethos in the Thought of Anna-Teresa Tymieniecka. In A.-T. Tymieniecka (ed.), *The Origins of Life*. Dordrecht: Springer Netherlands.

Miksic, J. 1990. *Borobudur: Golden Tales of the Buddhas*. Hong Kong: Periplus Editions.

Minchin, T. 2011. Storm. Retrieved from www.youtube.com/watch?v=HhGuXCuDb1U (accessed 26 December 2014).

Mini, P. V. 1974. *Philosophy and Economics: The Origins and Development of Economic Theory*. Boca Raton, FL: University Presses of Florida.

Mishra, P. 2012. *From the Ruins of Empire: The Revolt against the West and the Remaking of Asia*. London: Penguin.

Moin, B. 1999. *Khomeini: The Life of the Ayatollah*. London: I. B. Taurus.

Molloy, R. P. 2004. *Law in a Market Context: An Introduction to Market Concepts in Legal Reasoning*. New York: Cambridge University Press.

Moore, G. E. 1903. *The Ideal: Principia Ethica*. Amherst, NY: Prometheus Books.

Moore, J. W. 2014. The End of Cheap Nature, or, How I learned to Stop Worrying about "the" Environment and Love the Crisis of Capitalism. In C. Suter and C. Chase-Dunn (eds), *Structures of the World Political Economy and the Future of Global Conflict and Cooperation*, 291–305. Berlin: LIT Verlag.

Moore, J. W. 2015. *Capitalism in the Web of Life*. London: Verso.

More, T. 1516. *Utopia*, ed. S. Dunscombe. New York: Minor Compositions. Retrieved from http://theopenutopia.org/wp-content/uploads/2012/09/Open-Utopia-fifth-poofs-facing-amended.pdf (accessed 1 September 2014).

Morgan, D. 2011. Beyond Epistemological Pluralism: Towards an Integrated Vision of the Future. *Futures* 43: 809–819.

Morin, E. 2007. Restricted Complexity, General Complexity. In C. Gershenson, D. Aerts and B. Edmonds (eds), *Worldviews, Science and Us: Philosophy and Complexity*, 5–29. Singapore: World Scientific.

Morowitz, H. J. 2002. *The Emergence of Everything: How the World Became Complex*. Oxford: Oxford University Press.

Morozov, E. 2013. *To Save Everything, Click Here: The Folly of Technological Solutionism*. New York: Public Affairs.

Morris, I. 2014. *War! What is it Good For? The Role of Conflict in Civilization, from Primates to Robots*. London: Profile Books.

Moshman, D. 1998. Identity as a Theory of Oneself. *The Genetic Epistemologist: The Journal of the Jean Piaget Society* 26(3). Retrieved from www.piaget.org/GE/1998/GE-26-3.html.

Mukerjee, M. 2010. *Churchill's Secret War: The British Empire and the Ravaging of India During World War II*. New York: Basic Books.

Mulgan, G. 2013. *The Locust and the Bee: Predators and Creators in Capitalism's Future*. Princeton, NJ: Princeton University Press.

Mulgan, G. 2014. The Wicked Problems Remain Wicked: Has the Craft and Science of Transforming Whole Systems Moved Forward, and How Could We Do Better? Congreso Wosc 2014, Universidad de Ibague, 15 October.

Mumford, L. 1922. *The Story of Utopias*. London: Forgotten Books.

Mumford, L. 1934. *Technics and Civilization*. New York: Harcourt, Brace & World.

Mumford, L. 1941. *Faith for Living*. London: Secker & Warburg.

Mumford, L. 1946. *City Development: Studies in Disintegration and Renewal*. London: Secker & Warburg.

Mumford, L. 1951. *The Conduct of Life*. New York: Harcourt Brace Jovanovich.

Mumford, L. 1954. *In the Name of Sanity*. New York: Harcourt, Brace.

Mumford, L. 1956. *The Transformation of Man*. New York: Harper & Row.

Mumford, L. 1961. *The City in History: Its Origins, Its Transformations, and Its Prospects.* San Diego, CA: Harvest, Harcourt, Inc.

Mumford, L. 1967. *The Myth of the Machine: Technics and Human Development.* New York: Harcourt Brace Jovanovich.

Mumford, L. 1970. *The Myth of the Machine: Pentagon of Power.* New York: Harcourt Brace Jovanovich.

Mumford, L. 1979. *My Works and Days: A Personal Chronicle.* New York: Harcourt Brace Jovanovich.

Munger, C. 1994. A Lesson on Elementary, Worldly Wisdom As It Relates To Investment Management and Business. Retrieved from www.ritholtz.com/blog/2012/02/a-lesson-on-elementary-worldly-wisdom-as-it-relates-to-investment-management-business (accessed 7 November 2014).

Murphy, J. M. and Gilligan, C. 1980. Moral Development in Late Adolescence and Adulthood: a Critique and Reconstruction of Kohlberg's Theory. *Human Development* 23: 77–104.

Murray, G. 2003. *Five Stages of Greek Religion.* New York: Dover Publications.

Murray, J. F. N. 1969. *Principles and Practice of Valuation.* Sydney: John Andrew & Co.

Musschenga, A. W., Van Haaften, W., Speiker, B. and Slors, M. 2002. *Personality and Moral Identity.* Dordrecht: Kluwer Academic Publishers.

Muthu, S. 2008. Adam Smith's Critique of International Trading Companies Theorizing "Globalization" in the Age of Enlightenment. *Political Theory* 36: 185–212.

Nader, R. 2014. *Unstoppable: The Emerging Left-Right Alliance to Dismantle the Corporate State.* New York: Nation Books.

Nagel, T. 1986. *The View From Nowhere.* Oxford: Oxford University Press.

National Commission on Terrorist Attacks upon the United States. 2004. *The 9/11 Commission Report: Final Report of the National Commission on Terrorists Attacks upon the United States.* New York: Norton.

Ndlovu, M., Dlamini, C. S. and Nkambule, B. 2014. Towards a Theoretical Framework for Sustainable Smallholder Irrigation Farming: A Case Study of Lusip Smallholder Sugar-Cane Farmers in Swaziland. *African Journal of Agricultural Research* 9: 3205–3214.

Nelson, R. H. 2002. *Economics as Religion: From Samuelson to Chicago and Beyond.* Philadelphia, PA: Pennsylvania State University Press.

NESCI. n.d. Multiscale Methods. Retrieved from www.necsi.edu/research/multiscale (accessed 11 July 2016).

Neve, M. 2015. Through the Looking-Map: Mapping as a Milieu of Individuation. In A. Sarti, F. Montanari and Francesco Galofaro (eds), *Morphogenesis and Individuation*, 111–140. Berlin: Springer.

Newton, I. 1974. *Newton's Philosophy of Nature: Selections from his Writings*, ed. H. S. Thayer. New York: Haffner Press.

Ney, S. M. and Verweij, M. 2014. Messy Institutions for Wicked Problems: How to Generate Clumsy Solutions. Retrieved from http://ssrn.com/abstract=2382191 (accessed 11 September 2015).

Nicolescu, B. 2006. Transdisciplinarity – Past, Present and Future. In B. Haverkort and C. Reijntjes (eds), *Moving Worldviews: Reshaping Sciences, Policies and Practices for Endogenous Sustainable Development.* Leusden: ETC/COMPAS.

Niebuhr, R. 2001. *Moral Man and Immoral Society: A Study in Ethics and Politics.* Louisville, KY: Westminster John Knox Press.

Nielsen, J. A., et al. 2013. An Evaluation of the Left-Brain vs. Right-Brain Hypothesis with Resting State Functional Connectivity Magnetic Resonance Imaging. *PLoS ONE* 8(8): e71275.

Normand, R. 2016. *The Changing Epistemic Governance of European Education: The Fabrication of the Homo Academicus Europeanus?* New York: Springer International Publishing.

Norththrup, T. A. 1989. The Dynamic of Identity in Personal and Social Conflict. In L. Kriesberg and T. A. Northrup (eds), *Intractable Conflicts and their Transformation.* Syracuse, NY: Syracuse University Press.

Nugapitiya, M., Boydell S. and Healy, P. 2009. Engaging "Meaning" in the Analysis of the Project. Presented at IRNOPIx International Research Network on Organizing by Projects, Berlin, Germany, October 2009.

Nussbaum, M. 1997. Flawed Foundations: The Philosophical Critique of (a Particular Type of) Economics. *University of Chicago Law Review* 64: 1197–1214.

O'Brien, B. 2015. Buddhism and Compassion. Retrieved from http://buddhism.about.com/od/basicbuddhistteachings/a/compassion.htm.

Odin, S. 1982. *Process Metaphysics and Hua-Yen Buddhism: A Critical Study of Cumulative Penetration vs Interpenetration.* New York: State University of New York.

Oh, K. 2000. The Taoist Influence on Hua-yen Buddhism: A Case of the Scinization of Buddhism in China. *Chung-Hwa Buddhist Journal* 13(2): 277–297.

O'Keefe, K. 2011. Where Kotter's 8 Steps Gets it Wrong. Retrieved from www.cebglobal.com/blogs/where-kotters-8-steps-gets-it-wrong (accessed 24 July 2016).

Okoth-Ogendo, H. W. O. 1998. Land Policy Development in Sub-Saharan Africa: Mechanisms, Processes and Outcomes. International Conference on Land Tenure in the Developing World with focus on Southern Africa, Cape Town.

Okoth-Ogendo, H. 2000. Legislative Approaches to Customary Tenure and Tenure Reform in East Africa. In C. Toulmin and J. Quan (eds), *Evolving Land Rights, Policy and Tenure in Africa.* London: DFID/IIED/NRI.

Oliver, K. 2007. Stopping the Anthropological Machine: Agamben with Heidegger and Merleau-Ponty. *PhaenEx* 2: 1–23.

Oliver, K. 2009. *Animal Lessons: How They Teach Us to be Human.* New York: Columbia University Press.

Olson, G. 2012. *Empathy Imperiled: Capitalism, Culture, and the Brain.* New York: Springer.

Olwig, K. and Besson, J. 2005. Introduction: Caribbean Narratives of Belonging. *Caribbean Narratives of Belonging: Fields of Relations, Sites of Identity.* Basingstoke: Palgrave Macmillan.

Ormerod, P. 1994. *The Death of Economics.* London: Faber & Faber.

Ormerod, P. 2014. How Decisions are Made. NESS Policy Conference, London, October.

Orrell, D. 2018. Economics is Quantum. Retrieved from https://aeon.co/essays/has-the-time-come-for-a-quantum-revolution-in-economics (accessed 8 January 2018).

Osborn, P. G. 1964. *A Concise Law Dictionary.* London: Sweet & Maxwell.

Overton, W. F. 2013. A New Paradigm for Developmental Science: Relationism and Relational-Developmental Systems. *Applied Developmental Science* 17: 94–107.

Pace, S. 2012. Writing the Self into Research Using Grounded Theory Analytic Strategies in Autoethnography. In N. McLaughlin and D. L. Brien (eds), *Creativity: Cognitive, Social and Cultural Perspectives.* TEXT special issue 13. Retrieved from www.textjournal.com.au/speciss/issue13/Pace.pdf (accessed 27 March 2018).

Page, S. 2007. Type Interaction Models and the Rule of Six. *Economic Theory* 30: 223–241.

Palm, D. J. 1997. *The Red Herring of Usury: This Rock.* San Diego, CA: Catholic Answers.

Palmer, H. 2014. Steps towards Fourfold Vision: From the Myth of Power to a Cybernetic Unity of Healing. Retrieved from www.academia.edu/8773220/Steps_towards_fourfold_

vision_From_the_myth_of_power_to_a_cybernetic_unity_of_healing (accessed 7 May 2014).

Palmer, R. 2007. *Literature Review of Governance and Secure Access to Land*. London: Prepared for DfID through the North South Consultants Exchange through the Governance and Social Development Resource Centre Framework.

Panaritis, E. 2007. *Prosperity Unbound: Building Property Markets with Trust*. New York: Palgrave Macmillan.

Panikkar, R. 1989. *The Silence of God*. New York: Orbis.

Panikkar, R. 1989a. *Epistula de Pace: A Booklet Response to Philosophica Pacis*. Homenaje a Raimon Panikkar. Madrid: Simbolo Editorial.

Panksepp, J. and Panksepp, J. B. 2000. The Seven Sins of Evolutionary Psychology. *Evolution and Cognition* 6: 108–131.

Pascal, B. 1669. *Pensées*. Salt Lake City, UT: Project Gutenberg. Retrieved from www.gutenberg.org/ebooks/18269 (accessed 15 July 2014).

Passuello, L. 2007. Top 3 Reasons to Improve Your Vocabulary. Retrieved from https://litemind.com/top–3-reasons-to-improve-your-vocabulary/ (accessed 19 August 2014).

Patriquin, L. 2004. The Agrarian Origins of the Industrial Revolution in England. *Review of Radical Political Economics* 36: 196–216.

Patterson, P. J. 2006. The Promise of Caribbean Unity. 20th Dr Eric Williams Memorial Lecture, Central Bank Auditorium, Port of Spain, Trinidad and Tobago, May 2006.

Patterson, N., Moorjani, P., Luo, Y., Mallick, S., Rohland, N., Zhan, Y., Genschoreck, T., Webster, T. and Reich, D. 2012. Ancient Admixture in Human History. *Genetics* 192: 1065–1093.

Payne, G. 1997. *Urban Land Tenure and Property Rights in Developing Countries: A Review of the Literature*. London: Intermediate Technology Publications/Overseas Development Administration.

Payne, G. 2001. Urban Land Tenure Policy Options: Titles or Rights? *Habitat International* 25: 415–429.

Pearson, Z. 2008. Spaces of International Law. *Griffiths Law Review* 17: 489–514.

Peden, J. R. 1977. Property Rights in Celtic Irish Law. *Journal of Libertarian Studies* 1: 81–96.

Pedersen, M. A. 2011. *Not Quite Shamans: Spirit Worlds and Political Lives in Northern Mongolia*. Ithaca, NY: Cornell University Press.

Pedersen, M. A. 2012. Common Nonsense: A Review of Certain Recent Reviews of the "Ontological Turn." Retrieved from http://aotcpress.com/articles/common_nonsense.

Pels, D. 1986. *Property or Power? A Study in Intellectual Rivalry*. Amsterdam: University of Amsterdam.

Penalver, E. M. and Alexander, G. S. 2012. *An Introduction to Property Theory*. Cambridge: Cambridge University Press.

Perc, M. 2014. The Matthew Effect in Empirical Data. *Journal of the Royal Society Interface* 11: 20140378.

Pereira, J. M. M. 2016. Modernization, the Fight Against Poverty, and Land Markets: An Analysis of the World Bank's Agriculture and Rural Development Policies (1944–2003). *Varia Historia* 32: 225–258.

Perlman, J. 2010. *Favela: Four Decades of Living on the Edge in Rio de Janiero*. New York: Oxford University Press.

Pieper, J. 2009. *Leisure: the Basis of Culture*. San Francisco, CA: Ignatius Press.

Pierce, R. 2017. Nature, The Golden Ratio and Fibonacci Numbers. Retrieved from www.mathsisfun.com/numbers/nature-golden-ratio-fibonacci.html (accessed 27 January 2018).

Pierson, C. 2013. *Just Property: A History in the Latin West, Volume One: Wealth, Virtue, and the Law*. Oxford: Oxford University Press.

Piketty, T. 2014. *Capital in the Twenty-First Century*. Cambridge, MA: Belknap Press of the Harvard University Press.

Pilote 1996. The Public-Debt Problem. In L. Even (ed.), *In This Age of Plenty*. Rougemont, Ontario: Pilgrims of St. Michael.

Pines, D. 2014. *Emergence: A Unifying Theme for 21st Century Science*. Santa Fe, NM: Santa Fe Institute. Retrieved from https://medium.com/sfi-30-foundations-frontiers/emergence-a-unifying-theme-for-21st-century-science-4324ac0f951e (accessed 8 December 2014).

Pinker, S. 2011. *The Better Angels of Our Nature: Why Violence Has Declined*. New York: Viking.

Pirsig, R. 1974. *Zen and the Art of Motorcycle Maintenance*. London: Bantam Books.

Pirsig, R. M. 1991. *Lila: An Inquiry into Morals*. London: Corgi.

Ploog, D. W. 2003. The Place of the Triune Brain in Psychiatry. *Physiology and Behavior* 79: 487–493.

Poblador, N. S. 2014. Finding a Common Framework for the Analysis of Social and Institutional Change: A Retrospective and an Exploration. *Philippine Science Letters* 7: 146–154.

Polanyi, K. 1957. *The Great Transformation: The Political and Economic Origins of Our Time*. Boston, MA: Beacon Press.

Polanyi, K. 2001 [1944]. *The Great Transformation: The Political and Economic Origins of Our Time*. Boston, MA: Beacon Press.

Pollack, J. 2013. Pluralist Project Research: Drawing on Critical Systems Thinking to Manage Research across Paradigms. In N. Drouin, R. Müller and S. Sankaran (eds), *Novel Approaches to Organizational Project Management Research: Translational and Transformational*. Copenhagen: CBS Press.

Popper, K. R. 2002. *The Logic of Scientific Discovery*. London: Routledge.

Porges, S. W. 2003. The Polyvagal Theory: Phylogenetic Contributions to Social Behavior. *Physiology and Behavior* 79: 503–513.

Poteete, A. R. 2003. Challenging the Property Rights Paradigm: Professional Norms and Policies for Private Ranching in Botswana. Retrieved from www.academia.edu/12285209/Ideas_Interests_and_Institutions_Challenging_the_Property_Rights_Paradigm_in_Botswana.

Poundstone, W. 2013. *The Recursive Universe: Cosmic Complexity and the Limits of Scientific Knowledge*. New York: Dover.

Presland, G. 2013. Core Values in Aboriginal Religions. *The Beacon*, July: 6–9.

Proshansky, H. M., Fabian, A. K. and Kaminoff, R. 1983. Place-Identity: Physical World Socialization of the Self. *Journal of Environmental Psychology* 3: 57–83.

Qutb, S. 2000. The America I Have Seen: In the Scale of Human Values (1951). In A.-M. Kamal (ed.), *America in an Arab Mirror: Images of America in Arabic Travel Literature: An Anthology*. New York: St Martin's.

Radin, M. J. 1982. Property and Personhood. *Stanford Law Review* 34: 957–1988.

Ramp, D. and Bekoff, M. 2015. Compassion as a Practical and Evolved Ethic for Conservation. *BioScience* 65(3): 323–327.

Rand, A. 1974. Ayn Rand Quote of the Week. Retrieved from http://aynrandcontrahumannature.blogspot.com.au/2007/10/ayn-rand-quote-of-week-51007.html.

Raphael, R. 2010. Debunking Tea Party Myths. *American History* 45(2): 60–65. Retrieved from www.historynet.com/debunking-boston-tea-party-myths.htm (accessed 26 January 2015).

Ravn, I. 2015. Explaining Money Creation by Commercial Banks: Five Analogies for Public Education. *Real World Economic Review* 71: 92–111.

Rayman, R. A. 2013. *A Multi-Gear Strategy for Economic Recovery*. Basingstoke: Palgrave Macmillan.

Reich, W. 1946. *The Mass Psychology of Fascism*. New York: Orgone Press.

Reuter, T. 2006. *Sharing the Earth, Dividing the Land: Land and Territory in the Austronesian World*. Canberra: ANU Press.

Riem Natale, A. 2016. Lords of Peace, Lords of War. *Simplegadi* 14–15: 6–15.

Rinaudo, T. 2014. Regreening Ethiopia. In J. Green (ed.), *Sunday Extra*. Sydney: Australian Broadcasting Corporation.

Ring, A. A. and Boykin, J. A. 1986. *The Valuation of Real Estate*. Englewood Cliffs, NJ: Prentice-Hall.

Rittel, H. W. J. and Webber, M. M. 1973. Dilemmas in a General Theory of Planning. *Policy Sciences* 4: 155–169.

Roar, R. and Martos, J. 1992. *The Wild Man's Journey*. Cincinnati, OH: St Anthony Messenger Press.

Robertson, I. 2000. *Mind Sculpture*. London: Bantam.

Robins, N. 2003. Loot: In Search of the East India Company, the World's First Transnational Corporation. *Environment and Urbanization* 14: 79–88.

Rockström, J., W., Steffen, K., Noone, Å., Persson, F. S., Chapin, E., Lambin, T. M., Lenton, M., Scheffer, C., Folke, H., Schellnhuber, B., Nykvist, C. A., de Wit, T., Hughes, S., van der Leeuw, H., Rodhe, S., Sörlin, P. K., Snyder, R., Costanza, U., Svedin, M., Falkenmark, L., Karlberg, R. W., Corell, V. J., Fabry, J., Hansen, B., Walker, D., Liverman, K., Richardson, P., Crutzen, P. and Foley., J. 2009 Planetary Boundaries: Exploring the Safe Operating Space for Humanity. *Ecology and Society* 14: article 32.

Rockwell, W. T. 2005. *Neither Brain Nor Ghost: A Nondualist Alternative to the Mind–Brain Identity Theory*. Cambridge, MA: MIT Press.

Rohr, R. and Martos, J. 1992. *The Wild Man's Journey*. Cincinnati, OH: St Anthony Messenger Press.

Rollins, W. G. 2011. The Three Faces of Evil in Jungian Psychology: The Shadow Side of Reality. In J. H. Ellens (ed.), *Explaining Evil*. Santa Barbara, CA: Praeger.

Roosevelt, K. 1979. *Countercoup: the Struggle for the Control of Iran*. New York: McGraw-Hill.

Rosado, C. 2003. What Is Spirituality? Memetics, Quantum Mechanics and the Spiral of Spirituality. Retrieved from www.eastern.edu/academic/campolo/inst/gcar/PDF/Spirituality-SD.pdf (accessed 18 April 2014).

Rosado, C. 2008. Context Determines Content: Quantum Physics as a Framework for "Wholeness" in Urban Transformation. *Urban Studies* 45: 2075–2097.

Rose, S. 2006. *The 21st Century Brain: Explaining, Mending and Manipulating the Mind*. London: Random House.

Rosenbaum, S., Nguyen, D., Lenehan, T., Tiedemann, A., van der Ploeg, H. and Sherrington, C. 2011. Exercise Augmentation Compared to Usual Care for Post Traumatic Stress Disorder: A Randomised Controlled Trial (the REAP Study: Randomised Exercise Augmentation for PTSD). *BMC Psychiatry* 11: 115.

Ross, S. N. and Commons, M. L. 2008. Applying Hierarchical Complexity to Political Development. *World Futures* 64: 17.

Ross, S. N., et al. 2014. Toward Defining Order 16 and Describing its Performance for the Model of Hierarchical Complexity. *Behavioral Development Bulletin* 19(3): 33–36.

Roszak, T. 1972. *Where The Wasteland Ends: Politics and Transcendence in Postindustrial Society*. Garden City, NY: Doubleday & Company.

Roth, J. 2004. *The White Cities: Reports from France, 1925–39.* London: Granta Books.

Rowson, J. 2011. Transforming Behaviour Change: Beyond Nudge and Neuromania. Retrieved from www.climateaccess.org/resource/transforming-behaviour-change-beyond-nudge-and-neuromania (accessed 13 February 2015).

Rowson, J. 2014. Spiritualise: Revitalising Spirituality to Address 21st Century Challenges. Retrieved from www.thersa.org/globalassets/pdfs/reports/spiritualise-report.pdf.

Rowson, J. and McGilchrist, I. 2013. Divided Brain, Divided World. Retrieved from www.thersa.org/globalassets/pdfs/blogs/rsa-divided-brain-divided-world.pdf (accessed 17 July 2016).

Rucker, R. 1987. *Mind Tools: the Five Levels of Mathematical Reality.* Boston, MA: Houghton Mifflin Company.

Rucker, R. 1997. *Infinity and the Mind.* London: Penguin.

Ruhl, J. B. 1996. Complexity Theory as a Paradigm for the Dynamical Law-and-Society System: A Wake-Up Call for Legal Reductionism and the Modern Administrative State. *Duke Law Journal* 45(5): 849–928.

Rumsey, D. 2005. When Location Matters: The Past and the Future of Mapping. Retrieved from http://web.archive.org/web/20130729211228id_/http://itc.conversationsnetwork.org/shows/detail633.html (accessed 28 February 2017).

Russell, B. 1956. *Portraits from Memory.* London: George Allen & Unwin.

Russell, P. H. 2006. *Recognising Aboriginal Title: The Mabo Case and Indigenous Resistance to English-Settler Colonialism.* Toronto: University of Toronto Press.

Rutherford, A., Harmon, D., Werfel, J., Gard-Murray, A. S., Bar-Yam, S., Gros, A., Xulvi-Brunet, R. and Bar-Yam, Y. 2014. Good Fences: The Importance of Setting Boundaries for Peaceful Coexistence. *PLoS ONE* 9: e95660.

Sachs, J. 2015. By Separating Nature from Economics, We Have Walked Blindly into a Tragedy. *The Guardian*, 10 March. Retrieved from www.theguardian.com/global-development-professionals-network/2015/mar/10/jeffrey-sachs-economic-policy-climate-change.

Sagan, C. 1990. *Cosmos: A Personal Voyage.* Sydney: Random House.

Sagan, C. and Druyans, A. 1992. *Shadows of Forgotten Ancestors: A Search for Who We Are.* Sydney: Random House.

Sagoff, M. 2012. The Rise and Fall of Ecological Economics. Retrieved from https://thebreakthrough.org/index.php/journal/past-issues/issue-2/the-rise-and-fall-of-ecological-economics (accessed 26 November 2017).

Salzman, D. A. and Zwinkels, R. C. J. 2013. *Behavioural Real Estate.* Tinbergen: Tinbergen Institute.

Samuel, R. and Thompson, P. E. 1990. *The Myths We Live By.* London: Routledge.

Samuelson, P. A., Hancock, K. and Wallace, R. 1970. *Economics: An Introductory Analysis.* Sydney: McGraw Hill.

Sardar, Z. 2010. Welcome to Postnormal Times. *Futures* 42(5): 435–444.

Sardar, Z. and Abrams, I. 2004. *Introducing Chaos.* Crows Nest, NSW: Allen & Unwin.

Sargant, W. 1963. *Battle for the Mind: A Physiology of Conversion and Brain-Washing.* London: Pan.

Sarker, R., Mohammadian, M. and Xin Yao (eds). 2002. *Evolutionary Optimalization.* Berlin: Springer.

Saul, J. R. 1997. *The Unconscious Civilization.* London: Penguin.

Sayama, H., Pestov, I., Schmidt, J., Bush, B. J., Wong, Yamanoi, J. and Gross, T. 2013. Modeling Complex Systems with Adaptive Networks. *Computers and Mathematics with Applications* 65: 1645–1664.

Scaramuzzi, I. 2014. *Francis: "Usury is Not Human, it is a Social Evil".* Vatican City: Vatican Insider, La Stampa.

Schleiermacher, F. 1958. *On Religion: Speeches to its Cultured Despisers.* New York: Harper.

Schmidt, C. U., Hertl, C. and Wicke, H. 2005. *Real Property Law and Procedure in the European Union: General Report.* Florence: European University Institute.

Schore, J. R. and Schore, A. N. 2008. Modern Attachment Theory: The Central Role Regulation in Development and Treatment. *Clinical Social Work Journal* 36: 9–20.

Schwartz, M. 2013. On Social Holons, Ideologies of Integral, and the Kosmological Call of Politics: Beyond Methodological Individualism in Integral Theory and Practice. *Journal of Integral Theory and Practice* 8: 163–174.

Scudder, T. 2005. *The Future of Large Dams: Dealing with Social, Environmental, Institutional and Political Costs.* London: Earthscan.

Sebring, E. 2015. Civilization and Barbarism: Cartoon Commentary and "The White Man's Burden" (1898–1902). Retrieved from https://ocw.mit.edu/ans7870/21f/21f.027/civilization_and_barbarism/cb_essay01.html.

Sedlacek, T. and Havel, V. 2011. *Economics of Good and Evil: The Quest for Economic Meaning from Gilgamesh to Wall Street.* New York: Oxford University Press.

Sejnowski, T. and Oakley, B, n.d. Introduction to the Focused and Diffuse Modes. Online Course on Learning How to Learn, Lecture 1. University of California, San Diego. Retrieved from www.coursera.org/learn/learning-how-to-learn/lecture/75EsZ/introduction-to-the-focused-and-diffuse-modes.

Selabalo, C. 2016. GLTN: Securing Land and Property Rights for All. FIG Working Week, 2–6 May 2016, Christchurch, New Zealand.

Selebano, B. 2016. Leaders to Promote Ubuntu. Retrieved from www.ann7.com/leaders-to-promote-ubuntu (accessed 12 May 2016).

Sen, A. 1977. Rational Fools: a Critique of the Behavioural Foundations of Economic Theory. *Philosophy and Public Affairs* 6 (summer): 317–344.

Serres, M. 1995. *The Natural Contract.* Ann Arbor, MI: University of Michigan Press.

Shanahan, E. A., Jones, M. D., McBeth, M. K. and Lane, R. R. 2013. An Angel on the Wind: How Heroic Policy Narratives Shape Policy Realities. *Policy Studies Journal* 41: 453–483.

Shand, M. A. 1994. An Annotated Bibliography of Vocabulary-Related Work. Champaign, IL: Johnson O'Connor Research Foundation, College of Education, University of Illinois at Urbana Champaign.

Sheehan, J. and Wahrman, D. 2015. *Invisible Hands: Self-Organization and the Eighteenth Century.* Chicago, IL: University of Chicago Press.

Sheehan, R. J. and Rode, S. 1999. On Scientific Narrative: Stories of Light by Newton and Einstein. *Journal of Business and Technical Communication* 13(3): 336–358.

Sheldrake, R. 2012. *The Science Delusion: Feeling the Spirit of Enquiry.* London: Hodder & Stoughton.

Shell, M. 1993. *Children of the Earth: Literature, Politics, and Nationhood.* Oxford: Oxford University Press.

Sheppard, R. Z. 1974. Books: The Enormous Vrooom. *Time* (15 April). Retrieved from http://content.time.com/time/magazine/article/0,9171,911198-2,00.html#ixzz0vP8WURV4 (accessed 28 March 2018).

Shipman, M. D. 2014. *The Limitations of Social Research.* Abingdon: Routledge.

Shipton, P. M. D. 2007. *The Nature of Entrustment: Intimacy, Exchange, and the Sacred in Africa.* New Haven, CT: Yale University Press.

Shipton, P. M. D. 2009. *Mortgaging the Ancestors: Ideologies of Attachment in Africa.* New Haven, CT: Yale University Press.

Shipton, P. M. D. 2010. *Credit Between Cultures: Farmers, Financiers, and Misunderstanding in Africa.* New Haven, CT: Yale University Press.

Sidebotham, N. 2009. "The White Man Never Wanna Hear Nothin about What's Different from Him": Representations of Laws "Other" in Australian Literature. PhD thesis, Murdoch University, Perth.

Silverman, L. K. 1994. The Moral Sensitivity of Gifted Children and the Evolution of Society. *Roeper Review* 17: 110–116.

Simberloff, D. 2004. Community Ecology: Is It Time to Move On? (An American Society of Naturalists Presidential Address). *The American Naturalist* 163: 787–799.

Sindic, D. and Condor, S. 2014. Social Identity Theory and Self-Categorization Theory. In T. Capelos, C. Kinvall, P. Nesbitt-Larkin and H. Dekker (eds), *The Palgrave Handbook of Global Political Psychology*. Basingstoke: Palgrave Macmillan.

Singal, D. J. 1991. The Other Crisis in American Education. *The Atlantic Monthly* 268(5): 59–74.

Singer, J. W. 2000. *Entitlement: the Paradoxes of Property*. New Haven, CT: Yale University Press.

Skolimowski, H. 1993. An Evolutionary Concept of Spirituality. *A Sacred Place to Dwell: Living with Reverence Upon the Earth*. Rockport, MA: Elements.

Sloman, S. and Fernbach. P. 2017. *The Knowledge Illusion: Why We Never Think Alone*. London: Pan Macmillan.

Small, G. and Sheehan J. 2005. Selling Your Family: Why Customary Title is Incomparable to Western Conceptions of Property Value. Retrieved from www.academia.edu/1396111/Selling_Your_Family_Why_customary_title_is_incomparable_to_Western_conceptions_of_property_value (accessed 18 February 2017).

Smarandache, F. 2010. *Multispace and Multistructure Neutrosophic Transdisciplinarity*. Hanko, Finland: North-European Scientific Publishers.

Smith, A. 1776. *The Nature and Causes of the Wealth of Nations*. London: W. Strahan and T. Cadell.

Smith, A. 1790. *The Theory of Moral Sentiments*. London: A. Millar.

Smith, A. 2001. The Spectrum of Holons. Retrieved from www.integralworld.net/smith2.html (accessed 14 July 2016).

Smith, C. E. 1993. The Land Tenure System in Ireland: A Fatal Regime. *Marquette Law Review* 76: 469, 481–483.

Smith, K. V. 2005. Tupaia's Sketchbook. Retrieved from www.bl.uk/eblj/2005articles/pdf/article10.pdf.

Smith, R. K. 2001. *The Dimensions of Value*. Dallas, TX: Clear Direction. Retrieved from www.cleardirection.com/docs/dimensions.asp.

Smocovitis, V. B. 2014. The Unifying Vision: Julian Huxley, Evolutionary Humanism, and the Evolutionary Synthesis. In G. K. H. Somsen (ed.), *Pursuing the Unity of Science: Ideology and Scientific Practice Between the Great War and the Cold War*. Farnham: Ashgate Press.

Snowden, D. J. and Boone, M. 2007. A Leader's Framework for Decision Making. *Harvard Business Review* 85(11): 68–76.

Sobel, D. 1998. *Longitude*. London: Fourth Estate.

Society for the Diffusion of Useful Knowledge. 1836. *The Penny Cyclopædia of the Society for the Diffusion of Useful Knowledge*. London: Charles Knight.

Sohst, W. 2009. *Prozessontologie: Ein systematischer Entwurf der Entstehung von Existenz*. Berlin: Xenomoi.

Soma, K. 2006. Natura Economic in Environmental Valuation. *Environmental Values* 15: 31–50.

Song, D. 2007. Non-computability of Consciousness. *NeuroQuantology* 5: 382–391.

Song, D. 2015. Consciousness Does Not Compute (and Never Will), Says Korean Scientist. Retrieved from https://wemustknow.wordpress.com/2015/05/06/consciousness-does-not-compute-and-never-will-says-korean-scientist.

Sonnert, G. 1994. Limits of Morality: A Sociological Approach to Higher Moral Stages. *Journal of Adult Development* 1: 127–134.

Sonnert, G. and Commons, M. L. 1994. Society and the Highest Stages of Modern Development. *Politics and the Individual* 4: 31–55.

Sornette, D. 2009. Dragon-Kings, Black Swans and the Prediction of Crises. *International Journal of Terraspace Science and Engineering* 2: 18.

Sosnitsky, A. V. 2011. Artificial Intelligence and Unresolved Scientific Problems. *International Journal of Information Theories and Applications* 18: 82–92.

Sousanis, N. 2015. *Unflattening*. Cambridge, MA: Harvard University Press.

Speel, H.-C. 1995. Memetics: On a Conceptual Framework for Cultural Evolution. Einstein Meets Magritte, Free University of Brussels, June.

Spinoza, B. D. 2002. *Spinoza: Complete Works*. Indianapolis, IN: Hackett Publishing Company.

Splash, C. L. 2012. New Foundations for Ecological Economics. *Ecological Economics* 77: 11.

Stankov, L. 2014. Comment: What Goes on in the Mind of a Militant Extremist? Retrieved from www.sbs.com.au/news/article/2014/08/19/comment-what-goes-mind-militant-extremist.

Stankov, L., Saucier, G. and Knezevic, G. 2010. Militant Extremist Mind-Set: Proviolence, Vile World, and Divine Power. *Psychological Assessment* 22: 70–86.

Stanley, K. 2013. When Algorithms Inform Real Life: Novelty Search and the Myth of the Objective. In L. Correia, L. P. Reis, J. Cascalho, L. M. Gomes, H. Guerra and P. Cardoso (eds), *16th Portuguese Conference on Artificial Intelligence (EPIA 2014)*, 2013 Angra do Heroismo, Azores, Portugal. Universidade dos Acores, Portugal: CMATI.

Stanley, K. O. and Lehman, J. 2015. *Why Greatness Cannot Be Planned: The Myth of the Objective*. Berlin: Springer International Publishing.

Stannard, D. E. 1992. *American Holocaust*. New York: Oxford University Press.

Stark, D. 2000. *For a Sociology of Worth*. Meetings of the European Association of Evolutionary Political Economy. Berlin: Center on Organizational Innovation.

Stedile, J. P. 2010. *Most Advanced Land Reform Project to Date is Still the One Presented by João Goulart's Administration*. Chicago, IL: Friends of the MST. Retrieved from www.mstbrazil.org/news/50410-republican-democratic-reform-necessary-brazil-pagina-64-interview-joao-pedro-stedile (accessed 27 August 2014).

Sterling, S. 2003. Whole Systems Thinking as a Basis for Paradigm Change in Education: Explorations in the Context of Sustainability. PhD thesis, University of Bath.

Sterman, J. D. 2002. All Models are Wrong: Reflections on Becoming a Systems Scientist. *Systems Dynamics Review* 18: 501–531.

Stern, D. S. 2013. *Essays on Hegel's Philosophy of Subjective Spirit: Imaginative Transformation and Ethical Action in Literature*. New York: State University of New York Press.

Stewart, I. 1998. *Life's Other Secret: The New Mathematics of the Living World*. New York: Wiley.

Stewart, I. and Cohen, J. 1995. *The Collapse of Chaos*. London: Penguin.

Stewart, I. and Cohen, J. 1997. *Figments of Reality: The Evolution of the Curious Mind*. Cambridge: Cambridge University Press.

Stewart, J. E. 2014. The Direction of Evolution: the Rise of Cooperative Organization. *Biosystems* 123: 27–36.

Stierli, M., Shorrocks, A., Davies, J. B., Lluberas, R., and Koutsoukis, A. 2014. *Global Wealth Report*. Zurich: Credit Suisse.

Stigler, G. J. and Kindahl, J. K. 1970. *The Behavior of Industrial Prices*. New York: Columbia University Press.

Stiglitz, J. 2012. Of the 1%, By the 1%, For the 1%. *Vanity Fair* (May). Retrieved from www.vanityfair.com/society/features/2011/05/top-one-percent-201105 (accessed 29 November 2014).

Stirling, A. 2011. *Sustainability and Transformation. Framing Future Studies: Science, Technology and Global Challenges*. Aachen: Aachen University, Sustainable Lifestyles Research Group.

Stirling, A. 2012. From Sustainability, through Diversity to Transformation: Towards More Reflexive Governance of Vulnerability. In A. Hommels, J. Mesman, W. E. Bijker (eds), *Vulnerability in Technological Cultures: New Directions in Research and Governance*. Cambridge, MA: MIT Press.

Stout, M. 2005. *The Sociopath Next Door*. New York: Three Rivers Press.

Strasser, U. and Vilsmaier, U. 2013. Coupled Numerical Modelling for Inter- and Transdisciplinary Integration in Climate Change Effect Research: Examples of Interface Design. First Global Conference on Research Integration and Implementation, Canberra, Australia, online and at co-conferences in Germany, the Netherlands and Uruguay.

Strehlow, T. G. H. 1968. *Aranda Traditions*. New York: Johnson Reprint.

Streithorst, T. 2014. *A Brief Glossary of Financial Cataclysm*. Glendale, CA: T. Lutz.

Streufert, S. 1970. "Complexity and Complex Decision Making: Convergences Between Differentiation and Integration Approaches to the Prediction of Task Performance." *Journal of Experimental Social Psychology* 6(4): 494–509.

Streufert, S. and Streufert, S. C. (joint author.). 1978. *Behavior in the Complex Environment*. New York: V. H. Winston.

Strogatz, S. 2004. *Sync: the Emerging Science of Spontaneous Order*. London: Penguin.

Strongman, L. 2008. "When Earth and Sky almost Meet": The Conflict between Traditional Knowledge and Modernity in Polynesian Navigation. *Journal of World Anthropology: Occasional Papers* 3: 48–110.

Strozenberg, F., Filhoa, W. S. G., Leitea, L. O. F. B., Raquel, E., Hogemanna, S., Nagiba, M., De Oliveiraa, H. C. S., Da Silvaa, M. N. and Antãoa, A. C. 2015. Ubuntu: Alterity as a Perspective for Peace. *Sociology* 5: 53–59.

Suchman, L. 1987. *Plans and Situated Actions: The Problem of Human-Machine Communication*. New York: Cambridge University Press.

Sumner, L. W. 1996. *Welfare, Happiness, and Ethics*. Oxford: Oxford University Press.

Suvini-Hand, V. 2000. *Mirage and Camouflage: Hiding behind Hermeticism in Ungaretti's "L'Allegria"*. Leicester: Troubador.

Swann, W. B. J., Jetten, J., Gomez, A., Whitehouse, H. and Brock, B. 2012. When Group Membership Gets Personal: a Theory of Identity Fusion. *Psychology Review* 119(3): 441.

Swanson, D. and Bhadwal, S. 2009. *Creating Adaptive Policies: A Guide for Policymaking in an Uncertain World*. London: IDRC.

Syly, L. P. 2014. Micro vs. Macro: On the Use and Misuse of Theories and Models in Economics. The Third Nordic Post-Keynesian Conference, Aalborg, 22–23 May 2014.

Tacey, D. 2004. *The Spirituality Revolution: The Emergence of Contemporary Spirituality*. London: Routledge.

Tagore, R. 1918. *Nationalism*. London: Macmillan and Company.

Tagore, R. 1994. To the Nation. In S. R. Das (ed.), *The English Writings of Rabindranth Tagore*. New Delhi: Sahitya Akademi.

Tajfel, H. 1986. The Social Identity Theory of Intergroup Behaviour. In G. Worchel (ed.), *Psychology of Intergroup Relations*. Chicago, IL: Nelson-Hall.

Taleb, N. N. 2007. *The Black Swan: The Impact of the Highly Improbable*. London: Penguin.

Taleb, N. N. 2012. *Antifragile: Things that Gain from Disorder*. New York: Random House.

Tanase, A. 1989. European Culture between Nuclear Holocaust and a Humanist Philosophy of Peace. In M. Siguan (ed.), *Philosophica Pacis: Homanaje a Raimon Panikkar*. Madrid: Simbolo Editorial.

Taonui, R. 2012. Canoe Navigation – Waka – Canoes. Retrieved from www.TeAra.govt.nz/en/canoe-navigation/page–1 (accessed 26 May 2015).

Taplin, N. 2015. *Taplin Family Business*. Adelaide: Wakefield Press.

Taylor, C. 1989. *Sources of the Self*. Cambridge, MA: Harvard University Press.

Taylor, C. 2001. On Social Imaginary: Contemporary Sociological Theory. Retrieved from www.nyu.edu/ classes/calhoun/Theory/Taylor-on-si.htm (accessed 25 February 2017).

Taylor, C. 2002. Modern Social Imaginaries. *Public Culture* 14: 91–124.

Taylor, C. 2004. Modern Social Imaginaries. Durham, NC: Duke University Press.

Taylor, C. 2007. *A Secular Age*. Cambridge, MA: Belknap Press of the Harvard University Press.

Taylor, M. 2015. The Voices in Your Head Offering Solutions. Retrieved from www.thersa.org/discover/publications-and-articles/matthew-taylor-blog/2015/05/the-voices-in-your-head-offering-solutions (accessed May 2015).

Taylor, S. n.d. The Origin of God. Retrieved from www.stevenmtaylor.com/essays/the-origins-of-god.

Tendulkar, D. G. 1960. *Mahatma*. New Delhi: Publications Division, Ministry of Information and Broadcasting, Government of India.

Terrill, L. 2015. *Beyond Communal and Individual Ownership: Indigenous Land Reform in Australia*. London: Taylor & Francis.

Thadani, N. V. 1932. *The Garden of the East*. Karachi: Bharat Publishing House.

Thaler, R. H. 1988. Anomalies: The Winner's Curse. *Journal of Economic Perspectives* 2(1): 191–202.

Thomas, W. I. and Thomas, D. 1928. *The Child in America: Behavior Problems and Programs*. New York: Alfred Knopf.

Thompson, E. 2015. Dreamless Sleep, the Embodied Mind, and Consciousness. In T. Metzinger and J. M. Windt (eds), *Open MIND, Philosophy and the Mind Sciences in the 21st Century*, vol. 2, pp. 1551–1569. Cambridge, MA: MIT Press.

Thompson, E. P. 1963. *The Making of the English Working Class*. London: Gollancz.

Thompson, F. 1917. Mistress of Vision. In D. H. S. Nicholson and A. H. E. Lee (eds), *The Oxford Book of Mystical English Verse*. Oxford: Clarendon Press.

Thompson, M. 2013. Clumsy Solutions to Environmental Change: Lessons from Cultural Theory. In L. Sygna, K. O'Brien and J. Wolf (eds), *A Changing Environment for Human Security: Transformative Approaches to Research, Policy and Action*. London: Earthscan from Routledge.

Thompson, W. I. 1989. *Imaginary Landscapes: Making Worlds of Myth and Science*. New York: St. Martin's Press.

Tilly, C. 2002. *Stories, Identities, and Political Change*, Kindle edition. Lanham, MD: Rowman & Littlefield Publishers.

Tippett, K. 2016. *Becoming Wise: An Inquiry into the Mystery and the Art of Living*. London: Little, Brown Book Group. Kindle Edition.

Todd, P. M., Gigerenzer, G. and the ABC Research Group. 2012. *Ecological Rationality: Intelligence in the World*. New York: Oxford University Press.

Tognetti, S. S. 2013. Revisiting Post-Normal Science in Post-Normal Times and Identifying Cranks. Retrieved from www.postnormaltimes.net/wpblog/wp-content/uploads/2013/01/pns-in-pnt1.pdf (accessed 9 June 2015).

Tonkinwise, C. 2015. Committing to the Political Values of Post-Thing-Centered Designing. Retrieved from www.academia.edu/14560093/Committing_to_the_Political_Values_of_Post-Thing-Centered_Designing (accessed 3 October 2015).

Torbert, W. 1991. *The Power of Balance: Transforming Self, Society, and Scientific Inquiry.* Thousand Oaks, CA: Sage.

Torbert, W. 2013. Listening into the Dark: An Essay Testing the Validity and Efficacy of Collaborative Developmental Action Inquiry for Describing and Encouraging the Transformation of Self, Society, and Scientific Inquiry. *Integral Review* 9: 264–299.

Torbert and Associates. 2004. *Action Inquiry: the Secret of Timely and Transforming Leadership.* San Francisco, CA: Brett-Koehler Publishers.

Toulmin, C. and Pepper, S. 2000. Land Reform North and South. Retrieved from www.caledonia.org.uk/land/nands.htm (accessed 16 January 2015).

Trinidad, A. M. 2014. Critical Indigenous Pedagogy of Place: How Centering Hawaiian Epistemology and Values in Practice Affects People on Ecosystemic Levels. *Journal of Ethnic and Cultural Diversity in Social Work* 23: 110–128.

Trucost 2013. *Natural Capital at Risk: The Top 100 Externalities of Business.* New Delhi: TEEB for Business Coalition.

Tse, K. S. M. 2000. Market Sentiments, Winner's Curse, and Bidding Strategy in Real Estate Auctions. Asian Real Estate Markets Conference, Beijing, July 2000.

Tuan, Y. F. 1977. *Space and Place: The Perspective of Experience.* Minneapolis, MN: University of Minnesota Press.

Tuan, Y. F. 1990. *Topophilia: A Study of Environmental Perception, Attitudes, and Values.* New York: Columbia University Press.

Tuckett, D. 2012. Financial Markets are Markets in Stories: Some Possible Advantages of Using Interviews to Supplement Existing Economic Data Sources. *Journal of Economic Dynamics and Control* 36: 1077–1087.

Tully, J. 2008. *Public Philosophy in a New Key,* 2 vols. Cambridge: Cambridge University Press.

Tuma, E. H. 2015. Land Reform. In *Encyclopaedia Britannica Online.* Retrieved from www.britannica.com/topic/land-reform.

Tung, C. 1997. Blake's Dialectical Vision. *Wenshi xuebao [Journal of the College of Liberal Arts, National Chung-hsing University]* 27: 193–211.

Turnbull, C. M. 1984. *The Mountain People.* London: Paladin.

Turner, M. 1986. English Open Fields and Enclosures: Retardation or Productivity Improvements. *Journal of Economic History* 46: 669–692.

Tzu, L. 1972. *Tao Te Ching,* trans. Ch'u Ta Kao. London: Unwin.

Uhlmann, A. 2001. Law Translating Life and Life Translating Law through Stories: Bringing Them Home and Benang by Kim Scott. *Australian Feminist Law Journal* 15: 41–54.

Underwood, E. 2015. Lifelong Memories May Reside in Nets around Brain Cells. *Science* 350: 491–492.

UNDP. 2015. *United Nations Global Sustainable Development Report 2015.* New York: UNDP. Retrieved from https://sustainabledevelopment.un.org/globalsdreport/2015.

UNEP. 2012. *One Plane, How Many People? A Review of Earth's Carrying Capacity.* Nairobi: UNEP. Retrieved from http://na.unep.net/geas/archive/pdfs/GEAS_Jun_12_Carrying_Capacity.pdf.

Unger, R. M. 2007. *The Self Awakened: Pragmatism Unbound.* Cambridge, MA: Harvard University Press.

Unger, R. M. and Smolin, L. 2015. *The Singular Universe and the Reality of Time.* Cambridge: Cambridge University Press.

United Nations. 2014. *World Urbanization Prospects 2014.* New York: United Nations.

Upadhyaya, D. 1988–1989. *Pandit Deendayal Upadhyaya: A Profile.* New Delhi: Deendayal Research Institute.

USAID. 2006. *Land Tenure Property Rights and Natural Resource Management*. Washington, DC: USAID.

Vago, D. R. 2014. Mapping Modalities of Self-Awareness in Mindfulness Practice: A Potential Mechanism for Clarifying Habits of Mind. *Annals of New York Academy of Sciences* 1307: 28–42.

Valeriano, B. and Owsiak, A. 2014. John Vasquez, Territoriality, and Staying Ahead of the Game. Retrieved from www.whiteoliphaunt.com/duckofminerva/2014/04/john-vasquez-territoriality-and-staying-ahead-of-the-game.html (accessed 15 April 2014).

Vallicella, B. 2009. Teleological and Axiological Aspects of Existential Meaning. Retrieved from http://maverickphilosopher.typepad.com/maverick_philosopher/2009/10/teleological-and-axiological-aspects-of-existential-meaning.html (accessed 10 May 2015).

Valters, C. 2014. *Theories of Change in International Development: Communication, Learning, or Accountability?* London: The Justice and Security Research Programme.

Valters, C. 2014a. Six Key Findings on the Use of Theories of Change in International Development. Retrieved from http://blogs.lse.ac.uk/jsrp/2014/08/18/six-key-findings-on-the-use-of-theories-of-change-in-international-development (accessed 27 June 2015).

Van der Molen, P. 2012. After 10 Years of Criticism: What is Left of De Soto's Ideas? FIG Working Week, 6–10 May 2012: Knowing to Manage the Territory, Protect the Environment, Evaluate the Cultural Heritage, Rome, Italy.

Van der Molen, P. and Tuladhar, A. 2007. Corruption and Land Administration. *Surveying and Land Information Science* 67(1): 5–21.

Van Eck, E. 2011. A Prophet of Old: Jesus the Public Theologian. In H. D. V. E. Bedford-Strohm (ed.), *Prophetic Witness: An Appropriate Contemporary Mode of Public Discourse?* Zurich: Lit Verlag.

Van Every, D. 1961. *Forth to the Wilderness: The First American Frontier 1754–1774*. New York: William Morrow and Company.

Varoufakis, Y. 2015. Greece's New Finance Minister Varoufakis Tells German Counterpart Schäuble to "Expect a Frenzy of Reasonableness". Retrieved from https://wallofcontroversy.wordpress.com/2015/02/05/greeces-new-finance-minister-varoufakis-tells-german-counterpart-schauble-to-expect-a-frenzy-of-reasonableness (accessed 30 May 2015).

Vasquez, J. A. 1993. *The War Puzzle*. New York: Cambridge University Press.

Vasquez, J. A. 2009. *The War Puzzle Revisited*. Cambridge: Cambridge University Press.

Vasquez, J. A. and Valeriano, B. 2010. Classification of Interstate Wars. *The Journal of Politics* 72: 292–309.

Veitch, S. 2007. *Law and Irresponsibility: On the Legitimation of Human Suffering*. London: Taylor and Francis.

Venkatesan, S. and Al., E. 2010. Ontology Is Just Another Word for Culture: Motion Tabled at the 2008 Meeting of the Group for Debates in Anthropological Theory, University of Manchester. *Critique of Anthropology* 30: 152–200.

Von Benda-Beckmann, F., von Benda-Beckmann, K. and Wiber, M. G. 2006. The Properties of Property. In F. Von Benda-Beckmann, K. von Benda-Beckmann and M. G. Wiber (eds), *Changing Properties of Property*. New York: Berghahn Books.

Von Foerster, H. 1979. Cybernetics of Cybernetics. (Opening Address of the American Society for Cybernetics, 1974.) In K. Krippendorff (ed.), *Communication and Control in Society*, 5–8. New York: Gordon and Breach. Retrieved from www.univie.ac.at/constructivism/archive/fulltexts/1707.pdf.

Von Glasersfeld, E. 1990. An Exposition of Constructivism: Why Some Like It Radical. In R. B. Davis, C. A. Maher and N. Noddings (eds), *Constructivist Views on the Teaching and Learning of Mathematics*, 19–29. Reston, VA: National Council of Teachers of Mathematics.

Waddock, S., Meszoely, G. M., Waddell, S. and Dentoni, D. 2015. The Complexity of Wicked Problems in Large Scale Change. *Journal of Organizational Change Management* 28: 993–1012.

Wade, J. 1996. *Changes of Mind*. New York: State University of New York Press.

Wahba, M. A. and Bridwell, L. G. 1976. Maslow Reconsidered: A Review of Research on the Need Hierarchy Theory. *Organizational Behavior and Human Performance* 15: 212–240.

Waldrop, M. 1992. *Complexity*. London: Penguin.

Walker, I. and Ostrom, E. 2007. Trust and Reciprocity as Foundations for Cooperation: Individuals, Institutions, and Contexts, Capstone Meeting of the RSF Trust Initiative at the Russell Sage Foundation. New York: RSF, May 2007.

Walker, S. P. 1973. A Note on Sense-Perception in the Poetry of Judith Wright. *Westerly* 18: 4.

Walport, M. 2015. Making Sense of Big Data. In P. Barclay (ed.), *Big Ideas*. Sydney: ABC RN.

Walter, K. 1996. *Tao of Chaos: Merging East and West*. Shaftesbury: Element.

Wang, B. and Christensen, T. 2017. The Open Public Value Account and Comprehensive Social Development: An Assessment of China and the United States. *Administration & Society* 49(6): 852–881.

Wang, L. and Ranjan, R. 2015. Processing Distributed Internet of Things Data in Clouds. *IEEE Cloud Computing* 2(1): 76–80.

Ward, M. 2001. *Universality: The Underlying Theory behind Life, the Universe, and Everything*. Oxford: Pan Books.

Watts, A. 1973. *The Book: On the Taboo against Knowing Who you Are*. London: Abacus.

Watts, A. 2014. Metaphysical Theories. Audio extract from the lecture "Consciousness and Rhythm". Retrieved from www.youtube.com/watch?v=CcXstUEpivo and www.youtube.com/watch?v=YD-DcrpZlm4.

Watts, D. J. 2004. *Six Degrees: The Science of a Connected Age*. London: Vintage.

Wells, D. 1986. *The Penguin Dictionary of Curious and Interesting Numbers*. Harmondsworth: Penguin.

Werner, H. 1957. The Concept of Development from a Comparative and Organismic Point of View. In D. Harris (ed.), *The Concept of Development*. Minneapolis, MN: University of Minnesota Press.

Werner, R. A. 2014. Can Banks Individually Create Money Out of Nothing? The Theories and the Empirical Evidence. *International Review of Financial Analysis* 36: 1–19.

Wesley-Esquimaux, C. 2007. The Intergenerational Transmission of Historic Trauma and Grief. *Indigenous Affairs* 4(7): 6–11. Retrieved from www.mooseriverpeople.org/wp-content/uploads/IA_4_07.pdf#page=6.

West, S., Haider, J., Sinare, H. and Karpouzoglou, T. 2014. *Beyond Divides: Prospects for Synergy between Resilience and Pathways Approaches to Sustainability*. STEPS Working Paper 65. Brighton: STEPS Centre.

Whitehead, A. N. 1967. *Adventures of Ideas*. New York: Free Press.

Whitehead, A. N. 1978. *Process and Reality*. New York: Free Press.

Whitehead, A. N. 1985. *Science and the Modern World*. London: Free Association Books.

Whitehead, A. N. 2010. *Process and Reality*. New York: Free Press.

Whitehead, A. N. 2011. *Science and the Modern World*. Cambridge: Cambridge University Press.

Whitall, J. and Barry M. 2005. *A Framework for Analyzing Change Management in Geomatics Development Projects: From Pharoahs to Geoinformatics*. Cairo: FIG: 16.

Whitman, W. 1860. A Song of Joys. Retrieved from http://classiclit.about.com/library/bl-etexts/wwhitman/bl-ww-joys.htm (accessed 6 May 2015).

Wilber, K. 1980. *The Atman Project*. Madras: Quest.

Wilber, K. 1995. *Sex, Ecology, Spirituality*. Boston, MA: Shambhala.

Wilber, K. 1996. *A Brief History of Everything*. Boston, MA: Shambhala.

Wilber, K. 1999. *One Taste*. Boston, MA: Shambhala.

Wilber, K. 1999a. *Integral Psychology*. Boston, MA: Shambhala.

Wilber, K. 1999b. Boomeritis vs. Spiritual Growth in the New Millennium. Retrieved from www.tikkun.org/archive/backissues/xtik9911/politics/991111a.html (accessed 11 July 2016).

Wilber, K. 2000. *Integral Psychology: Consciousness, Spirit, Psychology, Therapy*. Boston, MA: Shambhala.

Wilber, K. 2003. Excerpts from Volume 2 of the Kosmos Trilogy. Retrieved from www.integralworld.net/Excerpts.html.

Wilber, K. 2012. The Integral Operating System. Part III: Lines of Development. Retrieved from www.integrallife.com/member/ken-wilber/blog/integral-operating-system-part-iii-lines-development (accessed 3 April 2012).

Wilcox, A. 2013. *Lobamba Interpretation Centre of the Oral Arts and Landscape*. Johannesburg: School of Architecture and Planning, Faculty of Engineering and the Built Environment, University of the Witwatersrand.

Wildschut, T., Sedikides, C., Routledge, C., Arndt, J. and Cordaro, F. 2010. Nostalgia as a Repository of Social Connectedness: The Role of Attachment-Related Avoidance. *Journal of Personality and Social Psychology* 98: 573–586.

Williams, R. J. 2014. *The Buddha in the Machine: Art, Technology, and the Meeting of East and West*. New Haven, CT: Yale University Press.

Williamson, I., Enemark, S., Wallace, J. and Rajabifard, A. 2012. *Land Administration for Sustainable Development*. Redlands, CA: ESRI Press Academic.

Wilson, C. 1956. *The Outsider*. London: Gollancz.

Wilson, C. 1984. *A Criminal History of Mankind*. London: Granada.

Wilson, D. S. 2017. The Invisible Hook: How Pirate Society Proves Economic Self-Interest Wrong. Retrieved from https://evonomics.com/pirates-economics-self-interest-hayek-wilson (accessed 24 December 2017).

Wilson, D. S. and Mulgan, G. 2017. How to Create Collective Intelligence: Markets, Science, and Humanity Don't Automatically Generate Solutions. Retrieved from http://evonomics.com/how-to-creative-collective-intelligence-david-wilson-mulgan (accessed 8 January 2018).

Wilson, J. L. 2005. *Nostalgia: Sanctuary of Meaning*. Lewisburg, PA: Bucknell University Press

Wittgenstein, L. 1974. *Tractatus Logico-Philosophicus*. New York: Routledge & Kegan Paul.

Wodak, R., De Cillia, R., Reisigl, M. and Liebhart, K. 2009. *The Discursive Construction of National Identity*. Edinburgh: Edinburgh University Press.

Woodward, K. (ed.). 1997. *Identity and Difference*. London: Sage Publications.

Woollacott, M. 2016. Does the Brain Filter out a Wider Awareness? *Huffington Post*. Retrieved from www.huffingtonpost.com/marjorie-woollacott/does-the-brain-filter-out_b_9859158.html. (accessed 17 December 2017).

Wordsworth, W. 1798. The Tables Turned: An Evening Scene on the Same Subject. Retrieved from www.bartleby.com/145/ww134.html (accessed 26 May 2015).

Wordsworth, W. 1885. *Ode on Immortality, and Lines on Tintern Abbey*. London: Cassell & Company.

World Bank. 2013. *Land Policy: Sector Results Profile*. Washington, DC: World Bank. Retrieved from www.worldbank.org/en/results/2013/04/15/land-policy-results-profile.

Wren-Lewis, L. 2013. *Corruption in Land Administration: Role for Donors to Minimise the Problem*. U4 Anti-Corruption Resource Centre Brief. Paris: Paris School of Economics and Institut National de la Recherche Agronomique.

Wright, J. 1955. *The Two Fires*. Sydney: Angus & Robertson.

Wright, J. 1971 *Collected Poems, 1942–1970*. Cremorne: Angus & Robertson.

Wright, S. 1932. The Roles of Mutation, Inbreeding, Crossbreeding and Mutation and Selection in Evolution. In D. F. Jones (ed.), Proceedings of the Sixth International Congress of Genetics, Brooklyn Botanical Garden, Brooklyn, vol. 1, pp. 356–366.

WWF. 2014. *Living Planet Report: Species and Spaces, People and Places*. London: World Wildlife Federation UK.

Yang, Z., Tang, K. and Yao, X. 2008. Multilevel Cooperative Coevolution for Large Scale Optimization. In Proceedings of IEEE Congress on Evolutionary Computation, Hong Kong, pp. 1663–1670.

Yiftachel, O. 2006. *Ethnocracy: Land and Identity Politics in Israel/Palestine*. Philadelphia, PA: University of Pennsylvania Press.

Young, G. 2012. A Unitary Neo-Piagetian/Neo-Eriksonian Model of Development: Fundamental Assumptions and Meta-issues. *New Ideas in Psychology* 30: 241–249.

Yourgrau, P. 2005. *A World Without Time*. London: Penguin.

Yu, L., Cui, P., Wang, F., Song, C. and Yang, S. 2015. From Micro to Macro: Uncovering and Predicting Information Cascading Process with Behavioral Dynamics. Retrieved from arxiv.org/pdf/1505.07193.pdf.

Yunupingu, G. 1997. *Our Land is Our Life: Land Rights, Past, Present and Future*. Brisbane: University of Queensland Press.

Zaman, T. 2012. *The Noble Sanctuary: Interpreting Islamic Traditions of Asylum in the Contemporary World*. Doctor of Philosophy thesis, University of London.

Zbierski-Salameh, S. 2013. *Bitter Harvest: Antecedents and Consequences of Property Reforms in Post-Socialist Poland*, Lanham, MD: Rowman & Littlefield.

Zeidan, F., Johnson, S. K., Diamond, B. J., David, Z. and Goolkasian, P. 2010. Mindfulness Meditation Improves Cognition: Evidence of Brief Mental Training. *Consciousness and Cognition* 19: 597–605.

Zellmer, S. B. and Harder, J. 2007. Unbundling Property in Water. *Alabama Law Review* 59: 68.

Zipf, G. K. 1949. *Human Behavior and the Principle of Least Effort*. Cambridge, MA: Addison Wesley.

Zock, H. 2004. *A Psychology of Ultimate Concern*. Amsterdam: Rodopi.

Zovanyi, G. 2013. *The No-Growth Imperative: Creating Sustainable Communities Under Ecological Limits to Growth*. Abingdon: Routledge.

Case references

Daubert v. Merrill Dow Pharmaceuticals, Inc. (1993: 509 US 579).

Gulf, Colorado and Santa Fe Railway Co. v. Ellis (1891) 165 US 150.

Healthcare at Home Limited v. The Common Services Agency (2014) UKSC 49. UKSC.

State vs. Shack 58 N.J. 297, 277 A.2d 369 (N.J. 1971). United States v. Buchman, United States Court of Appeals, Seventh Circuit. Decided 16 May 2011, no. 10-2306. Retrieved from www.justice.gov/file/490021/download.

Index

Entries in *italics* denote figures; entries in **bold** denote tables.

Printed in the United States
by Baker & Taylor Publisher Services

Printed in the United States
by Baker & Taylor Publisher Services